Freedom
In Christ

A Scholarly, Bible-based Exposé
Revealing the Defiled Spiritual
Condition of Every Organized Church
and the Inherently Sinful Nature of the
Authorities Who Control Them

Herb Leisure

Copyright © 2020 by Herb Leisure
All rights reserved

Formerly published as *Free At Last* © 2008
Unpublished manuscript © 2007

Scripture references from Biblesoft's PC Study Bible, King James Version. Copyright © 2003

Hebrew and Greek word definitions from Biblesoft's PC Study Bible, Strong's Hebrew and Greek Dictionaries. Copyright © 2003

Published by Herb Leisure, Campbell, California
email: hleisure@aol.com

Printed in the United States

ISBN 978-0-578-03540-6
Library of Congress TX 8-195-016

This book is dedicated to those who have suffered under the oppression of ecclesiastical authority and, particularly, to those God may be calling out of organized churches and into the complete freedom of New Covenant faith in the Lord Jesus Christ.

Smith Rock State Park, Oregon
Cover photo by Herb Leisure

Table of Contents

	Acknowledgments	vii
	Preface	ix
1	The Nature of the Bible	1
2	The Nature of Covenant	13
3	The Nature of God	49
4	The Nature of Jesus Christ	87
5	The Nature of Law	103
6	The Nature of Sin and Judgment	129
7	The Nature of the Church	169
8	The Nature of Church Leadership	219
9	The Nature of Organized Churches	259
10	A New Perspective	293
	Appendix	331

Acknowledgments

With humble gratitude I thank the great Creator God for carefully preserving His inspired words for more than thirty-two hundred years, so that even I could have the personal privilege to delve into His mind and contemplate His thoughts. I am also grateful to my mother, whose diligent instruction taught me from my earliest recollection about the men and women of faith in the Bible. Her love for the word of God inspired me to study to show myself approved unto God, just as she had done in her life. I deeply appreciate my dear brother in the faith, David Conrad, whose life exemplified godly compassion more than any other church leader I have known. Our frequent discussions and arguments over issues of doctrine and faith played a significant role to sharpen my knowledge of the Word and to lay the groundwork for reliance on the Spirit, as God prepared to call me to the freedom I now enjoy in Jesus Christ. I am also greatly indebted to my loving wife, Luanna, who makes my life worth living and challenges me regarding each new perspective until it either stands firm or crumbles under the scrutiny of the inspired text of scripture.

Additionally, I appreciate those who have labored diligently to create and publish the scholarly works upon which I have based the conclusions presented in this work. Without these independent scholars, the precious truths of the Bible might remain hidden from our view. I am also grateful to the creators of Bible software, who provide students of the Bible ready access to those scholarly works. The following individuals or companies made a direct contribution to provide insight into the meaning of words, the tense of verbs, the grammar of sentences and the historical context or meaning behind the various passages of scripture underlying the biblical concepts discussed herein; but I am also indebted to many, many others, whose comfort, admonition, rebuke, sermons, doctrines and examples have contributed over the years, whether positively or negatively, to illuminate my perspective of God and to help me understand His precious handbook of life.

Biblesoft, Inc. *PC Study Bible, Version 4.0*. Seattle, WA, 2003

Clarke, Adam. *Clarke's Commentary*. Nashville, TN: Abingdon, c. 1975

Ehrman, Bart D. *Misquoting Jesus*. San Francisco, CA: Harper, 2005

Jones, Timothy Paul. *Misquoting Truth*. Downers Grove, IL: IVP Books, 2007

Mounce, William D. *Basics of Biblical Greek*. Grand Rapids, MI: 2003

Mounce, William D. *Complete Expository Dictionary of Old and New Testament Words*. Grand Rapids, MI: 2006

Newman Jr., Barclay M. *A Concise Greek-English Dictionary of the New Testament*. Stuttgart, Germany: 1993

Pratico, Gary D. and Van Pelt, Miles V. *Basics of Biblical Hebrew*. Grand Rapids, MI 2007

Strong, James S.T.D., LL.D. *Strong's Exhaustive Concordance of the Bible* with the *Hebrew Dictionary of the New Testament* and the *Greek Dictionary of the New Testament*. McLean, VA: MacDonald Publishing Company. c. 1975 (disc version from Biblesoft's *New Exhaustive Strong's Numbers and Concordance with Expanded Greek-Hebrew Dictionary*. 2003)

Thayer, Joseph Henry. *New Thayer's Greek-English Lexicon of the New Testament*. Lafayette, IN, 1979

Vine, W. E. *Vine's Expository Dictionary of Biblical Words*. Nashville, TN: Thomas Nelson Publishers, 1985.

Zodhiates, Spiros. *The Complete Word Study Old Testament* and *The Complete Word Study New Testament*. Chattanooga, TN: AMG Publishers, 1992. (disc version from Biblesoft's *The Complete Word Study Bible*. 2002)

Preface

Hierarchical organization and human authority have been entrenched in Christian churches since at least the third century. Contemporary historians have endeavored to determine how the churches were transformed from the cooperative communal congregations of the first century to the highly structured and controlled organizations of the present era, but that record has vanished along with second century church history. Undoubtedly scriptural illiteracy, which resulted from the lack of access to the writings of the apostles, combined with the desire of men to have preeminence, which resulted in the control of the writings of the apostles, contributed significantly to the change. The inspired words of God have long been restricted to the custody of an elite few.

Before the printing press, access to a personal copy of the Hebrew Scriptures or the canonized text of the New Testament, either in the original language or in translation, was limited to those who were educated enough to make themselves a copy or wealthy enough to employ a scribe. When mass produced Bibles became available, church authorities attempted to restrict their distribution outside of the church hierarchy; consequently, prohibition was added to inaccessibility, and the revelation of scripture remained in the custody of church authorities, who continued to control and interpret the words of God according to their long established heretical doctrines. Thus, they continued to teach without question their mixture of truth and error, which had become a theological substitute for the pure and simple truths of God.

Early in the sixteenth century Martin Luther began to expose some of the heresies taught by the Catholic Church, and his work paved the way for the Protestant Reformation. Luther's translation into the German language and, later, the King James translation into English began to loosen the control Catholicism held over trusting believers; however, the most reprobate heresy of them all continued to elude scrutiny. Since the hierarchical structure of the Catholic Church was generally assumed to be the correct model for the emerging churches, hierarchical organization was simply reinvented in Protestantism, which correctly concluded that faith is expressed in Jesus Christ alone, but which failed to grasp the full reality of God's sovereignty over the Church. Consequently, Catholic and Protestant authorities continued to control and manipulate believers through the same hierarchical system of human government which had long reigned in the mother church. Hierarchical organization continues to be the structure of choice for church governments today.

After the last apostle was quietly laid to rest and the first century faded into the second, the true nature of the government of the early churches became increasingly clouded in mystery. In more recent periods Bible historians have patiently and meticulously searched the scriptures for clues to the organization and operation of the first century churches without being able to discern their function at all. The fragmented hints offered by the apostles in their letters have left no tangible clues allowing historians to accurately reconstruct the organization of the early fledgling churches or to determine with any degree of certainty how they functioned. Although most historians admit the organization of the first century churches is completely obscured from their view, theologians and church authorities have ignored the absence of any explicitly stated hierarchical order in scripture and have assumed hierarchical organization is at least implicit in the text. Even without a single scriptural example of the transfer of authority from one member to another, church leaders simply assume divine authority passes by ordination from leader to leader, and they continue to rule and direct the members of their churches based on that assumption. Since hierarchical organization has always been the accepted form of government in world, new converts don't even question the assumption that God's direction passes from the denominational head through a chain of command to the local pastor and then to each member of the church. Most churchgoers are unaware that hierarchical order demands mediators and that such governments invariably place one or more human mediators between believers and God.

Also lacking a biblical pattern for the style of their hierarchy, churches have employed every imaginable form of human government to direct their members. Although widely diverse styles of organization appear in churches, each organized church naturally assumes biblical authority for its particular hierarchical system and claims its government follows the biblical model, even though none has biblical justification. When new churches form, faithful members look to the Bible for guidance and pray for divine insight to reveal God's will for their church, however, their church leaders inevitably create churches organized under federal and state regulation, wherein members are expected to follow men having questionable divine authority and trust in a system of questionable scriptural foundation. Since none of these structures or styles is firmly anchored in scripture but rather in humanly devised systems of government, we should not be surprised that the organization of most churches reflects the same hierarchical structure found in civil governments or the corporate world, except that church authorities reserve an imaginary position at the top of their structures for God. In reality, many churches give Jesus Christ the top job and virtually ignore the divine Father, Who is the Creator, the Sustainer and the sovereign Ruler of the Church.

The subject of church government frequently raises intense debate and sometimes even fractures church fellowships. Even when a congregation can agree, its style of government is likely to be at least somewhat different from the church down the street. Some see a minimum of governmental structure, while others see the framework of an exotic hierarchical organization. Churches often begin with minimal structure and grow into greater administration. Division in the Christian community has become so obvious that ecumenical councils have been convened in an attempt to reconcile the multitude of rival Christian denominations and their opposing governmental structures, but even high ranking church leaders, all claiming to be guided by the Spirit, have been unable to discern the framework of a united church government. Given the wide diversity of organizational systems, structures and styles within the Christian community and the irreconcilable division among the various church denominations, one might wonder why God did not inspire the apostles to reveal the nature of the divinely established first century church government explicitly.

However, rather than being an obstacle, the obvious ambiguity of the structure of the early churches should have long since been recognized as a significant clue to resolve the menacing problem of the correct form of government for a church. In retrospect, it seems remarkable that church authorities have not even dared to think, let alone suggest, that the government God described in the pages of scripture might not require any human intervention at all. None of these theologians seems to have even entertained the possibility that men have no ability or authority to organize a church or that God has indeed reserved the right to place members in the body of Christ entirely to Himself. The body of Christ is a living body, yet it has completely escaped these theologians' cognitive perception that God alone has the power to create and organize a living body. These men are completely oblivious to the reality that God alone possesses the divine ability to create eyes, shape ears, form hands, mold feet and place them in the spiritual body He is creating for His Son.

The Bible explicitly describes the Church as a body. (Col 1:18) Jesus Christ is designated as the Head of the body, (Eph 5:23) indicating the body has only one Head, yet every denomination and most churches designate multiple heads to govern their churches, and the structure of these churches can only be described as an organization, not a body. When Jesus walked on this earth, He had no trouble living in and directing His physical body, yet most theologians today do not even consider the possibility that the Lord might be able to live inside His body today and direct it without their help. Is it possible that these high ranking theologians and church leaders have missed the point of the apostles' analogy? Is it possible that church authorities have usurped the Lord's divine prerogative to direct His own body? Would you allow someone else to direct the members of your body?

I have been associated with several organized churches over my lifetime. I was born into one mainstream Protestant denomination, attended another in my youth and frequently visited others. I was later involved with a fundamentalist cult for over thirty years before our denomination of about 150,000 members experienced a radical transformation from a law-keeping church to a faith-based church. Our pastor-general led the entire denomination back to a mainstream evangelical perspective. The unprecedented doctrinal changes were heralded in *Christianity Today,* proclaimed to be a miracle in the Christian community and described as parallel to the experience of first century Jews when the gospel was first preached to them. Unfortunately, the transformation hardly received universal acclaim among our own members. Previous doctrinal changes caused little disruption in the organization, but, when the head of the denomination abandoned the law of Moses and began teaching salvation by faith, the church split down the middle. Less than fifty percent of the membership followed the denominational leadership.

I felt blessed to be among those whose minds God opened to His amazing grace. I found new covenant faith to be a significant improvement over old covenant law, and I smugly felt I had arrived at the gates of the Kingdom. I thought I finally understood Christianity. Little did I know that God had yet another important lesson—a vital lesson—to teach me. I had yet to learn that grace cannot be extended without freedom. I had yet to learn that God requires His people to be free from human direction before we can truly experience salvation or live by the faith of Jesus Christ.

In the meantime I began to wonder why God had called me out of a mainstream Protestant church to wander in the legalistic wilderness of the law for thirty years just to bring me back to Protestantism. Why had I spent those years keeping the law? What could I learn from my experiences? From a certain perspective, the old covenant was not a bad way to live, and certainly there is no sin in keeping the law, but I was shocked and felt embarrassed before God when I began to realize my greater sin was not necessarily my faith in the law, but my faith in the self-appointed apostle, who founded the denomination, and his hand picked ministers. If the Lord had personally led me to keep the law through my own study of the Bible, I could have kept it the way the Lord directed, but I had spent thirty years following a man—indeed lots of men—men who claimed they were authorities on God. In a mistaken allegiance to these men, I allowed them to order my spiritual life, and I allowed them to enforce a religious code upon me which had been obsolete for nearly two millennia. How could this deception have been possible? Did God have something yet for me to learn? Certainly those authorities had something to learn. When the new covenant doctrine was introduced to our denomination, every ordained minister should have immediately realized he was no authority on God at all, and godly humility should have forced every one of them to resign on the spot. Unfortunately, many of those same authorities still control the organization, and many of those pastors still oppress and manipulate their unsuspecting congregations to this day.

As a result of those unprecedented doctrinal changes, the organization nearly dissolved, but those same events which rocked the church to its foundations served to further strengthen my faith in God and in His ability to lead His people to Himself. The doctrinal upheaval opened my mind to the reality that even denominational authorities are only men, that men make mistakes, and that sometimes men make big mistakes. My mind opened to the possibility that even high-ranking church authorities may not know any more about God and the Bible than you or I do. The reality of those events allowed me—indeed forced me—to question every doctrine, and it even led me to question the biblical basis which had seemed to allow men to have authority in churches in the first place.

The early period of my seventy year life was occupied with my mother's Bible stories, then from early teenage with regular personal study of the Word, of course with occasional lapses along the way. Perhaps your experience has been similar. As a member of the aforementioned church, daily Bible study was required, and our church service was conducted more like a classroom than a place of worship. The fluttering noise of turning pages arose every time the minister quoted a scripture, and, when the commotion settled down, everyone diligently took notes to record the speaker's "inspired" interpretation of the passage. The weeks, months and years of personal study—from examining individual verses to reading the Bible from cover to cover—allowed me to become very familiar with the stories, the history and the subject matter contained in the Bible, but all that prescribed study did not bring me any closer to faith, and certainly not to freedom. I knew what the Bible said. I just didn't realize what much of it meant until God forced the doctrinal changes in the organization which initially opened my mind to the new covenant faith of Jesus Christ.

A faith-based perspective almost automatically improved my understanding of much of the New Testament, but the shock of the experience changed the way I studied the Bible. For the first time I began paying very close attention to the context—the greater context as well as the immediate context—of every passage I read. Context, I learned, is critical. I also began to consider words very carefully to understand their simple meanings, many of which had needed interpretation before. I carefully avoided the previous assumptions which had colored every passage of scripture. I learned the principles of biblical interpretation, hermeneutics, and their proper application, exegesis, and I diligently applied those principles, even when the conclusions challenged my cherished beliefs. As a result of a more educated approach to Bible study while having lost trust in the authorities who seemed to fix every contradiction with an inspired interpretation, I began finding irresolvable contradictions in more than just a few passages of scripture. These contradictions inevitably sent me to the Hebrew or Greek text for resolution, and, in every case, the original language text exposed the translators' errors and brought harmony to the scripture. Passage after passage came into clearer focus as each discovery brought increasing harmony to the poorly translated English text. I have since discovered several keys to unlock the simple meanings of perplexing passages of scripture, but my most remarkable discovery was finding no scriptural basis for the rite of ordination or for human authority in churches. Indeed, the Greek New Testament contains no such words as ordain, office, minister, deacon or authority.

When I discovered the shocking absence of hierarchical church government in the inspired text of scripture, I suggested to my Bible study class that men should not assume positions of authority in churches. The class was shocked that I would even suggest such a thing. Our study leader gave an impassioned testimonial calling for sanity, and another suggested she knew what my problem was, although she never overtly stated what she thought it might be. Since no one offered a single scripture to refute my allegation, I stood my ground. I have since found few who would even engage me in a discussion of the subject; therefore, I have determined to make the evidence available in this book, so interested Bible students may judge for themselves whether or not men should hold authority over those in whom God dwells.

Subsequent study has unquestionably convinced me that God never intended men to rule or stand in authority in His churches. The message of this book proclaims God to be the Ruler of the Church and Jesus Christ to be the sole Authority in the Church. The message of this book is a message of freedom. It describes how believers may become unshackled from the oppression of church organizations and the human rulers and authorities who control them. This book also explains how believers may come to experience the full freedom of new covenant faith in Jesus Christ as God has revealed it through the inspired writings of the apostles and prophets.

Just as the Jewish authorities hated Jesus' message, church authorities hate the message contained in this book. Jesus' message threatened the exalted positions the Scribes and Pharisees held in Jewish society; the message of this book threatens the exalted positions men have assumed in the Christian community. Jesus' message exposed the pride and arrogance of Jewish authorities; this message exposes men's pride and feelings of superiority in churches. This book reveals the presumptuousness of those who look down on trusting believers from their exalted positions in the pulpits of organized churches and dare to think they have the spiritual insight to know how to construct a spiritual body or the divine authority to direct Christ's own body. This message reveals how ludicrous it is to think mortal men could possibly be authorities on God or authorities over those in whom God dwells. While this message will threaten the entire system of organized Christianity, I believe this same message will encourage and support believers' faith in God and show them how they can be released from the power of fallible, pride-filled, arrogant men and be safely placed in the loving hands of the omniscient and omnipotent God. This message is a message of freedom for those in whom God dwells, and I believe it strikes at the very heart of the already-failing system of organized religion. This book boldly acknowledges and proclaims the central and essential truth that Jesus Christ alone is Lord.

Although I could tell many heart-wrenching stories, this work is not an exposé of the sins or shortcomings of any particular church leader, nor is it a diatribe against the organization with which I was associated for so long. I hold no grudges, and I have no regrets. I could have walked away at any time. If I had it to do over again, I would join that church again, because I believe the training and experience I received there was essential to my spiritual growth. I believe God chose that way to draw me personally to His Son. I would gladly endure the bondage again as long as God would bring me once again to the full freedom of faith in Jesus Christ.

Rather than focusing on the misdeeds of individuals or the blundering of an organization, it is my intention to expose the nature of all church authorities and the nature of all church organizations. I will expose who and what they are rather than what they have done. Believers need to know the nature of the individuals who call themselves authorities in churches, and believers need to know the nature of church organizations which assume the right to rule our spiritual lives. We need to know who these authorities are and what church organizations are, and we need to know what they are from a biblical point of view—from God's point of view—rather than depending on our senses to determine for ourselves what is good or evil. Humanly, it is impossible to discern for ourselves what is right or wrong. We may think we know, but we don't. We may think we can discern for ourselves, but we can't. It takes spiritual vision. It takes unquestioned faith in the inspired words of God. I thought I was on the right road, but I was headed blindly down the road to destruction. Even after the previously mentioned organization became a mainstream evangelical church, I was still groping in the dark until I began to read the New Testament in Greek. When I did, the whole facade of hierarchical organization and ecclesiastical authority crumbled before my eyes and lay exposed and shattered in a pile of mistranslation and misinterpretation.

In spite of copyist errors, scribal manipulations and translator abuses, God has carefully preserved and protected the essence of the inspired texts. He has preserved the means through which diligent students of the Word can break the grip of Catholic and Protestant oppression and enter the full freedom of new covenant faith in Jesus Christ. The pompous facade of organized Christianity can be exposed by anyone who is willing to question authority, question the translators, and go directly to the inspired Hebrew and Greek texts to see if the assumptions the translators have made can stand the test of scholarly investigation. Beginning with the concordance, and particularly now with the invention and proliferation of computers, even a casual Bible student has direct access to the inspired words of the prophets and apostles written in the original Hebrew and Greek languages without necessarily knowing a single word of Hebrew or Greek. Although the inspired words of scripture have been available for our scrutiny for well over a century (if one is willing to turn pages endlessly), the text now falls open to our view by the click of a mouse or the touch of a key. Consulting a concordance is slow and laborious, but a Bible student armed with a Bible program on the computer can click his or her way through the definitions of words and the grammar of sentences at almost lightning speed. Finally, in our age, the computer has opened the original language writings to the scrutiny of anyone who cares enough about God to study His inspired words. The intentional and unintentional errors of the translators now lie exposed to anyone who cares enough to check their work. We can no longer blame the translators. God has left the computer generation without excuse.

The purpose of this book is to expose the corrupt state of church organizations and the sinful nature of the authorities who run them. In the process I will also show how recklessly and irresponsibly the translators have mishandled the inspired texts entrusted to them, and, although there is no reason to expose the misdeeds of church leaders or the organizations they control, I will indeed expose the misdeeds of the translators, because their misdeeds appear plainly on the pages of every English Bible for all to see. The translators' misdeeds directly influence our perception of God's thoughts, so they must be exposed to reveal the inspired meaning of the Hebrew and Greek texts and the inadequacy of every English translation.

As mistranslation after mistranslation becomes exposed for your scrutiny, carefully consider that each individual error is a very small part of a broad deception. Individually, these mistranslations may seem relatively benign, but, taken collectively, they constitute a deception I believe only Satan himself could have devised. No individual or church is to blame, because the deception permeates the Bible and is evident throughout the Christian community. Satan alone is certainly responsible for the depraved state of organized Christianity, but his culpability cannot absolve any faithful believer of a personal responsibility to seek God through the message He has so diligently and carefully preserved for us over the centuries. We each have a personal responsibility to study and examine the inspired words of God, because we are responsible to work our own salvation with fear and trembling.

The more churchgoers study English Bibles to memorize and internalize the official-sounding rhetoric of every translation, the more difficult it will be to overcome the collective force of these mistranslations, because they all tend to reinforce one another and support the assumption of ecclesiastical authority in churches. Undoing this deception will not be a simple task, but I believe God can overcome any obstacle human beings may have placed in the path of salvation, so I have produced this book in the hope that He might be at work in your life. All I can do is explain what I have learned, but the Spirit of God will reveal the Truth. I have learned that the inspired Bible is a very different book from the ones I have read all my life, but you must see for yourself that English Bibles are full of mistranslations. You must see that these mistranslations camouflage a remarkable and almost unbelievable truth. You must see for yourself that, when these mistranslations are corrected by the work of published scholars, ecclesiastical authority vanishes from the Bible. I believe hierarchical organization in churches is a house of cards destined for collapse, and every believer who truly loves the Lord and desires the salvation God has promised should be warned to abandon church organizations, reject ecclesiastical authority and depend on the Lord alone for spiritual direction as faithful believers fellowship together as equals in the Lord—as equals in His Church.

In an effort to accomplish the above-stated purpose, I rely on the works of published scholars to define the inspired Hebrew and Greek words and explain the grammar of the inspired texts of the Bible. I claim no scholarly authority of my own, but I defend my criticism of the translators by quoting the works of Hebrew and Greek scholars themselves. These scholarly works abound in the Christian community, and they are readily available everywhere to anyone who truly desires to seek and know God.

Although I believe this book reflects the truth of scripture, I have relied on scholars to teach me what the inspired text says. I am not a scholar. I am not a pastor. I am not a prophet. God has not given me a special revelation of truth. I am not inviting you to join my church or to send me money. I have no need of your money. I am simply a believer of average intelligence possessing a desire to know my Creator, and I have trusted God to teach me through the Book which claims to reveal His identity. I have tested that claim and found that, although translations are very corrupt and full of errors, the inspired Hebrew and Greek texts exhibit remarkable integrity. Only God's authorship can account for such integrity. I have found truth in the inspired texts, and I believe you can too, if you are willing to study God's inspired words diligently and trust the Lord to teach you personally through the Spirit rather than trusting the uninspired work of paid translators.

Although every English translation is corrupt, our native tongue is English, so we must at least start with an English translation. The King James Version (KJV) of the Bible serves as my designated English text, not because I believe it is any better than other translations, but because it is basically a word for word translation, which can be more easily used to point out and correct specific translation errors. I have chosen to use Strong's *Hebrew and Greek Dictionary of Old and New Testament Words* as the reference I quote for word definitions. Since nearly every serious Bible student has a copy of Strong's Concordance, my work can be easily verified by consulting his dictionary or any other contemporary dictionary of Hebrew and Greek words. I use Zodhiates' *Word Study Old Testament* and *Word Study New Testament* to resolve questions of Hebrew and Greek grammar, including the tense of verbs and the number of pronouns, both of which influence the meaning and interpretation of passages significantly. Grammatical issues may be further researched by consulting Mounce's *Basics of Biblical Greek* or any number of other recognized textbooks which explain the grammar of the Koine Greek language.

Simply as a matter of personal preference, I have chosen to refer to church in two distinct ways: I capitalize Church when I refer to the whole body of Christ; I use the lower case church when I refer to a denomination (such as the Catholic church), local congregation or small fellowship. Nouns and pronouns referring to Deity are also capitalized, so some noteworthy names of old covenant types, which are customarily capitalized, such as the law of Moses, the sabbath and the ten commandments, I have intentionally left in lower case to avoid confusion with the antitypical Deity. Quotations from the Bible were electronically inserted unedited from Biblesoft's *King James Version of the Bible*, except for bracketed corrections. The definitions of Hebrew and Greek words were all electronically inserted entirely unedited from Biblesoft's version of *Strong's Expanded Greek-Hebrew Dictionary*.

I ask God's blessing and inspiration upon each of you who is willing to face these issues with an open mind. I offer this work, not intending that you accept it without question, but to encourage you to diligently investigate the words of God in personal study as you further research the allegations I have presented here. God expects each of us to learn and grow as we live in His grace, and we must continue to revise our perspectives and align our practice to conform to our Lord Jesus Christ; consequently, this book will be a work in constant progress in order to refine and correct its details. Should you find any error in thought or logic, or if you find evidence contrary to the purpose of this work, I invite scholarly discussion. Please feel free to contact me by email at hleisure@aol.com.

Chapter 1

The Nature of the Bible

True freedom abides in the living Word of God—Jesus Christ. He is the Truth of God, and only the Truth will free us from death and from the bondage of this world. Faithful Christians look to Him alone as the source of spiritual truth and freedom, and we carefully listen as He speaks to us through the Spirit. He alone is able to guide our lives, just as He led first century Christians, who possessed no personal copies of either the writings of the prophets or the writings of the apostles, let alone a complete copy of the Bible as we know it. The Lord is equally able to direct us from within today.

The Bible is a masterful work of art composed by God through no fewer than thirty-two human authors over a period of fourteen hundred years. The remarkable integrity of these forty-nine inspired books reveals their divine authorship. God has continued to preserve and protect the inspired revelation of His divine purposes over the last two millennia, so that even you and I can peer eagerly into the mind of God. We are blessed beyond measure to have direct access to our Maker's handbook for life.

Although we may certainly find truth and freedom in the living Word of God, we will not likely find them in the words of our English Bibles. Over nineteen hundred years of corrupt religious practice has distorted the perspective of the most well intentioned translators, and they have ignorantly injected contemporary church practice into the words of scripture and polluted the inspired writings with lies and half-truths from Genesis to Revelation. Every English Bible from the King James Version to the most modern translation is filled with mistranslations, and they all validate the generally accepted system of organized religion, which masquerades as the source of truth and freedom for believers. The Word of God is holy, but the Bible on your shelf is far from it.

Christians often assume the Bible is a holy book, when in fact no writing—no epistle—no book is holy. God has designated nothing to be holy in our lives as Christians. The old covenant was filled with holy times, holy places and holy things, but there are no holy times, no holy places and no holy things in the New Covenant. God is holy, Jesus Christ is holy, and those who live in Him are holy. We are holy, because the Holy Spirit lives in us, not because we read the Bible. Bible study is not required for salvation. Faith is required for salvation. We faithfully depend on Jesus Christ for our daily direction and possess within ourselves the pure and unchangeable Word of God. The living Word of God within us is beyond the reach of the meddling hands of human beings who, by nature, pollute and besmirch everything they touch. "Jesus Christ is the same yesterday, today and forever." (Heb 13:8)

However, the Bible is very important to us, and it is incumbent upon all of us to understand the nature of the book we call the Holy Bible. Although the Bible as a book is not holy of and by itself, the inspired writings contain holy thoughts. God's Thought is holy, and the Bible was intended to convey some of God's thoughts to His people. Holy men were inspired by the Spirit to record the thoughts of God and create a written record of truth, which God preserved for believers of all ages to examine. These inspired writings, reflecting either historical, prophetic or spiritual truth, are the only basis by which we can authoritatively resolve questions of faith, doctrine and practice. Unfortunately, the original writings of the prophets and the histories and epistles of the apostles, called autographs, have all long since been lost. All we have remaining of the inspired autographs of the biblical writings are copies of copies of copies.

The surviving copies of the apostles' inspired writings fall short of perfection, but the thoughts of God recorded in them are remarkably well preserved, and their texts largely agree in content. Where they do not, the science of textual criticism provides the means to recognize many of the intended and unintended changes, which have occurred by the hands of men in the process of copying and recopying the original writings over the centuries, and the present day Nestle text has been largely restored to reflect the original content of the apostles' letters. You may hear or read about the hundreds of thousands of variations in the three thousand or so surviving whole or partial Greek texts, but you should consider that the vast majority of those variants are either unintentional copyist's errors, which have been easily found and corrected, or intentional insertions, which are recognizable and have, in many cases, been removed from the text and from modern translations. The overall impact these thousands of variants have on the meaning of the text is negligible, and even the intentional insertions have little impact on belief or practice. Keep in mind that textual critics are a very fussy group of people. They work tirelessly to reproduce the exact text of the autographs of the apostles, whereas very, very close is entirely sufficient to determine the mind of God on any particular question of belief or practice.

The inspiration of the Bible is unquestioned, except by those who doubt God Himself. Jesus put His stamp of approval on the Old Testament writings when He attested that not one jot or tittle would pass away from the law until all was fulfilled, (Matt 5:18) and the apostle Paul verified that all scripture (the Old Testament) was given by inspiration of God. (2 Tim 3:16) The apostle Peter directly associated the New Testament writings of the apostle Paul with scripture, (2 Pet 3:16) and the Lord prayed for those of us who would embrace a life of faith through the words the apostles wrote. (John 17:20) Those who carefully examine the Greek text should notice the remarkable integrity of thought and expression shared among the various writers of the books of the New Testament. Additionally, the New Testament perfectly complements the Old as its fulfillment and serves to complete the revelation of God for His new covenant people. The hand of God is clearly visible in the canonization of the New Testament, and the critically edited Nestle Greek text reflects both inspiration and completeness.

Although the original words written by the apostles were divinely inspired, the inerrancy of the inspired texts is a subject open to endless discussion and debate. We cannot examine the autographs of the apostles to see whether they were inerrant or not, because we do not possess them. The original writings have all long since disintegrated and turned to dust, so any discussion about inerrancy is an exercise in futility; but, even if we possessed an inerrant original text, our English Bibles could not retain the inerrancy. Translation always produces an interpretation. Translations cannot be inerrant. Whenever the original texts are interpreted by a man or a group of men, they are no longer the same and, therefore, no longer inerrant. Inerrancy is impossible in respect to a translation. For those interested in an authoritative and informative discussion of biblical inerrancy by textual critics working in the field, I recommend Bart Ehrman's recently published work, *Misquoting Jesus,* and Timothy Paul Jones' rebuttal work, *Misquoting Truth.* Although these two scholars disagree about the severity of the impact these scribal errors and additions have upon the Greek text of the New Testament, they are in complete agreement that the texts we possess contain errors. We do not possess any inerrant text of scripture.

In spite of the many minor errors in the existing copies of Greek manuscripts, I am convinced the reconstructed Nestle text is reliable. The integrity of the apostles inspired thoughts remains intact. All the discussion about these minor mistakes in the original language texts camouflages a much more significant problem. The technical points surrounding issues of textual criticism have raised a smoke screen of doubt regarding the original texts, and these issues effectively blind most people to the real problem existing in every Bible they read. Original language texts are not the problem. Translations are the problem. The translations, upon which most believers are entirely dependent, not only vary significantly from one translation to another, but they all vary significantly from the original language texts. You need only visit any Bible bookstore to see that there are dozens of different translations. You should be appalled to realize that there are so many translations, because logic should tell you no more than one of them could possibly be correct. In fact, none are. In addition to the difficulties inherent in accurately conveying any thought from one language to another, faithless translators have hidden the meanings of the inspired words by attributing their own theological paradigms to their translations. Every translator has interpreted, manipulated and changed the meaning of the precious words of God. Translations are inherently corrupt and unreliable. You should only trust the original texts in their original languages.

Although translations are far from accurate, you should feel blessed to be able to read the Bible in your native tongue. However, you should realize that each translator places his own personal spin on the meaning of words, the tense of verbs, and the structure of sentences, all of which function together in the original language to form the inspired message the author conveyed to his original audience. Difficulties will always arise whenever thoughts are translated from one language into another, and these difficulties are compounded when translators take liberties with the text and break the rules of responsible translation. The existence of dozens of translations obscures the reality that the inspired authors of the Bible wrote their histories and letters with one meaning to one audience in one context. Only one translation at the most could possibly be inspired, but the realization that none of them is inspired will be your first step toward freedom. Each translation is produced by a group of people who bring their personal religious experiences and perspectives to the translation. Thus, the crystal clear words of God invariably become colored when they are filtered through religiously biased human minds. The existence of this multitude of translations is clear evidence that religious organizations have been willing to bear the expense of translation and publication in order to validate, promote and codify their private interpretations of scripture.

Perhaps you can better appreciate the apostle Peter's concern in light of his admonition to the scattered Jewish brethren to avoid private interpretations of scripture. (2 Pet 1:20) Translation naturally results in an interpretation, because the exact thoughts the author expressed in the original language can never be precisely conveyed in another language. Peter, in fact, warned the recipients of his epistle to avoid translations. Peter wrote to Hebrew brethren who were scattered around Asia Minor, and some of them were getting used to speaking and reading Greek. Scholars had even produced a Greek translation of the Hebrew Old Testament, and the Septuagint was gaining popularity among Jews who could no longer read Hebrew. Peter was encouraging the brethren to retain their ability to read their ancient language, so they would always have direct access to the inspired thoughts God preserved in Hebrew, even though Greek had become the first language of many Jews. We may apply the same principle to the New Testament scriptures, which God inspired to be written in Koine Greek. God strongly implies through Peter that later generations of believers should continue to read and understand the Greek language, so every believer would always have direct access to the words God inspired for His Church.

Koine Greek is actually not that hard to learn. It is a relatively simple language, but it is very precise. English, on the other hand, is very sloppy. We have become complacent in the way we express thoughts. In recent centuries English speakers have abandoned some of the basic grammatical constructions which are essential to properly translate God's message for His Church, consequently, modern day English has lost the capacity to convey some simple Greek expressions accurately. In spite of those deficiencies, most of us don't read Greek and most are unwilling to even attempt to learn the language through which God spoke to the churches. Shame on us. Certainly everyone need not learn Greek, but there ought to be far more of us who are at least familiar enough with it to overturn the most egregiously misleading translations.

My personal study has revealed hundreds, indeed thousands, of significant omissions, additions and mistranslations in our English Bibles. These errors collectively skew major perspectives and individually misrepresent simple details God intended all of us to understand. Recent movements to modernize the language of older translations, to improve the readability of translations and to make translations gender neutral will only serve to further obscure the pure truths and thoughts God intended to convey to each member of His Church. Nearly sixty years of study has taught me that every word of scripture is important, that God inspired the tense of every verb for a reason and that I cannot ignore the cases of nouns without distorting the message God preserved for me to read and understand. Even the presence or absence of an article reveals a little something about the way God thinks.

Perhaps an example will begin to underscore the problem. Translators occasionally encounter passages containing what seems to be difficult language, not that the words themselves are difficult to translate, but that the literal meaning is difficult to believe. Just such a passage, which scholars call a "difficult reading," appears in 1 Peter 1:20. In every English translation of this short phrase, the translators allege that Jesus Christ was manifest or appeared in these last times for our benefit. The wording varies from translation to translation, but the translators invariably make the assertion that Christ <u>was manifest</u> (past tense) <u>for</u> us (showing benefit).

> [Jesus Christ]… <u>was manifest</u> in these last times <u>for you</u>, (1 Peter 1:20)

However, when I examined the Greek text, it plainly says Christ <u>is being manifest</u> (aorist participle) <u>through</u> us (showing means). The difference in meaning is profound. Remarkably, the translators have told us something which is true, but the thought Peter revealed to his audience is entirely hidden from our view. Translators have literally turned truth into a lie by substituting a truth taught elsewhere in the Bible for Peter's inspired thought. We can read elsewhere that Jesus appeared in the flesh and was sacrificed for our benefit, but nowhere else in the Bible can we plainly read that Jesus Christ can be seen in these last times as He is walking on earth today and speaking through the members of His Church. We may reach such a conclusion, if we understand the nature of the Church and realize He lives in each of the members of His body, but the Bible does not specifically express the thought in any other passage that the Lord is being manifest in these last times through us.

I do not believe the translators intended this errant translation to obscure any biblical truth, but it simply arises from the translators' lack of faith in the plain, inspired, Greek text. Socially elite and self-absorbed KJV translators simply could not believe that Jesus Christ was walking the streets of London in pauper's clothes or speaking through someone with a Cockney accent, but God wants every Christian to know the Lord is walking and talking today through the members of His Church regardless of our nationality, skin color, gender, life circumstance or manner of speech. This error in translation belies the translators' scholarly credentials. They knew what the text said. They just couldn't believe what it said. They lacked faith in the inspired words of God.

In order to effect this change, the translators had to introduce two errors. First, they had to change the tense of the verb from an aorist passive participle to the passive past tense, and second, they had to change the meaning of the Greek preposition, *dia*, to indicate benefit rather than means. This combination of errors, both of which were necessary to change the meaning of the verse, clearly indicates an intentional manipulation. Although obviously intentional, I do not believe it was malicious. Unfortunately, the KJV became so highly revered as an authoritative translation that those making subsequent translations have been loath to overturn these and other mistakes. Longstanding interpretative precedent compounded by theological and ecclesiastical authority still blocks our access to an accurate literal translation of the inspired texts today.

Although the original Hebrew and Greek texts are reliable, most of us cannot read Hebrew or Greek. Most of us are dependent on English translations, which largely convey the translators' perceptions of what the original text says. The Bibles we read are quite adequate to inspire each of us personally to good works, but English Bibles are woefully inadequate to determine what ought to be taught in churches. We may read them for personal inspiration and edification, but church leaders should not use them to counsel or instruct believers in their walk with God. Every Christian teacher needs to be trained in Hebrew and Greek and be able to read the Bible in its inspired languages.

Nearly twenty centuries of errant ecclesiastical doctrine and practice has largely obscured God's purpose for mankind and the true nature of the Christian life. Translated versions of the Bible are primarily responsible, but the convenience of translation in these end times does not exempt any of us, particularly not church leaders and teachers, from becoming familiar with the original language texts. Responsible pastors and teachers must be able to read the original languages and study the inspired texts without prejudice. They cannot afford to depend on another man's opinion about the meaning of scripture. Many of the subtleties of the inspired languages are lost in translation, and they can only be seen through direct access to the words God inspired. Pastors and teachers especially need access to the inspired writings, so they are able to teach and counsel confidently based on first-hand knowledge of inspired texts; however, all those who deeply desire to know God and seek a personal relationship with Him will be richly rewarded for their efforts to approach Him through the words He inspired.

Inquisitive Bible students may consult a number of Bible programs, reference books and study helps to gain insight into the original texts. Independent scholarly works may be reasonably trusted to help those who cannot read Hebrew or Greek. Although contemporary practices have corrupted every translator and every translation, scholars of Hebrew and Greek remain largely independent of organizational theologies and the authorities who promote them, because scholars have no doctrine to defend and no theological axe to grind. Integrity in scholarship demands that they truthfully reveal the literal definitions of words, explain the true nature of the tenses of verbs, show the proper cases of nouns and convey every part of speech accurately to maintain their standing in the community of scholars. The scholars' focus is language, not religion, so they may be reasonably, but not blindly, trusted to teach us the truth of the inspired texts. Even scholars make mistakes, so interpretations based on contemporary ecclesiastical practice have also crept into scholarly works, but we may usually separate these interpretations from actual language function, if we analyze their work carefully, because their scholarly work is nearly always separated in some way from their personal interpretations.

Concordances and word study reference books provide a wealth of basic information necessary to shed light upon the inspired meaning of the Hebrew and Greek texts. In addition, Bible programs for the computer offer powerful research capability for serious Bible students. Use of these tools presupposes only an understanding of English grammar, because words function the same way in every language. Nouns, for example, in one language will be translated into nouns in the other language. Likewise, verbs will be translated into verbs, and adjectives into adjectives, etc. When you encounter a noun in the original text, but you see a verb in your English Bible, you will have, at the very least, found a subtle manipulation of the inspired text. Unfortunately, subtle manipulations of words are not uncommon, and they frequently conceal some small, but significant, revelation of the truth of God.

A concordance is a Bible student's most basic tool to check translation, and it provides scholarly insight into the pronunciation and meaning of every word in the Bible. Strong's concordance has two parts: 1) the alphabetical listing of every English word in the Bible with its numerical key to the original language definition; 2) a Hebrew and Greek dictionary of numerically keyed word meanings, which can be found in the back of the concordance. To find the definition of the original word supporting any English word, first look up the English word alphabetically, and then scan down the list of verses until you find the specific verse where the word you would like to examine is used. Observe the fragment of the verse with the word included, specifically noting the number at the right end of the partial verse. That number is the key to find the definition of the original language word. Next, turn to the back of the concordance and find the appropriate Hebrew or Greek dictionary. Numbers in block type are found in the Hebrew dictionary. Numbers in italics are found in the Greek dictionary. In the appropriate dictionary, find the number of the word. You have now found the original language word and its literal definition.

Once you find the original word and its definition, it is important to know how to interpret the information contained in the definition. Immediately after the key number you will find the following information: 1) the word in the original language; 2) the word transliterated to English; 3) the phonetic pronunciation of the word; 4) the root or word family from which the word was derived, usually indicated by "from" and another reference number; 5) <u>the definition of the word in italics</u>; 6) various additional and often helpful bits of information indicated by implication (by imp), literally (lit) or figuratively (fig), technically (techn), etc.

The original language definition you are seeking will usually be the fifth piece of information in Strong's concordance, and it will always appear in italics. Carefully compare the definition with the English word in your translation. Mistranslations frequently occur when translators do not faithfully translate words according to their literal definitions. While scholarly definitions rarely stray from a literal meaning, the most dangerous part of Strong's otherwise scholarly work is the sixth bit of information, which follows the literal definition of the word. Although these are usually helpful, notations here can be misleading or in error. Be particularly careful of technical (techn) meanings or those designated "concretely" or "especially." These frequently reflect contemporary ecclesiastical practice. Some scholars format their dictionaries differently, but in Strong's you will only find interpretations in this last group of usually helpful information (6). Depend first and foremost on the literal definition (5), then consider how the appended notations (6) might apply in certain contexts. If you are still in doubt, consult another Hebrew or Greek dictionary. "In the multitude of counselors there is safety." (Prov 11:14)

As your study expands beyond word definitions and into grammatical considerations, Zodhiates' *Complete Word Study Old Testament* and *Complete Word Study New Testament* are valuable study tools. Each word in the Bible is coded in Dr. Zodhiates' books to show the word's function in each instance as a part of speech, i.e., verb, noun, pronoun, adjective, preposition, conjunction, etc. A key card connects the grammar code to the grammatical notations in the Study Helps section, which further explains how each word functions grammatically in a sentence. Although you can find all sorts of grammatical errors by carefully comparing a word's use in the inspired text with the function of its counterpart in any English translation, the most significant mistranslations arise when translators assume the authority to take liberties with the literal definitions of words and the expressed tenses of verbs. These two types of manipulations are easiest to make and have the most significant impact on the meaning of the text, but they are also the easiest to find and correct. These two types of textual manipulations lead to more mistranslations and misinterpretations than any other.

By far the most powerful study help is a Bible program for your computer. Make sure the program offers Hebrew and Greek research capability. Bible programs not only contain a wide diversity of study helps, but good programs contain the Old Testament in Hebrew and the New Testament in Greek, all keyed with Strong's numbers to provide instant access to word definitions by the click of a mouse. Zodhiates' Word Study Bibles are also available on disc and combine with Bible programs to provide the most powerful study tools available without actually learning the languages.

For those who would like to learn the ancient Hebrew and Koine Greek languages, basic grammar textbooks and on-line classes are available. Interactive pronunciation and tutoring discs along with workbooks and grammar charts will allow a diligent Bible student to investigate the nuances of the original languages with nearly the precision of a biblical scholar. In this end time God has left us with no excuse for allowing ourselves to be fooled by the translators.

Although Bible study is not required for salvation, it has become imperative in an environment where the proliferation of translations, all seeming to convey the thoughts of God, and the abundance and diversity of church organizations, all claiming to teach according to the inspired thoughts of God, have rather hidden and twisted the inspired thoughts of God. Since we speak a different language than the apostles spoke and we are nearly twenty centuries removed from the churches the apostles established, we not only need to study the Bible to show ourselves approved unto God, but we especially need to study the inspired texts to avoid being misled by those who base their doctrines on English translations and pridefully desire to draw a following after themselves.

In an effort to whet your appetite for personal study and research in the original language texts, I have peppered the remainder of this book with references to the scholarly works of James Strong and Spiros Zodhiates, whose works I have quoted to expose dozens of translation errors relevant to the subject of this book. Their dictionaries and word studies provide a scholarly basis for the conclusions I have reached in this book, and I quote from their work and insert it into the discussion whenever the KJV translation is in question. Please check my work independently to verify its accuracy and to make sure you know how to use a concordance or a word study reference book effectively for your own research.

Although the original language texts are very reliable to guide us in our walk with God, we should always remember that the Judge and Head of our personal lives is Jesus Christ. Access to the written words of God is an additional blessing to anchor us firmly in the faith, but the motivation for our actions should come primarily from the personal relationship we have with the Lord and the personal direction we receive from Him daily. The living Word of God within us—our Lord Jesus Christ—is just as able to direct us today as He was in the first century when believers possessed no personal copies of scripture to read.

Chapter 2

The Nature of Covenant

True freedom becomes a reality when a sinner enters into a covenant relationship with God. A sinner cannot approach God, know God or have a relationship with God without entering into Covenant with God. Are you in Covenant with God? Do you understand the covenant relationship which makes you one with God? Do you know what the New Covenant is? Far too many churchgoers today have little or no concept of the nature of biblical covenants. The sole purpose for the Bible is to reveal Jesus Christ in order that those whom God calls to His Son may have a covenant relationship with their Creator. The Bible is the written record of God's Covenant for every faithful believer.

God created Adam and Eve in a sinless state, so they walked in the Garden of Eden in harmony with God. God allowed them to live freely in His garden and eat the fruit from every tree God had created, except for the infamous tree of the knowledge of good and evil. Since God knew human beings had no inherent capacity to differentiate between good and evil, He tested the first couple to see whether they would trust His Word or trust their own observation and intellect to determine right from wrong. Sadly, they failed the test and ate the forbidden fruit. That one sin changed their nature and separated all humanity from God.

The essential evil which separates mankind from God is their steadfast refusal to allow God to set the standard which determines right from wrong in their lives. As long as human beings continue to use their own senses to determine what is good and what is evil, sin keeps them separated from God, and, as long as they are separated from God, they are as good as dead. Sin requires the life of each individual to pay the debt for sin, and every sin debt will be paid. "The wages of sin is death." (Rom 6:23) The only way a human being can pay his own sin debt is to give up his life and die. When he dies, his death satisfies God's law of sin and death and frees him from sin, (Rom 6:7) but once dead, he has no ability to resurrect himself out of the grave. He can pay his own debt, but he remains separated from God, because human beings do not possess eternal life within themselves.

God alone possesses eternal life, and only God is sinless. God exists in a state of perfection, and He cannot abide where sin dwells. Sin has separated mankind from God, and humans have no capacity to reverse their sinful state. They are entirely dependent on God to reach out to them and offer them His solution to redeem them from sin and reconcile the relationship broken by their insistence that they make their own decisions. Fortunately, the Creator deeply desires a personal relationship with His creation, and toward that end He has provided the means by which those of us who are willing to allow Him to personally direct our lives may be reconciled to Him and live pleasingly in His sight. The means through which God personally lives in us and directs our lives is covenant.

Through covenant God cleans up our sinful lives and restores our relationship with Him. We become clean, or holy, and our sins are expunged, so we may walk in harmony with God. The only way sinful human beings can have a relationship with God is through covenant. We have no instinctive sense of godly love, faith or even hope. The only way we can express what the Greek language calls *agape* love or live by what the Bible calls *the* faith or rest in the *hope* of eternal life is to allow the One Who created us to live inside of us and direct us from within. Without covenant, natural human beings cannot have any relationship with God, leaving them with no capacity for godly love or any other godly attribute. They may talk about love. They may believe they have faith. They may even claim to hold a hope for life beyond the physical realm, but the fulfillment of faith, hope and love is impossible without a covenant relationship with God. The covenant relationship and its attending features pervade the Bible from cover to cover, and a firm grasp of the basics of covenant is imperative for believers to achieve an understanding of our relationship to God, our relationship to Jesus Christ and our relationship to all faithful believers.

The central and essential feature of any covenant is the covenant sacrifice. The life of the covenant becomes a substitute life for the life of the one who sinned, and the blood of the covenant covers or removes the sin of the one who sinned. The life of an individual or animal is in the blood, (Lev 17:11) so the blood of the covenant is a substitute life for the life God requires for sin in every case. When the covenant is cut, or slain, God's law of sin and death is satisfied, and God is obliged to forgive us of any sin we may have committed.

We become holy—spiritually clean—before God, and He restores the relationship broken by sin.

We should not be too surprised to find that the first implication of a covenant was recorded in the Bible on the occasion of Adam and Eve's sin in the Garden of Eden. The Bible very simply states that God made coats of skin and clothed Adam and Eve, (Gen 3:21) but the reality that God had sacrificed an animal in their place and shed the animal's blood to symbolically cover their sin should be apparent. God made clothes for them from the skin of the sacrificed animal and literally covered them to alleviate their embarrassment from the effects of their sin—their awareness of nakedness—and to symbolically restore their relationship with God. God determined that we should all wear clothes to remind each of us that human beings are sinful by nature and that all of us must be clothed in a covenant Sacrifice in order to have a relationship with God.

God offered the first explicitly stated Covenant to Noah, a just man who walked with God. Noah was not sinless or perfect, as some translations imply, but the Hebrew word indicates he was morally complete—a man of integrity. God promised Noah that this Covenant would be established at some future time, (Gen 6:18) so a covenant sacrifice was not cut on that occasion, but God's promise was sufficient to afford him protection from the flood which God brought upon the earth. We should be able to appreciate the vital importance of a covenant promise from God in this instance, since only Noah and his family survived the cataclysmic event which wiped human existence from the earth, save eight souls.

After the flood God announced another aspect of His Covenant to Noah. He promised Noah, his descendents and every living creature that He would never destroy all flesh again by a flood. (Gen 9:9-17) Since this Covenant was also yet to be established, God placed the first sign of His Covenant—the sign of the rainbow—in the sky and gave us this sign of the Covenant to remind us of His promise to spare mankind from another flood. We not only appreciate God's promise to spare us from another flood, but this sign also reminds us that our physical existence is entirely dependent upon the Covenant God promised through Noah.

The next two covenants recorded in the Bible were announced to Abraham, but only one applied to him. God's first covenant promise to Abraham provided a land as an inheritance for his descendents, the children of Israel. (Gen 15:9-21) This covenant is unique, because Abraham did not personally benefit from the promises announced to him. Remarkably, he was asleep at the time God established this covenant. On this occasion many interpreters believe God Himself passed like "a smoking furnace and a burning lamp" between the cut pieces of the covenant animals. This land covenant was necessary to provide a home for the children of Israel, as God prepared to establish the old covenant with the nation of Israel. It is important to observe exactly what God said, or did not say, on this occasion when He cut this land covenant with Abraham.

> In the same day the LORD [cut] a covenant with Abram, saying, Unto thy seed have I given this land, from the river of Egypt unto the great river, the river Euphrates: (Gen 15:18)

God instructed Abraham to divide, or cut, the sacrificial animals into two pieces and lay them out on the ground. In our culture we write covenants and we make agreements. We don't cut them. The nature of biblical covenants is very different. In ancient cultures the animal was the covenant, and the animal was cut, or sacrificed, to establish the covenant. When English Bibles say that a covenant was made, the inspired Hebrew text always says it was cut. The sacrificial animal was the covenant. Covenant and sacrifice were synonymous terms. A firm grasp of the nature of biblical covenants is imperative in order to understand the nature of the New Covenant.

Zionists claim God gave the land of Canaan to the descendants of Abraham for a perpetual inheritance, so modern day Jews assume they have a divine right to possess the same land called Palestine today. However, careful scrutiny of the covenant text above reveals a promise of land, but not a promise of land forever. This covenant was exclusively for the nation of Israel during the period of the old covenant. Some historians place the river of Egypt in the Negev and indicate the territory under David's and Solomon's influence did indeed extend from there to the great river Euphrates.

Although God cut "a covenant" with Abraham that day and had given (past tense) the land to Israel, God later promised He will raise up (future tense) "My Covenant" with Abraham. (Gen 17:7) In this future Covenant, God promised that He will give (future tense) the land to Abraham "and to thy seed" forever. (v.8) In Galatians 3:16 Paul explained that God limited the application of His promises to Abraham "and to thy seed" to a singular interpretation of the word "seed," therefore, we must interpret the phrase "and to thy seed" to refer to Christ alone. Under the terms of this eternal Covenant—My Covenant—which God promised to establish with Abraham, the promise of land "forever" only applies to Jesus Christ.

This eternal Covenant has become known as the Abrahamic Covenant. (Gen 17:1-11) The language of the terms and promises of this Covenant is marked by future tense verbs, and the blood of the Covenant is conspicuously missing from the biblical record. Since covenants were always established by shedding the blood of the covenant sacrifice, these circumstances combine to imply that the Abrahamic Covenant was intended to be established at a future time. In the meantime God placed another sign of the Covenant, circumcision, in Abraham's flesh until the blood of the Covenant could be shed to establish "My Covenant." The sign of circumcision designated Abraham as a covenant partner with God. (v. 10)

The aforementioned covenants were all covenants which God established with or promised to individuals. We will also consider the two significant covenants God has established with nations, but before we examine the nature of the old and new covenants, we should consider an important human covenant established between two men. Since all covenants are essentially marriage agreements, some have suggested that the covenant between Jonathan and David resulted from a homosexual relationship, but such an allegation is preposterous. David was a man after God's own heart, (Acts 13:22) and scripture tells us God condemns homosexuality. (Lev 18:22, Rom 1:27) Jonathan and David's mutual love for one another was a godly love, and there was no impropriety in their relationship at all. We should not read into the text what is not there but rather observe the masterful hand of God at work through the unity produced by Jonathan and David's covenant relationship.

> Then Jonathan and David [cut] a covenant, because he loved him as his own soul. And Jonathan stripped himself of the robe that was upon him, and gave it to David, and his garments, even to his sword, and to his bow, and to his girdle. (1 Sam 18:3-4)

Every covenant establishes a union between unequal partners. God is clearly the greater partner in covenants with individuals or earthly nations, but you may not so easily discern the greater and lesser partners in Jonathan and David's covenant. David's character stands so tall in biblical history that you might assume he was the greater partner. Such is not the case. Jonathan was King Saul's firstborn son and heir to the throne of Israel. He was an experienced warrior and a ranking officer in his father's army. Young David had been blessed with the victory over Goliath, but he had no experience at all on the battlefield. The narrative describes David as an adolescent, while Jonathan was a middle-aged man perhaps twice David's age. Jonathan's love for David was a pure godly and fatherly love. He had little to gain from a covenant relationship with David, but David's covenant relationship with Jonathan united them together as one and made David a co-heir to the throne of Israel.

Covenants aren't about sex but rather create unity. Covenant partners become one with each other. In a profound gesture of unity, Jonathan gave David his robe and weapons of warfare to symbolize the reality of their covenant relationship. The robe was a symbol of Jonathan's royalty and designated him as an heir to the throne, so, when Jonathan gave David his robe, David also became a rightful heir to the throne. When Jonathan gave David his armor and sword, David assumed his rank in the army of Israel. The symbolism of the exchange set up David to fulfill Samuel's prophecy that the kingdom would be removed from the house of Saul. (1 Sam 15:28) Subsequently, God sent Samuel to anoint David to be king over Israel, and this covenant with Jonathan confirmed David as the legitimate heir when Saul and Jonathan died together in battle.

Armed with an overview of some ancient covenants, which described the sacrificial animal as the substance of the covenant and unified the covenant partners as one, we may now consider the nature of the two covenants God established with nations. The first was established with a physical nation, Israel, and the second with a spiritual nation, the Church. Both covenants contain the central and essential element of a covenant sacrifice to purge sin and unite the covenant partners, but the essential nature of these two covenants is entirely different. The first covenant was established by sacrificing animals, and the second was established by sacrificing a Man. The first contained codified laws written in words on stone tablets, but the second is the Word of God and contains a complete, living Law. The first was mediated through Moses, but the second is mediated through Jesus Christ. The first had human high priests, but the second a divine High Priest. The first covenant kept the people clean by sprinkling them with the blood of animals and by observing holy times, holy places and holy things, but the second Covenant keeps God's people clean by His own blood, which instantly cleanses us from every sin and continually maintains our holiness in Him. The first was a covenant of types and symbols pointing to the second, but the second is the one and only living Covenant.

In all the previous covenants which God established with men, (if I may momentarily speak of them as separate), God assumed the role of the greater Partner. He gave His Word to provide blessings and protection for the patriarchs, and the patriarchs gave their word to obey God's Word in every aspect of their lives. God's Word forms the basis for any covenant relationship with God, just as an individual's word is the basis for any relationship with that individual. A covenant relationship is essentially a simple agreement, highlighted by a covenant sacrifice and an exchange of vows to remain faithful to the covenant partner. Covenants remain simple between trustworthy individuals, who may personally exchange their word to establish the terms of the agreement and exchange vows of commitment and fidelity, but covenants become more complicated when the partners are untrustworthy or one partner is a nation filled with unproven individuals. In such cases the greater partner must spell out the terms of the relationship, and each partner must affix a signature to the covenant, so the greater partner may legally prosecute offenders according to the terms of the covenant agreement.

The ancient covenants God cut with the patriarchs were packed with unwritten symbolism, but, when God entered into His first relationship with a nation, all the aspects of a modern day contract were evident in the covenant God established with Israel. In our contemporary world, men and women are assumed to be untrustworthy, and they are often required to enter into legally binding contracts, which must be validated by signatures and which contain the rules or terms of the covenant agreement. Various benefits may be specified for each party, often including that which each may receive in the form of goods, services or the exchange of money. Contracts frequently include the penalties which may result from any failure to fulfill the contract. If either party fails to uphold the agreement, the language of the contract itself will mediate the dispute, sometimes with the help of a judge. Although the nature of contracts has changed significantly over the centuries and today the official document is usually a piece of paper upon which the terms of the agreement are written and the signatures of the parties appear, every contract or covenant will contain all these basic elements and serve to unite the parties in agreement. The first national covenant God established with Israel specified each of these elements, which were always present but not necessarily obvious in the ancient covenants God cut with the patriarchs.

The Bible is naturally divided into two parts: the old covenant and the new covenant, not necessarily the Old and New Testaments. The word "testament" is a spurious reference to the first covenant because the relationship described by the old covenant was an agreement or contract, not just a will. It is misleading in the New Testament, not because we do not see the death of Jesus Christ and the expression, establishment and revelation of the will of God, but because the relationship we have with God according to His will is a covenant relationship. Christians enjoy a new covenant relationship with God, and the last twenty-seven books of the Bible particularly focus on the life, work and teaching of our Covenant and our relationship to Him.

The Old Covenant

All biblical covenants contain several essential elements either overtly or symbolically, and all these elements are particularly evident in the old covenant. First, there must be covenant partners interested in a relationship, and there must be a mediator between the covenant partners. There must also be a covenant document, and the document must have a sign, i.e., a signature. The terms of the covenant appear in the covenant document, and the sign of the covenant must always appear on the document itself. Lastly, every covenant must have a covenant sacrifice, and the covenant is established when the blood of the covenant sacrifice is shed.

The covenant partners under the old covenant were God and Israel. God called Israel out of Egypt to be His chosen people and promised them the protection of His divine favor and blessings in exchange for obedience to the laws He gave them at Mount Sinai. Since covenants unite the partners as one, the old covenant was essentially a marriage covenant between God and Israel.

Any covenant between covenant partners requires a mediator, more commonly known as a judge, and Moses was the mediator of the old covenant. Moses personally received the law from God, and he was directed to record all the commandments, statutes and judgments in the book of the covenant and to instruct Israel regarding God's laws. As the mediator of the covenant, Moses judged the people according to the words of the covenant. On several occasions when Israel sinned grievously, Moses intervened on their behalf and stood before God as an advocate for Israel.

The covenant document is a key element of every national covenant, and it reveals the terms of the agreement—the rules—the laws which define the relationship between the covenant partners. Two stone tablets were the covenant documents which bound Israel to God in the old covenant marriage relationship. God's covenant law for the nation of Israel, written on each of those tablets, was the ten commandments. (Deut 4:13) These two covenant documents embodied Israel's covenant law—the constitution—the basis for their covenant relationship with God, which was expanded into the law of Moses, or the *torah*, for the nation of Israel.

The signatures of both parties to an agreement authorize the covenant relationship. The signatures must appear conspicuously on the document, and any covenant without signatures is invalid. The signature, or sign, God placed on the old covenant was the sabbath. (Ex 31:13) The sabbath injunction was not only visible on the covenant document, but it was also readily apparent in the life of each Israelite. The sign of the sabbath set Israel apart from the nations and designated them as the people of God. To fulfill her responsibility to sign the covenant, Israel placed her mark on the covenant documents when Moses broke both stone tablets.

God outlined the terms of the old covenant marriage agreement on the covenant documents. The ten commandments, or, in Hebrew, the ten words, were the heart of the law which governed Israel in her relationship with God under the old covenant. Each of the six hundred thirteen statutes and judgments God gave Moses had their basis in the ten words. God placed explicit restrictions on changes to the law and forbade any Israelite, whether judge, king or average citizen, to add to or to diminish from the law God had established for Israel. (Deut 4:2) The law was unchangeable. No one was authorized to make laws for Israel. God alone ruled Israel.

An essential element of every covenant with God is the covenant sacrifice. The sinful nature of human beings requires the shedding of blood to cover or remove their sins, and the sacrificial blood reconciles them to God and restores the relationship broken by sin. Under the old covenant, animals served as typical covenant sacrifices. Moses sprinkled their blood on the people to symbolically purge their sin and restore them to a proper relationship to God.

As mentioned previously, every covenant unifies the partners in agreement, so God and Israel became unified together as one. Even though the human mind has difficulty imagining two separate entities being one, particularly when one partner is God and the other is a physical person or nation, the concepts of covenant and unity cannot be separated. We may at least partially grasp the unity of covenant by considering a husband and his wife in conjugal union, but we may still have difficulty understanding that God sees a husband and his wife as one flesh continually. The unity of covenant is a spiritual reality viewed through the eyes of God. In God's eyes the consummated marriage relationship cannot be broken, except in death, and God requires believers to acquire and maintain His perspective in every human marriage relationship. Those who do not fully realize the spiritual unity of every marriage relationship will have difficulty visualizing the spiritual unity Israel (and later the Church) had with God in the covenant relationship.

The divinely influenced culture of ancient Israel viewed engagement and marriage from a different perspective than we do in our culture. Although our modern engagements end with a covenant, vows of commitment and conjugal union on the wedding day, Hebrew engagements began with a covenant and a vow to be faithful, and then a period of time elapsed before the wedding feast was held and the marriage was consummated. The couple was legally married as husband and wife from the time they established the covenant agreement, even though they did not come together sexually. After the groom paid a certain marriage price to the father of the bride, the groom went to prepare a place for the couple to live. During this engagement period of separation, the couple remained chaste and each carefully guarded his or her virginity. After the groom returned, the couple held a week-long wedding feast and came together in sexual union. This manner of wedding tradition forms the basis for God's instruction regarding marriage in the Bible. Those who ignore the Jewish wedding custom will have difficulty understanding the biblical instructions regarding marriage, and the present relationship between Christ and the Church will likely remain unclear.

Animals served as the symbolic covenants, and Moses sacrificed animals to establish the marriage relationship between God and Israel. Our English Bibles introduce a conceptual error to our minds when we read that covenants were "made," even though we "make" covenants today by signing a piece of paper, but ancient covenants were entirely different. In ancient times covenants were "cut," as is evident in the corrected translations of the verses on pages 16 and 17 above, because the covenant was not a piece of paper but an animal, which was sacrificed to establish the relationship. The animal was cut, not made. When the covenant was cut, or sacrificed, each partner agreed to defend and protect the interests of the other. If either partner failed to keep his word to uphold the covenant agreement, the offending partner would be subject to death.

Israel's covenant with God was cut and established at Mt. Sinai. Under the direction of God, Moses led Israel out of Egypt through the Red Sea and on a seven-week trek in the wilderness to Mount Sinai, where God presented the terms of the marriage covenant to Moses and then exchanged wedding vows with Israel. God spoke to Moses before He went up the mountain to receive the covenant documents and explained the law He later engraved on the tablets. Moses told the people all the words of the Lord including God's promise that "ye shall be a peculiar treasure unto me above all people." (Ex 19:5) When Israel heard the terms of the covenant, "all the people answered together and said, 'All that the LORD hath spoken we will do.'" (Ex 19:8) God's expressed promise to take Israel as His special treasure and the people's explicit "I do" constituted the exchange of wedding vows.

When Moses had read all the words of the covenant from the book of the covenant and Israel repeated her promise to obey everything God required her to do, Moses took the blood of the covenant sacrifices and sprinkled it on the people to cover their sins.

The sacrifice and exchange of vows established a binding covenant between God and Israel, (Ex 24:8) but God and Israel had yet to come together as one. Israel was engaged to God through covenant, but they were not yet living together as one.

On the occasion of Moses' first trip up Mt. Sinai, God engraved the covenant documents and gave Moses instructions to prepare the tabernacle, so God could dwell with Israel and consummate the marriage covenant. However, during Moses' forty day absence, the people built a golden calf and began worshipping it instead of God. Their idolatry constituted spiritual fornication. God would have been justified to rescind His covenant agreement and divorce Israel, but Moses intervened on their behalf. God was satisfied to blot out those responsible rather than to divorce the whole nation. (Ex 32:33) Very few Bible students really grasp the magnitude of this single act of idolatry and the potential consequences fornication can precipitate in the Jewish tradition of an unconsummated covenant relationship.

Following God's forgiveness, Moses began construction on the tabernacle, which was placed in the center of the camp flanked on each of the four sides by three of the twelve tribes of Israel. Within a year the tabernacle was finished and all the furniture was installed. "Then a cloud covered the tent of the congregation, and the glory of the Lord filled the tabernacle." (Ex 40:34) God had come to dwell in the midst of Israel, completing the marriage between God and Israel. Divorce was no longer lawful for any of Israel's sins. (Matt 5:32)

God's presence within the tabernacle in the midst of the camp pictured the consummation of the marriage and Israel's unity with God, but the old covenant relationship was only a type of the relationship between God and the Church. God preserved the historical record of the marriage between God and Israel to prepare us to understand that He will even more fully live in the Church through Jesus Christ. God's presence *in* us is an even more intimate relationship than His presence *with* Israel.

An Israelite groom had the responsibility to build the couple's home prior to the wedding feast, so the couple had a place to live together as husband and wife. God had already made provision for Israel's home in the land of Canaan through His first covenant promise to Abraham four centuries before His covenant with Israel. God promised to give Israel the same land where Abraham sojourned. When the Sinai covenant was established, God gave

Israel instructions for occupying the land of Canaan. God promised to deliver the inhabitants of the land into Israel's hands as long as Israel did not enter into covenants with the people God intended to drive out of the land. God directed Israel to execute His judgment upon the occupants of the land, therefore, Israel was forbidden to cut any covenant with them or with their gods.

> Thou shalt [cut] no covenant with them, nor with their gods. (Ex 23:32)

Israel's ability to cut a covenant with the people of another nation is easy to understand, but you might legitimately ask how Israel could possibly cut a covenant with a stick of wood or a stone image. Bible students frequently assume these heathen gods were wood or stone images—and in some passages, depending on context, images may be implied—but such an assumption cannot be true in this context. The heathen kings of the nations around Israel made the laws for their people, and, in their role as rulers, they had usurped God's privilege to rule and stood in the place of God. The gods to which God referred were not inanimate. The heathen people were not bowing to laws made by wood or stone images. The people were bowing to their kings. The people's gods were their rulers. Consequently, when Israel cut a covenant with a ruling king, she cut a covenant with their god. These gods were not made of sticks and stones but rather were flesh and blood human beings. God's instruction in this verse prohibited covenants with the people of another nation or with their human rulers.

Israel was united in marriage with God, and any covenant Israel cut with the people of another nation or the ruler of that nation constituted adultery. God's restriction on covenants was an extension of the seventh commandment, which prohibited adultery. God required Israel to remain faithful in her marriage and avoid extramarital relationships, which would violate her covenant with God. God knew covenant relationships with other nations would turn Israel's attention away from His laws and lead to respect for the rulers of those nations and the recognition of their human laws. National adultery invariably led to idolatry, because a covenant with a Gentile ruler always required Israel to bow before the ruler and obey his laws. When Israel bowed in obedience to the laws of the human ruler, she also committed idolatry. Adultery and idolatry stand apart as Israel's greatest sins, and they were the inevitable and inseparable products of covenants with the nations.

In spite of God's instructions, Israel cut covenants with the occupants of the land and committed adultery and idolatry in God's sight. Joshua was cleverly tricked into the first covenant Israel cut with the Gibeonites shortly after entering the promised land, but, afterward, Israel cut covenant after covenant with the rulers of the nations around her. Israel depended less and less on God for her protection and more and more on the nations and city-states which occupied the surrounding territories. As Israel increasingly entered into covenants with the nations and rejected God's rulership, she slipped deeper and deeper into adultery and idolatry. When God's repeated warnings went unheeded, God withdrew all His blessings. Later, He removed Israel from the land, sent her into captivity and, after the covenant ended, scattered her people throughout the world.

The Transition from Old to New

A covenant with God is forever in the sense that the covenant agreement will be binding as long as the partners to the covenant continue to live. A covenant can only be broken by the death of one of the covenant partners. The covenant between God and Israel was an eternal covenant as long as both God and Israel lived. Within the old covenant were numerous perpetual injunctions and everlasting statutes, yet they all came to an end when the old covenant came to an end. Death terminates a covenant relationship.

Marriage is an eternal covenant established by God. Whether the marriage is between a man and a woman or between God and a nation, the marriage covenant is forever. The marriage cannot be terminated, except by the death of one of the covenant partners. When one mate dies, both are free from the law which bound the relationship. The marriage law does not cease to exist, but the covenant relationship is broken. If you keep in mind how covenants are terminated, you should be able to understand how the transition occurred from the old covenant to the New Covenant.

Israel had long since forsaken her covenant responsibilities to God and had become an unfaithful wife. She trusted the covenants she made with the nations around her more than the promises she received from God through the old covenant. Israel had rejected her covenant Partner. God and Israel were functionally separated, but God was bound to Israel as long as they both lived.

Additionally, God had already promised Israel a new and better Covenant than the codified law God originally gave her, but God could not establish the New Covenant until He terminated the old covenant. Only the death of one of the covenant partners could terminate the old covenant. Coincidentally, the New Covenant required the death of a covenant Sacrifice to become valid. In the fullness of time the omniscient mind of God accomplished both at once. God our Savior died.

Jesus was not only a man: He was divine. He was the physical manifestation of the eternal *Logos*, or the Word, Who existed from the beginning. (John 1:1, 14) Through the Word, the Father and the Spirit also dwelt in Christ. "For in [Jesus Christ] dwelleth all the fullness of the Godhead bodily." (Col 2:9) The Father, the Word and the Holy Spirit dwelt in Jesus Christ, but the existence of God as Father, Word and Holy Spirit was not diminished in the least by Christ's death, because Jesus died, not the triune God. Jesus' divine death terminated the marriage relationship between God and Israel. When Jesus died, His death freed God and Israel from the vows of their old covenant marriage relationship.

According to God's divine purpose, He sent His Word to end the first covenant and to establish the second. As God in the flesh, His divine death terminated the old covenant and, simultaneously, His divine Sacrifice established the New Covenant. The same death which ended the old covenant was also the covenant Sacrifice to establish the New. How elegant are the thoughts and plans of God!

Paul explained the transition from the old covenant to the New Covenant in the passage below, and he used the law, which bound God and Israel in their marriage, to describe the transition. Paul explained that the marriage relationship defined by the marriage covenant which bound Israel to God had been set aside because of the death of Jesus.

> For the woman [Israel] which hath an husband [God] is <u>bound by the law</u> [the marriage covenant] to her husband [God] so long as he liveth; but if the husband [God] be dead, she [Israel] is <u>loosed from the law</u> [the marriage covenant] of her husband

> [God]. So then if, while her husband liveth, she be married [by a covenant] to another man, she shall be called an adulteress: but if her [Israel's] husband [God] be dead, she [Israel] is <u>free from that law</u>; [the marriage covenant] so that she is no adulteress, though she [Israel] be married to another man [Christ]. Wherefore, my brethren, ye [the Roman church] also are become <u>dead to the law</u> [the marriage covenant] by the body of Christ; that ye [the Roman church] should be married to another [Christ], even to him who is raised from the dead, that we should bring forth fruit unto God. (Rom 7:2-4)

If Jesus had not died, the old covenant marriage would still be binding and Israel would still be married to God. In a selfless act of love, God offered His Word to free Israel from the bondage of her old covenant marriage and provide a New Covenant of freedom. As God in the flesh, Jesus' death loosed Israel from the ritualistic system of animal sacrifices and provided a new covenant Sacrifice for all believers. Jesus' sacrifice allowed both Jews and Gentiles to be united together into one living Covenant with God and began preparations for the yet future wedding feast of the Lamb when God in Christ will be united with the holy, virgin Church.

The New Covenant

About the time God executed His judgment upon the house of Judah and sent them into captivity, He sent Jeremiah the prophet to announce the New Covenant, which God would later cut with the house of Israel and the house of Judah. Jeremiah prophesied that the nature of the New Covenant would be completely different from the covenant God cut with Israel at Mt Sinai.

> Behold, the days come, saith the LORD, that I will [cut] a new covenant with the house of Israel, and with the house of Judah: <u>Not according to the covenant that I [cut] with their fathers</u> in the day that I took them by the hand to bring them out of the land of Egypt; which my covenant they brake, although I was an husband unto them, saith the LORD: But this

> shall be the covenant that I will [cut] with the house of Israel; After those days, saith the LORD, I will put my law in their inward parts, and write it in their hearts; and will be their God, and they shall be my people. (Jer 31:31-33)

This new and different Covenant would be "not according to the covenant that I [cut] with their fathers," which was a covenant of prescriptive laws written on tablets of stone and of animals cut as the covenant sacrifices, but this Covenant would be one that God would cut and resurrect to heaven to be placed inside His people in their hearts and their minds. The prophet Isaiah revealed Who this Covenant would be nearly seven hundred years before He came.

> Behold my Servant, whom I uphold; mine elect, in whom my soul delighteth; I have put my spirit upon him: he shall bring forth judgment to the Gentiles. He shall not cry, nor lift up, nor cause his voice to be heard in the street. A bruised reed shall he not break, and the smoking flax shall he not quench: he shall bring forth judgment unto truth. He shall not fail nor be discouraged, till he have set judgment in the earth: and the isles shall wait for his law. Thus saith God the LORD, he that created the heavens, and stretched them out; he that spread forth the earth, and that which cometh out of it; he that giveth breath unto the people upon it, and spirit to them that walk therein: I the LORD have called thee in righteousness, and will hold thine hand, and will keep thee, AND [I WILL] GIVE THEE FOR A COVENANT of the people, for a light of the Gentiles; (Isa 42:1-6)

Carefully examine this passage to be sure you see Whom God promised to give as the Covenant. In this profound pivotal passage in Isaiah, God proclaimed His love for His Servant—an unmistakable reference to Jesus Christ—and promised to give Him as the Covenant both for Israel and for the Gentiles. Jesus Christ was to be the New Covenant. God's Servant and only begotten Son became the Covenant God cut (sacrificed) and then resurrected and placed within His people, both Jew and Gentile. The New Covenant is not a sacrifice of bulls and goats or a covenant of inflexible prescriptive laws written on stones, but a living Covenant, a living Law and a living Sacrifice dwelling in His people. Jesus Christ Himself is the New Covenant.

The old covenant was a type of the New Covenant, and Jesus Christ fulfilled every element of the old covenant. The lambs and their blood, the tablets, the law and even Moses himself all pictured Jesus Christ in the various roles He fulfills as the New Covenant. Jesus Christ is the covenant Sacrifice. His blood is the blood of the Covenant. He is also the covenant Document in Whom God's laws are written. He is the outward expression of God's divine Thought, so He is the embodiment of God's Law for us, not externally, but written in us and on our hearts. He is our Mediator, and He judges us according to righteous judgment. God's people are no longer subject to the low standard of external prescriptive laws written on stone, but we are subject to the Law Who lives in us. Jesus Christ lives in us. Our High Priest lives in us. Our Judge lives in us. Our Covenant lives in us.

One Covenant of Faith

Jesus Christ fulfilled every element of the old covenant and opened the door to the whole world, both Jew and Gentile, to enter into a new covenant relationship with God. He is the Mediator of the Covenant, Who intercedes with God on our behalf whenever we serve, thank, praise, petition or cry out to God. He is our covenant Sacrifice, and His blood continually circulates in His spiritual body to bring us nourishment and to carry away our sin. He is also the covenant Document and the living Law of God. He individually and personally directs every action of the Church according to the will of God as the Father gives Him direction.

Although most theologians understand that Jesus Christ fulfilled the law in its entirety and became the substance of every type pictured in Israel's ritualistic worship, those same theologians remain unable to discern the sign of this Covenant or to make a connection between any ritual and the sign of this Covenant. I believe the main reason for this lapse is their failure to realize that there were two covenants running concurrently during the period when the old covenant was in force. From the time God promised His Covenant to Abraham, the

Abrahamic Covenant continued to be available to every circumcised individual. Many assume that circumcision was a sign of the old covenant, but circumcision was not even a law given by Moses, but by the patriarchs. (John 7:22) The practice simply continued under the law, because God required Abraham to circumcise his male descendents. The sabbath was the sign of the old covenant, but circumcision designated those who had access to the Covenant of faith promised to Abraham, even during the time of the old covenant.

Theologians and biblical scholars have intensely searched the New Testament from end to end and have failed to find the illusive sign of the New Covenant. The reason they have failed to find it in the New Testament is because the sign of the New Covenant is only revealed in the Old Testament. It only appears in the book of beginnings—the book of Genesis. It is overlooked, because the sign of the New Covenant was first placed in the father of the faithful when God promised His everlasting Covenant to Abraham. That sign was carried in the flesh of every faithful son of God until the sign of the Covenant was finally placed by divine prescription in the flesh of the Covenant Himself at the age of eight days old. (Luke 2:21)

The role of circumcision in Christianity is at once very clear and remarkably obscure. The plain teaching of the Bible leaves no doubt that the physical ritual of circumcision is not required for new covenant believers. Jesus Christ perfectly fulfilled every prescribed ritual, and, in so doing, He accomplished the ritual requirement of circumcision on the eighth day of His physical life. There is no biblical requirement that the Church generally or that any member in particular should continue to be ritually circumcised.

Although the Bible is very clear about how circumcision relates to individual Christians, the role of circumcision in regard to the New Covenant is not nearly as apparent. Most Bible students are aware that Jesus was circumcised, but few make any connection between Jesus' circumcision and the New Covenant per se, because no definitive biblical statement explicitly addresses that relationship. Most dismiss the significance of Jesus' circumcision as an irrelevant result of God's covenant relationship with Abraham and the subsequent requirement that Hebrew males continued to be circumcised under the law, but Jesus' circumcision is very important to us and should not be ignored.

The sign of the New Covenant is found among God's instructions and promises to Abraham, because Abraham is the father of the faithful. (Rom 4:16) Everyone who lives by faith lives under the same sign and the same everlasting Covenant of faith. After God imputed righteousness to Abraham through faith, God promised Abraham He would give him His Covenant and promised He would establish His Covenant between Himself and Abraham at a later time. (Gen 17:2, 7) In the meantime God invited Abraham and all of his descendents to participate in the Covenant by placing the sign of the Covenant in his flesh and in the flesh of his male descendents.

In order to establish circumcision as the sign of the New Covenant, one must necessarily show that the Abrahamic Covenant and the New Covenant are the same Covenant. I will briefly examine the various aspects of the Abrahamic Covenant and the New Covenant, and I believe the biblical record will show that all the signs and identifying features of the Abrahamic Covenant and the New Covenant are identical and that circumcision holds as much significance for those who live through faith today as it did for Abraham, our father in the faith. (Rom 4:16)

Theologians have long recognized the similarity between the Abrahamic and New Covenants. Both covenants are based on faith. (Gen 15:6, Rom 3:22) Both covenants promote the same standard of conduct. (Gen 26:5, Heb 10:16) Those who identify Christ with Melchizedek acknowledge the same High Priest in both covenants. (Gen 14:18, Heb 5:6) Both set perfection—or more correctly, completeness—as the result of faith. (Gen 17:1, Matt 5:48) Both are covenants of friendship. (Jas 2:23, John 15:15) Both were established forever. (Gen 17:7, Heb 13:20) Given such a host of similarities, one might wonder why intellectually gifted men have been unable to reconcile the two remaining obstacles—blood and sign—and acknowledge the complete unity of all covenants of faith.

You should be aware that scripture never names God's Covenant with Abraham as the "Abrahamic Covenant." Even the construction of the name is awkward and sounds contrived. Unfortunately, the naming itself contributes to the mistaken impression that the Abrahamic Covenant stands apart from other covenants of faith. It has been so named by theologians as a shortened way of referring to God's Covenant with Abraham, but the Bible does not overtly limit its application to Abraham. In fact, God extended the same

Covenant to Isaac (Gen 17:21) and to Jacob. (Ex 2:24) Since circumcision was the Covenant, (Gen 17:10) we should understand that the Covenant applied to everyone who was circumcised, so that all Israelites as well as proselyte Gentiles had access to the same everlasting Covenant originally promised to faithful Abraham.

The conspicuous absence of any specific connection between the two essential elements of covenant—blood and sign—is a major obstacle blocking the unity of all covenants of faith. Scripture does not equate the blood of the covenants or the sign of the covenants. Indeed the Bible lacks any reference to either the sign of the New Covenant or the blood of the Abrahamic Covenant. The sign of the Abrahamic Covenant is clearly designated (Gen 17:10-11), and the blood of the New Covenant was plainly shed (Matt 26:28), but the missing blood of the Abrahamic Covenant and the missing sign of the New Covenant seem to represent a significant obstacle to their unity. However, I rather see these missing elements as a significant clue to unite them. Could it be that Abraham's sign is the sign of both and Christ's blood is the blood of both?

When God offered His Covenant to Abraham, no animal's blood was poured out on that occasion. (Gen 17:1-22) Clearly animals provided the blood of the old covenant, (Ex 24:8) but why was there no sacrifice offered on the occasion of the Abrahamic? Is it because the blood of the Abrahamic Covenant was yet to be shed two millennia later? Animal sacrifices can only typify the sacrifice Jesus made on the cross, and any covenant of faith would necessarily and ultimately require the blood of Jesus Christ to atone for the sins of the believers.

In addition to the missing blood of the Abrahamic Covenant, there is the difficulty of the missing sign of the New Covenant. Although scripture specifically states that the sign of the Abrahamic Covenant is circumcision, (Gen 17:10-11) we know the ritual of circumcision has been set aside for new covenant believers, leaving no specifically stated sign of the New Covenant anywhere in the Bible. To the frustration of even the most diligent Bible students, endless searches of the biblical text reveal no plainly stated sign of the New Covenant.

These realities lead to the remarkable circumstance that the blood of the New Covenant is plain and the sign is obscured, while the sign of the Abrahamic Covenant is plain and the blood is obscured.

I believe the missing sign and the missing blood become apparent in the reality that the Abrahamic Covenant and the New Covenant are one Covenant of faith.

The Blood of the Covenant

Since the Bible makes no mention of the blood of the Abrahamic Covenant when God offered His Covenant to Abraham, (Gen 17) a distinct possibility remains that Jesus' blood is the blood of the Abrahamic Covenant. I offer here two points to lend credibility to such a conclusion.

First, there are two textual insertions which deserve our attention, one in Matthew 26:28 and the other in Mark 14:24. These are not necessarily mistranslations but are rather an attempt on the part of the translators to clarify the text according to what the apostles state elsewhere in the Bible. Had the translators not attempted to interpret this text for us, we might have more easily recognized the identical phraseology describing the sign of "the covenant" in Genesis and the blood of "the covenant" in Matthew and Mark.

> For this is my blood of the **new** [covenant], which is shed for many for the remission of sins. (Matt 26:28)

> And he said unto them, This is my blood of the **new** [covenant], which is shed for many. (Mark 14:24)

The translators inserted the word *new* into the KJV translation, but it is missing from the Greek text in both cases. Perhaps they assumed *new* here because Luke's and Paul's accounts of the last supper include the word *new* in the Greek text of their writings. I do not mean to imply that either of these accounts necessarily reflects an error, but I simply call your attention to these two remarkable gospel accounts where *new* is missing. A corrected KJV translation of Matthew's and Mark's gospels reads, "For this is my blood of the covenant," as if to imply that there may be only one Covenant of faith, that Jesus' blood might serve as the blood of all covenants of faith, and that it may not be necessary to make a distinction between the New Covenant and what many erroneously consider to be previously established and separate covenants of faith.

Of the four historians who record the events of the last supper, Matthew was an eyewitness of the event, and Mark likely wrote on behalf of Peter, who was also present at the last supper. Luke and Paul were not eyewitnesses. Therefore, Matthew and Mark are more likely to have recorded the exact words of Jesus, while Luke and Paul simply relate an essentially accurate history. Since it appears that our Lord did not personally speak of the "new" Covenant, but rather only of "the" Covenant, we may reasonably conclude that Jesus intended us to understand that His blood is the blood which purges the sins of all the faithful of every generation who participate in the one and only Covenant of faith.

Second, the book of Hebrews explains that Jesus' blood was "for the redemption of the transgressions under the first covenant," which all Bible students interpret to mean the old covenant, but fails to mention how the sins of the early patriarchs are redeemed. Is there no sacrifice for the sins of Abraham, Isaac, Jacob and Joseph?

> And for this cause he is the mediator of the new [covenant], that by means of death, for the redemption of the transgressions that were under the first [covenant], they which are called might receive the promise of eternal inheritance. (Heb 9:15)

If Jesus' blood redeemed those called under the law and removed their sins, how much more should His blood serve as the antitypical sacrifice for the sins of Abraham and the patriarchs who lived under the sign of the Abrahamic Covenant by faith. Has God forgotten the patriarchs? However, if the Abrahamic Covenant and the New Covenant are one Covenant of faith, there is no need to explain redundantly how sins committed under the Abrahamic Covenant are removed. Such an omission is only understandable, if the Abrahamic Covenant, the New Covenant and any other covenants of faith are one Covenant of faith and the blood of Jesus Christ satisfied the law to expunge the transgressions of all faithful men and women in the Bible from Genesis to Revelation.

The Sign of the Covenant

Before investigating how circumcision might serve as the sign of a single unified Covenant of faith, let us consider the nature of a sign. A sign identifies or authenticates a person, place or thing, and individuals place signs on or outside of that which they designate. A business owner may place a sign on the outside of the store or office, so everyone can see the location and name of the business. Town magistrates usually place signs on the perimeter of town, so everyone traveling knows the name of the town and that they have arrived at their destination. In the case of a legal document, the sign, or signature, must be placed conspicuously on the document itself. The sign of the New Covenant must be visible on the covenant Document, just as the sign of the sabbath was plainly visible on the two stone tablets of the old covenant. A sign is only valid, if it can be plainly seen on the document it authenticates.

Bible students point to several aspects of Christian life as possible signs of the New Covenant. Some may point to faith as the sign of the Covenant. (Eph 2:8) Others indicate that conversion (Rom 2:28-29) or that brotherly love (John 13:35) is the sign. Yet others assert that baptism (Rom 6:3-6) serves as the sign which reveals a Christian's Covenant of faith. Although these are all noble attempts to find the illusive sign of the New Covenant, realistically, none of these can be the sign of the Covenant. Faith, conversion and love are required for salvation, but they are not signs one can see as an outward visible symbol of the covenant relationship. These three attributes have to do with the heart and the mind, which are, unmistakably, internal functions. Baptism is an outward sign, but baptism is not required for salvation. (Luke 23:39-43) These guesses seem to indicate most interpreters are searching for a sign which can be associated with all of us as covenant partners rather than a sign specifically associated with the Covenant, but the sign we must look for is the sign God placed on the Covenant and not necessarily a sign associated with God or visible on any of the covenant partners. In any case the sign must be visible externally to be a valid sign, just as circumcision was visible on Abraham's body and plainly serves as the sign of the Abrahamic Covenant.

Lacking a scripturally designated sign, many churchgoers have adopted the sign of the cross as the symbol of their Christianity. Indeed, it fulfills the requirement of an external sign, and it certainly has become recognized for its association with Christianity. A cross was borne by the Covenant, but He does not bear it now, and there is no indication early Christians wore them. Crosses are found on most church buildings, but a building is not the church, and sometimes the church is in the building and sometimes not. Some Christians wear crosses, but not every believer does, and, of course, there is no biblical requirement to do so. In reality the cross is more a symbol of execution and death than it is a symbol of resurrection and hope, the former being the fate of our worldly life and the latter more clearly describing our New Covenant life of faith in Christ. A cross may serve as a personal sign of a given individual's faith, but it is not the sign of the New Covenant.

Those who correctly understand the nature of a sign may reasonably suggest that the nail marks in Jesus' hands and feet and the mark from the spear thrust into Jesus' side may serve as the sign of the New Covenant. These are clearly external marks, and they appear plainly on the body of the Covenant, so they may well serve as "a" sign of the Covenant, however, they are not likely "the" sign of the Covenant. In a covenant agreement it is appropriate that both parties sign the contract. The crucifixion marks were marks inflicted by the world, indeed by each of us, and they may represent our signature on the Covenant; however, our marks are not the primary authenticating marks. The Principal in the agreement—the Author of the Covenant—must also place His signature on the Document. The primary signature on the new covenant Document will be a sign God Himself has placed on His Covenant.

God prescribed the signature He wrote on His living Covenant when Jesus was still in the loins of Abraham. The sign of the Covenant God promised to Abraham is unmistakable. Abraham was circumcised. Circumcision is an excellent sign, because it is plainly visible on the body. Remarkably, God designated His signature for the New Covenant about 1900 years before the Covenant was cut.

> This is my covenant, which ye shall keep, between me and you and thy seed after thee; Every man child among you shall be circumcised. And ye shall circumcise the flesh of your foreskin; **and it shall be a token** [sign] **of <u>the</u> covenant betwixt me and you.** (Gen 17:10-11)

Among the more challenging questions I have had to face is how to reconcile the application of circumcision as the sign of the New

Covenant with the reality that Jesus Christ fulfilled the ritual requirement of circumcision, thus precluding circumcision as a requirement for Christians today. Fundamentally, the solution to this difficulty becomes apparent in the spiritual reality that a man and a woman are one in marriage.

> Therefore shall a man leave his father and his mother, and shall cleave unto his wife: and they shall be one flesh. (Gen 2:24)

Unless Bible students view marriage the way God views marriage, a correct understanding of marriage-based relationships in the Bible will remain illusive. Many view the Bible as a sexually biased book, because men are dominant in the text and women appear to be nearly invisible. Such is not the case. God simply sees the two as one, so when He addresses the husband, He addresses the wife. Some wonder what might have happened, if Adam had refused the forbidden fruit after Eve had already eaten it. In God's eyes the question is moot, because they were one. Thus, we may resolve seemingly complicated questions with very simple, straightforward answers when we view the spiritual realities of the Bible from the same point of view in which God has given them.

Paul explained a highly relevant spiritual reality, which describes all new covenant believers as members of a spiritual body in which Jesus Christ is the Head. Collectively, all believers are one body, called the Church, (Col 1:18) and he describes the Church as a woman. (Eph 5:23) In this spiritual marriage relationship, Jesus Christ and the Church are joined as one. In the following verses Paul explained the mystery of Christ and the Church, and then he repeated God's perspective of the unity of marriage.

> Husbands, love your wives, even as Christ also loved the church, and gave himself for it; that he might sanctify and cleanse it with the washing of water by the word, that he might present it to himself a glorious church, not having spot, or wrinkle, or any such thing; but that it should be holy and without blemish. So ought men to love their wives as their own bodies. He that loveth his wife loveth himself.

> For no man ever yet hated his own flesh; but nourisheth and cherisheth it, even as the Lord the church: For we are members of his body, of his flesh, and of his bones. **For this cause shall a man leave his father and mother, and shall be joined unto his wife, and they two shall be one flesh. This is a great mystery: but I speak concerning Christ and the church.** (Eph 5:25-32)

In these verses God provides insight to help us understand the unity of the marriage covenant, both physically between a man and a woman and spiritually between Christ and the Church. Our fleshly marriages only typify the relationship between Christ and the Church. Unless Bible students clearly grasp the reality of God's view of the oneness of marriage and how an even more profound unity exists in the relationship between Christ and the Church, they will struggle to understand the role circumcision plays in Christianity as the sign of the New Covenant.

In Paul's analogy a husband and his wife represent the marriage relationship between Jesus Christ and the Church. Jesus is the Man. The Church is the woman. Christ and the Church are united in a marriage Covenant, so God sees them united as one, even though they have not yet come together in the marriage supper of the Lamb. In this spiritual marriage, only the Man is circumcised.

The sign of circumcision was only borne in the male members of the family. Women were never circumcised under any covenant. The patriarchal injunction designated the eighth day after birth for circumcision, so Joseph and Mary circumcised Jesus when He was eight days old. (Luke 2:21) Jesus was circumcised with the sign of the Covenant in His flesh. He did not bear the sign of the old covenant. (Ex 31:13) Jesus was circumcised with the sign God prescribed to designate His Covenant with Abraham, just as the sign of circumcision was subsequently borne in the flesh of all faithful men until God caused it to be placed in the Covenant Himself.

Under the Abrahamic Covenant, Abraham was circumcised; Sarah was not. Abraham bore the sign of the Covenant in his flesh, but the Covenant was also in Sarah. She participated in the Covenant just as her husband did, even though she was not personally circumcised. Abraham and Sarah were one.

Under the old covenant, the men were circumcised; the women were not. Yet the Covenant was in the women, and the Covenant guided the women as much as the men, even though the men bore the sign of the Covenant in their own flesh. The husbands and their wives were one.

Likewise under the New Covenant, the Man is circumcised; the Church is not. Jesus Christ bears the sign of the Covenant in His own body, but the Covenant is also in the Church, and the Church participates in the Covenant under the sign borne in the body of her Husband. Christ and the Church are one.

The sign God prescribed for Jesus Christ—our Husband and Covenant—to bear in His body is circumcision. Since Jesus Christ is the New Covenant and the sign God caused to be placed in the body of the Covenant is circumcision, the evidence seems conclusive that the sign of the New Covenant is circumcision.

Spiritual Reality

This study of the nature of biblical covenants should bless you with a deeper understanding of the spiritual reality of your unity with God. Covenant partners become one with each other. When believers enter into Covenant—into Jesus Christ—we become one with God. We put on Jesus Christ and live in Him, just as He inhabits us and lives in us. "For as many of you as have been baptized into Christ have put on Christ." (Gal 3:27) "Hereby know we that we dwell in him, and he in us, because he hath given us of his Spirit." (1 John 4:13) He is in us, and we are in Him. He has inhabited us in the flesh, and we have become clothed in Him in the Spirit. Our unity with God is spiritual reality.

Those who write earthly covenants place the sign or the seal of their covenants on the outside of the contract and in plain sight, most often on the front page of the document. God has given His Covenant, not in the form of a written document, but in the Person of His Son. (Isa 42:6) Jesus Christ is the Covenant. He is the Document. This is not an analogy, but spiritual reality, so we should expect to find the sign of the Covenant on the Covenant Himself. God has prescribed circumcision to be the sign which designates and authenticates His Covenant. (Gen 17:10)

When we are baptized of the Spirit and become clothed in Jesus Christ, our appearance completely changes in the eyes of the Father.

When the Father looks at us, He does not see us. He sees His Son, because we are clothed in Jesus Christ, our Covenant. When the Father looks at us, He looks for the sign of the Covenant, which authenticates His Covenant and verifies the relationship He has with us. The sign He looks for is circumcision. Therefore, when the Father looks at us, He sees the sign of the Covenant in us, because we are one with, clothed in, and have put on Jesus Christ. This is the spiritual reality of covenant.

Theologians have long recognized a close relationship between the Abrahamic Covenant and the New Covenant. As pointed out above, the number of obvious similarities between the two covenants is remarkable. Each is a covenant of faith accompanied by promises. Each features an individual calling from a life of sin in a morally corrupt society to a life of completeness (KJV, perfection). The priesthood is the same in both. Each is a covenant of friendship. In each covenant the faithful individual listens to God as He speaks and follows His Word as the standard of his or her conduct. Both covenants are forever.

Although not generally recognized, I have also shown that circumcision serves as the sign of both the New Covenant and the Abrahamic Covenant. A corrected reading of Matthew's and Mark's accounts of Jesus' words at the last supper and the plain statement of Hebrews regarding the universal application of Christ's blood indicate that the blood of Jesus Christ serves as the blood of both covenants. Since all the significant features of each covenant are the same, the blood of each covenant is the blood of Christ, and the sign of each covenant is circumcision, I am led to the inescapable conclusion that the New Covenant and the Abrahamic Covenant are one Covenant of faith.

If you are interested in an item by item comparison between the various elements of the old, the new and the Abrahamic covenants, see the "Comparison of the Covenants" chart in appendix 4.

The New Covenant Relationship

Covenant unity with God is a spiritual reality. We must exercise spiritual vision through faith to comprehend the unity in our spiritual mind's eye. Faith takes practice, and the more we practice living like God lives and meditating on the truths He reveals to us in His word, the more apparent the reality of our spiritual existence in Him will become. The spiritual reality of our unity with Christ and with each other is more real than our perception of physical separation.

The Bible describes spiritual unity as each covenant partner in the other partner. We are united with God through His Covenant, because we are in Christ and He is in us. We are in Him as unique members of His body, and Christ lives in us, because He is the Spirit living in His body. We can't see the reality, because it's spiritual reality. We believe it's true, because God says it's true.

One of the most important words in the New Testament is the preposition "in." "In" is a covenant term. The unity of covenant is described by this preposition. Since it is such a simple little word, it is often overlooked or ignored, but it holds profound significance in scripture, because it describes the reality of our position—our location—our spiritual state of being "in" Jesus Christ. We cannot have a relationship with God, unless we are "in" His Covenant, and the apostles frequently described the Church as being in Christ, in the Lord, in Him or similar phraseology to indicate our spiritual location in the Covenant of God. When we are united in Covenant with God, we are in Christ and He is in us.

A serious misconception exists in the minds of most churchgoers regarding the meaning of the biblical expression "believe in God." Most interpret this phrase to mean "believe God exists," but such a belief is futile, because even the demons believe that God exists. (Jas 2:19) The demons receive nothing from God, because they have fallen away from God because of sin. They are no longer IN God. Christians must not only believe, but we must be IN God. We must be IN His Covenant. We must be IN Jesus Christ as a member of His body—as an integral part of His Being, and we must continue to believe in order to remain in Him. We cannot stop believing, and we must remain in Him continually. Our state of being in Him is a spiritual reality invisible to human eyes. God places each member into the body of Christ, and the Spirit connects all the members to one another. We can't see the Spirit connecting us, but we believe it's true, because God says it's true. (Eph 2:19-22) Faith validates the spiritual realities we cannot see with our eyes.

The covenant meal symbolizes unity with Christ and with one another. When we take the symbols of communion, we picture the reality that Christ is in each of us and that we are unified and complete in Him. The one bread symbolizes the unified body of

Christ, and the wine symbolizes the blood of Christ. As we each eat the covenant meal, we picture Christ in us and us in Him, symbolized by the one bread; we picture all of us cleansed and holy as the blood of the Covenant flows in and around us, symbolized by the wine. We become one with Christ, because we are in His body and His blood flows in us. We become one with each other, because every member takes nourishment from Jesus Christ—from the Word of God—and drinks from the spiritual blood of Christ. We are all in Christ, and we are all one in Him.

As we become one with our covenant Partner, each assumes the identity of the other by exchanging names. Our identities become one through Christ. God became human when He sent His Word to be clothed in the flesh and become a Man. Likewise, we assume God's name when we live in Christ and become Christians. God takes our identity by becoming human, and we take His identity by becoming sons and daughters of God.

In covenant each partner takes on the nature and role of the other partner. Jonathan and David became covenant partners and symbolically exchanged roles when Jonathan gave David his royal robe. (1 Sam 18:3-4) David assumed Jonathan's royal nature as Saul's son and heir to the throne of Israel, and Jonathan assumed David's nature as a common citizen of Israel. David became the rightful heir to the throne of Israel when Saul and Jonathan died in battle. The biblical record of Jonathan and David's covenant gives us divine insight into covenant unity and shows us that we rightfully possess divine nature when we enter into Covenant with God.

Similarly, God took on our nature when Jesus Christ came to the earth. He took on our human nature and became clothed in the flesh. While He lived in the flesh, God tested Him in every way He tests us, yet He remained without sin. In like manner we take on His divine nature, and we live as He lives. We live in the Spirit, and we become holy as God is holy. We become righteous as He is righteous. God imputes the qualities of His character to us by grace through faith. We are holy and righteous, because we continually believe IN Him and He grants us those aspects of His nature, not because we cease to sin.

Covenant partners also exchange their weapons. In another symbol of Jonathan and David's covenant, Jonathan gave David his belt, which carried the weapons he used in battle. In covenant with

God, we take on His battles with His weapons, and He takes on our battles with our weapons. We give up fighting our own physical battles our way, and we arm ourselves with the whole armor of God and fight spiritual battles His way. (Eph 6:13-18) Our loins are girt about with truth, and the breastplate we wear is righteousness. Our feet are shod with the gospel, and we hold the shield of faith. The helmet of salvation and the sword of the Spirit complete our spiritual armor. Our battle is spiritual, and we only use the spiritual weapons God has given us. (2 Cor 10:3-4) As the covenant Partner living in each of us, God controls the way we use our bodies, and He controls our physical weapons of aggression and retribution. He exercises the privilege to fight our physical battles for us, and He reserves the right to exact vengeance, or not, upon those who do us harm.

The old covenant pictures the New, and the New Covenant makes all the types and rituals of the old covenant a reality. Every covenant with God is a marriage relationship in which unity is the essence of the relationship. We are in Covenant when we live in our covenant Partner and He lives in us. We exchange natures by giving up our physical lives to Him and by living in the Spirit, and we exchange battles by giving up our weapons of warfare and by fighting His battles with His weapons by faith. Faith is the basis of our spiritual life and our covenant relationship with God.

Two New Covenant Marriages

As the sixth day of creation drew to a close, God saw everything He had made, and, behold, it was very good. God had finished the work of the physical creation, and He rested as the seventh day began. He blessed and sanctified the seventh day, because in it He planned to accomplish the pinnacle of His creative work. In the seventh day God began the work to create two spiritual creations. God will destroy the entire physical creation with fire, but His two spiritual creations will live forever. God's entire purpose for the physical creation is to produce a spiritual Man and a spiritual woman, of whom Adam and Eve are types. God sanctified the seventh day in order to create a Son and His bride.

God has named His two spiritual creations in scripture. The first is called the Lamb. The second is called New Jerusalem. God is presently creating the Lamb in this age, and He will create New Jerusalem in the age to come. Human beings can participate in

God's first spiritual creation by becoming members in the body of the Lamb. Human beings can participate in the second spiritual creation by becoming members in the body of New Jerusalem.

Human beings are particularly suited to be members of a body, because each member of a body is unique and each performs a unique function in the body. Therefore, those who allow God to determine what is right or wrong in their lives can become members in one of two spiritual creations. Those who live righteously in this age will become members in the body of God's first spiritual creation, the Lamb. Those who live righteously in the age to come will become members in the body of His second spiritual creation, the New Jerusalem. In the spiritual realm the type of a woman implies subservience not gender, so you should not assume that any given spiritual body is female. Covenant is the means through which sinful human beings in this age may become holy and form the body of the first spiritual Man.

In the fullness of time, God placed His divine Word into a virgin named Mary, and the divine Man Jesus was born. He lived a perfect life in the flesh, and He was crucified and resurrected as the First of the firstfruits—the Head of the Church—a perfect and complete Spirit to live in the members of His body. (1 Cor 15:45) The faithful of God from the time of Adam until Christ returns at the end of this age will become unique and equal members in the body of the Lamb, the first spiritual Man.

The first man Adam was the physical prototype of the first spiritual Man. God created a body from the dust of the ground and then breathed the breath of life—Adam's human spirit—into the body, and Adam became a living soul. Just as God created Adam before Eve, God is presently in the process of creating the first spiritual Man. In the same manner that God breathed the breath of life into Adam, God will place the breath of Life—Jesus Christ—into the Church. When Jesus Christ, the Head, is united in spiritual marriage to His body, God's first spiritual Creation will be complete. God will have completed the first spiritual Man. The age of building the first spiritual Man will end. Jesus Christ, the eternal Word of God, will have been fitted with a spiritual body, by which He will be able to do everything God directs Him to do. Jesus Christ and the Church—the Head and His body—will be united together as one spiritual Man at the marriage feast of the Lamb.

> Let us be glad and rejoice, and give honour to him: for the marriage of the Lamb is come, and his [woman] hath made herself ready. And to her was granted that she should be arrayed in fine linen, clean and white: for the fine linen is the righteousness of saints. And he saith unto me, Write, Blessed are they which are called unto the marriage supper of the Lamb. (Rev 19:7-9)

Two spiritual marriages are briefly outlined in the Bible, one before the 1000 year reign of Christ on earth (Rev 19:7-9) and the other following the millennium after the earth has been destroyed and renewed. (Rev 21:1-9) The first marriage will be between Christ and the Church. In this pre-millennial marriage God will complete His creation of the first spiritual Man by uniting the body with its Head. After the biblical record of that wedding, the Church disappears from scripture and is forever one with the Lamb. Wherever the Lamb goes and whatever the Lamb does during the millennium, the Church is there as the Lamb's body to perform the Lamb's work. Just as Christ is building His Church in this age, the work of the Lamb during the millennium will be to build His bride.

In His infinite wisdom God knew every man needs a mate, so He took a member of Adam's body and created a woman. Then God brought the woman to Adam, pronounced them man and wife, and declared them to be one flesh. The marriage between Adam and Eve was the physical prototype of the spiritual marriage between the Lamb and New Jerusalem, His bride. (Rev 21:2, 9)

God will begin His second spiritual creation—New Jerusalem—following the completion of the Lamb. Just as God took a member from Adam's body to create Eve, God will take a member of the Lamb's body—David—to be the exalted member living in and directing the body of the first spiritual woman. David's presence in the body of the bride will fulfill God's promise to build a house for David. (2 Sam 7:11) With David as the personality of the bride, the Lamb (Jesus Christ and the Church) will begin building the body of David. God will begin to fulfill His promise to complete the New Covenant with the house of Israel and the house of Judah and offer reunited Israel the opportunity to be the body of David, just as the Church will be the body of Christ. Gentiles may also become members of God's second spiritual creation by becoming part of spiritual Israel, and, consequently, all Israel will be saved under this millennial Covenant to create the Lamb's bride.

> And there came unto me one of the seven angels…and talked with me, saying, Come hither, **I will shew thee the bride, the Lamb's wife**. And he carried me away in the spirit to a great and high mountain, and shewed me that great city, the holy Jerusalem, descending out of heaven from God… (Rev 21:9-10)

When God has completely adorned the bride for her Husband, God will destroy the earth and create a new heaven and a new earth to provide a dwelling place for the Lamb and His bride. Then the Lamb's bride—New Jerusalem—will descend from heaven and wed her Husband, the Lamb. The New Jerusalem will be the living city of God, and the Almighty God and the Lamb (Christ and the Church) will be the living Temple in the great and glorious Holy City. (Rev 21:22) The Lamb will live forever in New Jerusalem, and, as the written record of God's eternal Covenant for mankind comes to a close, the first spiritual Man and the first spiritual woman will begin to produce the first spiritual offspring of the kingdom of God, the increase of which will never end. (Isa 9:6-7, Luke 1:33)

Chapter 3

The Nature of God

True freedom begins with God. He is the Creator and Sustainer of the universe and the Source of all life. God is sovereign. He rules the universe through His Word by the power of the Holy Spirit. We experience spiritual freedom when we enter into Covenant with God and acknowledge God's sovereign rulership over us. When God rules both our church and our individual lives, we are free to listen to the Lord Jesus Christ directing us and follow the Holy Spirit leading and empowering us.

Human beings can only possess true freedom in God, and a general understanding of the nature of God is fundamental to an understanding of the spiritual freedom available to all Christians. Christians live under the government of God, and the government of God for the Church is theocracy. As we explore the nature of God, I will explain how the Father, the Word and the Holy Spirit each fulfill a unique role in the government of the Church. The Father rules the Church. The divine Word expressed through the Son is the Head and sole Authority in the Church. The Holy Spirit empowers, encourages and protects the Church. A church remains free as long as the church lives under the government of God.

Divine governance in the Church is a natural function of the triune nature of God, but few understand its function, because theologians have muddled the simplicity of the triune God in philosophical terminology. The trinity is one of the most puzzling concepts of mainstream Christian theology. Believers struggle with the illusive reality that God is one and three at the same time, while atheists scoff at the apparent contradiction such a concept presents. Even within the Christian community, believers hold widely divergent views of the relationship between the three essences of the one God. The doctrine of the trinity emerged during the early centuries of the Christian era, partly because of the Arian and Macedonian controversies and partly because of secular criticism. The church fathers created the doctrine in an attempt to settle internal strife, but they also needed to quell secular incredulity and create a rational explanation for the apparent contradiction of three persons in a single divine Being. The doctrine of the trinity attempts to explain divine nature by means of rational human logic.

Few outside the theological community are able to understand the doctrine, because theologians have crafted their theological statement very carefully with words carrying specific, predefined meanings. We must first understand how theologians define these words to avoid misunderstanding the doctrine. Unless we speak the theological jargon, we may very easily reach irrational conclusions about the doctrine and about the nature of God. Since few outside the theological community avail themselves of the opportunity to learn exactly what the narrowly defined terms of this theological statement mean, individual believers may embrace a wide variety of views regarding the nature of God.

Most professionals, including theologians, create whole vocabularies to talk to one another precisely and concisely as they interact in a professional capacity. They create highly technical words, which help them to be very exact in their expression while avoiding repeated explanations of complicated concepts. When those outside a profession really want to know what a professional means when he uses a particular word, they can obtain a technical dictionary or a professional manual and read a definition of the word or a description of the procedure. In the case of the doctrine of the trinity, we may similarly consult various theological works to gain a more precise understanding of the implications of the doctrine; however, in this case we face yet another obstacle in our path to understand the triune nature of God. Theologians have not created a complicated technical word to define a key aspect of the doctrine, but they have rather chosen the very common word "person" to describe each of the three hypostases of God.

One of the main obstacles to an understanding of the theologians' attempt to explain the nature of God is their use of the word "persons" in the text of the doctrine, because the ordinary word "person" comes with a lot of baggage associated with its common usage. The difficulty to understand the trinity is compounded, in that we must not only understand the precise theological definition of a "person", but we must also overcome the tendency to attribute the commonly understood definition of a person to the persons of God. We must first extract the commonly understood definition from our minds before we can apply the theologian's carefully crafted definition of this very common word. Unfortunately, few students of the Bible realize theologians have chosen a very special definition for the persons of the trinity, and fewer yet take the time to find out how theologians define their word. The majority of believers assume the common-use definition and, even if they do not, it is almost impossible to fully extract the common-use concept of a person from our minds when we consider the nature of God.

We naturally think of a person as being separate from all other individuals. A person is one, and a person stands apart from all others. However, a serious theological contradiction arises, if we attribute separateness to the persons of the trinity. When theologians introduce persons into their description of the triune God, they do not mean these theological persons are separate from each other. God cannot contain three separate persons and still be one God. Separateness and unity cannot coexist. To maintain unity, we must reject separateness in God. Theologically, each person of the trinity is *distinct* rather than *separate* from another person of the trinity.

Perhaps I can explain the difference between distinct and separate better, if we consider a man who is a husband to his wife, a father to his son and an employee to his boss. We could say the husband, the father and the employee describe three distinctions of the one man, but we could not say the husband, the father and the employee are three separate people. The man functions in three distinct ways, but the man is not three persons. As with a man, no separation exists in God. Unlike God, however, a man can never function as husband, father and employee at the same time, whereas God always functions simultaneously as Father, Word and Holy Spirit. (This oversimplified example does not explain how God is three persons in one Being, but only the difference between distinct and separate.)

In addition to the misleading use of the word "persons" to define the nature of the triune God, I must also address a fundamental error in the assumption that the triune God is Father, Son and Holy Spirit. The Bible does not specifically say the Son is the eternal second person of the trinity, but rather says the Word, or the *Logos*, existed from eternity. (John 1:1) This detail may seem like splitting hairs, but I believe it is important to notice carefully what the Bible says and what it does not say. The Son is also eternal, because the Son is the fleshly manifestation of the Word, and, theologically, His fleshly existence as a Man cannot be separated from His eternal existence as the Word; but the eternal Word was not always the Son. The Word became the Son at a certain point in time. (Acts 13:33) This perspective does not deny that a father-son relationship also exists between the Father and the Word, just as it exists between the Father and the Son, but every student of the Bible should be aware that "Father and Son" does not define the eternal relationship in God which existed from the beginning. Therefore, I will not describe the eternal God as Father, Son and Holy Spirit, but more precisely as Father, Word and Holy Spirit.

God is One

Having established that the persons of the trinity are distinctions of God and not separate persons and also that the eternal God must be defined as Father, Word and Holy Spirit, I will now endeavor to explain the nature of the triune God, and I will begin with the most plain and basic teaching of scripture: God is ONE! The God of the old covenant—Father, Word and Holy Spirit—the very same God we worship under the New Covenant—made it plain to Israel that He is one God. Jews frequently recite what has come to be known as *The Shema*, taken from the first Hebrew word of Deuteronomy 6:4.

Hear, O Israel: The LORD our God is one LORD.

Throughout the Old Testament, and indeed in the New, God repeatedly emphasizes that He is one. In every case "one" is the Hebrew or Greek counting number one. One is absolute. It does not mean first. God is not the first among many gods. God always uses the counting number "one" to tell us that He is unique and that there is complete unity in Him. The Father, Word and Spirit are one God.

It is only because scripture plainly describes the Father as God, the Word as God and the Holy Spirit as God that we understand God exists in three distinct hypostases, or persons, of God. Scripture never says God is three,* however theologians and most Christians are led to the inescapable conclusion that the one God must be understood in three distinct, but not separate, ways.

---

*With one exception, 1 John 5:7. "However its genuineness is seriously questioned and it is very likely this verse was never part of the original letter penned by the apostle. It is omitted from every manuscript of John's epistle written before the invention of printing, except the *Codex Montfortii*. One hundred twelve manuscripts omit it." (Adam Clarke)

The Bible acknowledges the Father as God in dozens of verses. Jesus taught us to pray to the Father. (Luke 11:2) Jesus depended completely on the Father for His direction and claimed He only did what He saw the Father do. (John 5:30, 8:28) The apostle Paul acknowledged the Father as God in the salutation of almost every one of his epistles. These and many other biblical statements clearly indicate that the Father is God and that He exists as the preeminent member of the triune God.

The Bible also acknowledges that the Word was with God in the beginning and that the Word was God. (John 1:1) John described the Word as a participant in the creation, (v. 3) and the Word possesses life within Himself. (v. 4) Only God possesses life, therefore, the Word is God. The Word also came in the flesh (v. 14) in the person of Jesus, and the author of Hebrews reinforced John's claim that the Word was God when he wrote of the Son, "Thy throne, O God, is forever." (Heb 1:8)

The Bible also acknowledges that God is a Spirit. (John 4:24) The Spirit is essential to God's nature. Not every spirit is God, but the Holy Spirit is God. Just like God, the Spirit is life and has the capacity to give life, (John 6:63) thus, the Holy Spirit is God.

Scriptures abound to declare that God is one God, yet it is clear that the Father, the Word and the Holy Spirit are all God. It is no small dilemma for theologians to explain how these three hypostases of God can exist and be understood as a single divine Being. How can these three—Father, Word and Holy Spirit—be one God?

If I attempt to determine which hypostasis of God is actually the Creator, I can further magnify the interpretative difficulty. The Bible opens with the statement, "In the beginning God created the heavens and the earth," (Gen 1:1) so God claims full responsibility for the creation, but in other scriptures it is unclear whether God acted as the Father, the Word or the Holy Spirit when He acted in the beginning. Malachi says that the Father created us and implies the Father is the Creator. (Mal 2:10) Then John tells us all things were created by the Word. (John 1:3) Finally, the Bible, not wanting to leave out the Spirit, explains that the Spirit went forth to do the creating. (Psa 104:30) The Spirit also created Job. (Job 33:4) Indeed scripture ascribes responsibility to the Spirit for Mary's pregnancy with Jesus. (Matt 1:18) Who then is the Creator, and how can we interpret scripture to provide a clear picture of the creative efforts of

God in the Bible? Is it possible that God is one in the obvious sense, which seems to have eluded theologians?

In spite of the complicated and misleading doctrine of the trinity, God has provided a remarkably simple explanation of His existence as a triune God. As inherently complex as the nature of God might seem to be, God has filled the earth with examples of His triune nature. God has given us the profound revelation that human beings have been made in His image. (Gen 1:26) This insight implies we can understand the nature of God, if we are willing to believe and apply the truth that He made us in His image. He has revealed that there is a direct parallel between the nature of God and the nature of man. We know God is one, and we know a man is one, but, if God is three, then this truth implies that, in some way, a man is also three. We can understand God, if we understand the triune nature of our own being. The nature of man reflects the nature of God.

God is one as a man is one.
God is three as a man is three.

This analysis is simple in concept, but not so simple to reconcile with scripture. The doctrine of the trinity has baffled believers for centuries, and some even feel it is easier to simply believe the Father, the Son and the Holy Spirit are all God without further explanation than to believe three persons exist in one God. Human philosophy invariably results in more questions than answers. The only solid clue to resolve this dilemma is the revelation that we have been made in His image. Our quest to understand the triune God is integrally tied to a clear understanding our own triune nature.

Various biblical references seem to indicate that a person is a body, a soul and a spirit, and some may suggest that body, soul and spirit describe the triune nature of man. These three may indeed encompass the totality of a man, but they are not the essential elements which make a man three as God is three. The critical test of any assumed triune nature of man is the requirement that two of the three elements reflect a father and son relationship. Just as the first person of God is the progenitor of the second person of God, one of the three elements of a man must be the progenitor of one of the others. One element of man must produce or beget the other, and there must be a certain subordination of one element to the other. Since it is obvious that the soul of a man does not produce the spirit, nor does the spirit of a man produce the soul, and the body of a man can produce neither the soul nor the spirit, and visa versa, I can only conclude that body, soul and spirit do not represent the essential elements which make a man three as God is three.

Scripture has not explicitly defined the three distinct elements of the nature of man, but it has described the nature and function of the three persons of God. If we carefully examine each person of the trinity to determine how each functions in God, then we should be able to determine how a man functions in the same three essential ways. If we examine the function of the Father, the function of the Word and the function of the Holy Spirit, then we may be able to see how a man requires the same three functions to be complete, and then we should be able to see how the triune God is one.

When human beings endeavor to know one another, they do so through the exchange of words or thoughts. Unless we can communicate with one another, we cannot know one another. So it is between God and man. Unless God communicates with us, and we with Him, we cannot know God, and He cannot know us. Since God can read our minds, human beings are open books of communication whether we speak to Him or not, but unless God communicates with us in some way, we have no way to know God. Fortunately, God wants us to know Him, and toward that end God has provided His Word, the divine Expression of the Father, both in person and in written form, so we may converse with God and know Him. We can only know God through His Word.

The Word took on flesh and became a Man, and the physical manifestation of the Word, Jesus Christ, gives us access to God the Father and allows us to communicate with God. No man can come to the Father, except through the Son. (John 14:6) Through the Son, we have access by one Spirit to the Father. (Eph 2:18) There is one Mediator between God and men, the Man, Jesus Christ. (1 Tim 2:5) These and other scriptures inform us that the Father draws us to Himself and communicates with us through Jesus Christ, the Word of God. Since our purpose is to know God in His triune nature, these scriptures imply that the best way to begin to understand God might be to first explore the nature of the Son in His eternal existence as the Word. When we understand the role of the Word in God, we may then be able to understand the role of the Father because of the father and son relationship in the trinity. I will focus on the eternal Word rather than the Son or Jesus the Man, because the Word is the divinity Who existed in the beginning with God. As we gain insight into the function of the Word in God, we can use what we learn to unlock a clearer understanding of the Father in God and then the Spirit of God.

One of the most eloquent and profound revelations regarding the nature of the second person of the trinity is found in the first verse of John's gospel. Believers should understand this verse in its totality, because several heresies arise when individual parts of it are isolated and misinterpreted. John reiterates the opening words of Genesis, and it might have made an excellent introduction to the New Testament, had John's gospel been placed first. The opening statement of the book of John introduces us, not to the Father, but to the Word in His eternal existence with God.

> In the beginning was the Word, and the Word was with God, and the Word was God. (John 1:1)

This remarkable statement informs us that the Word existed before the creation, that the Word was with God in the creation, and that the Word was God. We should carefully consider the nature of the Word before we can effectively determine the nature of the Father. John reveals an important clue to the nature of the second person of the trinity in this verse, especially if we combine what he says here with other verses in his gospel. John was particularly attuned to Jesus' eternal existence as the Word, because he records a number of Jesus' statements about Himself which transcend the obvious nature of a man and give us a glimpse into the nature and role of the eternal Word of God.

> Believest thou not that I am in the Father, and the Father in me? the words that I speak unto you I speak not of myself: but the Father that dwelleth in me, he doeth the works. (John 14:10) I can of mine own self do nothing. (John 5:30)

These and other statements of Jesus, recalled uniquely by John, shed much light on the divine relationship between the Father and the Word rather than the relationship between the Father and the Man, Jesus. Jesus was not simply patronizing the Father, Who created Jesus' mouth, vocal cords and tongue and caused the words to come out of Jesus' mouth. As true as these realities certainly are, Jesus' statement is far more profound in its implication. Jesus was explaining that, as the eternal Word of God, He has no power at all to act on His own. A word cannot produce itself or speak itself, and a word has no power to accomplish anything, even after it has been spoken. A word emanates from the lips and the sound waves vibrate outwardly until the word disappears into the background noise of the cosmos. Of itself, a word can do nothing; so also the eternal Word of God has no power to act or accomplish anything of Himself.

In this particular context we should be careful not to confuse Jesus' ability to act humanly with the inability of the Word to do anything at all of Himself. Jesus was describing His divine existence as the Word apart from His physical existence as a Man. Jesus, the Man, had a physical body which gave Him the ability to speak and act and move about and accomplish physical tasks, while the eternal Word always remains distinct from the Spirit, Who gives the Father and the Word the power and ability to accomplish the purposes of God. Even though Jesus, as a Man, could speak and act of Himself through His physical body, Jesus, as the eternal Word, had no ability to accomplish anything at all of Himself. Jesus was attesting to the complete impotence of the Word in His divine role as the second person of the triune God.

Let us also consider what the Word is not. Some have suggested, since Jesus Christ is the Word, that He is a spokesman or one who speaks for God. This interpretation is an error. Spokesman and word are related functions but completely different concepts. A word is something which is spoken, whereas a spokesman is a person who speaks words. You may see the contradiction more easily, if we consider the difference between utterer and utterance. An utterer is the one who speaks. An utterance is the thing which is spoken. John tells us the Word was the Utterance of God, not the utterer. If John had intended a speaker, a spokesman or an utterer, he would have used that completely different form of the noun. John's choice of words precludes the possibility that the Word was a spokesman. The

Word is not an utterer, but rather He is the Utterance of God. This explanation also confirms a father-son relationship between the Father and the Word, because an utterance requires an utterer to come into existence, just as a word requires a speaker and a son requires a father to come into existence.

Continuing in John 1:1, the writer explains that the Word was not only present at creation, but that the Word had a distinct existence in God's Presence. The Word was "with God." However, if the Word was with God, then we cannot exactly identify the Word as God, even though some have asserted that the Word, or specifically Jesus Christ, was the God of the Old Testament. Others have said the Father was the God of the Old Testament. A correct perception of God will reveal that neither of these assumptions can be true.

In the original Greek language, the middle part of this verse reads, "and the Word was with THE God." The definite article "the" is omitted in English, being unnecessary for our translations because no other God is known in Christendom and the meaning is clear without the clarification of the definite article. For his audience, however, John emphatically states that this God was THE God, an unmistakable reference to the same GOD-WHO-IS-ONE revealed to the patriarchs in the Old Testament. Since the Word was <u>with</u> THE God, the Word cannot be THE God of the Old Testament. Likewise, the Father is a distinct person of THE God, so the Father cannot be THE God of the Old Testament either. It was neither the Father nor the Word Who was the God of the Old Testament, but it was the GOD-WHO-IS-ONE Who was. The Father, the Word and the Holy Spirit was God in the Old Testament, just as the Father, the Word and the Holy Spirit is God in the New Testament. Sometimes theologians fail to grasp what should be obvious.

The last phrase of this enlightening verse, "and the Word was God," may seem to contradict the paragraph above, but it does not. In this final phrase the definite article "the" is omitted before God, or *theos* in Greek, forming only a general reference to deity. *Theos* here simply means "divine." The Word was divine. John explained that the Word possessed divine nature in the beginning with THE God. Thus, this verse can be more clearly understood as follows: "In the beginning was the Word, and the Word was with THE God, and the Word was divine." That's the Greek sense of John's statement.

Immediately apparent in John's statement is an unmistakable condemnation of Aryanism, which claims Jesus Christ did not exist from eternity and was, therefore, merely a created being. You should recognize this gross error. The Word—the One Who took on flesh and became Jesus Christ—is divine. Jesus Christ is divine, because the eternal Word is divine, and the eternal Word took on flesh. Jesus Christ is divine, but He is not THE God of the Old Testament.

As I first began to carefully consider the nature of the Word, the simplicity and elegance of John's remarkable physical description of the second person of the trinity struck me profoundly. In spite of His divinity, John was inspired to describe Him in the most humble and physical way. A word is a purely physical expression which has no inherent life, power or substance connected with it. In the case of speech, a word takes its form as sound waves which emanate from the mouth of one who is speaking. They will radiate outwardly until they are blocked or absorbed into the background noise of the cosmos. The life of a spoken word is relatively short. In the case of written communication, a word is merely a spot of ink or some other mark on a piece of paper or other writing surface. The written word may last somewhat longer than the sound waves of the spoken word, but certainly a physical word cannot be considered eternal. How can such an intangible expression as "word" be used to describe the divine second person of the triune God?

Although a word is physical and temporary, a word is an element of thought. Thoughts exist in my mind as part of my being, but words are external expressions which represent my thoughts. When I communicate with someone, I use words to express the thought which I have created in my mind. When I express my thought verbally, the sound waves go out from my mouth to the ear of the one with whom I wish to communicate, and the hearer receives the words in his ear. Then they travel into his brain, where my thought is reproduced in the hearer's mind. When I express my thought in writing, I make certain marks on a piece of paper, and the reader's eyes perceive the shapes of the marks and transmit them to his brain, where the person interprets my words, and, similarly, my thought is reproduced in the reader's mind. In either case, if I have chosen the correct words, I can reproduce my thought in the mind of the person who heard or read my words.

As I am able to reproduce my thought in the mind of another, God is also reproducing His Thought in my mind. He has the same two ways to accomplish that purpose. He may speak to me directly, Person to person, or He may communicate with me through the physical mechanism of the printed word, which we call the Bible. When He speaks directly, He sends forth the divine expression of His Thought, His Word, and I receive His thoughts directly in my mind by the Spirit. When He communicates through the Bible, He must have first communicated His Word directly to the apostles and prophets, who wrote down the words, and then God's thoughts reach my mind through my eyes. In either case the result is the same. God has placed a small portion of His Thought into my mind.

God's written words, the Bible, are physical and temporary. With time the cover will come off, the binding will break, and the ink will fade from the pages. The book will turn to dust. However, God's Thought is eternal and divine. God has used "word," the outward expression of thought, to reveal the spiritual reality that the second person of the trinity is the living, eternal Thought of God.

Since the nature of the second person of the trinity is divine Thought, we may very quickly determine the nature of the Father. Words and thoughts do not represent a primary cause, but they must be produced. They neither exist nor act on their own. An utterance demands an utterer. If a thought exists, there must be a thought producer. There must be a thinker. A thought cannot think or produce itself any more than a word can speak itself. A thought requires someone to think the thought before the thought can exist. Therefore, we may reasonably conclude that the Father is the Creator and Producer of His divine Thought, which He may express as the Word of God. All divine Utterance begins with the Father. The Father is the primary Cause. The Father is the Thinker. Father and Word are Thinker and Thought.

As Thinker and Thought, God is a great divine Mind. As Father, God is Thinker. As the Word, God is Thought. Since the Thinker is the Creator of Thought, it becomes immediately apparent how the Word, and indeed the Son, can be both created by and coeternal with the Father. Since God is eternal, there has never been a time when God was not thinking. God has been thinking forever. As long as He has been thinking, the Father has always been producing His Thought. Therefore, God's Thought must also necessarily have always existed, because God has always existed, and God has always been producing His Thought. Therefore, the Father and the Word are coeternal members of the triune God.

Now let's consider the relationship between the Spirit and God's divine Mind—the Father and the Word. God is not only Father and Word, but He is a Spirit. (John 4:24) He is Holy Spirit. The Holy Spirit is the essence and power of His being. The Spirit gives God the ability to move and act. The Spirit gives the Father the ability to express His Thought. God creates, sustains, speaks, sees, hears, comforts, encourages and does everything He does by the Spirit. Without the Spirit, God would be impotent. The Father and the Word can do nothing without the Spirit. Without the Spirit, God would be a divine Mind without a divine body. The Spirit is the substance of God. The Spirit is God's spiritual "body," but we must be careful not to imply that God has a particular shape or that He is limited to a certain place. God cannot be limited in any way which the word "body" might imply. To avoid such a misunderstanding, the Spirit may be more appropriately described as God's Presence.

Therefore, the triune God can be described as Thinker, Thought and divine Presence, and each is mutually dependent upon the others for God to be a complete Being. If God were Thinker and Thought, but had no presence, God could not be anywhere or be able to do anything. If God were Thinker and Presence, but could not produce a thought, God would be like a man with total amnesia. If God were Thought and Presence, but could not think..., well, that makes no sense. God must be all three to be God. God must be Thinker, Thought and Presence to be a complete divine Being. God must be Father, Word and Holy Spirit to be one complete God.

In all of God's activities the Father, the Word the Holy Spirit act simultaneously and in perfect harmony. God can do nothing, except that all three hypostases of God act together. When scripture tells us the Father or the Word or the Spirit acted, we should understand that each hypostasis of God participated in His unique way to accomplish God's purpose. Recall that the Bible says in some places that the Father created us, in others that the Word was the Creator, and in yet others that the Spirit accomplished the work. It should now be clear that all three perspectives are true and that each passage of scripture reflects a unique perspective of the whole truth. The Father, the Word and Holy Spirit always act in unison to accomplish God's purpose. Whenever God acts, the Father must first think. When the Father produces His Thought, the Spirit sees the Thought of God, and the Spirit acts according to the direction of God's Thought. The Father thinks, the Thought (the Word) of God goes forth, and the Spirit makes it happen.

The apostles and prophets never specify the roles of each hypostasis of God when they record the various acts of God in scripture, but we should be able to see God in action, if we carefully analyze the biblical record. Remarkably, Moses recorded how the Father, the Word and the Holy Spirit functioned together to create physical light in the first chapter of Genesis. Keep in mind that the Father is the source of every action of God, so when God creates, the Father must first produce the Word before the Spirit acts.

> In the beginning God created the heaven and the earth. And the earth was without form, and void; and darkness was upon the face of the deep. And the Spirit of God moved upon the face of the waters. **And God said, Let there be light: and there was light.** (Gen 1:1-3)

The opening words of the Bible inform us that God—Father, Word, and Holy Spirit—created the universe. Subsequently, we learn exactly how each hypostasis of God functioned to produce the first physical light in the universe. God's Presence was apparent as the Spirit hovered above the waters, ready to act at the direction of the Word. Then the Father produced His Thought as recorded by Moses, *And God* (the Father) *said...* As the Father produced His Thought, the Word went forth from the Father, *Let there be light*. Upon seeing the Word sent out from the Father, the Spirit, hovering above the waters, acted instantly *and there was light*. Thus, we can plainly see the existing relationship between the three essences of the one God as each acted in the creation of physical light.

Now let's consider the nature of man. Man is made in the image of God, (Gen 1:26) but God does not explicitly describe the nature of the imagery, so men have misapplied this truth with disastrous consequences. Artists of all kinds have attempted to depict God based on this truth, resulting in a host of grotesque images of God. These artists seem to have assumed that the triune nature of God must reflect some feature of man in triplicate. The resulting images of God variously resemble Siamese triplets, a body with three heads or a man with three faces; but God does not say that He bears multiple features of a man. He says man is made in the singular image of God. We must first determine a plausible hypothesis for the triune nature of God, and then we ought to be able to confirm or deny our hypothesis by considering whether a man really bears that image. We cannot perceive God by manipulating the appearance of a man, but we may indeed perceive the nature of man by properly understanding the triune nature of God.

Since this analysis of the nature of God is irrelevant to the appearance of a human being but based on the revealed nature of the three hypostases of God, we will more likely achieve a result which will reveal the triune nature of man. Let's test this analysis regarding the triune nature of God by examining a man—for example, me—to see if I bear the triune image of God.

First, consider the nature of the Father. The Father is the One Who thinks and produces His Thought, which He may express as His Word. The Father is the Creator. The Father is the Source of every thought and action of God. Therefore, I must ask myself, do I think? Do I produce thoughts and express those thoughts in words to others? Am I the source of my thoughts and the initiator of every action of my body? Yes, I am. I can think. I produce thoughts. Just like the Father, I constantly think to produce directions for my body. I can create original ideas, refine old methods and produce solutions to problems. God has given me the ability to think creatively and produce thoughts. My mind, like God's divine Mind, is constantly thinking—constantly producing thoughts—constantly creating new ways to solve problems. Thinking is the highest function of my being. Just as the Father is the Thinker, I am also a thinker.

Next, consider God's Thought. The Father produces His Thought and God's Thought remains "with God." When I produce thoughts, do my thoughts remain "with me?" Absolutely! My thinking produces thoughts, and I am able to remember my thoughts by storing them in my memory. I do not produce thoughts which evaporate out of my mind, but I am able to remember my thoughts. My thoughts live in my memory. My thoughts remain "with me," and at any time I may recall my thoughts or send forth my word to accomplish my will, just as God can recall His thoughts and send forth His Word to accomplish His will. (Isa 55:11) My thoughts exist as long as I exist, just like God's thoughts are eternal as God is eternal. Unlike God, Whose Thought is eternal and perfect, I sometimes forget certain details of my thinking, but, generally, my thoughts will live as long as I live, and they are a distinct but integral part of my being. My ability to remember all my thoughts, even from early childhood, gives me identity and defines who I am. I am who I am, because my thoughts live "with me." Just as God's Thought is God, so my collective thoughts are an essential part of who I am. I am thought.

My abilities to think, produce thoughts and store and recall thoughts define the functions of the human mind. God is a great divine Mind—Thinker and Thought—Father and Word, and God has given me a human mind, which He has created to function just like His Mind. My mind contains the same dynamic duo—thinker and thought—required for any functional mind whether human or divine. The human mind directs the human being, just as God's Mind directs His Being. Like God, my mind is thinker and thought. I can think, and I can remember my thoughts, and both of these distinctions of my existence function in the bi-lobed brain which initiates and directs every purpose I desire to accomplish.

Lastly, consider the Spirit. The Spirit is the Presence of God and His power to act. Do I have a presence? Do I have the power to act? Most surely I do. God has given me a body. My body is the substance of my existence, and my body gives me the power and ability to do whatever my mind—thinker and thought—directs my body to do. I can produce the creations of my mind with my hands, move about with my feet, speak through my mouth, comfort with my arms, see with my eyes and do many other things just like God does by His Spirit. Everything I create comes into existence by the operation of my body. When I create, I first create a thought—an idea—an image of the thing I would like to produce. When I have fully developed the thought and considered the details of my creation, my thoughts direct my body to produce the idea I created in my mind. Instantly my body goes into action to produce the finished product.

All three of these functions of a human being are necessary to do anything I do. Without the ability to think, I would have no ability to produce thoughts, and I couldn't create anything. Without the ability to retain my thoughts or send forth my word, I could not remember anything I had thought, nor could I direct my body to do anything I wanted it to do. Without a body, I could never produce any of my thoughts or ideas nor could I communicate my thoughts to others. The human creative process is identical to the process God employed to create the universe. Just like God, I can think and retain my thought, and I have the ability to communicate my thoughts to my body or express my word to others, so I can realize the finished product of my creative thinking. Just as God is Thinker, Thought and divine Presence, I am thinker, thought and physical body. Truly, I am made in the image of God.

> I am thinker, thought and physical body;
> I am one.
> God is Thinker, Thought and divine Presence;
> God is one.

The triune God is not nearly as complicated as theologians try to make Him, and you need look no further than the bathroom mirror to understand how God is one and three at the same time. God has created a world filled with beings made in His image, and we need only consider how each of us reflects the nature of God to be able to grasp the oneness of God and the trinity of God. The concept is a bit difficult to explain, but once one perceives the reality, the simplicity of it is profound. Theologians have only complicated what most Christians take on faith, and they have done nothing more than contrive a philosophical solution instead of believing God's revealed solution for this conceptual dilemma. Their solution only barely avoids a contradiction. The doctrine of the trinity is a doctrine of smoke and mirrors. Although theologians created the doctrine in an attempt to quell internal quarreling, they also needed a rational explanation for the nature of God, because they desperately needed to save face with secular philosophers, who scoffed at the idea of three persons in one being. Ironically, the theologians beat the philosophers at their own game by redefining the terms of their explanation to produce the result they had predetermined to achieve. We no longer need to resort to deception. We can understand the nature of the triune God, if we simply believe and apply the divine revelation that we are made in the image of God.

The nature of God determines the government of God. The government of God is a function of God's triune Being. The government of God is theocracy. God's government is spiritual and requires no human function. Each hypostasis of God—the Father, the Word and the Holy Spirit—plays a unique role in the government of God. Unless each hypostasis of God fulfills His unique role in the theocracy, God would have no ability to govern either in the physical universe or in the spiritual realm.

Fundamentally, there are only three functions in any government, and the roles of the Father, the Word and the Holy Spirit fulfill the three functions of God's government. Paul summarized these three functions as rule, authority and power, (1 Cor 15:24) and, from a practical point of view, all three of these aspects of government must be functional in a government before the government can be effective. Each government must have a ruler to create laws, it must have authority(s) to direct citizens according to the laws, and it must have the power to enforce the laws it creates.

The nature of God contains rule, authority and power within Himself, and each of these three functions of government corresponds respectively to the Father, the Word and the Spirit. The Father rules, the Word (the Son) possesses all authority, and the Spirit is the power of God to enforce His rulership and authority. Since God contains all three within Himself, the true theocracy of God needs no external governmental function. God alone governs in the entire spiritual and physical realm by Himself. God has the ability within Himself to rule His people, the authority to command His people, and the power to comfort, protect, lead and heal His people as well as the power to remove or destroy those who reject His rulership or resist His authority. When I discuss theocracy in this book, I refer to the government of God apart from any human rule, authority or power. True theocracy exists without human rulers, human authorities or human power.

Just as each essential element of government is evident in God, so also these three elements are evident within each human being. Since God made us in His image, each human being has the ability, albeit in a limited way, to rule, to command and to exercise power to enforce his or her will. Just as the Father rules, we have the ability to rule, because our ability to create allows us to analyze relationships and create laws to govern ourselves and others. Just as the Word commands the Spirit, our thoughts command our own bodies, and our expressed word has the ability to command others. Just as the Spirit is God's substance and power, our bodies give us substance, and they give us the power to accomplish whatever we direct our bodies to do and the power to enforce the rules we make. Human beings can govern just as God governs, but only in a limited way.

Since human beings are physical, time and space severely limit our ability to personally govern more than a few individuals. As the number of family members or citizens of a city grows, and even as the territory one attempts to govern expands, an individual becomes increasingly unable to personally rule, command and exercise the power to enforce all the rules and commands or to protect all the citizens. Our human limitations make government vested in a single individual practically impossible. Consequently, men have devised a system whereby they divide the three basic functions of government into separate responsibilities, and separate individuals perform each of the three essential functions of the government. The system men have devised is a hierarchical system.

Every type of human government takes the form of a hierarchical system, and each separate responsibility in the hierarchy serves at lest one of the three basic functions of government. Men have determined, and the Bible confirms, that rulership is the highest responsibility in government, so a ruler rules over all. Authorities are placed under the ruler to interpret the laws for practical application, and these bureaucrats are distributed throughout a nation in order to direct citizens according to law in any given situation. The third and lowest responsibility in government is exercised by various law enforcement agencies, which are authorized to use power, when necessary, to enforce the laws of the ruler or the commands of authorities. Although rulership is often vested in a group rather than an individual and the functions of authority and power often overlap in hierarchical systems, the basic functions of rule, authority and power are essential to every viable government, and they can be seen in every hierarchical system. Every human government requires a hierarchical system, because the ability of a single human being to rule, command and force compliance with laws is severely limited.

A ruler is sovereign, and there is no higher governing function than rulership. A ruler possesses sovereign privilege to impose his will upon the citizens by enacting his rules, or laws, for the nation.

These codified laws apply broadly to everyone without exception. Everyone in the nation living under the protection of the ruler must obey his laws. No one is exempt, and there are no exceptions to the laws unless specified. A ruler possesses the sovereign right to create the broad principles of law which apply to everyone at all times under all applicable circumstances.

An authority is a person authorized by the ruler to give orders or commands, and the authority is charged to inform citizens regarding the nature of the laws enacted by the ruler and to explain how the laws may be interpreted and applied. Authorities give commands in specific situations and possess the authority to direct others to act according to the law of the ruler, but authorities do not rule. In various emergency situations, duly licensed authorities, particularly policemen, may act or give commands contrary to human laws to insure public safety, because human laws are flawed by their nature. God's Law is a perfect Law, but human laws must be amendable to allow authorities the discretion to deal with unusual situations. Authorities command, but authorities do not rule, because they do not create the rules or legislate the laws. Authorities give commands in specific situations based on the laws of a city, state or nation.

The power of force brings compliance when neither rules nor commands achieve the desired result. Policemen are trained to protect citizens by using overwhelming physical strength and the power of weapons to control those who live outside the law and refuse to obey the laws of the ruler or the commands of authorities. The ruler may also maintain military forces, so called, because they are trained to use force to protect the nation from external enemies.

Imprecise usage and mistranslation often blur the important differences between rule, authority and power, but when we understand the nature of God, the nature of man and how every government must use rules, commands and power to remain viable, we may more clearly understand the exact nature of government, not only in the hierarchy of physical nations, but, more importantly, in the theocracy of the omniscient and omnipotent God, Who solely governs His holy nation, the Church. God exercises rulership, authority and power solely by Himself, and the Father, the Word and the Holy Spirit each act continuously in their unique functions to sustain God's kingdom and sovereignty. God's laws apply to his people at all times, His Word commands us in specific situations, and He uses the power of His Spirit to strengthen us, lead us away from danger and subjugate the enemy. Theocracy is the only viable government in one Being.

Each hypostasis of God functions uniquely in one of the three functions of the theocracy. The Father is sovereign, and He rules His spiritual kingdom by creating the laws which He applies to everyone He places under His rulership. The Word in the person of the Son commands each citizen of the kingdom by giving unique directions to each individual placed under His authority. The Spirit is God's power to protect His holy nation and empower His people to obey the Father's laws. When believers understand the vital functions of rule, authority and power and how they operate in the Church, we hold the key to unlock one of the best kept secrets in the Christian community—the identities of the sovereign Ruler, the supreme Commander and the omnipotent Power of the Church.

The Father is the Creator and the Beginning of everything which exists, so the Father is the Source and Creator of all rules and all laws in both the physical universe and the spiritual realm. He has designed the laws of physics, thermodynamics, biology, chemistry and all the other laws which operate the physical universe, and He has also designed the spiritual rules—the principles—the laws which govern the spiritual realm, particularly the laws which govern interpersonal relationships. The Father is the Source of our existence, and He has created the laws which bring us into harmony with Him and with one another. Since the Father is the Creator of those laws, the Father is the Ruler.

Over nineteen hundred years of corrupt religious practice in churches has blinded churchgoers to the true nature of God. The people of God have lost sight of the rulership of the Father and role He plays in the government of the Church. Most churchgoers trust men to rule their churches, so the rules of men have been substituted for the laws of God. Believers cannot live by the rules of men and the laws of God, because churches cannot operate under two standards of conduct. Churches cannot function properly or please God until the Father rules the churches, the Word commands the churches, and the Spirit empowers, strengthens and sustains the churches while He protects them from harm and heresy. Churches cannot be free until the Father rules, the Word (the Son) commands, and the Spirit empowers each church to accomplish the will of God.

God Ruled Israel

The mystery of rulership in the Bible belies the simplicity of the concept, yet rulership has become a mystery, because the translators of the Bible have failed to understand Who always rules the people of God. A ruler, by definition, is the one who makes the rules. The rules, or, as we most often call them, the laws, are the means by which a ruler rules. A ruler rules by creating and enforcing rules. Fundamentally, it's no more complicated than that. Therefore, it should be obvious that the Ruler of Israel was God, particularly the Father. God ruled Israel, because God created the laws which governed Israel. God alone ruled Israel.

God gave the law through Moses, and Moses became the first judge of Israel. Although Moses was a judge, he was not a ruler. God the Father made the rules. Moses only interpreted what the law meant when the proper application of the law was unclear in a given situation. The judges judged the people by the law, but they did not create the law, and they did not rule Israel.

Judges perform the same vital function in our society today which judges performed in ancient Israel. They settle disputes over different interpretations of the law, and they make decisions or judgments, errantly called rulings, regarding the meaning and the application of the law in specific instances. From time to time the Supreme Court judges may appear to rule, and, when their decisions seem to infringe upon the constitution or appear to change the law, Congress and the President are quick to rebuke the Court for usurping their sovereign privilege to rule. Our judges judge cases by existing law, but they do not create laws, and they are not permitted to rule our country.

God's law applied to every individual in Israel, including the judges and, later, the kings. God placed every Israelite citizen under the law equally, including those who were responsible to make judgments regarding it. No one was exempt. Moses lived under the divine law as much as a newborn baby did. The law prescribed the conduct of everyone in Israelite society. Indeed God Himself fulfilled the law.

God protected the integrity of Israel's law by incorporating restrictions within the law itself, which prohibited human tampering. The following two verses contain God's instructions to Israel regarding His rulership.

> Ye shall not add unto the word which I command you, neither shall ye diminish ought from it, that ye may keep the commandments of the LORD your God which I command you. (Deut 4:2)

> What thing soever I command you, observe to do it: thou shalt not add thereto, nor diminish from it. (Deut 12:32)

General theological ignorance of the difference between laws and commands pervades the Bible, but you should not be deceived about the nature of the injunctions God gave Israel. God did not command Israel or give them commandments, but He ruled them and gave them laws. Every injunction Moses recorded was a law, and these laws applied generally to every Israelite citizen. Repetition adds extra emphasis, so God stressed the importance of His rulership by repeating His prohibition of human rulership in these two verses. God the Father wanted to make sure everybody in His chosen nation knew that He was sovereign and that He had created the old covenant laws. Even though God had given the law to Israel through a man, God did not allow any human to tamper with the laws He had made. God prohibited adding anything to the laws God gave Israel, and He prohibited taking anything away from those laws. God was Israel's sovereign Ruler. The Father alone ruled Israel.

In spite of the obvious reality that the Father ruled Israel, the translators of our English Bibles have arbitrarily and unscripturally imputed rulership to the judges and kings of Israel. Notice this uninspired translation, which erroneously attributes rulership to the judges of Israel.

> Now it came to pass in the days when the judges **ruled**, that there was a famine in the land. (Ruth 1:1)

We may very easily determine whether the author of the book of Ruth intended to impute rulership to the judges or whether the rulership indicated by the translators is a figment of their own uninspired imaginations. Strong's Hebrew Dictionary explains the exact meaning of God's inspired Hebrew word, *shaphat*, which was translated "ruled" above.

OT:8199
shaphat (shaw-fat'); a primitive root; **to judge**, i.e. pronounce sentence (for or against); by implication, to vindicate or punish; by extension, to govern; passively, to litigate (literally or figuratively):

The inspired word, *shaphat*, is a verb meaning "to judge." *Shaphat* has nothing to do with rulership. It does not mean to govern. God intended us to understand that the judges judged Israel. That's what judges do. They judge. They make decisions. They don't rule. God ruled. The Father created the laws for Israel.

One of Israel's more renowned judges knew exactly Who ruled Israel, and he adamantly defended God's rulership. God had called Gideon to judge Israel, and Gideon had been successful in several battles when a group of Israelites nominated him to be the ruler of Israel and offered to set up a Gideon dynasty. Notice how Gideon defended God's sovereign right to rule Israel.

> Then the men of Israel said unto Gideon, Rule thou over us, both thou, and thy son, and thy son's son also: for thou hast delivered us from the hand of Midian. And Gideon said unto them, I will not rule over you, neither shall my son rule over you: the LORD shall rule over you. (Judg 8:22-23)

In each case the Hebrew word *mashal*, to rule, is correctly translated in this verse. The Bible never says the judges ruled Israel, and the nature of judgeship and God's explicit prohibition of human rulership should have precluded the translator's assumption that the judges might have ruled.

While the Father ruled Israel through His law when Israel was at peace, God was obliged to use a different approach to governance when Israel was at war. Codified instructions work very well when everybody in a society obeys them, but they are incapable of solving problems when there are those who reject the sovereignty of the ruler and the laws he makes. Such is the case in times of war. God had to deal with those who lived outside of Israelite society and threatened the peace and safety of the nation in a different manner. When Israel required specific instructions, God directed them with commands rather than with laws, so they knew exactly what to do in order to overcome the enemy in each specific situation.

When ancient Israel went to war, they needed a commander to lay out the battle plans and direct the troops, so God sent His Word to direct the army of Israel, and He provided the specific instructions Israel needed to defeat the enemy. The exact means by which God made His Word known is not clear in scripture, but the Father seems to have communicated His Word to the high priest through what was known as the Urim and the Thummim. As long as the army remained ceremonially clean and followed the direction of the Word communicated to the high priest, Israel was successful in their battles. The Word was the Commander of the armies of Israel.

The government of ancient Israel was theocracy. The Father was the Ruler of Israel at all times. He governed through His written Word—the law—in times of peace. He governed through His spoken Word—the Commander of the army—in times of war. God personally directed the battle plans through the Word communicated to the high priest. When the troops exactly followed God's Word, the Spirit acted to achieve the victory. As Father, God was the Ruler, as the Word, He was Commander, and God gave Israel the victory by the power of His Spirit. God governed Israel by theocracy.

Israel's constant sins provoked God's wrath, and the repeated cycle of sin, punishment, repentance and restoration during the period of the judges wearied Israel with cyclical wars. Israel became tired of going out to battle, and they repeatedly failed to rely on God to direct the battle strategy. Israel wanted a commander they could see. They wanted a king. Corruption among the judges of Israel exacerbated the situation, and eventually the people rejected the judges and asked God's prophet Samuel for a king to judge them and to lead the army. Theologians and translators have assumed Israel asked for a human ruler. They did not. However, the change which established the monarchy in Israel was no less significant, because it broke the theocracy in Israel.

About two hundred and fifty years before Israel asked for a king, God had already determined the king's role in the government of Israel. God knew Israel would reject His Word and demand a physical king, so God prescribed the king's duties in the law to make sure the king would specifically know that he was also subject to God's law for Israel.

> And it shall be, when he sitteth upon the throne of his kingdom, that HE SHALL WRITE HIM A COPY OF THIS LAW in a book out of that which is before the priests the Levites: And it shall be with him, and HE SHALL READ THEREIN ALL THE DAYS OF HIS LIFE: that he may learn to fear the LORD his God, to KEEP ALL THE WORDS OF THIS LAW AND THESE STATUTES, TO DO THEM: That his heart be not lifted up above his brethren, and that he turn not aside from the commandment, to the right hand, or to the left: to the end that he may prolong his days in his kingdom, he, and his children, in the midst of Israel.
> (Deut 17:18-20)

The longevity of the king's reign was entirely dependent on his continued acknowledgment that God ruled Israel. When the king read in the law, and indeed when he made himself his own copy of the law, he would have necessarily read and copied the verses we examined before: "Ye shall not add to the word which I command you, neither shall ye diminish ought from it, that ye may keep the commandments of the LORD your God which I command you." (Deut 4:2) God directed the king to write himself a copy of the law to guarantee that the king knew he was not the ruler. The law prohibited adding to or diminishing from the law God gave Israel, but the king needed to be very well acquainted with the law in order to fulfill the responsibility to judge Israel as head of the hierarchical judgeship established by Moses. In this respect the king's role was no different than the role of the judges before him.

Most theologians and Bible students have failed to grasp the exact nature of the change which took place in the government of Israel when God gave Israel a king. Many have assumed that the monarchy established by Samuel transferred the rulership of Israel from God to the kings. Such is not the case. The kings reigned, but they did not rule. The kings simply continued the judgeship Moses established at the beginning of the kingdom, but the change which angered God involved the transfer of authority to direct the armies of Israel from the Word to the king. The armies of Israel were no longer under the direction of the Word. The king became the commander of the army in place of the Word. Israel wanted a man to lead them into battle like the nations around them, and they rejected the role of God's Word as the Commander of the army. Although the king assumed the added responsibility to command the armies of Israel, God continued to rule Israel through the law. God remained the sovereign Ruler of Israel.

Even with an accurate translation, one must read the biblical text very carefully and without bias to avoid imputing rulership to the kings. Ruling and reigning are two different functions. Israel's kings reigned, but they did not rule. The Hebrew text never says the kings ruled. A key passage in this regard is 1 Samuel 8. Even the English text of this chapter does not discuss rulership, but most assume rulership simply because the word "reign" appears here. Carefully notice in verses 5 and 6 that the people asked for a king to judge them, not to rule them. Also notice in verse 7 that God said the people had rejected Him from reigning over them, not from ruling over them. When Samuel finished explaining how much the monarchy would cost and all the difficulties the people would experience when the king became commander instead of the Word, Samuel encouraged them to reconsider, but to no avail.

> Nevertheless the people refused to obey the voice of Samuel; and they said, Nay; but we will have a king over us; that we also may be like all the nations; and that our king may JUDGE US, and GO OUT BEFORE US, AND FIGHT OUR BATTLES.
> (1 Sam 8:19-20)

The people's request for a king to judge them (v. 5-6) and their rejection of God's reign (v. 7) exactly parallel their final decision to have a king judge them and go out before them to fight their battles. (v. 20) This passage defines the two fundamental roles of the king. He was judge, and he was warrior. He judged Israel, and he commanded the army. As judge, he became the head of the judgeship established by Moses. As king, he was responsible to seek direction from God and carry out God's battle plans, so the Spirit could give the victory. The king became a human substitute for God's personal Word. The law did not change at all, but the king stepped into God's shoes as commander of the armies of Israel in place of the Word. The Father still ruled, and the Spirit still gave the victory, but the Word no longer commanded the armies of Israel. Thus the theocracy was broken.

Most Bible students ignore the biblical difference between rule and reign, and even theologians and translators frequently use the terms interchangeably. The difference should become clearer, if you consider the difference between the two families of Hebrew words. Three words encompass rulership in Hebrew.

OT:4910
mashal (maw-shal'); a primitive root; **to rule:**

OT:4474
mimshal (mim-shawl'); from OT:4910; **a ruler** or (abstractly) rule:

OT:4475
memshalah (mem-shaw-law'); feminine of OT:4474; **rule**; also (concretely in plural) a realm or a ruler:

These three Hebrew words are a family of words, and you can easily see from the indicated derivation that the latter two are derived from the first. *Mashal* is the root verb, to rule. *Mimshal* is the person, a ruler, and *memshalah* is a noun which collectively describes the realm of a ruler, including the people in his territory. Every reference to rulership in the Bible will include at least one of these three Hebrew words.

Unlike the family of words which describes rulership in Hebrew, the words which describe the role of a king and his reign in a kingdom form a completely different family of words.

OT:4427
malak (maw-lak'); a primitive root; **to reign**; inceptively, to ascend the throne; causatively, to induct into royalty; hence (by implication) to take counsel:

OT:4428
melek (meh'-lek); from OT:4427; **a king:**

OT:4438
malkuwth (mal-kooth'); or malkuth (mal-kooth'); or (in plural) malkuyah (mal-koo-yah'); from OT:4427; **a rule**; concretely, a dominion:

Carefully notice one of the few errors Strong has introduced into his definitions. *Malkuwth* is plainly derived from OT:4427, to reign, not from OT:4910, to rule. The theological community has long assumed that rule and reign are interchangeable terms, so Strong has errantly imputed rulership to his definition of *malkuwth*, which should be defined as a kingdom or dominion wherein a king reigns, not a realm or rule where he is sovereign. *Malkuwth* is usually translated "kingdom." It is never translated "rule." There is no implication of rulership in the meaning of any of the latter three Hebrew words.

In the Bible a ruler is sovereign, and laws come forth directly from the ruler, but the king who only reigns makes no laws or rules of his own. Carefully examine the definition of the verb, *malak*. The king reigns when he has been inducted into the royal (God) family and ascends to the throne (of God) to take counsel (of God), not to usurp God's rulership, but to seek His advise regarding how he should reign, specifically how he should lead the army in battle to secure the victory. Notice the king "takes counsel" when he ascends the throne to reign. He does not give counsel. You should immediately recognize that a reign is particularly distinguished from rulership in this way. It is very unbecoming a sovereign ruler to take counsel. Israelite kings were responsible to receive counsel from the Word of God through the high priest in order to effectively direct Israel's battle strategy.

Unfortunately, translators have assumed the kings of Israel ruled, so those of us who read English Bibles will be errantly led to believe that the kings of Israel ruled Israel. They did not. Every such reference is a mistranslation of the inspired Hebrew text. Space does not allow the presentation of an exhaustive list of mistranslated verses and their corrections, but you can find them by examining the words rule, ruled, ruler, etc. in an English concordance. The errant translations will become apparent where none of the three Hebrew words of rulership supports the English word.

The Hebrew concepts of rule and reign cannot be interchanged. These two families of Hebrew words must be faithfully translated according to their literal meanings, or else the obvious misconceptions embraced by theologians and laymen alike will inevitably result. Unfaithful translations obliterate a correct perception of God's sole responsibility to rule His people in ancient times, and these arbitrary interpretations will in turn obscure God's sole responsibility to rule His people today. Similarly, if we fail to grasp the stated role of the kings to judge Israel and to command the army, we will in turn misunderstand Christ's role, not to rule, but to judge and command the Church. We may not assume the kings ruled when the Hebrew text specifically tells us they reigned.

However, you should be able to determine whether rulership played any part at all in the king's job description, if you track the three Hebrew words which define rulership in the Bible. These three words are used, collectively, over 100 times from Genesis to Zechariah to describe various rulers, rules and realms in the Old Testament. If the reigning kings of Israel also ruled, one of the prophets would have surely revealed the reality of kingly rulership during the 400 year reign of the Israelite kings. An organized search should reveal such rulership, if it exists, and you may search for it in at least two ways. You can use a Hebrew concordance and examine each passage where *mashal, mimshal,* and *mimshalah* are used, or you can do the same thing in a fraction of the time by using a Bible program on a computer.

An exhaustive examination of all these verses is not possible here, but I encourage you to undertake this study on your own. You will be able to see for yourself that Israelite kings never ruled over Israel. However, I will summarize here the results of a study I did several years ago. When I examined each appearance of *mashal, mimshal* and *mimshalah* in the Old Testament, I categorized each instance of rulership and reached the following general conclusions regarding rulership during the period of the kings of ancient Israel:

1) Gentile kings ruled over Gentiles.
2) Gentile kings ruled over Israelites.
3) Israelite kings ruled over Gentiles.
4) No Israelite king ruled over Israel.

Remarkably, the inspired Hebrew text never says Israelite kings ruled over Israel. This is a curious circumstance revealed in God's inspired words, while our English Bibles allege that several Israelite kings ruled Israel during their history. Is the lack of kingly rulership in the inspired text an oversight? Has God simply failed to make a notation for us that the kings of Israel ruled Israel, or has God always been solely responsible to rule His people?

This noteworthy circumstantial evidence serves to reveal the mindset of the prophets who wrote these books and recorded these histories. The prophets simply did not think in terms of rulership when they wrote about the relationship between the kings of Israel and the people. The prophets knew the law. They knew God was the Ruler, and they knew God did not allow any man—and maybe particularly not the king—to make laws for Israel. I personally feel God inspired the prophets to write their histories the way they did so anyone who cared to examine the inspired text would easily be able to see through the smoke screen of interpretative translation.

Although the Bible never explicitly says that the kings ruled, we should not be blind to the reality that the kings sinned by creating their own laws. The Bible does not describe the king's sins as ruling, but several of the kings, not so much of Judah but certainly of Israel, clearly made laws for the people contrary to God's will. One of the first things Jeroboam did after the rift in the kingdom was to set up golden calves in Dan and Bethel and institute a new religion with different festivals and his own priesthood. (1 Kings 12:28-33) His actions clearly violated God's rule against adding to and diminishing from the law. Jeroboam obviously changed the rules. He did away with some of the laws, and he made new rules of his own. Please don't think I'm saying the kings never made laws. They did, but my point is that God's design and intention was to reserve rulership entirely to His own discretion. His laws prohibited the rulership of others, and eventually God sent Israel into captivity, at least in part, because the kings assumed the right to stand in the place of God and make laws for the people of God.

While God did not permit the kings of Israel to rule His people, the kings of the neighboring nations did indeed rule their people. The archeological and historical records from Egypt, Babylon and Assyria inform us that these kings not only ruled, but that they were considered to be sons of their gods, and they were worshipped as gods by their people. Although we might cringe to even imagine bowing down to a mere mortal man as if he were a god, from God's perspective the heathen people's perceived identity of a ruler with a god is not a stretch at all, because anyone who rules usurps the sole prerogative of God to rule His creation. These heathen kings functioned in the role of gods simply because they assumed the prerogative to create laws and rule over their people.

The Bible subtly describes Israel's neighboring kings as gods, but most Bible students misinterpret Moses' reference to these ruling kings, because many interpreters mistakenly assume their gods were made out of sticks and stones. Such is not always the case. God gave Israel the land of Canaan, but the land was full of heathen people living in the city-states of the land, and these people were ruled by kings. To make room for Israel in the land, God promised to help Israel conquer the inhabitants and drive them out of the land, and, toward that end, He forbade Israel to cut any covenants—to make any peace agreements—with the people or with their gods.

> I will deliver the inhabitants of the land into your hand; and thou shalt drive them out before thee. Thou shalt [cut] no covenant with them, nor with their gods. (Ex 23:31-32)

Bible students tend to think of the gods of these nations in terms of carved sticks of wood and graven stone images, but the context of this verse precludes that interpretation here. It is impossible to cut a covenant with a piece of wood or a stone image. God's direction clearly forbade Israel to cut any covenants with the rulers of these nations, not with sticks and stones. The rulers of these nations were their gods, and God acknowledged these kings' de facto role as gods when He prohibited cutting any covenants with their gods. In God's sight the heathen kings were ruling in His stead. Anyone who usurps God's prerogative to rule makes himself a god. If all those who rule stand in the place of God, dare anyone make rules for the people of God today? Dare anyone rule a church?

God Rules the Church

The heavens declare the glory of God, but the people of God remain largely ignorant of the glory and majesty of His sovereignty and rulership. The inanimate creation praises its Ruler, but those who officiate in the churches of America have denied His sovereign right. God reveals Himself through the creation, so we may clearly see the invisible things of God, even His eternal power and divinity, (Rom 1:20) yet His people, like Israel, still prefer to worship human beings rather than the Creator and bow to the rules of men rather than acknowledge the laws of God.

We have seen that God created the laws for Israel and gave them to Israel through Moses, who preserved them in the book of the covenant. Likewise, God has created His laws for the Church, given them through Jesus Christ, and the apostles have preserved them in the words of the New Testament for us. Even without any specific biblical statement, we ought to take for granted that God is the Ruler and Lawgiver for all His people and especially for His holy nation, the Church; but, sadly, fleshly human beings have a proclivity to worship what they can see and touch, and they tend to bow to human rulers and obey gods of flesh.

All Christians ought to assume God's sovereign rulership, yet the concept is virtually lost on both the leadership and the membership of churches. Ask your pastor, "Who rules our church?" and see what he says. If you receive any reply at all, you'll probably get a wrong answer. I asked that question in a home Bible study one time, and twelve people who had been eagerly participating in the study suddenly became very quiet, their eyes glazed over and they gazed motionlessly back at me with blank stares. Why doesn't every believer know Who rules the people of God? How is it possible that churchgoers have lost sight of the sovereign Ruler of the Church?

The realization and understanding of God's sovereign rulership over His people has been largely lost in the Christian community today. God has allowed the world to go its own way, but He has always reserved the right to rule the people He has chosen as His own. God reserved the prerogative to rule the patriarchs from the beginning, (Gen 26:5) He alone ruled the ancient nation of Israel, (Deut 4:2) and today God still rules His chosen people. (Jas 4:12) The holy Church remains under the sole rulership of the Father.

James the apostle knew God is the Lawgiver, (Jas 4:12) but a very long time ago the church fathers lost sight of the Father's lawgiving role. When the church fathers no longer taught the truth about God's rulership, believers began to assume men ruled the churches. Later, when the Bible was translated into English, the translators assumed men had the authority to rule God's people, and their translations attributed rulership to men throughout the Bible, including judges, kings and church leaders. Ever since that time, God's rulership has been camouflaged by mistranslation, and church leaders have been emboldened to flaunt their spurious biblical proof that they possess God's blessing to rule the people of God.

Yet we have seen that only God the Father ruled Israel, and He denied any man, particularly the king, the privilege to make laws for God's physical nation of Israel. Thus, it ought to be intuitively true that the Father alone rules His spiritual nation, the Church, and that He does not allow anyone to make laws for His holy people today. Indeed, we will see that it is impossible for men to make rules for the Church because of the nature of new covenant Law, but that is a subject to be addressed in chapter 5. Here we may simply rely on the revelation of the apostle James to verify that there is only One Who makes laws for His people, and there is only One Who gives those laws to afford salvation to His people and to pronounce destruction upon those who reject His rulership.

> There is one Lawgiver, who is able to save and to destroy: (James 4:12)

God the Father was the Lawgiver for Israel, and God the Father is the Lawgiver for the Church. A flawed understanding of rulership is inherent in the problem most Bible students face to correctly understand the nature of government in either Israel or the Church. Confusion will reign when it is not clear who rules. Our English translation (KJV) compounds the problem by leading us to believe that the judges of Israel ruled, (Ruth 1:1) the kings of Israel ruled, (1 Kings 1:35) Jesus Christ will rule Israel, (Matt 2:6) and church leaders rule the churches. (Heb 13:17) Consult Strong's Hebrew and Greek dictionaries to confirm that these are all mistranslations.

We live in a world filled with rules, yet the world is confused about the nature of rulership. Some claim that dogs rule, that surfers rule, that hot chicks rule or that any arbitrary group may rule, when, in fact, what they really mean is that such individuals and creatures seem to function without any sense of restraint whatsoever. In a contradictory society where good is bad and bad is good, we should not be surprised that those who are lawless are attributed rulership. However, sometimes the confusion arises from serious, but misguided, attempts to describe rulership. We've coined the expression "the rule of law" in an attempt to describe our equitable system of government, but laws don't rule us at all. Men rule. Laws may command us in specific situations, but laws do not rule. Laws can't create themselves. The ruler is the one who creates the laws.

The nature of governments is to govern, and all governments make rules to govern their subjects. Rulership is the highest order of governance within any group of people, and the Bible describes rulers as gods, since they usurp God's sovereign privilege to rule His creation. In the United States we have constituted a bifurcated body of rulers called the Congress, which, in collaboration with the President, rules our nation and adds hundreds of laws each year to the countless thousands of laws already legislated, as our fleshly gods attempt to regulate our lives in what we call a free society. Yet with the passage of each new law, our freedoms are further eroded, if ever so slightly.

Our lives are filled with rules, and civil laws impact every aspect of our physical lives from IRS agents to local inspectors. When we go to work, there are corporate rules we must follow to maintain our jobs and facilitate the efficient running of the company. If we are union members, we must also comply with union rules. We are responsible to make sure our children obey the school rules, and such rules even extend to some aspects of our own conduct. Depending on where we might live, renter's rules, homeowner's association rules and/or municipal codes regulate our lives and control and restrict an increasing array of activities in and around our homes. There are rules when we walk in the park, play at the beach, hike on the trail, fish on the pier and hunt in the forest. We must obey the rules of the road, maritime rules on the water and FAA rules when we fly. Even when we play games, we are obliged to follow the rules. Human rules and regulations pervade our lives.

We become so used to people making rules for us that we might naturally assume human beings must make rules for a church. We might assume men must also govern our spiritual lives, and we tend to ignore God's plain declaration that He is the only Lawgiver for His people. God's rulership ought to be assumed, yet on several occasions when I have asked Christians, "Who rules our church?" my question has been met with utter confusion and blank stares. The confusion about rulership may be compounded, because most understand they have been freed from the law of Moses, and some may be misled into thinking there are no laws at all for Christians. Most churchgoers simply do not think in terms of church rulership. Most churchgoers are oblivious to the Ruler of the Church.

As with rulership in Israel, the mystery of rulership in the Church belies the simplicity of the concept. Whether for Israel or for the Church, the ruler, by definition, is the one who makes the rules. The rules, or, as we most often call them, the laws, are the means by which a ruler rules. Again, it's no more complicated than that. Therefore, it should be obvious that the Ruler of the Church is God, because He is the One Who created and inspired the biblical laws to govern the Church. God is the Ruler and the Lawgiver. (Jas 4:12) The Father rules the Church.

Some may assume Jesus Christ rules the Church. Although one might easily make that assumption, it's not true. Jesus Christ is the Word of God, not the Father. He is King of kings and Lord of lords, but He is never called the ruler of the Church. The Son is the Head of the Church, and He is our Commander. He is our King. The law did not allow the king to rule. Jesus Christ commands His Christian soldiers, but He does not rule us. The Bible never says Christ rules God's people. The Father is the sovereign Ruler of the Church.

Translators have distorted the nature of rulership throughout the Bible, and the New Testament is no exception. Words of rulership, indicating laws, and words of authority, indicating commands, have been routinely interchanged at the whim of the translators, and the inspired titles of governance have been obliterated by so-called honorable themes, which are mostly arbitrary and meaningless titles. Old Testament rulership is often imputed where it does not belong, whereas rulership in the New Testament is more often obscured where we should be able to see it exists. Translators have not only obscured the rulership of God by attributing rulership to the judges and kings of Israel, but they have obscured the laws of God by turning them into commandments, whereas the inspired text makes no determination at all regarding the exact nature of the authoritative direction. Utter chaos pervades rulership in the text of our English Bibles. The role of the Father is entirely camouflaged in churches.

The Hebrew and Greek words underlying most appearances of the verb "to command" or the noun "commandment" in our English Bibles are enjoin and injunction, respectively. Enjoin and injunction are only general references to authoritative direction, and we must examine the context in each case to determine whether the indicated injunction is a law or a command. In such cases God has chosen to leave that determination to the Bible student, so translators should not have arbitrarily assumed the author intended commandments, particularly when the context plainly indicates laws. Translators have distorted the nature of most scriptural injunctions by arbitrarily lumping them together as commandments, whereas the vast majority of them are obviously laws. Certainly this multitude of translation errors doesn't fool most of us, because we intuitively understand that the commandments of God are really His divine laws, but the conceptual difference between laws and commands suffers significantly when translators fail to faithfully translate what God inspired to be written. It is important to maintain the biblical distinction between laws and commands, because laws apply to everyone in a society, but commands are situation specific and only apply to those addressed. These and other mistranslations we have yet to examine utterly scramble dozens of key threads in the fabric of the divinely designed biblical tapestry and obfuscate the magnificent portrait of the kingdom of God which the apostles and prophets were inspired to weave.

Christendom proclaims the name of Jesus Christ as the primary focus of its doctrine and faith, and the Lord certainly deserves our adoration and worship, but the intense focus on Jesus has caused most churchgoers to loose sight of the Father and the rulership He exercises in the government of the Church and the life of each believer. Organized Christianity has lost sight of the Ruler and Lawgiver, and few churchgoers are able to define the Father's role in their lives. Confusion will reign when God's people loose sight of Who rules, and Christendom has become hopelessly confused regarding rulership. Church leaders grope in the dark for solutions to problems, and they can find none, because men rule the churches and human reason has become a substitute for truth and the basis for doctrine. Human reason is completely inadequate to solve the spiritual, moral and social dilemmas church leaders repeatedly and increasingly face in twenty-first century ecclesiastical culture. Only the laws of God provide the straightforward solutions Christians need in this age to effect complete and lasting solutions to the increasing complexity of social problems. The people of God must acknowledge God as the sovereign Ruler of the Church and honor Him as the Creator of the eternal, immutable laws governing all human relationships before they can even begin to experience the freedom of the New Covenant through faith in Jesus Christ.

Our freedom as Christians is dependent upon God's sovereignty over each church, yet every organized church has rejected God's privilege to rule. Every organized church is bowing to the rulership of men. Does your church acknowledge God as its Ruler, or do men stand as gods to rule your church? Does your church rely on the laws revealed in the Bible, or does your church follow the rules of men outlined in a church administration manual? Do you acknowledge God as your Ruler, or do you follow the rules of your church organization, the rules of your pastor, or the rules of your Bible study leader? Are you experiencing spiritual freedom, or are you shackled to the rules and regulations of men? Who rules your church? Who rules your spiritual life?

God is sovereign. The Father's role as sovereign Ruler of the Church is the foundation of Christian freedom. God created the laws which governed ancient Israel, and He has created the laws which govern the Church. Churches must acknowledge the rulership of God and reject all human rulership, so the churches can be free from gods of flesh and the injunctions of men. When the Father rules the churches, the members will be free to obey the direction of the Lord and follow the lead of the Holy Spirit to accomplish the purpose of God in their lives. Churches must acknowledge the rulership of the Father and embrace a covenant relationship with Him before they can be free. Freedom begins with the sovereign God.

Chapter 4

The Nature of Jesus Christ

True freedom belongs to those who know Jesus Christ and love Him and live in Him. His selfless sacrifice freed us from the law of sin and death. He is our perfect Law of liberty, Who frees us from the bondage of the old covenant law of Moses. He is the Commander of each Christian soldier, and His authority in our lives frees us from the authority of men. He is our Mediator and Judge, Who frees us from the judgment of men. He is the Way, the Truth and the Life. Those who walk in the Way of freedom have access to all Truth and possess eternal Life in Him. The Church walks in freedom, because no codified laws are in Him. He has made the faithful free, and we are free indeed.

Church leaders preach the gospel of Jesus' perfect life, gruesome death and miraculous resurrection weekly in churches around the world, and sermon after sermon witnesses of His humble birth, short ministry, selfless sacrifice, ascension to glory and many other aspects of the perfect life He lived in the flesh. I will not attempt to review what pastors constantly teach everywhere, but I will rather discuss and clarify several aspects of His nature which have been ignored by theologians and obscured by translators. The nature of Jesus Christ and His role in the government of God have been willfully ignored by those who have access to the original language texts of scripture, and, consequently, His nature and His role in the life of each believer have been largely hidden in translation. We will examine some of those mistranslations and reconstruct the English text, so we can properly understand the nature of Jesus Christ and His function in the government of the Church.

God specifically gave the old covenant to picture the coming Messiah, and the prophets confirmed the law and clarified the picture the law painted. Every aspect of the old covenant pointed to Jesus Christ. The old covenant served as a window into the New. Although the Messiah has come and the New Covenant has superseded the old, God has preserved the record of the law of Moses and the writings of the prophets to give us insight into the roles Jesus Christ now fulfills as the New Covenant. Jesus Christ fulfills all the old covenant types in God's spiritual nation, the Church.

Just as mistranslation has largely hidden the role of the Father in the Church, it has similarly obscured the roles of the Son. Church leaders have contributed to the problem, because they have failed to teach their members the basics of a covenant relationship and failed to rely on the inspired texts to reveal the essential roles Jesus Christ fulfills in the Church. Church leaders focus their sermons on what Jesus has done and ignore Who He is. They focus on His physical life on the earth and ignore what He is doing in heaven today. They are largely unaware of the roles our Lord actively exercises in the Church, as He fulfills the old covenant types which pictured Him.

The old covenant was a union between God and Israel, and the New Covenant unites God with the Church. The Father retains the role of Ruler, but He has delegated every other function pictured by the types of the old covenant to His Son. Jesus Christ fulfills all the old covenant types. The high priest, the judges and kings were types of His leadership. The bulls, goats and sheep were types of His character. The tabernacle and sanctuary were types of His kingdom. The ark of the covenant typed His person. Although most Christians understand that these old covenant types pictured our Lord, few understand that the two stone tablets—the old covenant documents—pictured Him. Few grasp the reality that Jesus Christ is the new covenant Document.

Jesus Christ, the Document

The purpose for a covenant document is to present the covenant law, but mainstream Christianity has lost sight of the new covenant Document. Theologians have utterly failed to recognize this key aspect of covenant, so they also struggle to define new covenant Law, because the covenant laws are always found in the covenant document. For this reason organized Christianity is largely blind to the roles Jesus Christ fulfills in the government of the Church.

A biblical covenant has four essential elements: 1) a covenant document; 2) a covenant law; 3) the sign of the covenant; and 4) the blood of the covenant. In ancient covenants between individuals, an animal represented the document, but animals lacked the words of the covenant, and they were only imputed to the animal through the promises of the covenant partners. When God cut the old covenant with Israel, they required a written document, so everyone could obey the covenant laws. Moses described the ten words written on each of the tablets as the words of the covenant. (Ex 34:28) Since the words of any covenant are written on the covenant document, it should be clear that the stone tablets containing the ten words were the old covenant marriage documents. As the fulfillment of all old covenant types, Jesus Christ is the new covenant Document.

In ancient times most covenants between individuals did not require a covenant document separate from the animal, because a man's word was considered more valuable than ink spots on a piece of parchment. However, covenants between nations always required a covenant document with the terms of the covenant clearly stated for everyone to know and obey. The sign, or signature, of the covenant was conspicuously placed on the document itself.

As the New Covenant, Jesus Christ fulfills those types. He is the Covenant, (Isa 42:6) so He is the covenant Document. His blood is the blood of the Covenant. He is the Word of God, (John 1:1) so He is the covenant Law and contains within Himself the laws of the Covenant. The sign He bears in His body is the signature God placed on the covenant Document, circumcision. (Gen 17:10-11) Jesus Christ is the only complete, living Covenant.

Jesus Christ is our New Covenant. He is a profoundly different Covenant than the old covenant. He is a Person, not a dumb animal or a stone tablet. The animals and the tablets were only types, and they are all dead or broken, but Christ is the only living Covenant. He alone is the everlasting Covenant. (Heb 13:20) His blood is the blood of the Covenant. (Matt 26:28) If His blood is the blood of the Covenant, Bible students should have known He is the Covenant. These realities should be obvious, but they are often overlooked, because church leaders have failed to teach the fundamentals of the biblical practice of cutting covenant. Translators have further obscured the reality of cutting covenant by errantly claiming that the ancient covenants were "made."

Jesus Christ, the Law

The Bible tells us that the eternal Word of God took on flesh and became Jesus Christ. (John 1:1, 14) The identity between the Word of God and Jesus Christ leads to the inescapable conclusion that Jesus Christ is our Law. Among the various roles Christ fulfills in the Church, one of the most important is His role as the Law of God.

The Father rules both the spiritual realm and the physical world through His Word. The divine Expression of the Father commands the spiritual host, just as the divine Expression of the Father commands His Christian soldiers. God's Word directs our lives. God's Word is our Law. Since the Word took on flesh and became Jesus Christ, I can only conclude that Jesus Christ is the Law of God. He is our living Law. He is our perfect Law of liberty. Jesus Christ is the personification of the divine Expression of the Thought of God. He is the Word of God. Jesus Christ is our Law.

Under the old covenant God expressed His Word to Israel through a human mediator, so Moses received and recorded the Word of God—the law—for Israel. God engraved the essence of His Word for Israel on tablets of stone, which became the centerpiece of the old covenant law. He personally communicated the remaining statutes and judgments directly to Moses through His Word on Mount Sinai. Moses wrote the whole law in the book of the covenant, which contained a history of Israel, the ten words of the covenant and all the laws God spoke to Moses. The book of the covenant became known as the law of Moses, or the *torah*, and this law provided the basis for the civil, religious and moral practices of every Israelite citizen. However, the written law of Moses was only a type. Jesus Christ is the fulfillment.

Just as the written, codified words of God comprised the law for Israel, the resurrected, complete and perfect Word of God is the Law for the Church. Jesus Christ is the perfect and complete Law of the Father. God has not given us another codified law, but He gives us His Son as a living Law. God's Thought—His living Law—His complete and perfect Word lives in us and directs our lives moment by moment. Jesus Christ has superseded the old covenant law. He has become our new covenant Law.

God promised through Jeremiah that He would give a New Covenant and that the Law of this New Covenant would be written in the hearts and minds of His people. (Jer 31:31-33) We should not assume God promised He would write the law of Moses or the ten commandments in our hearts and minds. Do not confuse the law of Moses with the Law of God. Jesus Christ is the Law Whom God promised to write in our hearts and minds. We will consider the nature of law and the differences between the law of Moses and the Law of God in the next chapter.

Although Jesus Christ is the Law, He is not the ruler of the Church. The Bible does not designate Jesus Christ as the ruler of the Church. The apostle James revealed that there is one Lawgiver Who is able to save and destroy, (Jas 4:12) and we saw in the last chapter that the Father is the only sovereign Who rules both the physical world and the spiritual realm. The Father has created the laws which govern the Church, and Jesus Christ embodies those laws. Jesus Christ is the means though Whom the Father rules the Church. Jesus Christ is the Law of God.

Jesus Christ, the Mediator/Judge

The terms "mediator" and "judge" are basically synonymous, and scripture is clear that Jesus Christ fulfills both roles in the Church. Paul explained to Timothy that there is only one Mediator between God and men, the Man Jesus Christ, (1 Tim 2:5) and Jesus said that the Father had committed all judgment to the Son. (John 5:22) Paul also told the Corinthians that spiritually minded members of a church cannot be judged by any man. (1 Cor 2:15) Jesus Christ alone has the authority to judge the members of the Church.

Although Jesus Christ is the one and only Mediator between God and men, few churchgoers grasp the entire significance of His role as Mediator in the Church. Protestantism has correctly discerned that our Mediator frees us from all the judgments Catholicism places along the path of salvation, including purification in purgatory, confession to priests, penance and indulgences, but most churchgoers still fail to understand that our divine Mediator not only frees us from all judgment, but from all those who stand in authority to impose judgment upon us Paul warned the Colossians not to let any man judge them in any ritual practices, (Col 2:16) and Jesus taught the disciples that a member can only be judged by the congregation, (Matt 18:17) not by the unilateral judgment of a church authority. The whole church must agree that a member is acting contrary to the Standard of Christian conduct before the member may be removed from fellowship. When a congregation agrees in assembly that a member has become a heathen and a publican, such agreement indicates that Jesus Christ has judged the individual, and the whole congregation must honor the Lord's judgment and reject the member from fellowship. When the Lord has judged the member, we must refuse to associate with that member or share communion with that member. (1 Cor 5:11) Church leaders have no biblical authority to remove any member from the congregation unilaterally. Jesus Christ is our only Mediator and Judge. I will consider the nature of judgment more thoroughly in chapter 6.

Jesus Christ, the Commander

During the period of the judges, God's Word commanded the armies of Israel through the high priest. When Israel rejected God as the Commander of the army and asked for a human king, we saw in the last chapter that they asked for a man to lead them into battle against their enemies. Rather than depending on the Word of God to lead them into battle, they wanted a visible leader. They wanted a human king to maintain a standing army to protect them from their warring neighbors. The new head of state continued to exercise the former role of judge in Israel, but the king assumed the new role of commander of the armies of Israel.

God revealed the king's new role in a number of verses scattered throughout the Old Testament, but mistranslation totally obliterates the biblically designated role of the kings in Israel. Listed below are several verses in the KJV which offer conflicting descriptions of the vital role God revealed for several of the kings of Israel and Judah. One could become very confused by the various titles offered in our English translations. These titles provide absolutely no rationale or consistency. Different translations make different choices for the responsibility hidden in the inspired Hebrew text, but none translates the original word literally into English. Consider each title alleged by the KJV in bolded capital letters.

Saul

To morrow about this time I will send thee [Samuel] a man out of the land of Benjamin, and thou shalt anoint him [Saul] to be **CAPTAIN** over my people Israel... (1 Sam 9:16)

David

And it shall come to pass, when the LORD shall have done to my lord [David] according to all the good that he hath spoken concerning thee, and shall have appointed thee **RULER** over Israel... (1 Sam 25:30)

Solomon
And [Israel] did eat and drink before the LORD on that day with great gladness. And they made Solomon the son of David king the second time, and anointed him unto the LORD to be the **CHIEF GOVERNOR**, and Zadok to be priest. (1 Chron 29:22)

Jeroboam
Go, tell Jeroboam, Thus saith the LORD God of Israel, Forasmuch as I exalted thee from among the people, and made thee **PRINCE** over my people Israel... (1 Kings 14:7)

These four examples are typical of dozens of irresponsible translations of the plain Hebrew text. You should notice that captain, ruler, chief governor and prince are among the titles the KJV bestows upon the king. Other titles offered in other verses are leader, noble and chief ruler. Remarkably, these titles are all mistranslations of a single Hebrew word, *nagiyd*, which appears in the Old Testament forty-four times, frequently in reference to the kings of Israel. Not once did it occur to the translators that a literal translation might be appropriate or significant. Notice the literal definition of *nagiyd* from Strong's Hebrew Dictionary.

OT:5057
nagiyd (naw-gheed'); or nagid (naw-gheed'); from OT:5046; **a commander** (as occupying the front), civil, military or religious; generally (abstractly, plural), honorable themes:

We call our President the Commander-in-Chief, because he is the head and commander of the military forces of the United States, and so it was in Israel that the king was the commander of the armies of Israel. The king commanded the troops to do whatever he needed them to do to achieve the victory, but these four "honorable themes" in the KJV completely obscure the inspired role of the king.

Mr. Strong recognized that *nagiyd* had been widely interpreted by the translators to embrace a variety of "honorable themes," so he glossed the translators' errors with the notation he included in his definition. We should not conclude that this notation in any way justifies the use of these honorable themes. They completely obscure the inspired word, and they have no basis in the meaning of *nagiyd*.

Nagiyd means commander—nothing more, nothing less. Forty-four times the translators have hidden the simple and inspired meaning of *nagiyd* from English speaking Bible students in favor of a handful of arbitrarily selected and meaningless honorable themes.

In spite of the examples above as well as other similarly mistranslated verses in the Old Testament, God never intended the kings of Israel to be rulers, captains or governors. They were Israel's head warriors. They were Israel's commanders. This correction makes a world of difference when one attempts to understand the function of the kings who reigned in Israel, and, particularly, how the government of Israel relates to government in the Church. God designated the kings of Israel to be the commanders of the armies of Israel, not the rulers of the people or the princes of Israel. Israel never questioned God the Ruler, only God the Commander. The king did not usurp the rulership of the Father, but rather he replaced God's Word as the commander of the army.

By the time the human kings of Israel had utterly failed in their responsibilities, God designated the Messiah of the tribe of Judah to restore the theocracy of God to Israel and to become the King of Israel and Commander of the army. God the Father never delegated the responsibility of rulership, but at the proper time He planned to send the Messiah to repossess the throne of Israel and reinstate the theocracy. Messiah's role as Commander was prophesied in the Old Testament in two of the previously mentioned forty-four mistranslated verses where *nagiyd* appears. These two verses prophesied the coming of Jesus Christ the Commander, but the prophesied responsibility is mistranslated in both verses.

> For Judah prevailed above his brethren, and of him came the **CHIEF RULER**; but the birthright was Joseph's: (1 Chron 5:2)

The translators subtly acknowledge that the alleged ruler in this verse is Jesus the Messiah by granting Him the title of "chief ruler" instead of just an ordinary ruler like one of the previously mistranslated references to the kings of Israel. We may see the logic in the translators' choice, but it only compounds the error. We know the Father is the Ruler, so, if Jesus Christ is the chief ruler, this mistranslation makes Jesus Christ the ruler of the Father. Of course, the heresy is obvious. Once again the Hebrew word behind chief ruler is *nagiyd*, which is exactly the same Hebrew word used for the roles of the kings of Israel above. God wanted every Bible student to know that Jesus Christ, the coming Messiah, would assume the same role the kings held in Israel. God wanted Israel to know Messiah will be the Commander of Israel. God wants us to know Jesus Christ is the Commander of the Church.

The title in the prophecy below is similarly mistranslated.

> Know therefore and understand, that from the going forth of the commandment to restore and to build Jerusalem unto the Messiah the **PRINCE** shall be seven weeks, and threescore and two weeks: the street shall be built again, and the wall, even in troublous times. (Dan 9:25)

Nagiyd is the inspired Hebrew word behind both "chief ruler" in Chronicles and "prince" here in Daniel. These two mistranslations obliterate the vital truth that God expressly designated the Messiah, Jesus Christ, to be the Commander of Israel and Commander of the Church over five hundred years before He came to fulfill that role. Substitute "Commander" where the KJV offers "chief ruler" and "prince" in the verses above to regain the inspired meaning. Only then can we understand the key role designated in these prophecies for Christ the Commander, Who came from Judah as the Messiah.

God had fully intended to give Israel a king, but He knew they would ask for a king before it was time for the Messiah to appear. With omniscient perspective God placed ground rules for the king in the law of Moses, so the king would know how to reign over Israel as the type of Jesus Christ, Whom God intended to be the eternal King over Israel. The kings of Israel were types of Jesus Christ. Jesus Christ is the fulfillment of all the old covenant types, and thus He is the Commander of both Israel and the Church.

We can also discover the Commander of Israel in the pages of the New Testament, where Jesus Christ is variously called the King, the King of Israel, the King of the Jews and the King of kings in twenty-seven New Testament references. Each time we read Christ the King, we should remember His responsibility as Commander. King is His title. Commander is His job description.

Jesus Christ, the Lord

Jesus Christ also fulfills the role of King in the Church, because He is the Head and Commander of every Christian soldier. Although Jesus Christ is just as much our King as He is the King of Israel, the apostles never referred to Him as the King of the Church. (The one reference to the "king of saints" is a mistranslation—see Rev 15:3.) God has given Jesus Christ a new title to differentiate between His role in Israel and His role in the Church. The function is the same, but the title is different. We know the Commander of the Church as the Lord. Commander is still His job description, but Lord has become His new title.

Christ's most frequently used New Testament title is Lord, and there are about 680 such references to our Lord. Although most churchgoers have an intuitive sense that this title implies superiority in Christ's role in the Church, few are aware of the specific function the title "lord" implies. Few churchgoers think of the Lord as the Commander of the Church, and fewer still realize that the Lord is the only Commander of the Church. The passing of two millennia has shielded us from the cultural significance of the lords of the first century, but we may regain a sense of lordship, if we examine Jesus' simple statement in the middle of the Sermon on the Mount, where Jesus explained that a believer can only serve one master (lord). This statement not only reveals that Jesus Christ is the Commander of the Church but that He is the only Commander of the Church. There can be only one Lord. There can be only one Commander.

> No man can serve two masters. (Matt 6:24)

The Greek word translated master is *kurios*. Almost all of the 750 occurrences of the word *kurios* are translated either Lord or lord, but, in this particular context, the translators have preferred to translate *kurios* into our cultural understanding of the word rather than translating it literally. In our culture we understand the relationship between a slave and his owner to be that of a slave and his master. The master was the land or plantation owner in our culture. In first century culture they understood it in terms of a slave and his lord. The lord was the land owner. I do not criticize the translation, but we should understand that a literal translation of *kurios* is lord. "No man can serve two *lords*."

If there is any doubt about the relationship Jesus described, it can be dispelled it by examining the Greek word for serve, *douleuo*. This verb is directly derived from the noun, *doulos*, the Greek word for slave. Our English translation softens the true meaning of the Greek text, which literally reads, "No man can *be enslaved to* two lords."

Additionally, the Greek word translated "no man," *oudeis*, is a compound Greek word which means "not even one." The simple English sense of the word is "nobody." Jesus did not limit His instruction to men, but He includes every member of the Church. Now we have a more accurate sense of the Greek text. "*Nobody* can be enslaved to two lords."

It is imperative that you understand the relationship expressed in this statement, and, to do so, you should consider the relationship which existed between a lord and his slave in Jewish society of the first century. How did a lord direct his slave? Did he make rules for him, or did he command him? If you are in doubt, recall that the law forbade anyone who lived under the law to add any rules to the law. Aside from that clue, simple logic should tell you that the lord commanded his slave; he did not rule him. Both the lord and his slave lived under the law, but the lord commanded the slave in every aspect of his life, and the slave did everything exactly as the lord commanded him. The nature of slavery demands that a lord is the commander of his slaves, and so it was in the early years of this country when masters commanded their slaves. The relationship ought to be so obvious that everyone should understand it. Sadly, modern era Christendom has completely missed Jesus' point.

In His sermon to the Church, Jesus taught, in effect, that nobody can be enslaved to two commanders. Although the principle is given in a physical sense, it also applies in the spiritual realm. A believer cannot be enslaved to two lords either. A believer cannot have two spiritual authorities in his or her spiritual life. A believer cannot obey both the pastor and the Lord. Similarly, a church cannot obey two commanders. A church cannot obey both the civil government and the Lord. Only the Lord has the authority to command His Christian soldiers. Only Jesus Christ has the right to command the members of His own body. Jesus Christ alone possesses the divine privilege to direct His Church.

Jesus Christ, the Head

Jesus' role as Head of the Church is more than just a title or responsibility. It is a spiritual reality. The human spirit living in a human body is its head, and the divine Spirit living in a spiritual body is its Head. Jesus Christ is the divine Spirit living in His spiritual body; therefore, Paul confidently explained to the Colossians that Jesus Christ is the Head of the Church.

> And [Jesus Christ] is the head of the body, the church: who is the beginning, the firstborn from the dead; that in all things he might have the preeminence. (Col 1:18)

God is creating His Son. His Son will be the first spiritual Man. The Church is the body of this new spiritual Creation, and God is placing Jesus Christ in the members of the body as the Spirit living in the body—as the Head of the body. When God has placed Jesus Christ into His finished body, the Lamb will be a complete spiritual Creation. He will be God's first spiritual Man.

Jesus Christ is Head of His body and the Director of every action of His body. The members of His body are His slaves. He lives in and commands each of the members of His body individually and personally through the Spirit. Jesus Christ is the Head and Commander of each Christian soldier—each slave—each member of His body. Christ and the members of His body are one. There is no hierarchical order in any body. There is no hierarchical order in the body of Christ.

The analogy of the body and Jesus' headship in the body lead to the inevitable conclusion that there is only one Authority in the Church. No one can obey the direction of two commanders. Human authorities are unnecessary in the Church, because our Head—the Spirit living in the body—our only spiritual Authority—lives in us and commands us from within.

Jesus Christ, the Chief Leader

Our Lord holds yet another important title, which indicates His relationship to the leadership of the Church. Translators entirely camouflage this title behind honorable themes, just as the *nagiyd*, the commander, was camouflaged in the Old Testament. The Lord's role as Chief Leader in the Church is entirely hidden in translation.

Few revelations of scripture are repeated more than once or twice, yet God felt it was so important to reveal the Chief Leader of the Church that He inspired the title to be recorded four times in the New Testament. Unfortunately, the translators completely missed the significance of God's revelation, and they mistranslated it all four times. In these four scriptures the translators have arbitrarily assumed titles of their own choosing, including captain, author and prince. These titles are all mistranslations, and they hide the biblical truth that our Commander is the Chief Leader of the Church. Carefully examine the bolded titles in the four verses below and notice to Whom they refer.

> But ye denied the Holy One and the Just, and desired a murderer to be granted unto you; and killed the **PRINCE** of life, whom God hath raised from the dead; whereof we are witnesses. (Acts 3:14-15)

> Him hath God exalted with his right hand to be a **PRINCE** and a Saviour, for to give repentance to Israel, and forgiveness of sins. (Acts 5:31)

> For it became him, for whom are all things, and by whom are all things, in bringing many sons unto glory, to make the **CAPTAIN** of their salvation perfect through sufferings. (Heb 2:10)

> Looking unto Jesus the **AUTHOR** and finisher of our faith; who for the joy that was set before him endured the cross, despising the shame, and is set down at the right hand of the throne of God. (Heb 12:2)

In each of these verses, the Greek word behind the misleading title is *archegos*. The titles of prince, captain and author are figments of the translators' imaginations, and each mistranslation hides the Lord's vital and revealed role as Chief Leader of the Church. Notice Strong's definition of *archegos*.

NT:747
archegos (ar-khay-gos'); from NT:746 and NT:71; **a chief leader**:

Archegos is a simple, straightforward, compound word derived from *arche* (chief) and *ago* (lead). The translators have become so accustomed to assigning their own titles to the various roles inspired by God in the Bible that they have become oblivious to the vital revelations of scripture. These four verses reveal that Jesus Christ, Who is the only Commander, is also a Leader, but He is not the only Leader. The inspired text of the Bible reveals that Jesus Christ is the Chief of all those who lead the people of God. The Head of every faithful church leader is the Chief Leader.

Although scripture clearly designates the Lord as the Chief Leader of the Church, scripture does not designate Him as the chief authority. This omission strongly implies that no human authorities exist in the Church. Human leadership in a church is a gift of God, not a position of authority. Leaders lead the members of their church, but they do not direct or command them. God has reserved the role of Commander for Jesus Christ alone. He alone commands both the leaders and members of a church. The Lord is Chief over all those who lead as well as all those who follow.

Jesus Christ: the Way, the Truth and the Life

An instinctive sense that a divine Being exists somewhere outside the physical realm has driven humanity to seek every imaginable pathway to God. Religions of every sort claim to hold the key to fulfillment in this life and access to the spiritual realm in the next. These religions may seem different, but the common denominator perpetuating every religion is the assumption that human effort and/or ritualistic practice can please God and bring sinful human beings closer and closer to God. Churchgoers tend to think of their relationship to God in terms of nearer or farther, when in truth it is all about being in or out. Being near to God is no longer good enough. In a profoundly anti-religious statement, Jesus revealed that religion cannot provide the way to God, reveal the truth of God or lead to eternal life with God. Jesus summarily relegated all religion and all ritualistic worship to the rubbish heap of human endeavor.

> Jesus saith unto him, I am the way, the truth, and the life: no man cometh unto the Father, but [through] me. (John 14:6)

The physical world is real, but it is full of illusions. We tend to believe what we can see with our eyes, but our eyes are deceiving us. Everything we see is relative. Nothing in the world is absolute. There is no truth in the world, and there is no life in the world. The world does not know the way of truth or how to gain eternal life. Destruction is the way of the world, and everything men touch becomes defiled or dies. Men have even polluted the Bible and filled it with lies. Men cannot quantify Truth or reduce Him to a set of codified doctrines, because Truth transcends the physical realm. Church organizations do not know or possess Truth, because Jesus Christ does not live in an organization. Church leaders cannot say a particular set of facts is Truth, because Jesus Christ is not a set of facts. Men are not custodians of Truth, because men cannot keep or protect Jesus Christ. God alone is the Source and Protector of Truth. Believers know the Truth, because He lives in us. The Spirit leads us into truth, and God gives truth freely to those who live in Him. His personal direction frees us from all ritual and all religion.

Likewise, the physical life we live in the flesh is an illusion. Human life is temporary and short. We do not possess an immortal soul. (Matt 10:28) We cannot gain eternal life through membership in a church organization. Men have no power over eternal life. We cannot achieve salvation by following men or maintain salvation by obeying church rules. Our only hope for eternal life is through the Word of God. We only have access to truth and eternal life through Jesus Christ. He possesses life within Himself. Jesus Christ is our eternal Life, because we live in Him.

Jesus Christ is the Way to God. He is the Truth of God. He possesses Life in God. There is only one Way to truth and eternal life, and those who are not in the Way are way out. Ritualistic practice is not worship, and it will not lead to eternal life. We cannot see the Truth or enter eternal life by being baptized, going to church, preaching the gospel or doing laps around the beads, but only by knowing the Way and by being in the Way. Salvation is a state of being, not a list of dos and don'ts. We must be in the Way, because He is the only pathway to God—the only pathway to truth—the only pathway to eternal life. He is the straight and narrow Way, and few are able to find Him, because few really trust Him. Most church-goers trust men to interpret truth for them, and they see the pastor as their pathway to eternal life, because they think salvation can be achieved by trusting a man to tell them what to do. They fail to see that salvation depends on who they are rather than what they do. Believers must be in Christ, and, when we are who we must be, then good deeds will be a natural result of who we are.

Each aspect of the Lord's divine nature plays a unique role along our spiritual pathway to God. Jesus Christ is our Covenant, without Whom we can have no relationship to God. He is our Law, without Whom we cannot be governed by God. He is the Word of God, without Whom we can have no communication with God. He is our Judge, without Whom we cannot be justified before God. He is our High Priest, without Whom we have no intercessor with God. He is our Sacrifice, without Whom we have no forgiveness from God. He is our Lord, without Whom we can receive no direction from God.

In covenant we take on the nature and character of God and become the literal, spiritual body of Christ. We become an integral part of His Being. We become the visible image of Who He is, because we know the Truth of God and have eternal life in God. We live in the Covenant of God, obey the Law of God, listen to the Word of God, stand righteous before the Judge of God, pray to the High Priest of God, seek forgiveness through the Sacrifice of God and act according to the direction of the Lord our God. Jesus Christ is everything we need to enter salvation. God has freed the Church from all codified law and all human direction, because we live under the theocracy of God. We only worship the sovereign Ruler and the supreme Commander of the Church while following the lead of the Spirit. True freedom is evident in a church, when the members only obey the directions of our Lord and Savior, Jesus Christ.

Chapter 5

The Nature of Law

True freedom becomes a reality when a church abandons the rules of men and worships our new covenant Law and obeys only Him. Jesus Christ has become the new covenant Law written in our hearts. Our new covenant Law lives in us, and He directs us from within apart from any external human direction. We experience freedom from the law of Moses and the commandments of men, because we acknowledge the perfect Law of liberty and allow Him to command us moment by moment in our daily walk with God. Jesus Christ is the only Law of freedom.

Our new covenant Law is entirely different from the old covenant law. Christians should know the difference between the law of Moses and the Law of God. Christians need to understand the nature of the divine Law, Who is the Head of the Church and Who directs the Church and each individual believer personally. God has raised the standard of conduct under the New Covenant from a divinely inspired written law to a divine Individual.

The terms law and rule are essentially interchangeable, and both encompass the broad principles of life which apply to everyone in every situation. Laws and rules exist in contrast to commands, which are situation specific. Commands only apply to specific individuals in specific places and at specific times. Rulers make laws which apply universally to everyone living under the protection of the ruler, but human rulers usually delegate the authority to command in specific situations. A ruler is sovereign, but those who command derive their authority from the ruler. In the physical world, men have assumed to themselves the prerogative to rule, but we saw in chapter 3 that individual human beings only have a limited ability to rule. God alone has the power within Himself to create, express and enforce His laws. God alone rules both the physical universe and the spiritual realm. God is the only true sovereign. God is the Ruler. God alone is the Lawgiver. (Jas 4:12)

As we attempt to sort out the multitude of laws and commands in the Bible to determine which apply to Christians and which do not, it is of paramount importance to pay very close attention to the context of each biblical passage containing injunctive directions.

The first and most important rule of sound exegesis is: CONTEXT GOVERNS THE INTERPRETATION. We cannot interpret any passage properly until we understand the context. Theologians have written many books on the subject, and they explain complicated procedures they see as necessary to arrive at proper interpretations, but common sense and careful observation of the text will serve us very well to avoid major mistakes in most cases, and a little education regarding the translators' errors and deceptions will help to nearly eliminate contextually related misinterpretations. Contextual ignorance leads more theologians, scholars, pastors and well-intentioned students of the Bible to embrace false conclusions than any other single reason. Faithful Bible students should always carefully observe the context.

The Bible is divided into two general contexts: the Old Testament and the New Testament. The Old Testament contains laws, prophecies and writings which mostly applied to the nation of Israel and to her individual citizens. Scripture plainly states that God gave the law to Israel, and the context reinforces the interpretation that the law only applied to God's physical nation as a whole and to His people individually. Context demands that the laws God gave to Israel were for Israel, and they were for Israel alone. Fundamentalist teachers who attempt to syncretistically apply old covenant laws in new covenant circumstances will invariably find themselves mired in a divided theology filled with irreconcilable contradictions. We must always carefully observe the context in which laws are given in order to accurately determine to whom they apply.

When the New Covenant superseded the old covenant, God provided a new Law containing a different type of laws for His new spiritual nation. The New Testament generally contains the record of the laws God gave to the Church, and those laws were intended to apply to churches as a whole and/or to their individual members. The New Testament contains the words Jesus taught the disciples, and it also contains some of the letters the apostles wrote to various individuals and church congregations. Most Bible students discern the context of the New Testament accurately and understand that the laws described there apply to faithful churches generally and/or to their members individually.

Although the general context of the New Testament is taught accurately in most churches, most twenty-first century exegetists have difficulty making a distinction between laws which apply to churches and laws which apply to individual members of a church. The difficulty is partly a function of linguistics and partly a result of mistranslation, but it is fundamentally one of context. Koine Greek is a simple, but very precise, language. It retains the ability to differentiate between the singular and plural forms of the second person pronouns, and the writers of the epistles used these pronouns very specifically to distinguish between their directions for a whole congregation and their directions for each individual member. When they used the second person singular, "thou," they addressed individuals, and when they used the second person plural, "ye," they addressed the whole congregation. This contextual distinction forms the basis to know which laws apply to churches and which apply to individual members. The distinction is very important.

English, on the other hand, has become very sloppy over the centuries. We have become extremely lazy in the way we think and express thoughts. Unfortunately, the distinction between the singular and plural second person pronouns has become a casualty of our laziness, and, since we haven't even used second person pronouns accurately for so long, we no longer even think in terms of them. We simply say "you" and expect the audience to know whether we are speaking to "you" singular or to "you" plural. Indeed the ambiguity occasionally serves our ignorance when we don't even know whether our audience is one person or several, but the apostles were very specific when they gave directions to churches and gave directions to individuals. Thankfully, the KJV retains the archaic second person pronouns, so we will be able to plainly see the difference between laws for a church and laws for an individual when appropriate passages of scripture are quoted in this book; but we should be aware that English speaking interpreters often ignore the difference, even when it is placed squarely before them, simply because we are not used to thinking in terms of thou and ye.

Accurate interpretation not only requires us to be able to recognize the distinction between laws for churches and laws for individuals, but we also need to know the difference between laws and commands. The ambiguity between laws for churches and laws for individuals is primarily a function of linguistics, but the ambiguity between laws and commands is mostly a function of mistranslation. All English translations are filled with commands and commandments, when the vast majority of these injunctions are really divine laws. Translators seem to be ignorant of the difference between laws and commands, and they have assumed nearly all injunctions are commandments. An injunction is only a general reference to authoritative direction, so an injunction may indicate a law or it may indicate a command depending upon context. English translations invariably obscure the difference, and unsuspecting Bible students face a biblical text full of commandments, even though those injunctions are nearly always laws. The exact nature of injunctions must be contextually discerned, so the translators have no right to arbitrarily assume any given injunction is either a law or a command. Ironically, their ignorance of the difference between laws and commands has led them to make the wrong choice in nearly every instance. However, I believe most of us understand intuitively that the commandments of God are really laws. In most cases the context and the nature of the injunction will reveal the translators' errors even without the need to consult the Greek text.

Now that I have explained that a contextual difference exists between laws and commands and that second person pronouns indicate the contextual difference between laws for a church and laws for individual members, we may now consider the nature and application of the old and new covenant laws and the basic differences between them.

The Old Covenant Law

Christians fiercely disagree over the exact nature of the transition which took place when the old covenant became obsolete and the New Covenant was established. The disagreement centers on the fate of the law generally, but particularly regarding the ten commandments and how the sabbath should apply in our life of faith. Three perspectives encompass the majority of thought regarding the present state of the law. Some claim the law is: 1) still valid and ought to be kept; 2) entirely done away or abolished; and 3) still valid but does not apply to Christians (the correct view).

At the heart of this debate about the law is the sabbath. Some claim Christians should keep the whole law including the sabbath, ignoring the obvious difference in the nature of the new covenant laws. Some believe Christians should keep the law, but claim the sabbath was changed to Sunday. Still others claim God destroyed the law and the sabbath with it when the covenant changed. Without the ritual requirement of the sabbath, the ten commandments would not garner nearly as much controversy as they do. Scripture upholds the other nine laws elsewhere among the new covenant instructions either to magnify their application or to simply leave them intact, but the New Testament is largely devoid of direction which specifically reiterates or abolishes the sabbath. Whichever position one takes, it ought to be obvious that the sabbath and the other nine laws stand or fall together. (Jas 2:10)

Before we can determine how the transition from the old covenant to the New Covenant resulted in different laws for the Church, we should first understand the nature of the old covenant. We should understand what the old covenant was. The name "old covenant" only appears once in the Bible, (2 Cor 3:14) but various biblical references call it "the" covenant, the "first" covenant and "His" covenant. The most revealing description of the old covenant is found in two passages of Moses' own writings, which specifically define the nature of the old covenant.

> And [Moses] was there with the LORD forty days and forty nights; he did neither eat bread, nor drink water. And he wrote upon the tables the words of **the covenant, the ten commandments**. (Ex 34:28)

> And he declared unto you **his covenant**, which he commanded you to perform, even **ten commandments**; and he wrote them upon two tables of stone. (Deut 4:13)

We should not overlook the near identity of the old covenant with the ten commandments. Those who are keeping the ten commandments are keeping the old covenant law. They are keeping the old covenant. This document constituted the marriage contract which bound God to Israel. Although the expression ten commandments never appears anywhere in the inspired texts, these ten laws were the essence of the old covenant. In the Greek New Testament they are simply called the injunctions, but in the Hebrew Old Testament they are called the "ten words." The numbered expression, ten words, only appears in the two verses above. The ten words were the words of the covenant joining Israel with God in marriage. God instructed

Israel to protect the words of the covenant—the ten words—which God had written on each tablet of stone. These ten words along with the statutes and judgments written in the book of the covenant became known as the law of Moses, or the *torah*, for the physical nation of Israel.

The marriage covenant between God and Israel required Israel to protect the law and obey everything God required them to do in exchange for blessings and protection. As long as Israel was obedient, God was obliged to fulfill the promises He made to them. Of course they failed to live up to the standard God set, so Israel's faithlessness released God from His obligation to bless and protect them; but, regardless of their disobedience, the marriage covenant itself remained binding. God does not enter into covenant lightly, and He continued to encourage Israel to return and receive the blessings He had promised them. From God's perspective covenants are binding until one of the covenant partners has died. (Rom 7:3) The nation of Israel continued to exist at least in part, but, when God came in the flesh, His death terminated the covenant. The old covenant ended, and the marriage relationship between God and Israel ended, but the law continued to define sin and mark out a humanly recognizable minimum standard of godly conduct.

Keep in mind that Christ's death terminated the covenant relationship between God and Israel, but not the words of the law written on the covenant documents. The marriage ended, but not the laws which govern covenant relationships. Just as the death of a spouse does not abolish the civil laws regarding marriage, so the death of Jesus Christ did not abolish God's laws of marriage. The spiritual nature of the law precludes its abolition. (Rom 7:14) Jesus Himself confirmed the validity of the law to His disciples.

> For verily I say unto you, Till heaven and earth pass, one jot or one tittle shall in no wise pass from the law, till all be fulfilled. Whosoever therefore shall break one of these least commandments, and shall teach men so, he shall be called the least in the kingdom of heaven: but whosoever shall do and teach them, the same shall be called great in the kingdom of heaven. (Matt 5:18-19)

The law has not been completely fulfilled even to this day. Jesus personally fulfilled those parts of it which applied to Him, but Israel has yet to fulfill a multitude of prophecies, one of which declares Israel will become a kingdom of priests and a holy nation. (Ex 19:6) Another declares that Israel will keep the sabbath throughout their generations for a perpetual covenant. (Ex 31:15-16) God did not form the so-called ten commandments with imperative or injunctive statements, but with prophetic language delivered in the future tense. These are not commandments or laws, but prophecies that Israel "will not steal," "will not lie," and "will not commit adultery," etc. Nearly all interpreters fail to see what God plainly said, and the KJV use of the expression "ten commandments" further obscures the reality that the "ten words" were mostly prophecies about a future Israel, which will not have other gods, will not bow down to them, and will not take God's name in vain. Ancient Israel never fulfilled any of those prophecies, but at some future time Israel will indeed fulfill every word of the law, most likely beginning after Christ returns to gather the nation of Israel from the four corners of the earth in order to reestablish a physical nation of Israel.

The Law Not Abolished

God wrote the ten words on stone, emphasizing the permanence and inflexibility of the law. The Hebrew text tells us God engraved the words on stones, thereby making it unlikely that they could simply be blotted out, as some interpreters of Colossians 2:14 believe. Under the inspiration of God, Paul described the law as holy, just, good and spiritual. (Rom 7:12, 14) God intended the law to remain in place until He fulfills every jot and tittle of it. Even though the covenant and the marriage relationship have been terminated, the law remains in force and its prophecies remain valid. Notice Paul did not say the law WAS holy. He said the law IS holy, just, good and spiritual.

> Wherefore **the law is holy, and the commandment holy, and just, and good**...For we know that **the law is spiritual**: but I am carnal, sold under sin. For that which I do I allow not: for what I would, that do I not; but what I hate, that do I. If then I do that which I would not, **I consent unto the law that it is good**. (Rom 7:12, 14-16)

Fully a quarter century after everything which was nailed to the cross would have long since been abolished, Paul consented to the law that it is good. In effect, Paul asserted that the law still existed. How could Paul say the law is good, if it had been done away? He might have said it WAS good, but he could not have said it IS good. Far from being done away, Paul said the law is spiritual. (v. 14) The verb "is" is in the present indicative active tense in the Greek text. Zodhiates' *Word Study New Testament* explains that present indicative verbs indicate "something which is occurring while the speaker is making the statement," so Paul implied the law existed and was continuing to exist. Paul could not have written it that way, if he thought the law had been abolished.

In spite of these plain biblical statements affirming the law, the translators of the Bible still assumed the law had been abolished or done away, and they translated their paradigm into the text of our English Bibles. The passage below is the first of four passages I will examine in the Greek text. In this first passage the English text plainly states that the law has been done away or abolished.

> But if the ministration of death, written and engraven in stones, was glorious, so that the children of Israel could not stedfastly behold the face of Moses for the glory of his countenance; which glory was to be **done away** (NT:2673): How shall not the ministration of the spirit be rather glorious? For if the ministration of condemnation be glory, much more doth the ministration of righteousness exceed in glory. For even that which was made glorious had no glory in this respect, by reason of the glory that excelleth. For if that which is **done away** (NT:2673) was glorious, much more that which remaineth is glorious. Seeing then that we have such hope, we use great plainness of speech: And not as Moses, which put a vail over his face, that the children of Israel could not stedfastly look to the end of that which is **abolished** (NT:2673): But their minds were blinded: for until this day remaineth the same vail untaken away in the reading of the old testament; which vail is **done away** (NT:2673) in Christ. (2 Cor 3:7-14)

Sloppy translation is primarily responsible for the prevalent misconception that God abolished or did away with the law. The underlined words in this passage were all translated from the same Greek word. Carefully observe the exact meaning of *katargeo*.

NT:2673
katargeo (kat-arg-eh'-o); from NT:2596 and NT:691; **to be (render) entirely idle (useless),** literally or figuratively:

In all four cases where *katargeo* is used in the passage above and translated "done away" or "abolished," Paul said the law was entirely idle or useless, particularly in respect to a new covenant Christian. To render the law useless is an entirely different concept than to do away with it or abolish it. The law has been rendered useless, because it has been replaced by the much higher standard of the new covenant Law, Jesus Christ. The low standard of the old covenant law is useless, because Christians guard the high standard of new covenant Law, which always fulfills the law. The Father has given Christians His living Word as our new standard of conduct, but the law still exists and its prophesies remain valid.

A second weaker example, which may indicate to some that the law has been abolished, is offered here for your consideration:

> For he is our peace, who hath made both one, and hath broken down the middle wall of partition between us; Having **abolished** (NT:2673) in his flesh the enmity, even the law of commandments contained in ordinances; for to make in himself of twain one new man, so making peace; And that he might reconcile both unto God in one body by the cross, having slain the enmity thereby: (Eph 2:14-16)

This passage describes the union of Jews and Gentiles under the New Covenant. God has "made both one," indicating that Jews and Gentiles have been brought together under one Covenant of faith, no longer separated by the wall of prescriptive rituals found in the old covenant law. Without even examining the Greek text, we can see that only the enmity between Jews and Gentiles has been allegedly abolished, not the law. Indeed the enmity has not even been abolished, but only rendered idle, because the same Greek word, *katargeo*, is also used here. The enmity is defined as "the law of commandments contained in ordinances," so these verses do not even say the whole law has been rendered useless, but only a certain portion of it. This verse focuses on the ritual practices which made Jews different from the nations around them, and those laws did indeed foster enmity between Jews and Gentiles. However, it is impossible to conclude from this passage that God even rendered the whole law idle, let alone abolished it entirely.

The third verse, which some use to do away with the law, is another excerpt from Paul's writings.

> For Christ is the end of the law for righteousness to every one that believeth. (Rom 10:4)

The primary obstacle to a correct understanding of this statement is the translators' choice of words here. This translation is not necessarily in error, but it may be misleading. We often think of an end as the conclusion or finish, but that is not what the Greek word *telos* (NT:5056) means. Strong defines *telos* as "the point aimed at as the limit," hence *telos* is a "goal" or "purpose." Paul intended us to understand that Christ is the goal of the law or the purpose for the law. The law looked forward to Christ. The law was a schoolmaster to bring us to Christ (Gal 3:24), but once having come to Christ, our need for the schoolmaster ends. There should be no reason to take the schoolmaster out and shoot him, but he simply becomes useless and irrelevant for our further education.

The last and most confusing passage about the law appears in a statement regarding some rather obscure handwritten ordinances, which had been figuratively nailed to the cross. At first glance one might be tempted to jump to the conclusion that the law was taken away or abolished, but such is not the case.

> And you, being dead in your sins and the uncircumcision of your flesh, hath he quickened together with him, having forgiven you all trespasses; blotting out the handwriting of ordinances that was against us, which was contrary to us, and took it out of the way, nailing it to his cross; (Col 2:13-14)

In a typically Hebrew expression, Paul states redundantly that God has forgiven every sin of every Christian. "The handwriting of ordinances that was against us" is the self written or hand written note of debt for our sins which we owed God before conversion. We have each written a figurative note of debt with our hands evidenced by the sinful actions our hands have done—indeed the sinful actions we have done. Jesus Christ took our legally enforceable sin debt out of the way by figuratively nailing it to the cross. I will not undertake a discussion here of the underlying Greek words used in this verse, but, if you are interested, please see a more complete explanation of this verse in appendix 3.

To my knowledge there are no other verses anywhere in the Bible which overtly appear to do wrath to the law. Those who maintain such a position build their case on very flimsy evidence, all of which is overturned by correct translation and by carefully avoiding assumptions. Jesus plainly stated that He did not come to destroy the law or the prophets, (Matt 5:17) so we certainly should not assume His actions did away with the law, nor can we assume the law was abolished by some other biblically unsupportable means.

The Sabbath

Scripture upholds nine of the ten commandments for Christians, and, indeed, God has raised the standard of most of them. Christians understand that gods are no longer limited to the type made out of wood and stone, and we realize we have taken God's name in vain when we are not living by His Standard of conduct. We realize we have murdered in our heart when we harbor hate for an individual, and we have committed adultery when we have lusted for anyone besides our respective mates. These are all principles found among the laws of God, which render the law of Moses irrelevant. If we are living by the Law of God, we cannot break the old covenant law.

However, there is one commandment (law) which cannot be raised to a spiritual level of application, because it is not a moral principle. The sabbath is a ritual. One cannot rest more on the sabbath in a way to make the day more holy, because the day is either holy or it is not. If the law is still in force, and it certainly is, why don't Christians still keep the sabbath?

The surprising answer is that we do keep the sabbath, or, better said, we fulfill the sabbath the same way Jesus Christ fulfilled it. We don't need to ritualistically observe it through physical rest, because we fulfill it spiritually through faith. All the rituals of the law are irrelevant as long as we live by the faith of Jesus Christ.

Fundamentally, the sabbath law is a call to faith in Jesus Christ. The sabbath is a most meaningful law, and it points to faith in Jesus Christ through the various elements contained within it. When we fulfill its essential elements through faith in Christ, we keep it in the spirit. The essential elements of the old covenant sabbath ritual are: 1) to cease from our own work (Ex 20:9-10); 2) to rest (Ex 16:30); and 3) to remain in our place (Ex 16:29).

When God calls a person to His Son and that individual believes and is placed in Jesus Christ, the law convicts the believer of sin and the person dies. The spiritual reality of each believer's death is a key to understand how Christians fulfill the sabbath law.

> Therefore **we are buried with him by baptism into death**: that like as Christ was raised up from the dead by the glory of the Father, even so we also should walk in newness of life. For if **we have been planted together in the likeness of his death**, we shall be also in the likeness of his resurrection: (Rom 6:4-5)
>
> **I am crucified with Christ**: nevertheless I live; <u>yet not I, but Christ liveth in me</u>: and the life which I now live in the flesh I live by the faith of the Son of God, who loved me, and gave himself for me. (Gal 2:20)
>
> **For ye are dead**, and your life is hid with Christ in God. (Col 3:3)

Now that our human spirits are dead on earth, and Jesus Christ is living in us and working through us: 1) we have ceased from our own works; 2) we are at rest (dead); and 3) we remain at rest where we have been placed awaiting resurrection. Our rest in Christ is seven days a week, not just one day a week. We are no longer doing our own work, because the Lord is doing His work through us. As long as our human spirits remain at rest where they have been placed, the Lord is always working through us to fulfill God's will.

The sabbath was the sign of the old covenant, but we do not live under the old covenant. There are no rituals—no holy times, no holy places and no holy things—in the New Covenant. We are holy, because the Holy Spirit lives in us. The Holy Spirit living in us makes US holy, and our holy state of being makes ALL our time holy. Since all our time is holy, faith in Jesus Christ renders the sabbath ritual useless and irrelevant.

I don't just rest one day; I rest every day. I continually rest from my own works and do the Lord's will through faith in Him. All the work I do is the will of the Lord, because He is my Head, and He is directing all the work I do. Even though I work on Saturday, I am resting from my work, because the Lord is fulfilling God's will through me. When others ask me if I keep the sabbath, I reply, "Yes, I absolutely do." Christians should understand that the fourth commandment is just as valid as the other nine, but we must see ourselves as God sees us: at rest—dead—in His Covenant.

Purpose for the Law

Over time the law will have served several purposes. The original purpose for the law was to contain sinfulness and promote godliness in Israel. When the descendents of Abraham grew from a family of seventy souls in Canaan to a nation of over two million leaving Egypt, Israelites needed a standard for acceptable conduct in their society. Without laws, sin could not be condemned or controlled. "Wherefore then serveth the law? It was added because of transgressions, till the seed should come to whom the promise was made." (Gal 3:19). Every nation on earth has incorporated many of the same principles God gave Israel into their laws, and they now serve to generally limit and control sin in the world.

God knew the old covenant would fail, so God not only gave them a law which would serve their civil and moral needs, but He gave them a law which would point them to the promised Messiah and help them recognize Him when He came. "Wherefore the law was our schoolmaster to bring us unto Christ, that we might be justified by faith." (Gal 3:24) The law still serves to bring sinners to Christ even today. I came to Christ through the law.

Now that the Seed to Whom the promise was made has come and the old covenant has become obsolete, the new covenant Law has superseded the law as the standard for Christian conduct. Although the law is not our standard of conduct, the law makes us aware of our occasional sinfulness. "For by the law is the knowledge of sin." (Rom 3:20) The law has become a tool for us to recognize sin in our lives without the necessity to suffer the penalty of death. The law cannot judge or condemn believers, because believers are not under the law. (Rom 6:14) Believers live by the law of the faith of Jesus Christ. (Rom 3:21-28) Believers may sin, but believers are not sinners, because the blood of Christ removes all our sins; therefore, we are exempt from the judgment of the law. Now the law serves to reveal the mind of God and enlighten us without condemning us.

The great white throne judgment will follow the thousand year reign of Jesus Christ on earth. Everyone who does not believe will be judged by the law. The law stands to condemn those who are under the law, but not those who live under grace. "Now we know that what things soever the law saith, it saith to them who are under the law: that every mouth may be stopped, and all the world may become guilty before God." (Rom 3:19) The law judges sinners, not believers. "Knowing this, that the law is not made for a righteous man, but for the lawless and disobedient, for the ungodly and for sinners, for unholy and profane, for murderers of fathers and murderers of mothers, for manslayers, for whoremongers, for them that defile themselves with mankind, for menstealers, for liars, for perjured persons, and if there be any other thing that is contrary to sound doctrine." (1 Tim 1:9-10) The law remains valid and serves several purposes, but we do not live by the law. We live by faith.

The Old Covenant Abolished

If the law was not abolished, what changed? The book of Hebrews holds the key to understand what was abolished when Jesus died and the New Covenant was established. Hebrews was written, not by Paul, but by someone who was equally familiar with the function of the old covenant ritualistic system of worship, and its author not only tells us what had become old and was ready to vanish away, but he also tells us what laws God has written on our hearts to govern us in our new covenant marriage with God.

The old covenant was a marriage agreement between God and Israel, (Jer 31:32) and that marriage agreement bound Israel to obey the law, specifically the ten words, which God enjoined upon them. In spite of their disobedience, the marriage covenant itself remained binding. From God's perspective all covenants are binding until the death of one of the partners to the covenant. Israel continued to exist, but when God came in the flesh and died, the covenant relationship ended.

The language of the old covenant was specifically the ten words, and from a certain perspective they were the same, but the law and the covenant marriage between God and Israel were not exactly identical, because they did not stand or fall together. The marriage has been abolished, but not the law. The relationship ended, but not the words of the covenant—nor the covenant law.

> In that he saith, A new covenant, he hath made the first old. Now that which decayeth and waxeth old is ready to vanish away. (Heb 8:13)

> Then said he, Lo, I come to do thy will, O God. He taketh away the first [covenant], that he may establish the second. (Heb 10:9)

The first covenant—the old covenant—had become obsolete, was decaying and was ready to vanish away, and God made sure the old covenant disappeared. Within a decade of the writing of the book of Hebrews, Jerusalem was sacked by the Romans and the temple was destroyed. Without a temple and, particularly, without an altar for sacrifices, the old covenant ritual worship could not be practiced. Shortly after the writing of these prophetic verses, the old covenant, which was abolished by Christ's death, did indeed fade away. The covenant marriage between God and Israel ended.

It is imperative to understand that the scriptures above state that the covenant was taken away, but no scripture says the law decayed or was abolished. The covenant relationship between God and Israel has been abolished, but not the law. Just as the death of a spouse does not abolish the laws of marriage, so the death of Jesus Christ did not abolish divine law. Only the covenant relationship has been terminated. Now we live under the grace of the New Covenant with a new set of laws. The higher standard of Jesus Christ—our new covenant Law—renders the lower standard of the ten commandments—the old covenant law—useless and irrelevant.

The New Covenant Law

Although the law still exists and its prophecies remain valid, it is a substandard and useless code for Christians. God does not judge our actions based on the law, but according to the new covenant Standard. Jesus Christ judges us. Christians should certainly avoid breaking the law, not because the law is our standard of conduct, but because we should not become sinners again. We don't live by the law of Moses. We live by the Law of God.

> For sin shall not have dominion over you: for ye are **not under the law**, but under grace. What then? shall we sin, because we are **not under the law**, but under grace? God forbid. (Rom 6:14-15)

Paul's statement simply means the law is not the standard of conduct for a Christian. We do not live under the law of Moses. We live by the new covenant Law, Who far exceeds the standard of the old covenant law. We live by Jesus Christ. He is the new covenant Standard. As long as we believe in Him and we are at rest, we are free from the law of sin and death. He is living in us and His faith is directing us. Through faith, we reflect His image, because He is doing the work. In Covenant with God, He has made it possible for the Church to achieve the character of Jesus Christ and fulfill the righteousness of the law, just as Jesus did.

> For the law of the Spirit of life in Christ Jesus hath made me free from the law of sin and death. For what the law could not do, in that it was weak through the flesh, God sending his own Son in the likeness of sinful flesh, and for sin, condemned sin in the flesh: **that the righteousness of the law might be fulfilled in us, who walk not after the flesh, but after the Spirit.** (Rom 8:2-4)

The righteousness of the law is a standard the law contained but could not be achieved simply by obedience. Israel could not attain the righteousness of the law even by keeping the law perfectly. Similarly, if we attempt to keep the law, we will never achieve the righteousness of the law, because the righteousness of the law can only be achieved through faith. When we live by the faith of Jesus Christ, He fulfills the righteousness of the law in us. The righteousness of the law is the standard of law which the Church exhibits in Jesus Christ under His direction.

Among the many old covenant types, the two stone tablets—the old covenant marriage documents—as well as the words written on those documents—the ten words—picture Jesus Christ. He is both the new covenant Document and the new covenant Law. Just as the old covenant documents contained many laws, our new covenant Document contains many laws, but the laws contained within Jesus Christ are different in nature from the old covenant laws. Within Jesus Christ are the laws of God, and God describes the laws He has placed in His Son as "My laws." Once again we turn to the book of Hebrews to verify exactly which laws God puts in our hearts and writes in our minds under the New Covenant.

> This is the covenant that I will make with them after those days, saith the Lord, I will put **my laws** into their hearts, and in their minds will I write them; (Heb 10:16)

The law of Moses is always "the law" in scripture, and it always appears in singular form. There is no general reference to it in the plural form. Israel kept "the law" by obedience, not by faith. God is not going to write the law of Moses in our hearts, nor has He any intention to write the ten commandments in our minds. He has written "My laws"—plural—in our minds through faith, just as the author of Hebrews indicated. "My laws" are not the laws of Moses. They are the laws of God. They are the descriptive laws of the New Covenant. They are the same laws Abraham obeyed long before the law of Moses existed. (Gen 26:5)

A codified law like the law of Moses was an inflexible law which could not be written on the heart, but the living Law of God, Jesus Christ, lives in us, and "My laws"—the eternal laws of God—have been written on our hearts and placed in our minds. "My laws" are functioning in us through Jesus Christ. We are not under the law of Moses, because we have "My laws" directing our actions from within. The new covenant laws of God supersede and surpass the old covenant standard of law for all faithful believers.

The following new covenant laws are specified in scripture among the apostles' writings. These laws, as well as many others found throughout the New Testament, broadly describe the basic principles of Christian conduct under the New Covenant. These laws may individually focus on a particular aspect of Christian conduct, but they all point to Jesus Christ, Who is our Standard of conduct. Jesus Christ Himself is the new covenant Document, and God has placed all the new covenant laws in Him. He has superseded the old covenant law for God's spiritual nation.

> Bear ye one another's burdens, and so fulfil the **law of Christ**. (Gal 6:2)
>
> By what law? of works? Nay: but by the **law of faith**. (Rom 3:27)
>
> For the **law of the Spirit of life** in Christ Jesus hath made me free from the law of sin and death.
> (Rom 8:2)
>
> But whoso looketh into the perfect **law of liberty**, and continueth therein, he being not a forgetful hearer, but a doer of the work, this man shall be blessed in his deed... So speak ye, and so do, as they that shall be judged by the **law of liberty**.
> (James 1:25, 2:12)
>
> If ye fulfil the **royal law** according to the scripture, Thou shalt love thy neighbour as thyself, ye do well: (James 2:8)
>
> But Israel, which followed after the **law of righteousness**, hath not attained to the **law of righteousness**. (Rom 9:31)

Notice that these laws are completely different in nature from the old covenant laws. These laws do not define what we should do, as the law of Moses did, but they describe who we should be. They describe our state of being. New covenant laws are descriptive laws.

They describe the character of Jesus Christ, and they describe our character in Him. We must first be in Covenant with God, and we must be in Christ, and, when we have become who we must be, then our Law directs each of us by the Spirit individually and personally, moment by moment to accomplish the purpose of God. There are no rituals or prescriptive laws in the New Covenant.

Jesus Christ is now our Standard of conduct, and the apostles described our new Law in these various ways in the New Testament. The law of faith (Rom 3:27) describes the faithfulness of Christ, so Christians must BE faithful. The law of righteousness (Rom 9:31) describes the character of Christ, so Christians must BE righteous. The law of liberty (Jas 1:25) reveals the freedom we enjoy in Christ, so Christians must BE free. The royal law (Jas 2:8) embraces the love of Christ we share in Christ, so Christians must BE loving. The law of the Spirit of life (Rom 8:2) proclaims the salvation and eternal life the Church possesses in Christ, so the Church must BE in the Spirit at all times. Collectively, these and many other laws are My laws. (Heb 10:16) My laws are "BE" laws, not "DO" laws, and God has written these laws in the hearts and minds of all those who are living in Christ. No "DO" laws exist in the New Covenant.

Jesus was born under the law, but the law was not His standard of conduct. He lived by faith, and He fulfilled the law through faith. He lived by the higher standard of the new covenant laws and thereby fulfilled the lower standard of the law of Moses. Jesus accomplished the ritual prescriptions of the law, because they foreshadowed Him, but He lived through faith according to My laws—the descriptive laws—the "BE" laws of the New Covenant.

Likewise, those of us who live in Jesus Christ live the same way He lived. We fulfill the law the same way He fulfilled it. We do not keep the letter of the law by obedience, but we fulfill the righteousness of the law through faith, because we live by the "BE" laws of the New Covenant. We fulfill the requirements of these laws by remaining in Covenant with God and listening to the Lord as He speaks by the Spirit. His direction fulfills all the laws of the New Covenant, including patience, humility, peace, hospitality, goodness, honesty, etc., not because we consciously work to achieve them, but because we are in Him and live by His faith. The new covenant laws are entirely descriptive, because they describe who Jesus Christ IS and who we must BE. There is no "letter" of new covenant laws.

The Nature of Law

Different types of covenants contain different types of laws. We can determine the nature of any particular covenant law by considering the nature of the mediator of the covenant. If the mediator is human, the covenant will be a prescriptive covenant with prescriptive laws. If the mediator is divine, the covenant will be a descriptive covenant with descriptive laws. Carefully consider the significant differences between these two types of laws.

The old covenant was a document of stone with a prescriptive law; the new Covenant is a living Document with a descriptive Law. The old covenant contained laws which led to death; the New Covenant is a Law Who gives eternal life. The old covenant law was temporary; the new covenant Law is forever. These differences arise because the mediator of each covenant is profoundly different. The mediator of the old covenant was human. The Mediator of the New Covenant is divine. This fundamental difference in covenant law can be further contrasted, if we examine the nature of the laws contained in each of these covenants.

Covenants mediated by man will contain prescriptive law. The old covenant was a covenant mediated by Moses and contained prescriptive laws, which define specific behaviors in specific circumstances. Indeed every law of man—every human constitution of law—every set of rules men might legislate will invariably be prescriptive. Prescriptive law demands everybody must act this way in this situation, and everybody must act that way in that situation. Those who fail to obey such laws can be prosecuted based on a determination of who did what, when and in which particular circumstance. Prescriptive law defines what we do, where we do it and when we do it. Prescriptive law attempts to control the activity of human beings through humanly enforceable laws created to apply in normal circumstances with an outlook towards the general well being of all citizens. Unfortunately, all such laws will become oppressive in certain circumstances. The normal distribution of the Bell Curve predicts that some individuals will inevitably fall outside the "normal circumstances" addressed by prescriptive laws. Some individuals will invariably feel oppressed when forced to comply with prescriptive laws. Endless amendments and exceptions to prescriptive laws futilely attempt to address every possible situation.

On the other hand, a covenant mediated by a divine Mediator will contain only descriptive law. Descriptive laws describe appropriate behavior in general terms, but such laws stop short of prescribing specific behaviors at specific times and in specific circumstances. "Love thy neighbor" is one example of descriptive law. "Be holy" is another. "Be humble" is a third example. Descriptive laws frequently use state-of-being verbs to describe the nature of our character, i.e., who we should be, but they do not specifically prescribe what we should do. Descriptive law enjoins believers to act in a godly way but contains no provision to do specific deeds.

Men only write prescriptive laws, because superior descriptive laws are humanly unenforceable. Men lack spiritual vision to be able to discern a person's character Men cannot determine who a person is by observation. Only God can search human hearts, (Jer 17:10) because the Word of God "is quick, and powerful, and sharper than any two-edged sword, piercing even to the dividing asunder of soul and spirit, and of the joints and marrow, and is a discerner of the thoughts and intents of the heart." (Heb 4:12) Descriptive laws are useless to human authorities, because men have no power to discern the human mind or the thoughts and intents of human hearts. Lacking rules which define behavior in prescriptive ways, men are incapable to even determine who has broken the descriptive laws and become an offender, let alone be able to prosecute the offender.

Descriptive laws are by nature superior to prescriptive laws, and Jesus pointed out the superiority of descriptive law when a scribe asked Him which law was the greatest among all the laws of Moses. The scribe may have expected Jesus to quote one of the much revered ten commandments, but, instead of quoting from the covenant document, He quoted two passages from the book of the covenant found in Deuteronomy 6:4-5 and Leviticus 19:18.

> And one of the scribes came, and having heard them reasoning together, and perceiving that he had answered them well, asked him, Which is the first commandment of all? And Jesus answered him, The first of all the commandments is, Hear, O Israel; The Lord our God is one Lord: And thou shalt love the Lord thy God with all thy heart, and with all thy soul, and with all thy mind, and with all thy strength: this

is the first commandment. And the second is like, namely this, Thou shalt love thy neighbour as thyself. There is none other commandment greater than these. (Mark 12:28-31)

Jesus quoted the old covenant version of the royal law of love to reveal that the ten commandments were hardly the most important injunctions in the law. Descriptive law is always superior to prescriptive law. In spite of the fact that the descriptive royal law is clearly superior to the "big ten," some professing Christians still become incensed, if anyone dares to suggest that the ten commandments should be removed from public display. General ignorance of the role of the ten commandments in the life of a Christian can result in bizarre Christian behavior, because many churchgoers still revere the useless standard of the ten commandments, while they ignore the higher standard of the new covenant laws of faith, righteousness, liberty and love, among others. Many professing Christians still worship the engraved stone tablets of the old covenant law and ignore the living laws of the New Covenant.

Our new covenant Law is entirely descriptive law. We are saved according to who we are, not by what we do. Who we are dictates what we do, and our nature dictates the nature of our deeds. When we are who we should be, then our deeds will reflect who we are. Our deeds will reflect Jesus Christ. Nothing we can do earns us salvation, and the circumstance of the thief on the cross is clear evidence that we are saved by faith alone. (Luke 23:39-43) Even water baptism and communion are not requirements for salvation. God makes no prescriptive laws for the Church, and there are no prescriptive laws in the New Covenant. Jesus Christ gives each of us prescriptive direction individually and personally through the Spirit. Those who assume the authority to impose prescriptive laws upon a church usurp God's prerogative to rule that church. God alone rules every faithful congregation.

Since Jesus Christ is our Law and all the laws of God are in Him, God rules the Church through Jesus Christ. He is the Law of God living in us. Christians need no other law than the Law Who lives in us. Whenever Christians are in doubt about God's direction through His living Law, we may consult the written record of God's descriptive laws preserved in the New Testament, which describe

Who Jesus Christ is. New covenant laws do not tell us what Jesus did and then direct us to do what He did, but rather they describe Who He is, and they command us to be the same way He is. The descriptive laws of the New Covenant command us to be what we ought to be rather than to do what we ought to do. New covenant laws do not command us to do a certain thing in a certain place at a certain time. God has left such prescriptive direction to Jesus Christ Himself, Who lives in us and directs us from within. There is no need to write prescriptive laws into the New Covenant, because our moment by moment direction comes from our Commander, Who lives in each Christian soldier.

We generally find the written laws God has specifically designed for the Church in the New Testament. Jesus' Sermon on the Mount forms the written constitution of law for the Church, and the apostles' writings expand on the principles of Jesus' sermon. The prophets' writings in the Old Testament supplement the apostles' writings and more fully reveal God's mind for practical application in specific circumstances. New covenant laws apply universally to every church and/or to every member of the church, and they never need amendment. They are forever. God alone rules each church and each believer through these descriptive laws.

The primary laws for the Church are faith and love. "And whatsoever we ask, we receive of him, because we keep his [injunctions], and do those things that are pleasing in his sight. And this is his [injunction], that we should <u>believe</u> on the name of his Son Jesus Christ, and <u>love</u> one another, as he gave us [injunction]." (1 John 3:22-23) One cannot prescriptively define faith or love as it applies in every situation. We assume the responsibility to apply these fundamental principles to the best of our ability according to the lead of the Spirit as we deal with unique people under unique circumstances and in real time. Descriptive laws never become oppressive. Christians are free to pursue the best course of action to effect the best solution under the circumstances at the time, because God does not handcuff us to a prescribed course of action, which may or may not even result in an adequate solution.

In addition to the differences found in the nature of prescriptive and descriptive laws themselves, we may also contrast these laws by the nature of the results which follow their application. Prescriptive laws inevitably result in the oppression of some individuals, but descriptive laws can produce non-oppressive solutions and offer freedom to all individuals. If the laws are codified prescriptive laws where people must do this or that in this or that situation, the laws will invariably result in the oppression of certain people in certain situations. If laws are descriptive principles, which allow believers the freedom to assess specific situations and act in the best interest of those involved, then God's purpose "to loose the bands of wickedness, to undo the heavy burdens, and to let the oppressed go free, and...[to] break every yoke" (Isa 58:6) can be achieved.

We could all site endless examples of the failure of prescriptive laws, but a recent news report comes to mind. A building in a city where thousands were suffering with homelessness was vacant. The owners were willing to allow the city to use the building as a homeless shelter during the winter, because renovation was not scheduled to begin until the spring. Unfortunately, city codes did not allow anybody to occupy the building unless the elevator was in working order, and it could not be immediately repaired. Consequently, the hundred or so homeless people, who might have had shelter through the worst winter months, were denied access to the building. We can clearly see that prescriptive laws may even threaten human life because of their inflexible nature.

The bottom line: all prescriptive law is oppressive, and men only write prescriptive laws. The only laws which offer true freedom and relieve oppression are the principles God has given the Church and under which it operates. This, of course, begs the question: If God has set aside the prescriptive laws of the old covenant (Rom 6:14) and the Church lives entirely by the higher standard of descriptive Law, (1 John 3:23) is it logical to assume that God allows men the privilege to make prescriptive laws for a church like the laws He has removed? Is it logical to assume God set aside a holy, just and good prescriptive law, (Rom 7:12) so He could authorize church leaders to write inferior rules and regulations, which cannot even approach the standard of the law He set aside?

Every church organization claims to be administering divine law through its authorities. They all claim the rules they impose upon their members are God's laws, and they all claim the Bible as the basis for their rules. But are they really teaching divine law? Can we verify their claims to know if they are telling the truth? I think we can. We simply ask: Do their rules conform to the standard of descriptive Law? Do they faithfully reiterate the same descriptive principles the apostles taught, or are their rules prescriptive? Do they require members to be godly and do everything they do in a godly way, or do they require members to do specific things in specific places at specific times? If their rules are descriptive in nature like God's descriptive laws, they are administering divine Law, but, if their rules are prescriptive laws, then they have stepped away from the protection of divine sanction and have entered the realm of heresy and sacrilege. Since all human laws are prescriptive and every church organization imposes prescriptive laws upon its members, I have concluded that every church organization is corrupt and none of them is speaking for God. All those who impose prescriptive laws upon churches or upon their members are standing in the place of God. (2 Thess 2:4) They have all usurped God's divine privilege to rule His people.

Many churchgoers feel church leaders must analyze God's laws and interpret them for a church; however, such a perception assumes men have the ability to interpret God's laws. If we carefully reconsider the assumption, I believe the absurdity of it will become apparent. The nature of descriptive laws precludes the possibility that they can be defined legalistically. God's laws for the Church are descriptive laws, and, by nature, descriptive laws defy prescriptive interpretation. Descriptive laws cannot be codified. Men cannot reduce them to a set of dos and don'ts. Love, for example, cannot be prescriptively defined; neither can patience, kindness, moderation, compassion, honesty or any of the other descriptive laws of the Church. God's laws apply differently toward different individuals in different situations, and they may even apply differently at different times. God's laws for the Church are descriptive for the expressed purpose of allowing each member the freedom to apply them uniquely in each situation according to the lead of the Spirit. When men define God's laws prescriptively, they turn Christianity into a religion. Christianity is not a religion. Christianity is a faith.

Ultimately, each individual Christian is responsible to interpret the laws and apply them in his or her life as the Spirit leads. It makes no difference how an individual prescriptively interprets God's laws for personal application, but no member may impose his interpretation upon another member. Individual members may even embrace practices which cannot be applied to other members and should not be taught in churches. A member may choose to observe Saturday as a day of rest; sabbath keeping is not a sin. One may choose not to marry; celibacy is not a sin. One may choose not to drink wine; abstinence is not a sin. One may choose to give a tenth of one's income to a church; tithing is not a sin. However, when anyone assumes the authority to prescribe or prohibit any activities such as these, he is sinning, and he has usurped the rulership of God and the authority of Jesus Christ to direct each of the members of His Church individually and personally. Each of us may practice whatever rituals we prefer, but, above all, we must <u>be</u> believers, and we must <u>be</u> holy. We must <u>be</u> loving and apply every principle of God in love. Whatever we do, we must <u>be</u> patient. We must <u>be</u> kind. We must <u>be</u> humble. We must <u>be</u> compassionate. Christian Law is all about who we are, not about what we do.

God alone rules the Church, but His laws are not prescriptive laws. He has given us His living Law to live in us and direct all our activities personally. No church leader may make rules for a church or for any individual member of the church. When the people of God obey the rules of men, they will accomplish the purpose of men rather than the purpose of God. When the people of God allow men to rule their church, God cannot rule that church, and that church is cut off from God's rulership. When some members obey the descriptive laws of God and some members obey the prescriptive rules of men, the church is divided. A house divided against itself cannot stand. God will remove every leader from the body of Christ who dares to stand in the place of God and make rules for a church. God will also remove idolatrous members from the body of Christ, if they are allowing men to rule them or bowing in obedience to human directions. Believers cannot worship God by obeying the rules of men or the commands of authorities. Our Ruler has placed "My laws" in the Church, and the Church must be directed by those descriptive laws at all times. Our perfect Law of liberty has freed us from the prescriptive laws and commands of men. Jesus Christ alone commands us in our daily walk with God. Jesus Christ alone is our new covenant Law.

Chapter 6

The Nature of Sin and Judgment

True freedom cannot exist where sin dwells, and free moral agency will invariably lead every human being into sin and bondage. Human beings naturally trust what they can see and reject the revelation of God, blissfully unaware that this physical world is full of illusions and snares. We possess no natural spiritual vision to be able to look past the moment, past the desire or past the physical circumstances to comprehend the spiritual consequences of our actions. If you and I had been in the Garden of Eden, we would have done exactly what Adam and Eve did.

Few subjects are so frequently discussed in churches and yet so completely misunderstood than the nature of sin. Some members live in fear that they might have sinned and not repented or that they might have committed the unpardonable sin. At the same time many members sin habitually without shame, even lacking the awareness that they are offending the body of Christ. Since most theologians and church leaders have lost sight of God's perspective of the nature of sin, most professing Christians have lost the ability to live godly lives in a confident manner.

God created human beings without spiritual vision, so God was not ignorant of our proclivity to sin, nor was He caught by surprise when Adam sinned. Every human needs spiritual direction through a relationship with God, because we have no innate ability to direct our own steps to avoid sin. Apart from God, none of us can govern ourselves or properly distinguish right from wrong, so we naturally cater to the desires of the flesh, which invariably produce sin.

By nature all human beings exist in an unholy state, and we are naturally slaves to sin. Sin is endemic in the human condition. As long as we live in the flesh, we will sin, and we have no hope to ever become sinless in the flesh. Sinlessness, otherwise described as perfection, is not possible in our physical lives, and God does not even place sinlessness as a stated goal for Christians. The Bible says we should avoid sin, but it does not even suggest we should become sinless. The concept of sinlessness and the goal of perfection have been created by faithless translators and perpetuated by ignorant church leaders. God is not so naïve.

Although the concept of perfection appears in dozens of verses throughout our English Bibles, the underlying Greek word is almost always "complete." It is never "perfect." We are probably most familiar with Jesus' mistranslated words in the Sermon on the Mount: "Be ye therefore **perfect**, even as your Father which is in heaven is **perfect**." (Matt 5:48) In most cases, as here, the Greek word underlying "perfect" is *teleios*.

NT:5046
teleios (tel'-i-os); from NT:5056; **complete** (in various applications of labor, growth, mental and moral character, etc.); neuter (as noun, with NT:3588) completeness:

Perfection is a figment of the translators' imaginations. We will never be perfect as God is perfect. God places completeness, not perfection, before us as an achievable goal, and indeed completeness describes the spiritual condition of everyone who lives in Christ. Human beings are incomplete by nature, because our physical existence does not allow us to comprehend spiritual reality through the five senses. We lack spiritual direction. However, human beings may become complete when we enter into Covenant with God and allow Jesus Christ to direct our lives. God's governance completes us as human beings. "We are complete in Him." (Col 2:10) We are neither perfect nor sinless, but we are complete.

Another requirement for believers is holiness. (1 Pet 1:15-16) Christians must be holy. The Christian life of holiness also begins with a covenant relationship with God and continues as long as we remain in Christ. Holiness cannot be achieved through good works or by living a sinless life, because we cannot achieve holiness by our own effort. Holiness, like completeness, is entirely the work of God. It is achieved by the indwelling of the Holy Spirit, not by avoiding all sin. We become holy when the Holy Spirit dwells in us.

Although we cannot achieve holiness by our own effort, human beings have a role to play in holiness, because God has given each of us free moral agency. Each person makes choices along the spiritual road of life, as God is working to produce His new spiritual Creation. We must continually choose to live a godly life. God does not force us to do anything. God reveals the right Way to us, but the responsibility inevitably falls upon each of us to choose that Way.

Repentance

A life of completeness and holiness begins with repentance, but the biblical concept of repentance has been muddled in mainstream Christian theology, because repentance and confession have become virtually synonymous. The English concept of repentance is based on a Latin root associated with penitence and means "to feel regret," so most churchgoers think of repentance as sorrow for sins, but the Greek language offers an entirely different concept. Notice Strong's definition of *metanoeo*.

NT:3340

metanoeo (met-an-o-eh'-o); from NT:3326 and NT:3539; **to think differently** or afterwards, i.e. reconsider

Repentance has nothing to do with being sorry for sins or seeking forgiveness. The Greek verb underlying "to repent" means "to think differently." When the authors of the New Testament wrote about repentance, they were encouraging their audience to experience a paradigm shift which would result in a change of nature and a change of thought process. They were encouraging us to allow God to place Jesus Christ in charge of our lives to give us spiritual direction. The change does not require us to search our past lives to dig up all our past sins but demands a change in our thinking process from that point forward. Repentance does not look backward but looks forward with a new perspective and a different thought process. We may express sorrow for past sins and sin again, but we cannot think differently without acting differently.

Repentance places Jesus Christ in us as our Head. He completes us so we can think spiritually and see things the way God sees them. Christ living in us changes our nature. We have truly repented when we no longer are who we used to be. When we no longer are who we used to be, then we should no longer act the way we used to act. Repentance is a gift of God which changes our nature, gives us spiritual direction and allows us to think and act differently.

As God calls sinful people out of the world and toward His Son, they must first choose to think differently about God and about who they are. Unbelievers must recognize God and recognize that they are sinners. They must recognize their lives are corrupt to the core and without hope in this life or the next. Sinners are not required to search their minds to recall every sin they ever committed, so they can confess all their sins. It would be an exercise in futility for them to even attempt to remember all their sins, let alone take the time necessary to confess each one. Sinners need not confess their sins, but God requires sinners to think differently about their nature. Sinners must repent of being sinners. They must come to abhor who they are. When they choose to acknowledge God and choose to turn toward God and allow God to apply His covenant Sacrifice as the propitiation for their sins, God changes their nature and they become believers. They are no longer sinners. God reconciles them to Himself, and their spiritual state of being changes. Certainly the blood of Christ removes all their sins, but the reality most converts fail to understand is that God changes their nature and they become complete and holy. They become united with all of us who have previously changed our thinking through the indwelling of the Holy Spirit. Repentance results in immediate completeness and holiness.

Repentance places Jesus Christ in each of us, changes our nature and sets us on the path of righteousness toward salvation. The only repentance discussed in the New Testament is the repentance which changes the way a person thinks. This repentance is not from sin or from what a person has done, but it is repentance about a sinful state of being. Jesus Christ living in us allowed each of us to recognize that God alone is good and that we were unrighteous before God. A spiritual perspective allowed us to see that our sinful human nature produced no good deed regardless of how hard we tried. Even those deeds which appeared to be good deeds were not, because, as sinners, our evil nature had no capacity to produce anything good. Therefore, our first step toward completeness and holiness was to choose to acknowledge that God is righteous and that we were unrighteous sinners, and then God changed our nature so we could think differently. Having chosen life and chosen to turn our backs on sin, the ledger was wiped clean of every sin we had ever committed, and we began a new life in the body of Christ, where every subsequent sin is also removed by the blood of Christ.

When we repented as sinners, the blood of Jesus Christ removed all our sins, because God placed us in the spiritual body of Christ where His blood flows continually to remove our sins. His blood keeps His body free from sin at all times. Christ's blood not only cleans up our past life, but our present life and future life as well.

Sin no longer has any power over us. Occasional sin is not a threat to the body, because Christ's blood flowing through Christ's body cleanses the body and removes every incidental sin to keep the body holy continually. The Church—the spiritual body of Christ—must remain holy—spiritually clean—continually.

Repentance should be a one-time experience for most Christians. Further repentance is unnecessary, because the blood of Christ instantly removes each sin, so the body can remain holy at all times. The Lord continues to be the Head of our lives to provide spiritual direction at all times. When we sin, we acknowledge the sin and stop the sin. Regular confession of sin should preclude the necessity to repent again—to think differently again.

Confession

Following repentance, God raises new believers from the watery grave of baptism to embark on a new life of holiness. New believers become complete through obedience to the faith of Jesus Christ and the lead of the Holy Spirit. The Holy Spirit will not lead us into sin, but, from time to time as we walk the Christian life, our dying human spirits assert themselves and sin occurs. Sometimes we recognize our sins, sometimes not. When we do, we must always confess each sin. The Greek expression is usually "acknowledge." Acknowledgement of individual sins is the recognition that we fall short of new covenant Law and depend on the blood of Christ to keep us holy. Acknowledgement, or confession, is very different from repentance at conversion. Confession acknowledges individual shortcomings, so we do not repeat the same mistakes. Confession is for our benefit, but it has nothing to do with cleansing sin or keeping the body holy.

Confession is vital in the Christian life to help us regularly align ourselves to the Standard of the truth of God, or, the way many view it, to measure ourselves against the stature of the fullness of Christ. (Eph 4:13) Without confession we will not grow spiritually. If we do not grow spiritually, we will die spiritually. The lake of fire awaits all those who refuse to acknowledge sinful omissions or to confess sinful actions. It is absolutely necessary to make course corrections along the Christian road of life, so we are always moving toward the Standard of Christian conduct, even if we never fully achieve it.

However, realistically, God knew we would not always confess every sin, not because we refuse to acknowledge sin, but because we do not always recognize sin. In many cases we sin because of human reasoning, false beliefs or false teaching. We may think we are acting according to the word of God, when, in fact, faulty thinking has led to occasional sins we do not even recognize. Our human limitations only allow us to acknowledge a sin when we recognize the sin. This lag in our recognition of sin poses a potential problem with the holiness of the body, because holiness must be constantly maintained in the body of Christ. Fortunately, holiness does not depend on our recognition of every sin. The blood of Christ is continually at work to keep His body holy, even when we do not recognize and acknowledge every one of our sins.

The plain word of God says believers are holy. (1 Pet 2:9) In the Greek text of the Bible, God speaks of the holiness of the Church in terms of present indicative Greek verbs. Such verbs, as discussed earlier, indicate action which is occurring in the present. The holiness of the Church is a spiritual reality, and the holiness of the Church is a present reality. We live in a state of holiness. The body of Christ must remain holy at all times. This spiritual condition is initiated and maintained, not because human beings have an instant ability to recognize every sin and confess every sin, but because holiness is initiated in the Church by the indwelling of the Holy Spirit and continually maintained by the blood of Christ.

Any sin remaining in the body will defile the body and must be removed. Sin in the spiritual body is routinely removed by the blood of Christ, just as impurities in our physical bodies are routinely removed by the blood which continually flows through our veins. All our sins—past, present and future—are or will be removed by the blood of Christ whether we recognize, or will recognize, we have sinned or not. The purpose for confession is not to gain God's forgiveness or to remain under His grace. Confession does not reinstate holiness. Holiness is achieved by the indwelling of the Holy Spirit and constantly maintained by the blood of Jesus Christ.

Some Christians live in the fear that they may have been rejected from the grace of God, because they may not have confessed every sin they have ever committed. Such fear is unfounded, because every incidental sin a believer may have committed since his slate was wiped clean upon repentance has also been removed by Christ's blood. The blood of Christ is always at work removing sin from Christ's body and keeping all the members of the Church holy. The Church remains holy continually.

Our acknowledgement of individual sins is not for the purpose of holiness, but for the purpose of Christian growth. When we recognize sin in our lives, we must acknowledge our sin and realign our actions to God's Standard of conduct. We continually revise our conduct, so we do not repeat the mistakes of the past, and then we acknowledge further error, as we recognize our conduct still falls short of new covenant Law.

Although Christians need not confess every incidental sin, there is an ever-present danger when a believer allows any sin to remain unrecognized. If he remains oblivious to sin, the door is open for a completely different type of sin in his life. When he does not confess the sin and change his actions, the likelihood is greatly increased that the sin will be repeated, and, when it is repeated over and over again, there is a strong tendency for the sin to become habitual. Habitual sin is a serious problem in the spiritual body. God is not so concerned with incidental sins, but He is very concerned with habitual sins. Habitual sins defile and offend the body. Habitual sin must be stopped or the sinning member must be removed in order for the blood of Christ to maintain the holiness of the body.

God's Perspective of Sin

The human view of sin stands opposed to God's view of sin. Humanly, people tend to categorize sin according to its impact on society or according to its impact on each of them individually. Society considers murder to be a very heinous crime, and it may be punished by death, while robbery is never punished by death, and the perpetrator may receive only a short jail sentence or a fine depending upon the amount stolen. Civil law limits prosecution of those who lie to matters involving the court, but individuals may become quite angry if others lie to them. Adultery is unique in that society virtually ignores illicit relationships between consenting adults, while an individual may consider adultery to be a most heinous crime, particularly if his mate has committed the adultery. In each of these examples, individual sins are considered irrelevant, bad or worse depending on the impact those sins have on society generally or on an individual in particular. The standard will vary from society to society and from individual to individual.

However, God views every type of sin the same. Idolatry is just as bad as murder in God's sight, and coveting a neighbor's possessions is just as bad as outright thievery. Jesus had to die for little white lies just as much as He had to die for life-threatening deceptions, and God considers sexual lust equal to committing the act itself. God does not rate sins on a scale of one to ten and ignore the "lesser" sins and punish the "greater" ones. God required the death of Jesus for the least of our humanly ranked sins as much as He did for the greatest no matter how human beings may evaluate or categorize them. God has no sliding scale for various types of sin.

God does not categorize or grade sin by type, but God considers the frequency of any sin as the factor which determines whether sin is tolerable or intolerable in the body of Christ. God is concerned about all sin, but He becomes increasingly concerned as repeated sin begins to change one's spiritual state from believer to sinner once again. The blood of Christ eradicates individual acts of sin routinely, but God considers repeated acts of sin very grievous and continual sin intolerable. God severely judged Israel for her repeated acts of adultery and idolatry, and the only record of a New Testament disfellowship occurred when a man was committing the continual sin of living with his father's wife. (1 Cor 5)

The difference between incidental sin and habitual sin is clearly defined by the various verb tenses God inspired in the Bible, but, unfortunately, the difference has been entirely lost in translation. The verbs showing continuous action in the Hebrew and Greek texts are routinely translated by present tense verbs in our English Bibles, and these translations severely distort the meaning of the original Hebrew or Greek thought. English translations are primarily responsible for the general ignorance about sin, and those who trust English translations to determine the nature of sin will have God's perspective of sin entirely hidden from them. Mistranslated verbs can lead students of English Bibles to believe outrageous statements, which plainly contradict other statements in the Bible. Without access to the original texts, unsuspecting Bible students encounter an irresolvable haze of confusing and misleading statements, which postulate contradictory allegations as substitutes for the overall integrity of the inspired thoughts of God.

The KJV Bible abounds with examples of confusing and misleading statements, and even modern English translations perpetuate the flagrant errors the King James translators introduced into the text of scripture over four hundred years ago. Notice one example of such an error in the New American Standard Version (NASB), which has modernized the dated KJV language but has failed to correct the obvious errors in the translation of the verbs.

> No one who abides in Him sins; no one who sins has seen Him or known Him. (1 John 3:6, NASB)

Bible students are often puzzled by this verse, and, sadly, most English translations reflect the same errors. Since all believers sin, these translations allege believers cannot dwell in Christ, and they also allege believers cannot see Christ or know Him. Yet we know everyone sins—the apostles sinned—even king David, a man after God's own heart, sinned. If we believe this statement, we may only conclude that nobody can dwell in Christ or know Him, but that conclusion renders the sacrifice of Christ impotent and the promises of God void. We may resolve this grossly misleading statement by accurately translating the Greek verbs in the original text.

Zodhiates' *Word Study New Testament* explains the precise meaning of the verb tenses John used in this verse. The verb *abides* is a present active participle. "The present participle expresses continuous or repeated action." The first verb *sins* is a present indicative active verb. "The present indicative asserts something which is occurring while the speaker is making the statement." The second verb *sins* is the same tense as *abides* and indicates continuous or repeated action. Therefore, we may more clearly understand John's statement as the following: No one who is (continually) abiding in Him is (now) sinning; no one who is sinning (repeatedly or continually) has seen Him or known Him.

Greek and English verb tenses do not correspond well, but using an English present participle rather than the present tense verb very closely approximates the Greek thought conveyed to John's original audience by ongoing and continuous Greek verb forms. Since both the present participle and present indicative Greek verbs require an English present participle, translators must occasionally insert the word "now" (present indicative) or "continually" (present participle) to insure that an accurate grammatical sense of each verb tense is conveyed to English readers.

John wanted believers to know that no one who is continually abiding in Christ—who is thinking differently—who is living the Christian life—is presently sinning any sin over and over again. He wanted us to know that no one who is sinning continually—whose sins are habitual—who is living in sin—has seen or known the Lord. Repeated or continual sin is evidence of unbelief, and it is evidence that the member has turned away from God again. If any member discovers that he has been sinning, he must repent again—he must think differently again—he must experience another change in his thought processes which will allow God to direct his life again.

The difference between incidental sin and habitual sin becomes evident when we properly understand the underlying Greek and Hebrew verbs. Sadly, the translators have failed to honor God's inspired text, and wholesale mistranslation of verb tenses has resulted in all sorts of misunderstandings and contradictions in English translations. These errors particularly affect New Testament theology, but the Old Testament suffers from the same symptoms of careless and inaccurate translation of verbs. A similar example of an improperly translated Hebrew participle occurs in Ezekiel 18:4, and the mistake was repeated in verse 20.

>...the soul that sinneth, it shall die. (Ezek 18:4)

>The soul that sinneth, it shall die. (Ezek 18:20)

Of course we know that every soul will die, because everyone has sinned, but that is not what Ezekiel intended to explain here. The children of Israel were well aware of their mortality, and they did not need a prophet from God to inform them that their sins would eventually result in physical death. God was speaking spiritually through His prophet to explain that the soul who is "sinning" will die spiritually. Anyone who is sinning repeatedly or continually will experience the second death. Occasional sin was not the issue, but those who are habitually sinning over and over again—those who are making sin a lifestyle—God will destroy by the fire of Gehenna. "The soul that is sinn<u>ing</u>, it shall die [forever]" was Ezekiel's warning to them and to us.

Lifestyle Sin

Every incidental sin a believer might commit is removed by the blood of Jesus Christ and immediately forgiven by God. Whether a member might tell a little white lie or murder someone, God forgives every sin. If he recognizes the sin, he must acknowledge that sin and stop doing whatever is unbecoming of his walk with the Lord and detrimental to the body of Christ. He must acknowledge that he has acted contrary to God's character, stop the sin, turn away from that sin and resume a faithful walk with God.

Although the blood of Christ removes every sinful act a member might commit whether he recognizes the sin or not, danger may lurk in his life, if he does not recognize and confess every sin. Human nature may cause a member to repeat a sinful action when he faces a similar problem in a similar situation. He will likely try the same sinful solution again, if it seemed to work previously. If he repeats that sin over and over again, he runs the risk of slipping into a habitual sin. If someone lovingly points out the sin, the cycle may be broken, but, if he continues to sin in the same way repeatedly, he is living in sin. Lifestyle sin causes a change in his spiritual state of being, and those who are caught up in lifestyle sin have lost their status as believers and become sinners once again.

A believer may sin in many ways and always receive forgiveness from God, but, if the believer is living in sin, he has become a sinner once again. He must stop the lifestyle sin and turn from the sin before God's grace can restore him to life. A believer may become intoxicated from time to time, but, if he is repeatedly drunk, he has become a drunkard, and he is living in sin. A believer may commit adultery from time to time, but, if he leaves his wife and moves in with his lover, he has become an adulterer, and he is living in sin. A believer may steal from time to time, but, if he steals repeatedly, he has become a thief, and he is living in sin. When a believer is living in sin, his spiritual state has changed, and he has made himself a sinner once again. A believer may not continue in a lifestyle sin, and a church may not allow a fallen believer to remain in its fellowship.

Lifestyle sin is like cancer in a physical body. A physical body remains healthy as long as cells in the body die and new cells continually take their place. When a cell continues to live and refuses to die, it begins to grow quickly and spreads throughout the body. When a cell grows and spreads in a body, doctors call that condition cancer. If the cancer is not removed from the body, it will inevitably spread to vital organs, and the whole body will die.

Spiritual cancer can also occur in a spiritual body. Lifestyle sin in a church is like cancer in a physical body. When a member of a church is sinning and does not acknowledge the sin and stop the sin, spiritual cancer has occurred in the congregation. Lifestyle sin is highly infectious, and God knows this spiritual cancer will spread rapidly in a spiritual body until it infects the whole congregation. As cancer must be removed from a physical body, lifestyle sin must be removed from a spiritual body, so a congregation may remain clean and holy in the sight of God. If the one living in sin is not removed from the congregation, the whole congregation will die. Lifestyle sin is sin unto death, and God does not tolerate it in a church.

Many have assumed sin unto death (1 John 5:16) is a specific sin, but it is not. Sin unto death is any sin which continues unchecked in a believer. The difference between ordinary sin and sin unto death is the same as the difference between incidental sin and lifestyle sin. A believer may sin various sins on occasion, but a believer may not sin the same sin repeatedly. Christ's blood removes every incidental sin a member or a church may commit, but, when a sin becomes habitual—when a sin becomes a way of life—when a Christian or a church is sinning repeatedly, then that person or that church is living in sin. Lifestyle sin is sin unto death.

The Holy Spirit strongly resists lifestyle sin in our lives, because the blood of Christ cannot remove lifestyle sins, just as physical blood cannot remove physical cancer. When a Christian engages in lifestyle sin, he is resisting the lead of the Holy Spirit, and he is on the road to spiritual death, but he is not necessarily committing the unpardonable sin. Forgiveness is possible, but repentance is necessary. He must repent of his evil nature again and stop his lifestyle sin before God will extend forgiveness and reinstate him in the body of Christ. A member may not commit sin unto death—he cannot live in sin—he cannot allow sin to change his nature and still remain in a holy spiritual state as part of the holy body of Christ. Lifestyle sin is not necessarily an unpardonable sin, but the salvation of those who are living in sin has become very precarious.

The mitigating factor which separates forgivable lifestyle sin from the unpardonable sin is ignorance. Although ignorance extends the opportunity for repentance, ignorance cannot excuse lifestyle sin. Repentance is necessary for every lifestyle sin, but repentance cannot occur until the sinner acknowledges the sin, stops the sin and turns away from the sin. Knowledge must precede repentance, and therein exists the salvation-threatening difficulty for every fallen believer. A fallen believer nearly always requires the assistance of a faithful teacher before he or she can repent. It is nearly impossible for a fallen believer to extract him or herself from living ignorantly in sin. As long as one is alive, there is hope, but, if a fallen believer dies living in sin, whether in ignorance or willfully, the judgment of God is eminent. Truly it was spoken by the prophet Hosea, "My people are destroyed for lack of knowledge." (Hosea 4:6)

Although lifestyle sins of ignorance offend the body and resist the Spirit, sinning in ignorance is always forgivable. However, those who possess the knowledge of the truth and intentionally resist the Holy Spirit have committed blasphemy against the Holy Spirit, and there is no more forgiveness for sin. Blasphemy against the Holy Spirit is lifestyle sin with knowledge. It is the unpardonable sin.

> But he that shall blaspheme against the Holy Ghost hath never forgiveness, but is in danger of eternal damnation: (Mark 3:29)

Few commit the unpardonable sin, because a person must first know he or she is sinning, and the person must be living willfully in that sin. Willful sin and willfully living in sin are two different things. All of us do things we know are sin. All of us commit sin willfully, but few are willfully living in sin. The point at which one is knowingly and willfully committing a lifestyle sin is the point at which sin becomes unpardonable. Those who are knowingly and willingly walking contrary to the Word and resisting the Spirit in repeated or continual sin will take their place in the lake of fire. There remains no more sacrifice for those who are committing the unpardonable sin.

> For if we sin [are sinning] wilfully after that we have received the knowledge of the truth, there remaineth no more sacrifice for sins, but a certain fearful looking for of judgment and fiery indignation, which shall devour the adversaries. (Heb 10:26-27)

Notice this verse carefully. I have indicated the proper translation of the present active Greek participle (continuous) in brackets, but I have left the KJV verb in place, so you can see the difference in the meanings of the two verb tenses. Observe the contradiction most translations introduce into the Bible. If God withholds the sacrifice of Christ from every Christian who sins willfully, nobody will be in the kingdom of heaven. We all sin willfully after receiving the knowledge of the truth, but only those who are sin<u>ning</u> willfully will face the certain judgment of God's fiery indignation. Willful lifestyle sin is unpardonable sin, and permanent death in the lake of fire is the promised consequence.

Some Christians live in fear that they might have committed the unpardonable sin, but it is impossible for those who are concerned about committing the unpardonable sin to have actually committed it. As long as a Christian is willing to repent, there is hope for salvation. The unpardonable sin cannot be committed in ignorance. May the merciful God of grace bring knowledge and repentance to those who are ignorantly living in sin.

Willful lifestyle sin has no forgiveness, but God will forgive all those who ignorantly live in sin when they recognize their sin and repent. Forgiveness is possible, but repentance is necessary. Unlike incidental sins of ignorance, which are forgiven without recognizing them and confessing them, those who fall into lifestyle sin must recognize their sin, stop their sin and think differently again before they can receive forgiveness from God. Forgiveness is possible, but those who are living in sin must stop the sin and repent. Churches which are living in sin must stop the sin and repent. They must turn their hearts and their minds to God and focus their spiritual eyes on the Lord, Who will forgive and cleanse their sin as soon as they recognize it and repent. The consequence of continuing ignorance is the same as willful resistance.

As weak and fallible human beings, we all sin, and the blood of Christ removes all our sins, but when a member sins repeatedly or continually, that member is defiling the spiritual body of Christ and offending the church. The whole church becomes spotted and defiled when a member sins continually. Each member of the body who engages in lifestyle sin and refuses to repent must be removed from the church. The blood of Christ cannot remove lifestyle sin.

> And if thy right eye [is offending] thee, pluck it out and cast it from thee: for it is profitable for thee that one of thy members should perish, and not that thy whole body should be cast into hell. And if thy right hand [is offending] thee, cut it off, and cast it from thee: for it is profitable for thee that one of thy members should perish, and not that thy whole body should be cast into hell. (Matt 5:29-30)

This passage has been wholly misunderstood, because most interpreters attempt to apply Jesus' words to the physical body of an individual rather than to the spiritual body of Christ. Jesus is not suggesting we cut off our physical hand or remove our physical eye if that member sins, but He used the analogy of the body to explain that members of a church who are sinning and offending the church must be plucked out and removed from the church, so the church can remain without spot or wrinkle. Notice I have replaced the KJV present tense verb *offend* with the English participle *offending* to more accurately reflect the present indicative tense of the Greek verb, which indicates ongoing action occurring in the present. Jesus explained that members of the spiritual body who are presently offending the spiritual body by committing a sin over and over again must be plucked out and removed from a church congregation, so the whole congregation may remain without spot or wrinkle. Jesus' words are a stern warning to every congregation that it should not allow lifestyle sin to remain in the church. Faithful members should not fellowship with a member who allows lifestyle sin to spot and wrinkle his life. Spiritual cancer cannot remain in a spiritual body, because it infects and defiles the whole body. If a church fails to comply with Jesus' instruction to remove sinners from the body, God will cast the whole congregation into hell.

God's thoughts are higher than our thoughts, and He looks at sin differently than we do. He considers every sin an offense, but He abhors repeated sinning. When we align our thoughts about sin to His thoughts and think about sin the way God thinks about sin, only then will we begin to gain a more accurate perspective of how sin impacts our lives as Christians. We will be empowered to boldly live the Christian life, free from the fear of God's wrath and confident that the blood of Christ will remove every sin we commit.

Believers vs. Sinners

The reality of lifestyle sin expressed through participles in the inspired texts should lead directly to an understanding of the nature of a person—an understanding of who a person is, because a direct grammatical parallel exists between participles and nouns of being. When a person is doing something continually or repeatedly, that action becomes part of the person's nature. An individual who is believ<u>ing</u> is a believer. An individual who is sinn<u>ing</u> is a sinner. The words "believ<u>er</u>" and "sinn<u>er</u>" are nouns of being. Nouns of being describe the nature of a person and often end with "<u>er</u>." We can determine the nature of a person, if the person is doing something repeatedly, but we cannot determine the nature of a person simply by observing the person or observing a particular deed. Therefore, a complete picture of the nature of believers and sinners can only be discerned through the spiritual vision of the word of God.

All have sinned and come short of the glory of God, but not all people are sinners. Some people are believers. When God says all have sinned, He is describing what everyone has done, but when He speaks of sinners or believers, He is discussing their spiritual state of being regardless of what they have done. God uses spiritual vision to determine every person's state of being, but human beings cannot determine anyone's nature by observation, because our eyes cannot look into a person's mind to evaluate the person's nature. We cannot see the spiritual state of a person. We may observe what a person may have done, but we cannot determine who the person is by observation. When we make determinations about the nature of our fellow human beings, we must depend on the spiritual vision of God revealed in the Bible.

Scripture describes the faithful of God as believers. When it says we are believers, it is discussing our nature, not our deeds. It is discussing who we are, not what we do. When the word of God describes our spiritual state, it says believers are holy. (1 Pet 2:9) We are saints, *hagios* in Greek, which means "holy ones." (Eph 1:1) Believers are holy, because the indwelling of the Holy Spirit makes us holy, and the blood of Christ keeps us holy. Holiness is every believer's spiritual state of being. Believers may sin from time to time, but believers always remain holy, because the blood of Jesus Christ has removed all our sins and God has forgiven all our sins. Believers sin, but believers are not sinners.

Scripture also tells us some people are sinners, and it says they are unholy. These terms also describe their spiritual state. A sinner is unholy, not necessarily because we can observe him continually committing sinful deeds, but because he is in a continual state of sin because of unbelief. If a sinner has only committed one single sin in his whole life, he is still a sinner, because the blood of Christ has not removed his sin. The sinner is a sinner, because he is living in unbelief and not thinking differently, so the single sin he committed remains unforgiven and ever-present in his life. A sinner may appear to be a very good person, but he remains a sinner in God's sight continually no matter what he does or how he lives the rest of his life. The sinner lives in a spiritual state of sin and unforgiveness.

Sinners are often mistaken for good people, because the things they do may seem to be kind or helpful, but we cannot determine the spiritual state of individuals based on our observation of what they do. We must depend on the spiritual vision of the word of God to know for sure who they are, and only then may we properly evaluate their deeds. Unbelievers do many things in the world which appear to be good in our eyes, so some people have observed the seemingly good actions of unbelievers in the world and have concluded that some unbelievers are better people or live better lives than some believers do. Such a conclusion is typical of the deception of the physical world and is a result of poor spiritual vision. We cannot depend on our eyes to determine spiritual reality.

Similarly, we must depend on the spiritual vision of the word of God to determine whether deeds are good or evil. The quality of a deed is spiritually discerned. The apostle James used a fountain to explain that the type of water coming from a fountain depends entirely on the nature of the fountain. "Doth a fountain send forth at the same place sweet water and bitter?" (James 3:11) Just as a bitter fountain cannot bring forth sweet water, so an unholy man cannot bring forth good deeds. If a believer and a sinner do the very same thing—provide the very same service or say the same kind words or give exactly the same gift—if the actions we can observe are identical, the believer's deed is a good deed, but the sinner's deed is an evil deed. Only God is good, and only God living in and working through a believer can do good deeds. The believer's deed is good, because he is holy. The sinner's deed is evil, because he is unholy. As a man is, so are all his deeds.

As we further explore the biblical difference between who we are and what we do, another biblical concept should become clearer. The same principle which allows us to differentiate between incidental sin and lifestyle sin also forms the basis for making proper Christian judgments. Since most theologians and pastors are ignorant of the difference between who we are and what we do, their members have lost sight of the nature of proper and improper judgments, and righteous judgment has become yet another casualty of failed church leadership and teaching. The same ignorance which pervades the nature of sin also pervades the nature of judgment, because the concepts are related. When we understand the difference between who we are and what we do, then we can also understand the difference between proper and improper judgments.

The plain words of the Bible forbid us to judge people at all, (Matt 7:1) and we are even forbidden to judge the incidental sins of unbelievers, (1 Cor 5:13) but we are responsible to edify our church and judge sin in our own congregations. (Matt 18:15-17) One sin invariably leads to another sin, so the Lord has made each of us responsible to one another to condemn sin and make sure we all recognize and acknowledge every sin before incidental sin escalates into lifestyle sin. Unfortunately, many churchgoers shy away from making any judgments at all regarding the actions of their fellow Christians, even though God holds each member responsible to admonish those who sin in the congregation.

Scripture expressly directs believers to make certain judgments from time to time, but very few churchgoers are able to pinpoint the exact difference between righteous judgment and the sin of condemnation, partly because the difference is not explicitly defined in the Bible and partly because few understand the grammatical difference between different types of judgments in a sentence. Remarkably though, the essence of this most important principle of non-condemnation has been taught to most children by the time they finish kindergarten. I remember my kindergarten teacher instructed all of us that it is not nice to call other students derogatory names. Actually "not nice" is an understatement, because the practice of "name calling," which is merely a secular term for judgment, is sin. Even beyond that, unlawful judgment of another individual can jeopardize the salvation of the errant believer who from time to time still requires the grace of God to remain free from judgment.

Among the more important teachings of our Lord is His instruction to the disciples that they should not judge other people. As modern day disciples of Jesus Christ, all Christians are obliged to heed His clear warning in order to avoid the stern judgment which will be allocated to all those who judge other people. Yet Jesus also taught that we should judge righteous judgment. (John 7:24) On the surface these statements may seem contradictory. How can we judge righteous judgment and avoid being judged ourselves for making judgments? Is there a distinction to be made between types of judgments and, if so, which judgments are permitted and which have been forbidden?

A correct understanding of judgment begins with clear biblical instruction, and Jesus taught His disciples the simple, foundational principle regarding judgment in the Sermon on the Mount.

> Judge not, that ye be not judged. For with what judgment ye judge, ye shall be judged: and with what measure ye mete, it shall be measured to you again. (Matt 7:1-2)
>
> Judge not, and ye shall not be judged: condemn not, and ye shall not be condemned. (Luke 6:37)

Jesus' words address judgments which condemn individuals. A Christian should not condemn any human being. If I judge a person, I will be personally judged. To the extent that I condemn a person, I will be personally condemned. Jesus' words are clear. Personal attacks are strictly forbidden, and any believer who improperly judges another member and rejects that individual from fellowship has placed his own salvation in jeopardy, because a personal condemnation is a lifestyle sin. Improper judgments are among the few sins God has lifted to the level of a salvation issue, because God will condemn all those who make personal judgments or condemn other human beings. Any Christian who condemns any individual, particularly one of the household of faith, and removes that individual from his presence has violated Jesus' words and placed his own salvation in jeopardy. God will judge and condemn all those who condemn and reject others.

Given the potential severity of the consequences, some have concluded that Christians should not make any judgments at all, but leave every judgment to Jesus Christ, the Judge of all. Such a strict policy of non-judgmental behavior may seem prudent, but it is indeed unworkable, because it is in conflict with the plain direction of scripture. We must all make judgments at the proper time and place and in the appropriate manner.

When any member of a church recognizes any sin in the body, love for the offender must lead the member to fulfill the scriptural responsibility to confront the offender and make an effort to repair the damaged relationship. Any relationship broken by sin must be restored, because division should not remain in a church. The church must remain unified by the Spirit.

> Moreover if thy brother shall trespass against thee, go and tell him his fault between thee and him alone: if he shall hear thee, thou hast gained thy brother. But if he will not hear thee, then take with thee one or two more, that in the mouth of two or three witnesses every word may be established. And if he shall neglect to hear them, tell it unto the church: but if he neglect to hear the church, let him be unto thee as an heathen man and a publican. (Matt 18:15-17)

The Greek word in this verse translated "tell his fault" literally means "admonish." Any member of the church who is offended by the trespass of another is required to tell the person his fault and admonish the offender, but personally and privately. Members must be able to recognize sin and condemn sin without condemning the individual. We must be able to judge sin without offending the individual we are trying to help. We must be willing and able to walk the very fine line between judging deeds and judging people.

Once a member takes the initial step to confront an offender, the process described above may be set in motion to involve the judgment of a small group of believers or possibly even the judgment of the whole congregation. If the offender fails to respond to personal admonition, the offended individual must include one or two others to bring additional pressure on the offender to recognize the sin. When the group fails to convince the offender, the matter must come before the entire congregation. Since sin offends every member when it occurs, every member must be able to judge sin whenever any sin occurs in the congregation.

The Lord's direction above initially involves an incidental sin, but it may escalate to a lifestyle sin, if the offender repeatedly refuses to acknowledge the fault. By the time the incident finally comes before the congregation, the incidental sin may no longer be the issue but rather the individual's adamant refusal to acknowledge the sin. Such refusal to confess a sin may have become a lifestyle sin of itself, so the end result of refusing congregational rebuke is evidence that the member's spiritual state has changed and that the member has become a heathen and a publican. Such a member is sinning, and he has become a sinner once again. Faithful members may no longer fellowship with that individual. (1 Cor 5:11) We are not only responsible to judge the original incidental sin, but a church must be able to recognize when a member has become a sinner again and treat the individual as such.

Although incidental sins require the process outlined above, lifestyle sins must be brought before the entire congregation immediately. Paul was well aware of the cancerous nature of lifestyle sin, so He instructed Timothy to immediately and publicly expose all lifestyle sins.

> Them that sin [are sinning] rebuke before all, that others also may fear. (1 Tim 5:20)

Notice once again the improper translation of the present active Greek participle (continuous) in KJV. Similarly, most translations lead us to believe that those who sin ought to be rebuked before all, but Greek active participles demand present participles in English to convey the proper sense. Paul grants no permission to expose every sin a member may commit, but he only instructs faithful members to publicly rebuke those who are sinning repeatedly. When lifestyle sin becomes evident, the normal procedure Jesus prescribed to expose incidental sin, quoted above, must be set aside, and faithful members must expose the lifestyle sin to the whole congregation immediately. Sinners cannot remain in the congregation of the righteous, (Ps 1:5) so members may be required to recognize and condemn lifestyle sin when a professing believer is sinning once again.

These biblical instructions should impress upon all believers that proper judgments are an integral part of the Christian life. Jesus' words expressly require believers to make judgments from time to time. The responsibility to make judgments in any number of circumstances will inevitably befall every individual member of a church, possibly some groups of members and, perhaps more rarely, the congregation as a whole. Christians need to be both willing and able to make righteous judgments and to analyze and judge the actions of our brothers and sisters when we are called on to do so. Do you know how to make righteous judgments? How can an individual be admonished without condemning him? How can the sins of an individual be judged without judging the individual?

Good judgment begins with a pure heart, but our hearts must be educated to know the right words to say. Every Christian needs to understand the exact difference between righteous judgment and the sin of condemnation and be able to distinguish between the type of judgments Christians may make and those we should avoid. Although proper personal judgments arise out of revealed truth and judgments of sin are based on observable evidence, all judgment is a function of the words we use to express the judgment. I will discuss the righteous judgment of persons in the next section, and, in the following section, I will discuss the basics of properly judging deeds by demonstrating how action verbs and state-of-being verbs form different types of judgments in a sentence.

Judging People

Jesus described the difference between righteous judgment and judging by appearance, and the apostle John recorded His statement, so we can know how to judge a believer who appears to sin. Jesus had healed a man on the sabbath, and some unbelieving Jews, who would circumcise a baby on the sabbath, had dared to criticize the Lord for making someone entirely whole on the sabbath. To defend His actions, Jesus encouraged the Jewish leaders not to condemn Him for His apparent actions in respect to the sabbath law, but to judge righteous judgment according to Who He was.

> Judge not according to the appearance, but judge righteous judgment. (John 7:24)

Human beings apart from God have no capacity to judge righteous judgment, so the Jewish authorities only had the ability to judge by physical appearance, and they loved to nitpick the rituals of the law. Believers guided by spiritual discernment are able to look past the physical circumstances and the letter of the law to judge an individual based on who he is rather than what he has done. Spiritual discernment allows us to see people the way God sees them and judge them based on their nature—based on who they are—rather than by the five senses or the arbitrary standard of a ritualistic code.

Jesus lived under the law, but He lived His life by faith, so what He did was not done by His own will. Jesus claimed to do nothing of Himself, (John 5:30) so, when He healed, spiritually minded men should have been able to see God working through Him, because only God can heal. They should have been able to see Who Jesus was. They should have seen that Jesus was the Messiah, because God had described Him in minute detail in the Holy Scriptures, which the Pharisees, Sadducees and scribes claimed to know very well. Therefore, Jesus encouraged the Jewish leaders to look beyond the appearance of a sabbath law violation and judge Him based on Who He was rather than on what He appeared to do.

God always judges with righteous judgment. He does not judge us according to what we do. God judges us according to who we are. We are believers, so He judges us as believers, not as unbelievers. He judges us holy and righteous, not because we do not sin, but because we live in His Son and His Son is holy and righteous. We are guiltless before Him, because Christ's blood cleanses us of all unrighteousness, not because we live perfectly sinless lives. Righteous judgment judges individuals according to who they are.

Since God judges with righteous judgment, He expects us to judge with righteous judgment also. He expects us to judge the way He judges. We must look beyond what a person has done and judge the person according to who he is. The law only judges deeds, and it was designed to condemn us and has concluded us all under sin, but God expects us to look beyond the law and righteously judge the person rather than the deed. We must look beyond the evidence, which may indeed be incriminating, and judge righteous judgment. Our physical senses are useless as a basis for righteous judgment, so we must use the spiritual vision of the word of God in order to make righteous judgments.

Since human beings are incapable of righteous judgment on their own, God has provided a simple standard for personal judgments, which faithful believers can easily follow. We do not judge people based on what our eyes see or our ears hear nor on the inflexible legalistic dogma of ritualistic codes, but we judge people according to God's direction revealed in the Bible. God has one Standard for judging people, and His Standard judges both believers and unbelievers, but He gives us specific direction for judging each type of individual. In the case of believers, we may freely judge them according to His Standard of revealed truth. In the case of unbelievers, we may see and understand how His Standard applies to them, but we may not judge them according to it. We do not freely judge unbelievers, because God has given us specific instructions in scripture regarding the Christian approach to the judgment of each of these two types of individuals.

God has revealed in the Bible that Christians are holy and righteous and that He holds us guiltless before law in spite of our occasional sins. Since God expects each of us to judge one another according to the same Standard of righteous judgment He uses, we must, therefore, esteem each of our fellow Christians holy and righteous and innocent of any sin a believer may commit from time to time. We must judge believers to be beyond reproach, holy and blameless, not because we are looking at them through rose colored glasses, but because we judge with spiritual vision the way God judges. All God's people are pure and innocent in His eyes. We may not condemn any Christian, because all true Christians are holy and righteous before God continually.

Although believers are pure in God's sight, unbelievers are vile in God's sight. Unbelievers are sinners. They are lawless and reprobate. They are unholy, unrighteous, profane and evil. Unbelievers have no capacity to do anything good. God calls unbelievers sinners, because, in His righteous judgment, they are in a continual state of sin because of unbelief in spite of all the apparently good deeds they may seem to do. God can see through the facade of good works right into their evil hearts, and He condemns them according to their nature—according to who they are. They are unbelievers, therefore, they deserve condemnation, and He will condemn them.

However, we learned from Jesus' instruction to the disciples in the Sermon on the Mount that Christians should not condemn any individual, believer or not, without jeopardizing our salvation. Even though unbelievers are the embodiment of everything vile in God's eyes and His righteous judgment deems them unholy, profane and evil, we may not condemn unbelievers. Even though unbelievers are sinners, we may not call them sinners or judge them as sinners. We may be able to recognize who they are, but we should not judge them according to their vile spiritual state of being.

In Paul's direction to the Corinthian church regarding the man committing fornication, he explained an important distinction we must make between those within a church and those outside the church in respect to judgment.

> For what have I to do to judge them also that are without? do not ye judge them that are within? But them that are without God judgeth. (1 Cor 5:12-13)

Writing to believers—members of the church at Corinth—Paul described believers as those within the church and unbelievers as those without. We must treat each group differently when we judge, so Paul limited the application of righteous judgment to the church. Believers only judge believers. Unbelievers are entirely excluded from our judgment. Unbelievers are God's responsibility. Even though God has revealed their nature and He has shown us who they are, He has forbidden us to judge either them or their unholy actions.

We may now clearly understand why Jesus said, "Judge not, that ye be not judged." Although God has revealed the entire spiritual truth about the nature of believers and unbelievers, our application of righteous judgment is limited to believers. We may not judge unbelievers at all. Since believers are innocent indeed and we may not judge unbelievers at all because we are forbidden to condemn them, we should be able to see that Jesus' direction is the simple and correct instruction for every human being. Christians should not be condemned as sinners, because it's not true. Unbelievers should not be condemned as sinners, because we are forbidden to judge them. As a matter of fact, we can never tell for sure who is a believer and who is not by observing the person, so God has made it simple. Don't judge people. Don't condemn anybody.

Many have assumed they can determine who is a believer and who is not by observation, but that misconception arises because they have ignored the context of Jesus' instruction regarding false prophets. The context has nothing to do with determining who is a believer and who is an unbeliever, but Jesus wanted believers to be able to recognize when a church leader is a false prophet. Members must be able to recognize when a church leader is teaching the truth of God and when he is teaching the doctrines of men.

> Beware of **false prophets**, which come to you in sheep's clothing, but inwardly they are ravening wolves. **Ye shall know them by their fruits**. Do men gather grapes of thorns, or figs of thistles? Even so every good tree bringeth forth good fruit; but a corrupt tree bringeth forth evil fruit. A good tree cannot bring forth evil fruit, neither can a corrupt tree bring forth good fruit. Every tree that bringeth not forth good fruit is hewn down, and cast into the fire. **Wherefore by their fruits ye shall know them.** (Matt 7:15-20)

In our Bible study, we strictly follow the principle that context governs the interpretation. More Bible students reach erroneous conclusions by ignoring the context than for any other reason. The context of this passage does not involve a comparison between believers and unbelievers, but it is a comparison between genuine believers and false believers. The context is limited to believers, and specifically to those who prophesy or teach. Jesus words describe the means by which believers can expose the fraudulent nature of those who pretend to be faithful church leaders. Jesus explained that believers can recognize which church leaders are false prophets and false teachers by examining the fruit of their prophecies or the truth of their instruction. An Old Testament prophet of God recorded a similar statement.

> To the law and to the testimony: if they speak not according to this word, it is because there is no light in them. (Isa 8:20)

The words of Jesus and Isaiah collaborate to reveal how we may recognize anyone who claims to speak for God but instead teaches false doctrine. We should not accept them based on whether the majority of their words are true or false, but we are to reject any prophet or teacher whose words are not in complete alignment with the inspired words of God. Inspired men of God cannot teach some truth and some error. Just as a fountain cannot bring forth both sweet and bitter water (Jas 3:11) and a good tree cannot bring forth both good and bad fruit, (Matt 7:18) so an inspired teacher cannot speak both truth and error. A teacher is a false prophet when we find even one doctrine or prophecy to be false.

We can never determine whether an individual is a believer or an unbeliever by observing the individual, but we can test the words of prophets and teachers against the words of God. When a believer claims to speak by the inspiration of God, he opens the door himself for other believers to determine whether he is from God or not. Out of his own mouth we can know if he is a false teacher. We still have no right to judge him, but we certainly ought to recognize him, and God expects us to remove ourselves from him and avoid him.

Everyone inspired of God knows and teaches the foundational principles of a Christian life. Every man of God teaches the biblical nature of a covenant relationship. Every godly leader teaches God's perspective of sin, repentance and judgment. Every inspired teacher knows the members of a church are holy, and every true prophet teaches that those who are sinning will not inherit the kingdom of God. Godly teachers will proclaim God to be the Ruler of the church and Jesus Christ to be the Head a sole Commander of the church.

Judging Deeds

Although Christians should not condemn any person, whether believer or unbeliever, we may certainly judge those of the household of faith, and we may also judge their deeds. We judge believers to be holy, righteous and innocent of any sin they may have committed, but we must also judge their sin to condemn sin in the church. We may judge the person and deeds of fellow believers, but we should not judge unbelievers or their deeds.

The Church is the temple of God, and it is holy, righteous and blameless in the sight of God because of the atoning sacrifice of Jesus Christ and because His blood continually cleanses the Church. Christ's blood removes every sin committed by the members of the Church, so His body remains holy at all times. Christ's body must be holy as He is holy. Although we have no role in maintaining the holiness of the body, each of us has a responsibility to do our part to avoid sin and arrest sin in the body. As we recognize sin in our own lives, we must acknowledge the sin, turn from the sin and walk in holiness through faith. As we recognize sin in the lives of our fellow Christians, we are responsible to humbly admonish them, condemn their sin and encourage them to avoid walking in unbelief.

Although the body remains holy at all times, some sins may occasionally remain unrecognized and unconfessed by those who commit them. In order to avoid repeated sinning, each of us has a responsibility to confront and admonish members when they sin and, particularly, to point out sins our fellow believers may not have recognized in their lives. We briefly examined the process Jesus prescribed in Matthew 18:15-17 regarding the role of an individual, a group and the whole congregation to admonish those who sin.

When church members sin and we humbly point out the sinful actions of other members of the congregation, we edify the body of Christ. Jesus' direction requires us to confront those who sin in any manner which does not exemplify the new covenant Standard of Christian conduct. The blood of Christ immediately removes each one of those sins, so the body remains holy at all times, but God's forgiveness does not necessarily result in confession unless the errant believer recognizes his sin. Toward that end we humbly judge one another's actions in the congregation.

Unfortunately, the vast majority of professing Christians have lost sight of the proper manner in which they can judge another Christian's actions. Many times members think they are judging an individual's actions when, in fact, they are judging the individual. We saw that God has strictly prohibited any condemnation of an individual, particularly of a believer, and we saw that doing so may place our own salvation in jeopardy. Therefore, it is incumbent upon every member to understand the grammatical difference between statements judging an individual and those judging his deeds.

Although the difference between judging righteously and judging by appearance is a spiritual matter and can only be determined with spiritual insight, the difference between statements judging a person and those judging his deeds is a purely academic matter. We only need good eyesight or good ears and a proper understanding of the academic principles of sentence structure to insure we are making a proper judgment of a person's deeds. In order to demonstrate the grammatical difference between statements properly judging the deeds of an individual and those judging the individual himself, I have prepared a chart (below) showing in two columns an arbitrary collection of both types of judgments. The chart is arranged to compare each judgment of a deed with a similar judgment of the person as you read across the chart.

Judgment of Deeds	**Judgment of Persons**
You idolized the singer.	You are an idolater.
She worshiped the Buddha.	She is a heathen.
He hit his wife.	He is a batterer.
You disgraced the family.	You are a disgrace.
They killed that man.	They are murderers.
Sam stole the purse.	Sam is a thief.
You committed adultery.	You are an adulterer.
She told my secret.	She is a gossip.
He drank too much wine.	He is a drunkard.

The sentences in the left hand column of the chart above are examples of judgments Christians are permitted to make regarding another Christian's deeds. Each statement uses an action verb and describes an action one may observe, and each statement is a judgment of that action based on the observations of the one making the judgment. Since any two people may see things differently, the offender may deny or dispute the truth of any of these or similarly constructed statements, and the offender may offer evidence to the contrary, if the observer's perspective was obscured or otherwise incomplete. Since the action is the focus of the judgment and not the individual, the lines of communication should remain open to offer a new perspective, an explanation, or possibly a confession and an apology for the offense.

Since we may judge the deeds of other Christians, we may make statements similar to the ones in the left hand column, always using an action verb to describe the perceived errant activity. All the statements in the left column use action verbs. Action verbs describe specific actions, and Christians may judge the actions of other Christians by using action verbs in this way. Any Christian who observes another Christian commit any sin according to Christian standards may humbly, yet directly, confront the perceived offender regarding the errant activity by judging the member's actions. Statements judging deeds always use action verbs.

For example, if a believer tells me something I think is not true, I may say, "You lied to me." My judgment focuses on the action of the individual. My judgment is based on my understanding that the statement the person made was false, and the new covenant law of honesty forbids Christians to make false or misleading statements. "You told me a lie" or "You have not told the truth" expresses the same thought, and these are appropriate judgments of actions which a Christian may make in this circumstance.

The sentences in the right hand column of the chart are examples of condemnations. Each statement uses a state-of-being verb and a noun of action to describe the nature of the person rather than his deed. The statement may or may not be a statement of fact, because an individual's state of being depends on his spiritual condition, as was discussed earlier, not on what he does. We cannot determine an individual's spiritual condition by observation. Additionally, neither party will be able to academically verify or dispute these personal judgments. Unfortunately, people everywhere indulge themselves in such unsubstantiated judgments, which serve to drive a wedge of offense, not only between individuals but also between nations, ethnic groups, the sexes, social classes and every other individual or group which can be called a name or stereotyped as being a certain way. Name-calling is sin. Personal judgment is sin.

Christians may not make condemnations, so God does not permit Christians to make statements such as those in the right hand column. All the statements in that column are constructed with state-of-being verbs rather than action verbs. State of being verbs combined with nouns of being describe the nature of a person. They describe an individual or group as being a certain way or having a certain character all the time. State-of-being verbs describe who a person is, not what he does. Only God can discern a person's nature to determine his spiritual state of being. Christians may judge another Christian's sinful actions, but not the person. We judge sin, but not the one who may have sinned.

For example, I may not say, "You are a liar," even though I may have heard the person say something which was not true. Such a judgment focuses on the nature of the individual rather than on his sinful action. Even though the person may have told a lie, he may or may not be a liar, so I may not judge him to be a liar simply based on my knowledge of a single lie. The Lord has forbidden us to make judgments of this nature, and they are reserved for His judgment alone. It is not humanly possible to positively discern the spiritual state of an individual by observing one particular deed.

Whether an individual is a liar or not depends on the nature of the individual. If the individual who told the lie is a believer, the blood of Christ has already removed his lie, and he is guiltless before God. Therefore, the believer cannot be condemned as a liar. If the individual is an unbeliever, he is most certainly a liar, because the blood of Christ has not removed his lie. His sinful action remains unforgiven, but the Lord has forbidden us to judge an unbeliever.

For the same reasons, a Christian may sin, but a Christian is not a sinner. Unfortunately, many churchgoers believe they are sinners, because pastors have told them they are sinners. Pastors who call the members of their congregation sinners have improperly and unrighteously judged the members of their congregation. Their faulty theological education has rendered them ignorant of the way Christians should make righteous judgments. Christians are forgiven and guiltless before God. We are not sinners. Unbelievers are sinners, because they are unforgiven. A believer who tells a lie is guiltless, while an unbeliever who tells the same lie is a sinner. His sin continues until he becomes a believer or pays the ultimate penalty for his sinful nature and his rejection of God's grace.

Although we may judge the actions of other Christians, we may not judge the actions of those outside the church at all. Paul said he had nothing to do with those outside the church, because they are reserved for God's judgment. Therefore, even though a man may be an unbeliever and a liar, Christians neither rebuke him for his sinful action nor condemn him for being the sinner he is, because only God judges him. We neither judge an unbeliever's lie nor call him a liar.

Righteous judgment acknowledges the holy state of believers, but our judgment of believers' sinful deeds fulfills our responsibility "to edify the body, as we speak the truth in love and grow up into Him, which is the Head, even Christ Jesus." (Eph 4:15) When we judge the actions of other Christians, we make our judgments based on the spiritual principles of the new covenant laws, which are descriptive rather than prescriptive, and which set a much higher standard for Christian conduct than was the case with the old covenant law. Sin occurs in a church when a believer acts without faith— "Whatsoever is not of faith is sin." (Rom 14:23) —or without the guidance of Law— "Whoever commits sin also commits lawlessness, and sin is lawlessness." (1 John 3:4 NKJV) Believers have the ability to recognize sin long before a person breaks the law, because spiritual discernment gives us the ability to recognize sinful attitudes, which fall short of faith and love. Our perfect Law living in us enables us to recognize and judge all sinfulness. New covenant laws are our basis for judgment. Jesus Christ Himself is our Standard.

The Nature of Deeds

With a background in righteous judgment and the proper judgment of Christian deeds, we can turn our attention to the nature of deeds. A good deed is just as much an illusion in unbelievers as sinfulness is in believers, and many can be deceived, if they depend upon their eyes to evaluate deeds. We cannot judge the nature of deeds by observation any more than we can judge the nature of people by observation. The nature of deeds can only be determined by employing the godly discernment of righteous judgment.

Righteous judgment based on the revelation of scripture demands we acknowledge that God alone is good. (Matt 19:17, Mark 10:18) Scripture reveals that human beings are corrupt by nature, and all human righteousness is like filthy rags. (Isa 64:6) Human beings are evil by nature, and, of ourselves, we have no capacity to do good deeds. Since all human righteousness is like filthy rags, every deed a human being can do is an evil deed. Apart from God, human beings can only do evil deeds.

Righteous judgment reveals that unbelievers are unholy and that all their deeds are evil. We do not judge them or their deeds, but we should know how God sees them and their deeds, so we are not deceived when unbelievers appear to do good deeds. Even the good deeds an unbeliever may appear to do are evil in God's sight, so we should be aware that our eyes can be deceiving us when we observe deeds. We must remember that we cannot depend on observation to determine which deeds are good and which are evil.

God is good, so every deed God does is a good deed. When Jesus walked the earth, His deeds were also good, yet He took no credit for the deeds He did. He allowed the will of the Father to direct His actions, so He did nothing of Himself. (John 5:30) The deeds He did were done through faith in God, so the Father was the One Who did whatever Jesus did. All the deeds Jesus did were good deeds, because God directed the work. Only God can do good deeds.

When believers enter into Covenant with God, we die and Christ comes to dwell in each of us. We are no longer alive in the flesh, but Christ lives in us, and He directs our actions by His faith.

> I am crucified with Christ: nevertheless I live; yet not I, but Christ liveth in me: and the life which I now live in the flesh I live by the faith of the Son of God, who loved me, and gave himself for me. (Gal 2:20)

The only way human beings can do good deeds is to enter into Covenant with God and allow God to work through us. When God places His Son in us, God is living in us through Jesus Christ. The presence of Jesus Christ in us completes us and changes our nature. Now we have the capacity to do good deeds. We are living by the faith of Jesus Christ, and God has taken over the responsibility to do the work we do. God is now working through us, so every deed we do through faith is a good deed. As long as God directs our actions, all our deeds are good.

Righteous judgment reveals that unbelievers' deeds are evil and believers' deeds are good. We cannot depend on our eyes to make a proper judgment of any person's deed, because our eyes have no capacity to judge the nature of the person who is doing the deed. We have no capacity to judge a person's character. We may think we are observing a good deed, but we really can't know, because a deed cannot be judged on its own merit. Of and by itself, a deed is not good or bad. The nature of a deed depends entirely upon who is doing the deed. (Matt 7:18, Jas 3:11)

Some people have observed that Christians fall short in their efforts to reach out to the community in comparison to many secular groups or unbelieving individuals. Unbelievers are frequently given high praise for their philanthropy and their personal efforts in the community, while Christians may be criticized for not contributing as much or for not setting as good an example as some unbelievers may seem to set. Of course these observations are based on what eyes can see rather than on the revelation of scripture. Christians ought to always wear spiritual glasses in order to maintain a spiritual perspective and see things the way God sees them. All the billions of dollars unbelievers contribute to worthy causes and all their personal efforts to advance the nation, the state or the community are all evil in respect to the unbeliever who accomplished them, because they did those deeds by their own effort and God did not participate in them or receive credit for their accomplishment. An unbeliever has absolutely no light in himself and has no capacity to accomplish any good deed in this world.

On the other hand, a believer's light is constantly shining, and the believer is constantly doing good deeds. Doing good deeds is the lifestyle of a Christian. Every deed a Christian does through faith is a good deed, because God is working through each of us, and we give God the praise for doing everything we do. Even menial tasks are good deeds, because God is working through us to do the work. We bring praise to God when we clean house, mow the lawn, wash the car and even when we walk down the street. God's light is constantly shining through us as we do everything we do. The five dollars we contribute to the community when the Girl Scouts come selling cookies door to door is better than the millions of dollars unbelievers may contribute to worthy causes in order to gain a tax break or personal recognition in the community. Believers seek no recognition at all but direct all praise to God for every deed He accomplishes through us.

We should not be deceived by all the good which appears to be done in the world. God is the only One Who does good in the world. God does most of the good done in the world through believers, but God can, of course, do good without us, so He can even turn the evil deeds of unbelievers into good for His people and use unbelievers as tools in His hand to deliver blessings to His people. When we are blessed by the action of an unbeliever, the deed which is evil in respect to the unbeliever is turned into good for us, because God can even use the evil deed of an unbeliever to bless us. The unbeliever may think to gain praise for himself, but spiritually minded believers are not deceived about the nature of unbelievers and all their deeds, nor are we deceived about the true Source of all our blessings.

Although the focus of this chapter has been to understand sin, judgment and the nature of people and deeds, a Christian should not feel inhibited to attribute praise to unbelievers or to make positive statements about those who are evil by nature in God's sight. We may certainly express thankfulness and say good things about all human beings. It is not a sin to call unbelievers good people or to thank them for their good deeds and kindnesses, even though God has revealed that their nature is corrupt, and, spiritually speaking, they have no capacity to do good deeds at all. We need not withhold adjectives of praise from unbelievers just because we wear spiritual glasses and have been blessed with spiritual vision. We may rightly edify an unbeliever just as we do believers. Since we really don't know who is a believer and who is not, we should offer praise to every person. Who knows where God might be working?

A Practical Example

As residents in the United States of America and citizens of a democratic society, Christians may be called upon to fulfill their civil obligation to serve as members of a panel of jurors in a civil or criminal matter and pass judgment upon the defendant(s) in the case. Unfortunately, our civil duty to judge stands in conflict with God's direction not to judge. Christians must follow the direction of the Lord to always judge a believer with righteous judgment and avoid any judgment of either the person or the deeds of unbelievers. Therefore, it is always prudent to avail ourselves of the opportunity to be excused from such governmentally imposed service. We must obey God rather than men.

Christians may not judge any individual, believer or unbeliever, and jury verdicts are judgments by nature. The judge always instructs the jury to determine whether the defendant is guilty or innocent. The jury not only determines whether or not an individual has done a certain deed, but it must pass judgment upon the defendant's state of guilt or innocence. Such a judgment assumes a single action can change the nature of the one who committed the act. Humanly, many of us may assume so, but, from God's point of view, a single deed has no impact upon the nature of an individual. A believer does not become an unbeliever by committing a crime, just as an unbeliever cannot become a believer by doing a so-called "good" deed. A single action cannot change who a person is.

God views all human beings from a spiritual perspective, so faithful Christians must judge according to righteous judgment and according to the direction God gives us in the Bible. From God's perspective guilt or innocence is a function of the person's spiritual state and not a matter of what the person has done, so Christians may not presume to know whether the individual is innocent or guilty based on the facts of the case. We cannot determine guilt or innocence by observation or by evidence presented in court. The nature of the individual determines guilt or innocence. He is guilty or innocent depending upon who he is. He is guilty or innocent depending upon whether he is a believer or an unbeliever. A believer is innocent even though he may have committed a crime, and an unbeliever is indeed guilty whether or not he committed the specific crime in question.

Some mistakenly assume jury service is a sin. Such is not the case. It is a sin to condemn a person based on facts. It is a sin to judge any person guilty. It is a sin to obey the judge rather than God. We may certainly serve on a jury as long as we make our judgments according to God's direction and ignore the judge's orders. Since Christians make judgments based on God's direction rather than by considering the facts in the case, we have an obligation to inform the court of our faith and request to be excused from jury service more for the sake of the court than for our own.

There are a number of reasons which legally allow a juror to be excused from service, and we may avail ourselves of any one of them as long as we are honest. Among the legitimate reasons for an exemption is a conflict of religious belief, however, the judicial system may not automatically excuse a juror for alleging a religious conflict with jury duty. Most courts now require the summoned juror to appear before a judge to state his or her beliefs and the reason for the request to be excused. Such is usually an excellent opportunity to witness your Christian faith to the court.

Although a simple statement to the effect that the faith of Jesus Christ working in your life forbids you to judge a fellow human being should be enough to grant your request to be excused, some judges may require a deeper understanding of your beliefs, so he or she may be assured that you are not just making a religious pretense in an effort to abdicate your responsibility to serve the court. I had just such an experience recently when a judge questioned me rather intensely for about five minutes regarding specific details of my beliefs. The following is the essence of what I explained to him.

I first explained to the judge that I would be glad to serve on the panel of jurists, but that my God requires me to render judgments based on His standards, not necessarily on those of the court. My citizenship in the kingdom of heaven takes precedence over my citizenship in this nation, so I must make my judgment based on the Standard of spiritual laws rather than on the standard of civil laws. Therefore, I told the judge, I may not be able to follow some of his directions regarding how I reach my verdict.

Each judge will invariably give instructions to the jury regarding their deliberations, usually after all the witnesses have been called and their testimony given. Among the judge's instructions will be an order to render a verdict based solely on the facts entered into evidence in the case, but I cannot determine guilt or innocence based on the facts of the case. I cannot judge a person based on what he has done. I must render a verdict based on the instruction God gives me in His word, so my verdict must be based on the nature of the defendant, that is, who the defendant is, not on what he has done. The facts, I told him, have no bearing on my judgment. The facts have no bearing on the verdict I render.

From a Christian perspective, I told the judge, there are two types of defendants passing through his courtroom—believers and unbelievers. I judge each defendant based on who he is rather than on what he has done. I must follow God's direction to judge these two types of defendants, and, although each type of defendant is judged differently, the verdict in each case will be the same.

In the case of a Christian defendant, I would certainly condemn his actions, if the charges were true, and admonish him to walk uprightly before God in the future. However, every Christian, who is indeed a Christian, acknowledges sin as soon as he recognizes the sin, and his arrest would have made the sin painfully apparent. A Christian would certainly have acknowledged the sin long before passing through the doors of the courtroom. Since God is faithful to forgive every believer who acknowledges sin, (1 John 1:9) God would have immediately forgiven the Christian defendant, and he would stand in the courtroom innocent before God. Therefore, I may not judge guilty the one who stands innocent before God. My verdict in the case of every Christian defendant will always be innocent, since God has declared him innocent because of the blood of Jesus Christ. The Christian is innocent, because he is a Christian. Every Christian is innocent indeed.

In the case of the unbelieving defendant, the biblical instruction is entirely different, because an unbeliever is a different type of person, and I must judge him according to God's direction based on who he is. The Lord allows me to judge the person and the deeds of my fellow Christians, but He forbids me to make any judgment at all regarding someone who is not of the household of faith. Under no circumstances may I judge a person who does not believe in God. I neither condemn his person nor his actions. Therefore, my verdict in the case of the unbeliever is not guilty, not because he is actually innocent before God or without fault according to civil law, but because God has forbidden me to condemn the unbeliever at all, either to judge his actions or to condemn his person. Since I may not condemn him, my verdict must be not guilty.

Therefore, I told the judge, my verdict in every case will be not guilty. Christians are innocent indeed, and I deem unbelievers not guilty, because God says I should not judge them. The judge thanked me for a clear and understandable explanation of my beliefs and promptly excused me from service.

Remarkably, God has so arranged for Christians, who judge righteous judgment and follow His direction regarding judgment, to always be nonjudgmental. The verdict in every case must be not guilty. Of course such an approach flies in the face of everything for which a court of law stands, and the relatively simple explanation of it will guarantee you an exemption from jury duty in every case. Even if the judge does not excuse you, no self-respecting prosecutor would allow you to remain on the panel and thereby guarantee himself either a hung jury or an acquittal.

A Humble Attitude

Faithful Christians take the responsibility to judge very seriously. The spiritual insight of the word of God gives us the ability to judge righteous judgment, and we have the added responsibility to condemn sinful actions in our church and to admonish those who participate in them. We never judge the world. Our responsibility to edify the body of Christ and promote holiness in the congregation is the entire focus of our judgment, and we must be careful to avoid vain personal judgments or jumping to conclusions about what we observe. We must always consider the possibility that the individual may be able to add some perspective to what we may think we have seen or heard. When confronting an individual, be ready to listen to his explanation, consider his circumstances and extend humility with meekness, lest we ourselves become puffed up with pride and fall into temptation and sin.

> Brethren, if a man be overtaken in a fault, ye which are spiritual, restore such an one in the spirit of meekness; considering thyself, lest thou also be tempted. Bear ye one another's burdens, and so fulfil the law of Christ. (Gal 6:1-2)

Faithful leaders and members of a congregation should always guard against pride and arrogance. When we observe a brother or a sister commit a sin, the human tendency is to feel superior to the member who sinned, but we should always remember the principles of righteous judgment when we confront members about their questionable actions. Righteous judgment teaches us that a believer is innocent of every sin, because the blood of Christ immediately removes every sin. The faithful in Christ approach those overtaken in a fault as being without sin in the congregation and righteous before God. We must consider our own proclivity to sin and carefully walk the very fine line between the proper judgment of sin and improper condemnation of the individual. We carefully focus on sinful deeds in the spirit of meekness, so pride does not puff us up and turn a well-intentioned attempt to help a member walk faithfully with God into an unrighteous condemnation of the individual. Paul's instruction encouraged the Corinthians not to let an incidental sin in an individual become a catalyst for lifestyle sin in themselves.

God's perspective of sin has been turned upside down in churches. Church leaders vainly attempt to create perfect churches by eliminating incidental sins, seemingly unaware that the sins of members are immediately removed by the blood of Christ and forgiven by God. At the same time church leaders allow lifestyle sin, because English Bibles obscure it, civil law promotes it and their faulty theological education blinds them to it. Since churches are focused entirely on incidental sins, their church leaders can errantly remove a member for nothing more than a single sin, if they perceive the member is threatening the organization in any way. Indeed church leaders themselves can be summarily removed from a church when they do nothing more than dip into the offering basket or commit adultery, even though such incidental sins have already been forgiven by God. Churches have no biblical right to remove any member because of an incidental sin.

God's perspective of proper Christian judgment has also been turned upside down in churches. Most church leaders are ignorant of the nature of righteous judgment, consequently, most churchgoers lack the ability to make the proper judgments God requires of every faithful believer. They seldom hesitate to judge those outside the church, yet they readily abdicate their God-given responsibility to judge the actions of their fellow Christians. They depend on church authorities to handle church discipline and solve problems, so they tattle their grievances to the pastor instead of confronting offenders to deal with problems personally and privately. Offended members may become angry or frustrated when problems are swept under the rug because of politics and favoritism.

The fundamental problem underlying these and other issues is a lack of congregational faith in God to govern the churches. Most churches have rejected God's rulership, and they depend on the authority of church leaders to solve problems. Church leaders ignore God's principles of problem resolution taught by the Lord, and they assume the prerogative to judge members unilaterally. When difficulties arise, human reason substitutes for righteous judgment and a sliding scale for sin determines which sins are tolerated and which require disfellowship. Churches cannot function under two sets of laws. Churches cannot live by the descriptive laws of God and the prescriptive regulations of men. The people of God can only achieve freedom from oppression, injustice and condemnation when God alone rules the churches and the word of God becomes the sole basis for judgment in the Christian community.

Chapter 7

The Nature of the Church

True freedom can only be attained through membership in the spiritual Church of God. The Church is a spiritual body, and God places each member in the body as He sees fit. Human hands have no role in the creation of a spiritual body or the placement of the members in the body. The Church dwells in the heavenly places in Jesus Christ, where rulers and authorities have no power over us, and where God alone governs us by theocracy. God rules the Church, Jesus Christ is the Head and sole Authority in the Church, and the Holy Spirit empowers the Church to worship and serve God in the full freedom of His glorious New Covenant.

The true nature of the Church is clouded in the minds of most churchgoers, not because they lack an intuitive sense of its spiritual nature, but because most people tend to think of church in physical terms. If you repeatedly think of church in physical terms, you will tend to speak of church in physical terms, and common usage will reinforce the illusion that a church is physical. You will likely substitute the physical illusions of the presence of a church for the reality that it is entirely spiritual and cannot be seen.

Common usage has led many people to believe that a church is a building or a place where believers worship God. Some may think of church as a meeting where people of God talk about God. Others may see the church as the men who lead the people and speak as authorities to direct them in their relationship with God. Some may even think of a church as the organization which governs its members and sets the doctrine and standards of conduct. To the extent that you allow yourself to think of church in physical terms, your spiritual perception of the Church will increasingly dim. When you are not in the habit of thinking in spiritual terms, you may allow physical illusions to override the spiritual realities revealed in the word of God. You may allow the illusion of what you can see to override what is true. The only way to perceive the true nature of the Church is to trust the words of the apostles to teach you. You can only perceive the entirely spiritual nature of the Church through unquestioned faith in the inspired words of God.

The most effective way to understand the true nature of the Church and the freedom we enjoy as members of that spiritual body is to examine the biblical text to discover how the apostles described the Church under the inspiration of the Spirit. When we examine the many analogies the apostles used to describe the nature of the Church, the unity described by these analogies should stand in stark contrast to the irreconcilable division evident between various denominations and church organizations. The Bible describes the Church as a spiritual body, not a physical body, and it says the spiritual body is a unified body. If you try to impute the long cherished paradigm of physical churches and church organizations into the text of scripture, you may continue to miss the profound instruction and truth which God reveals through the apostles in their gospels and epistles. You may fail to grasp the reality that a church is entirely spiritual in nature.

We may begin to explore the spiritual nature of a church, if we examine a few simple analogies used to describe the Church in the Bible. The Church is variously compared to a body, a woman, a temple, a house, a loaf of bread and other unified things. The nature of all these analogies demands a spiritual Church, not a physical one, because physical churches can never achieve the inseparable unity each of these analogies implies. Separate members can never be one body physically as long as we are separate physical beings. God could not compare us physically to a single temple or single loaf of bread as long as we are physically separated and scattered around the world. These analogies each point to a spiritual unity we cannot see with human eyes. A church must be a spiritual body, a spiritual temple and a spiritual loaf of bread in order to make any sense of the apostles' words at all. The integrity pictured by these types can only describe a spiritual Church.

Further, God has not inspired these analogies with a view to the future. They do not describe a state we have yet to achieve at the resurrection, but they describe a present reality we must embrace now. We cannot enter salvation unless each of us is part of the unified spiritual Church now. The various authors of the New Testament unanimously describe the Church as a single spiritual entity when they describe it as a body, a temple, a loaf of bread, etc., and they unanimously describe it in terms of present active Greek verbs. These Greek verbs explicitly declare that the Church is a unified body now. The Church is one temple now. The Church is a single loaf now. The tense of these Greek verbs precludes the possibility that the unity of the Church is a circumstance God will bring about at a future time. Since we cannot see the Spirit uniting the members of the one spiritual Church, we must trust God to tell us what is true and trust the spiritual vision of His word to know that it is true. God inspired the apostles to use present indicative verbs, so we would know that the unity of the Church is a present reality and that the Church is an entirely unified spiritual Church today.

The unity of the Church depends on the reality of one spiritual Church. If we attempt to understand the unity of the Church without understanding the Church is an entirely spiritual reality, we will face all sorts of contradictions in the Bible. Unity demands integrity, not separateness, and the physical bodies of the members of a church are unmistakably separate entities. The physical members can never achieve physical unity. Before we can consider the unity of the Church, we must necessarily understand the spiritual nature of the Church. Since the Church is spiritual, we will need spiritual vision to see it. We cannot see the Church with physical eyes.

When Jesus declared, "I will build my church," He did not say He was going to build many churches. He is building one Church. He is building His Church. Although Paul's epistles frequently addressed specific groups of members in specific locations, he referred to them as "the" church in whatever place the members lived. He made no distinction between a local congregation and the Church as a whole, except to designate the location of the congregation to which he wrote. He viewed each member as a member in the local body and each local body as a part of the greater Church. In biblical times some of the members were in Corinth, some were in Ephesus, some were in Colossae, and other congregations were scattered around Europe and Asia Minor. Today congregations may be scattered around the world, but every faithful member of every faithful congregation is an integral part of the greater Church—the one spiritual house of God.

> Ye also, as lively stones, are built up **a spiritual house**, an holy priesthood, to offer up spiritual sacrifices, acceptable to God by Jesus Christ.
> (1 Peter 2:5)

Speaking to the scattered Hebrew brethren and, by extension, to the Church as a whole, Peter used the second person plural, "ye," to explain that the collective membership is built up a spiritual house. The Church is not a physical house. The Church is not many houses. The Church is one spiritual house. There is no division in the spiritual Church, because the Church is one house.

All physical boundaries disappear in the spiritual Church. Geographical, denominational, doctrinal, racial, sexual, social and even temporal boundaries are irrelevant to the Church, because the Church is not a physical entity. Remarkably, God does not even make a distinction between believers who are living and believers who are dead. All the faithful of God live before Him. Christians of every generation are all alive in His sight. God has united the living in Christ and the dead in Christ, and we are all one united Church. Such a circumstance is absurd in the physical realm.

> Now that the dead are raised, even Moses shewed at the bush, when he calleth the Lord the God of Abraham, and the God of Isaac, and the God of Jacob. For he is not the God of the dead, but of the living: **for all live unto him.** (Luke 20:37-38)

Several references to the God of Abraham, Isaac and Jacob are scattered throughout the Bible, and in every case those references were made after the patriarchs were long dead physically. Jesus shocked the Sadducees when He explained that Abraham, Isaac and Jacob were indeed alive in God's sight. Unbelievers are dead in God's sight, even if they are still alive physically, (Matt 8:22) but believers are alive in the sight of God regardless of the state of our physical existence.

Our eyes are limited, and they will distort our perception of the Church, if we base our perception of the Church on what we can see. Without spiritual vision, we will see members and congregations separated by distance and time. The only way to make an accurate evaluation of the nature of the Church is to depend on the word of God to provide us with spiritual vision. We must believe what the Bible says about the Church and reject what we see with our eyes. The Church is one spiritual house.

Three simple biblical truths challenge the commonly taught and generally accepted mainstream Christian beliefs regarding the nature of the Church. Organized Christianity has been teaching so many lies for so long that members read over profound truths and fail to grasp the spiritual reality. Pastors twist passages written from a spiritual perspective, attempt to explain them from a physical perspective and end up in a quagmire of convoluted interpretations. Translation has concealed some spiritual realities, while theologians have redefined others to suit their organizational perspectives. Consequently, most churchgoers are largely unaware of their own spirituality or the spiritual state of their church.

God does not teach us about the spiritual realm with complicated terminology requiring a PhD or an IQ above 150 to grasp the concepts, but He uses very common terms in their ordinary sense to confound the wise of the world. These common terms are necessarily spiritual descriptions, because they contradict everything we can observe through our physical senses. These unsophisticated descriptions absolutely require faith to believe they can be true, because they are not true in the physical realm. False teachers and faithless churchgoers will either reject the plain words of scripture or attempt to manipulate the concepts in a way to make them seem to be figuratively true physically. God separates true believers from those who only pretend to believe by using simple concepts which cannot be understood without the faith of Jesus Christ.

One plain teaching of the Bible, which only the faithful can believe, is the holy state of every believer. It seems preposterous to most that all members of a church might actually be holy, since we all sin. We have all come short of the glory of God, (Rom 3:23) and even unbelievers can observe that we occasionally fall short of His glory. The general holiness of the Church has been rejected by theologians and lay members alike, generally because Christians sin, but more fundamentally because most people assume holiness is synonymous with sinlessness. It is not. Holiness and sinlessness are two different concepts. Holiness is a spiritual state of cleanness, whereas sinlessness is a spiritual state of perfection. The Church is clean, but it is not perfect. Human beings will never be perfect. The Bible plainly teaches that the members of the Church are spiritually clean. We are holy.

> If any man [is defiling] the temple of God, him shall God destroy; for the temple of God is holy, which temple **ye** are. (1 Cor 3:17)

Some have assumed that each of us is a temple of God and that Paul was criticizing individuals for defiling their bodies with sin. Although individual members would do well to avoid sin and even to avoid destructive physical practices, such an interpretation misses the point Paul intended to make. Interestingly, the Bible never says an individual is a temple of God. Notice carefully Paul's use of the second person plural pronoun, "ye," to designate the temple. The plural pronoun clearly indicates that the whole congregation is the temple of God, not each individual member apart from others. God surely lives in each one of us, but we can only be the temple of God in a collective sense. There is only one temple of God, and that temple is holy. Believers, collectively, are the one holy temple.

Notice also that I have corrected the tense of the verb *defile* to reflect the present indicative tense of the Greek verb. We all sin, but our occasional sins do not defile the temple, because Christ's blood eliminates each sin we commit. Paul used a present indicative verb to indicate members may not be sinning and thereby be defil<u>ing</u> the temple and threatening their salvation. Although the greater temple of God remains holy, Paul warned individual members (any man) to avoid defil<u>ing</u> the temple by living in sin. God carefully guards the holiness of the one temple by assuming the responsibility to remove "any man" from the holy temple, even if the individual's sinning remains hidden from a faithful congregation. The temple of God is holy, and it must remain holy at all times. Lifestyle sin cannot remain in a spiritual church, because the church must remain holy.

The Corinthian congregation was one of the most spiritually immature congregations Paul served, and they were struggling with a number of problems, yet Paul encouraged them by explaining that they were the temple of God and that they were holy, not that they were a separate temple from other congregations, but part of the one temple of God. (1 Cor 12:12) We may similarly apply Paul's words today. Each Spirit-led congregation around the world is part of the greater temple of God, and each Spirit-led congregation is holy regardless of the members' occasional sins and shortcomings.

In addition to general references to the holy temple, a number of passages of the Bible also inform us more directly that believers have been made holy, but many of those references are hidden in translation. Theologians have chosen to use the Latin root rather than the Greek root for holy, so the verb "to sanctify" substitutes for "to make holy" in English Bibles. Theologians have subtly redefined the concept of sanctification, and now it completely camouflages the holiness of the members of a church. Most members believe they are sanctified, but remarkably few understand that they are holy. Churchgoers have not been taught that the only difference between sanctify and holy is merely the difference between a Latin based and a Greek based word. The Greek verb *hagiazo* is the root word behind each occurrence of sanctify, sanctified or sanctification in our English Bibles. Notice Strong's definition of the verb *hagiazo*.

NT:37
hagiazo (hag-ee-ad'-zo); from NT:40; **to make holy**, i.e. (ceremonially) purify or consecrate; (mentally) to venerate:

Sanctify means "to make holy," and the apostles usually used it in the perfect tense to indicate the completed act of making us holy. Believers have been made holy. (Heb 10:10) Holiness describes our spiritual state of being. The indwelling of the Holy Spirit has made us holy. (Rom 15:16) Holiness is entirely the work of God, and our own effort can never achieve it. Holiness is all about who we are. Holiness has nothing to do with observable actions, so we cannot perceive it physically or verify it by observing what members do. Holiness is a spiritual reality only perceptible through the spiritual vision of the word of God. Faith verifies our holiness, because we believe what God has told us is true.

There is a lie related to our spiritual state of holiness, which many teachers have spread and many churchgoers have believed. The lie is: Christians are sinners. Such a belief contradicts the Bible. According to the Bible Christians are not sinners; we are holy. The Bible says we sin, but it does not say we are sinners. The Bible makes it plain that unbelievers are sinners. (1 Tim 1:9) Sinners are in a state of constant sin, either because of unbelief or because they are sinning habitually. The blood of Christ removes every one of a believer's incidental sins, so the believer remains holy at all times.

One cannot be a sinner and be holy at the same time. These concepts describe opposite states of being.

Due to the fundamental assumption that human beings cannot be holy, organized Christianity has created a logical sounding, but errant, definition for the concept of sanctification in an effort to separate the concepts of sanctification and holiness. Sanctify has been redefined in most theological circles to mean "set apart for a holy purpose," as if only the purpose is holy rather than the people. This definition not only obscures our holy state of being, but it turns our focus toward works and implies that we should focus our efforts to accomplish some undefined holy purpose instead of confidently knowing we are holy and that we continually accomplish God's holy purpose. The definition may lead us to believe that our sanctification depends on pursuing or accomplishing some alleged holy purpose. This errant definition implies there is an inherent holiness in deeds rather than in us. Theologians and church leaders notwithstanding, sanctify simply means "to make holy"—nothing more, nothing less. Holiness is a present reality for every faithful Christian.

In a further effort to obfuscate the holiness of believers, English Bibles call holy members of the Church "saints." English has inherited the word saint from the same Latin root underlying the word, sanctify. *Sanctus* is the equivalent for the Greek root, *hagios*, both of which mean holy. Sacred, sanctify and saint are simply the English equivalents for the respective Latin words which mean holy in either the adjective, the verb or the noun form. The Latin *sanctus*, the Greek *hagios* and the English *holy* are identical concepts. Since the etymological root of our English word holy comes directly from the Greek word *hagios* and holy is a virtually perfect translation for *hagios*, it is a mystery to me why Mr. Strong preferred to use the Latin form in his definition of *hagios*.

NT:40
hagios (hag'-ee-os); from hagos (an awful thing) [compare NT:53, NT:2282]; **sacred** (physically, pure, morally blameless or religious, ceremonially, consecrated):

Hagios means sacred or holy, but most translators prefer holy. *Hagios* appears 232 times in the inspired text, but sacred never appears in the KJV, because our English word holy is derived directly from the Greek word *hagios* and translates the Greek thought into English very well. Adjectives are far more versatile in Greek than in English, so *hagios* can function as either an adjective or a noun. When *hagios* occurs as an adjective, it modifies a noun and refers to holy things or holy beings, usually the Holy Spirit, but when it occurs as a noun, it always occurs in plural form and refers to the holy people of God. The Greek literally reads "the holies," or "the holy ones," but, unfortunately, the KJV always translates it as "saints" when it occurs as a noun. There is nothing special about the saints in respect to the members of a church generally. Members of a church are all saints, because all members of the church are holy. Saints are not limited to dead members of a church, but include all the holy ones, both living and dead. The Bible teaches us that the saints—the holy ones—are the Church.

We gain an important aspect of our spiritual life from holiness. Unless we are holy, we cannot be free. Unless the Holy Spirit lives in us, we will continue to be slaves to sin. When the Holy Spirit lives in us, we have life in us and the law of the Spirit of life has made us free from the law of sin and death. (Rom 8:2) When we become holy, we are free from prescriptive laws and free from those who assume the authority to enforce them. Holiness allows us to be free from unrighteousness and free from condemnation.

A second plain teaching, which few churchgoers comprehend, is the frequent biblical assertion that the Church is a body. Somehow church leaders have transformed the concept of a body, which has inseparable members, into the concept of an organization, which is composed of separate members. A body is completely different from an organization, yet church organizations imagine themselves a body, because the world creates corporations—from *corpus*, the Latin word for body—in spite of the fact that separate human beings cannot be a single body. Corporations form an illusion of a body, but the members of a corporation cannot be a literal body, because corporations have separate members. Similarly, the physical membership of a church cannot be a body, because the physical members of a church are separate individuals. Some may be members of the spiritual Church and others may not, but, in either case, the physical members of a church are not one body. They can only be an illusionary body of a human organization.

This divinely inspired analogy is not a figurative description. When the apostles described the church as a body, they spoke literally, but spiritually. They were not speaking physically. The Church is a literal spiritual body. We are Christ's body. Jesus Christ is spiritual, so His body must be spiritual. We cannot see the Church, because we cannot see a spiritual body. Some members of a church may be part of the spiritual body, and some may not. We cannot tell who is truly a member of the church from observation. That's why the Lord said we should allow the wheat to grow with the tares, (Matt 13:25-30) because human beings can never know for sure who is a member of the spiritual body and who is not. Anybody can join a church or be a member of an organization, but only the Spirit-led members are the inseparable members of the one spiritual body God calls His Church. Some members may try to fool their fellow human beings into thinking they are living uprightly, but they cannot fool God. Only God knows who is part of Christ's spiritual body, because God alone knows where His Spirit dwells and who are His. The Spirit of God does not dwell in a church organization, because any group can form a nonprofit corporation, and anybody can be a member of an organized church. The Spirit only dwells in the inseparable members of the one body of Christ.

While Jesus lived as a human being, He lived in a physical body, which allowed Him to go here and there and to do God's will, but after His crucifixion and burial, God resurrected Him as a perfect and complete Spirit to live in a spiritual body and do God's will through the Church. Jesus Christ lives in each of the members of His spiritual body and continues to accomplish the will of God here on earth through the members of His Church today. Wherever the members of the Church go, Jesus Christ goes. He does God's will through each member of His body individually and, in a greater sense, through His body as a whole. The collective Church is the literal, inseparable, spiritual body in which Jesus Christ walks to fulfill God's will on earth today. (1 Pet 1:20; see p. 6)

Paul explained the nature of the spiritual body of Christ in detail to the Corinthian church. He described the Church as one body with eyes, ears, hands, and feet. He described it as a literal body of many members placed in the body by God and integrally connected by the Spirit, not as a close association of separate members in a church organized by men.

> For as the body is one, and hath many members, and all the members of that one body, being many, are one body: so also is Christ. For by one Spirit are we all baptized into one body...and have been all made to drink into one Spirit. For the body is not one member, but many. If the foot shall say, Because I am not the hand, I am not of the body; is it therefore not of the body? And if the ear shall say, Because I am not the eye, I am not of the body; is it therefore not of the body? But now God hath set the members every one of them in the body, as it hath pleased him... But now are they many members, yet but one body.
> (1 Cor 12:12-18, 20)

    The Church is one body, not an organization. It is a real body, not an artificial body created by men through articles of incorporation. Don't allow anyone to deceive you about the nature of a body. A body is one. A body has integrity. There is no separateness in a body, therefore, any real body which may appear to have separate members must be a spiritual body unified by invisible Spirit. Physical eyes cannot see spirit, so physical eyes cannot see a spiritual body. Physical eyes cannot see the Church. The individual members cannot be discerned. No one knows for sure who is a member of the spiritual body and who is not, let alone be able to see the whole body. The Church is invisible. Men cannot organize what they cannot see. Men cannot organize a spiritual body any more than they can organize a physical body. God alone created Adam and placed the members of his body into his body, so God alone places the members of Christ's body into His body. Only God is able to place the members of the body into the Church and equip us to serve unique functions to accomplish His purposes on earth.

    In spite of the obvious contradiction, some pastors still claim the physical members of their church organization represent part of a physical, temporal body of Christ. Either these theorists are deluded about the nature of a body or else their eyes must indeed be able to see spirit. I doubt the latter, but, if they are deluded, then we should certainly avoid those who hold such a delusion. Did God inspire the apostles to use the analogy of a body when God really wanted us to know a church was an organization? Why didn't God inspire the

Greek word for organization instead of body? Perhaps He inspired the apostles to write *soma*, because He wanted us to know the Church is a *soma*—a body—a literal body—an integrally connected spiritual body.

There is no such thing as the physical, temporal body of Christ on earth today. Christ's physical, temporal body was beaten, shredded and hung on a stake, and now our immortal Savior is a complete and perfect Spirit in heaven. There will never be another physical, temporal body of Christ. A natural physical body has members integrally connected together by the physical stuff we call tissue, which unifies the various body parts into one physical body. In order to envision a physical body comprised of physically separate members, one would inevitably need to resort to spiritual connecting tissue to bind the members into a single physical body, which contradicts the assumption that the members of a church represent a physical temporal body. Physical tissue connects a physical body, and spiritual tissue—or more simply, spirit—connects a spiritual body. Separate physical members connected by spirit cannot be a physical body. Only biological tissue can unify a physical body.

Church congregations are not part of a physical body of Christ, because even a physical body of Christ would necessarily be holy, as was His former physical body. However, congregations consist of the holy and the unholy—those who truly believe, and those who do not—and we can never really tell the difference by observation. For that reason, Christ said we should let the tares grow with the wheat until the harvest, because He will be able to separate those who are making a pretense of faith from those who are connected by the Spirit and form a single spiritual body.

A physical body must be visible and be in a certain place at a certain time. Such a body should be able to have its height, weight, size and shape measured and its mass determined. A physical body has only one head. Yet when an organization claims to be a physical body of Christ, this hypothetical physical body cannot be seen, is alleged to be located in many places at the same time, and cannot be measured in any satisfactory way. This grotesque physical body would contain multiple heads and a hierarchical structure becoming only of a human organization.

A physical church congregation can only represent the corporate association of a physical, temporal organization, but not a body. A physical body exhibits obvious physical unity in both its appearance and its dedication to the purposes of its one head, i.e., the one who lives in the body. However, the physical congregations of the greater Christian community are not only divided among themselves in both appearance and purpose, but they are hopelessly divided by doctrine and hierarchical authority. The body of Christ cannot be so divided. If an earthly body of physical members were truly a physical body of Christ, Christ would also necessarily be the Head of such a body, and, if He were the Head of that body, He would also individually and personally direct each physical member, precluding the existence of any human head or hierarchical structure, even if we assume such a hypothetical physical body exists.

Every body has a natural integrity, which renders it indivisible. Physical bodies exhibit physical integrity. Spiritual bodies exhibit spiritual integrity. Whether a body is physical or spiritual, every body is one. A member of a body cannot be separated from the body or else the member will die, and great distress will be caused to the whole body when a member is removed from it. In some cases the whole body will die, if certain vitally important members are removed from the body.

A body and an organization differ by the nature of their integrity. A physical body has biological integrity, and a spiritual body has spiritual integrity, but an organization has neither biological nor spiritual integrity. Men create the artificial integrity of an organization on a piece of paper. A member of an organization may leave the organization or be fired without threatening the life of the member at all, and the organization may not suffer at all when a member leaves. There are no critical functions in an organization which another individual cannot perform, because an organization has no fundamental integrity. An organization may even remove and replace its head without serious consequences. Clearly, an organization is not a body, and it is either ignorant or deceptive to call an organization a body. The separate physical bodies of an organization cannot have biological integrity; therefore, the separate physical members of a church cannot be the members of a physical body of Christ. They can only be members of an organization. There is no physical, temporal body of Christ on earth today.

A third spiritual reality hidden from most Bible students and, consequently, not generally believed or understood in the Christian community is the spiritual slavery of the members of the Church. As members of the spiritual body of Christ, we are all slaves of Jesus Christ, and our slavery to Him frees us from our former slavery to sin. God specifically created human beings to function as spiritual slaves, and we can only be slaves of sin or slaves of righteousness. Slavery to righteousness frees us from slavery to sin.

> Being then made free from sin, ye became the **servants** of righteousness. I speak after the manner of men because of the infirmity of your flesh: for as ye have yielded your members **servants** to uncleanness and to iniquity unto iniquity; even so now yield your members **servants** to righteousness unto holiness. For when ye were the **servants** of sin, ye were free from righteousness. (Rom 6:18-20)

Translators have entirely hidden the reality of our slavery to righteousness and our slavery to Jesus Christ from our view. The reason for the general ignorance about the slavery of the members of the Church is the wholesale mistranslation of the Greek word for slave, particularly in the KJV. Notice carefully that each time the word "servants" appears in the passage above, the plural form of the word *doulos* occurs in the Greek text.

NT:1401
doulos (doo'-los); from NT:1210; **a slave** (literal or figurative, involuntary or voluntary; frequently, therefore in a qualified sense of subjection or subserviency):

Mr. Strong accurately defines *doulos* for us, but he had convinced himself that the slavery Paul asserted was somehow a figurative reference, because Mr. Strong attempted to use his eyes to determine the nature of the slavery instead of trusting the words of God through faith. Paul's words are literal, but we must understand that they only apply in the spiritual realm. They are references to our relationship to Jesus Christ. Paul did not use *doulos* here in a physical sense, which could be construed to imply a figurative or qualified sense of subjection, but rather he used *doulos* in a spiritual sense. Our slavery to Christ is literal, but it is spiritual.

Even without an understanding of Greek, we should all realize we are slaves of Christ, because Christ owns us. Numerous plainly written statements throughout the apostles' writings describe us in ways which can only imply slavery. We have been bought with a price. (1 Cor 6:20) We are a purchased possession. (Eph 1:14) He has purchased us with His blood. (Acts 20:28) We call Him Lord, so it should be obvious we are slaves of Christ. A lord was the owner of his slaves, because the lord had to purchase them for a price. Unfortunately, most churchgoers have lost the essential meaning of the term "lord" and the implicit reality the word conveyed to first century Christians. Anyone who calls someone lord is a slave.

The members of any body, physical or spiritual, are naturally slaves to the head of the body, i.e., the spirit living in the body. Physical members of a physical body are slaves to the physical head, just as the spiritual members of the spiritual body are slaves to our spiritual Head. Our spiritual slavery to Christ is just as literal as our eyes, ears, hands and feet are physical slaves to each of us. Just as the members of my body are my slaves, so the members of Christ's body are His slaves. I live in all the members of my body, and they all do exactly as I direct them. They work in perfect harmony to perform the various activities I command them to do, because they are all directed by one head—that is, by me. Thus, the spiritual members of the spiritual body of Christ are also slaves to Christ, and we must be free from human direction to do exactly as He directs us. The Lord alone directs His slaves, so the spiritual body will work in harmony to perform the work the Lord is doing through us.

Doulos occurs 127 times in the Greek New Testament, and it is nearly always mistranslated "servant" in the KJV. In more recent translations we find the blended, quasi-slave term "bondservant" offered as a substitute for slave, but such a translation is equally incorrect. The only way to properly understand our relationship to Jesus Christ is to understand it in terms of slavery. Our relationship to Christ is not that of a servant or bondservant, but a slave. The concept should become crystal clear, if you look up NT:1401 in a Greek concordance and read every reference to *doulos* in the New Testament. Space does not allow such a study here, but I encourage you to do so. My former perspective of the relationship of the members to Christ changed radically when I realized all the faithful members of the Church are slaves of the Lord.

On the other hand, the Bible teaches us that we are servants of Jesus Christ in respect to one another. Each member's relationship to the Lord is that of a slave, but each member's relationship to other members of the body is that of a servant.

> As ye also learned of Epaphras our dear **fellowservant**, who is for you a faithful **minister** of Christ; (Col 1:7)

This key verse shows the spiritual relationship of each member to the Lord as well as our spiritual relationship to one another, but, unfortunately, both key words are mistranslated. Paul first described the common slavery Epaphras shared with the rest of the Colossian church in relation to the Lord. Notice the literal definition of the Greek word errantly translated "fellowservant."

NT:4889
sundoulos (soon'-doo-los); from NT:4862 and NT:1401; **a co-slave**, i.e. servitor or ministrant of the same master (human or divine):

In the Greek text Paul described Epaphras as a dear *sundoulos*, or fellow slave, not a fellow servant. You may recognize *doulos* in this compound word, *sun* (together) and *doulos* (slave). We learn here that Epaphras was a "slave together" or a "co-slave" of the Lord together with the other members of the Colossian church. Next, Paul explained that Epaphras was a faithful *diakanos* for the brethren.

NT:1249
diakonos (dee-ak'-on-os); probably from an obsolete diako (to run on errands; compare NT:1377); **an attendant**, i.e. (genitive case) a waiter (at table or in other menial duties); specially, a Christian teacher and pastor (technically, a deacon or deaconess):

A *diakanos* is one who runs errands, waits at tables and performs other menial duties such as those an attendant or a servant might do. *Diakanos* describes our relationship to one another, just as Epaphras was a faithful *diakanos* for the brethren. We voluntarily serve one another, but we are slaves of the Lord. As a *doulos* of Christ, each of us receives his or her direction from the Lord, but, as a *diakanos* for the brethren, each of us voluntarily attends to the needs of the members according to the Lord's direction. We are not slaves of one another, because *diakanos* describes voluntary service. The *diakanos* is neither a slave to those served nor a master of those served. We are all *diakanos*, just as we are all *doulos*, and none is above or below another in our service to one another or in our slavery to the Lord. The spiritual playing field is level in the one spiritual Church. Consequently, an elder holds no respect or privilege over even the newest member of a congregation.

The KJV has variously and arbitrarily translated *diakanos* as servant, deacon or minister, so these inconsistent translations have resulted in Strong's erroneous special and technical definitions of *diakanos,* which rubber-stamp mainstream practice rather than reflecting biblical use. *Diakanos* means servant, but not deacon or minister. The latter two are inherently misleading, because the terms minister and deacon carry the baggage of previously established secular use and ecclesiastical practice, both of which obscure the unpretentious humble service described by the Greek word. Further, the authoritative connotation the words deacon and minister carry in mainstream Christian culture significantly compounds the deception. *Diakanos* carries no implication of authority. *Diakanos* means servant in the literal and menial sense of the word. The word deacon is not even a translation but has been loosely transliterated from the same Greek word, *diakanos*. Fundamentally, there are no ministers and no deacons in the Bible, particularly in the authoritative or bureaucratic sense of these words. In seventeenth century England a minister was a public official who acted under the authority of the king, and the office of a deacon was already an established function of the Anglican hierarchy. The words minister and deacon have no place in the Bible. *Diakanos* does not designate a servant in this verse, a deacon in that verse and a minister in others. *Diakanos* means servant—nothing more, nothing less. If translators would respect the inspired text and translate it accurately, ministers and deacons would disappear from the Bible.

In the Greek text of the Bible, there is one word for slave, *doulos*, and one word for servant, *diakanos*. There is no word for minister and no word for deacon. The inspired text describes our relationship to Jesus Christ as that of slaves, and it describes our relationship to one another as that of servants. We are all slaves of Jesus Christ, and we are all servants of one another. The simplicity of these spiritual relationships is entirely jumbled and hidden in errant translation.

The terms servant and slave describe two entirely different types of people and two entirely different relationships, yet contemporary American culture has virtually obliterated the distinction between servants and slaves. While the work of a slave is involuntary and the slave has absolutely no choice about what he does or when he does it, a servant's work is essentially voluntary. A servant is a free individual. A servant may perform acts of service as either an employee or a volunteer, but the servant is always free to continue or discontinue his service at any time. A slave must always obey the direction of his lord or master, but a servant may or may not submit himself to the direction of a boss, a friend or another believer. We must clearly understand the distinction between these two words as the apostles used them in their letters to the churches in order to understand our spiritual relationship to Jesus Christ and our spiritual relationship to one another. Spiritual vision depends on knowing and believing the inspired words of God.

As we develop spiritual discernment through faith in the inspired words of God, we can more clearly visualize the nature of the Church. The words of scripture sharpen our spiritual vision, so we may more easily peer through the dark glass of spiritual reality and understand the spiritual relationships set forth by the apostles. Thus, the Bible describes the Church as a spiritual house, not a physical house. The Church is also the literal, but spiritual, body of Christ, consisting of many unique members. The members are called saints, because all the members of the body are holy. The members of the body are slaves of the Lord in respect to the Head and servants of the Lord in respect to one another. We are all integral members of a literal spiritual body unified together into one indivisible living body by the Spirit. God is forming us into a new spiritual body to complete His Son, so He can fulfill God's will through us both today and in the age to come.

The word of God describes the Church as a spiritual body of holy slaves, and this reality demands that the Church is one unified Church. The unity of the Church is strongly implied in a number of passages scattered throughout the New Testament, and the realities implied by these passages can only be true in the spiritual realm, because each passage describes the Church in a manner which is impossible physically. As we examine several of these descriptions, we will further sharpen our spiritual vision, because each one describes a spiritual reality we cannot see with our eyes. Just as we cannot see the spiritual Church, the perfect integrity of the Church is likewise invisible to human eyes.

The unity of the Church is a spiritual unity, not a physical unity, but spiritual unity appears in the spiritual realm in exactly the same way physical unity appears in the physical realm. Unity in any body is invariably realized by the inseparableness of the members of the body—the integrity of the body—the indivisible nature of the body, not by the sameness of the members' appearance or activities. The heart and the liver have a different appearance and perform different functions, but they are each integral members of a body. A body is unified because each member is inseparably bound to the other members of the body, not because each member looks the same or is doing the same thing. Unity is a state of being which cannot be achieved by doing a certain prescribed set of activities, because the Holy Spirit is the unifying substance of a church. When a person becomes a member of a church, the Spirit instantly unifies the new member with every faithful member in the church as each spiritual church is unified with every other spiritual church. Thus, all are one, unified, spiritual Church. The Spirit unifies every member and every church, while each member retains a unique appearance and performs a unique function in the greater Church.

Function does not determine unity, so the leaders of a spiritual church should make no effort to organize or direct the activities of the members, because each member is personally and individually directed by the Head of the body to accomplish a unique purpose in the body. In a physically focused church, the members are strongly encouraged to participate in the "work of the church" or to work together to accomplish a church's "mission statement." These serve human attempts to create physical unity in a physical church. Some physically focused churches have imagined a "great commission" to preach the gospel, even though Matthew 24:14 is a prophecy which an angel will fulfill (Rev 14:6) and, even on its face, contains no imperative for churches to preach the gospel. Churches often assume preaching the gospel is a church-wide commission, and they assume it is a work in which every member must participate, even though scripture never defines "the work of the church." Physically focused pastors direct members to preach the gospel, even though few know what the gospel is, and they keep their members busy organizing activities, going to meetings and doing this ever-pressing work or, at the very least, praying for those who appear to be doing it. Physically focused pastors attempt to direct everybody to do the organizationally defined "work of God," as if human beings could possibly do God's work. Most church leaders have little concept of what God's work is, let alone to be able to direct it.

> Jesus answered and said unto them, This is the work of God, that ye believe on him whom he hath sent. (John 6:29)

God is about the spiritual business of creating believers. God's work causes those whom He calls to believe. Human beings cannot cause anybody to believe. Human beings cannot instill faith. Human beings can only do physical things, but God's work is spiritual. We can't do God's work. God is about the business of calling sinners to His Son and placing His faith in us, so we can believe the spiritual realities He teaches us in the Bible. Spiritual truths require faith, because they are not true in the physical realm. God's work equips us with the spiritual vision to believe the simple, yet profound, truths of the spiritual realm. When we believe <u>in</u> Him and we are believ<u>ing</u> what He says, spiritual vision may allow us to see the result of His work, but we don't do God's work. Only God can do His work.

The unity of the spiritually focused Church is found in the spiritual state of its being and the spiritual state of its members' being, not in the type, quality or uniformity of our activities. Everyone's state of being is the same, but each member's activity is unique, and individual members do not necessarily focus on a single humanly perceptible goal. Every member of the Church is holy, every member of the Church is righteous, and every member of the Church lives in Christ and depends on Him to direct his or her activities. We are all holy, because the Holy Spirit lives in us, and we are all righteous, because Christ is righteous and we live in Him. Each of us is one with Christ and one with each other. Who we are defines the unity of the spiritually focused Church, not what we do.

Although our state of being unifies us, the activities of each member of the spiritually focused church are different. Those in Christ focus on Christ, and we listen to Him as He speaks to each of us through the Spirit. Each of us takes direction in our spiritual lives from the Lord, not from the pastor. Each of us listens to the Lord as the Spirit leads us. One member cannot know what the Lord might require another member to do, so one member cannot direct another member in his or her walk with the Lord. A pastor practices the faith before the congregation, and he may describe the nature of a faithful walk with the Lord, but a faithful pastor will never rule, never command and never manipulate a member into doing what he may think might be best for the member to do. A spiritually minded pastor recognizes the uniqueness of each member and encourages diversity in the activities of the members. There are no corporate activities for the members of the unified spiritual Church.

Spiritual unity is the natural result of a covenant relationship with God and the acknowledgement of God's spiritual government over us. A faithful congregation retains its unity by worshipping God as the Ruler of the Church, exalting Jesus Christ as the Head of the Church and yielding to the Spirit to empower each member of the Church. A congregation may not allow any member to exalt himself in the congregation by assuming authority over the congregation or over any member. Human authority causes division between the Head and each member in a spiritual church and may lead to illicit spiritual relationships with civil governments. God keeps the Church unified by keeping it free from human government. When men assume authority and exalt themselves in a congregation, God will remove them from the spiritual Church, and God will remove any church which continues to be subject to human authority or to a civil government. God alone rules the Church, and He has granted authority to Jesus Christ alone to direct His Church by personally directing each member through the Spirit.

Human beings cannot see the Church or perceive its unity with physical eyes. Spiritual vision is required to see the Church and to grasp the reality that the Church is a unified Church, and spiritual vision only comes through faith in the word of God. Unity is a spiritual reality, and the apostles made the unity of the Church abundantly apparent in numerous passages: The Church is the one calling out of the Father. We are one virgin Church for Christ. The

Spirit unifies us into one nation. We live in one location. We live by one faith. We are subject to one government. We are formed into one spiritual body to complete Jesus Christ as the first spiritual Man, so He can do the will of the Father forever. As we examine each of these realities, notice the unmistakable unity each demands. Such unity cannot occur under any circumstances in any church organized by men. When we sharpen our spiritual vision through faith, we will more easily comprehend the plain truths of God.

One Calling Out (One Church)

When Jesus Christ came in the flesh and walked on the earth, He gathered His disciples around Him and proclaimed to Peter that He would build His Church. He did not say He would build many churches, nor did He say He would designate men to build churches for Him. Jesus Christ Himself is presently building His Church—the one Church—according to the Father's direction.

> And I say also unto thee, That thou art Peter, and upon this rock **I will build my church**; and the gates of hell shall not prevail against it. (Matt 16:18)

Throughout the history of Israel, God lived in either a house of wood or a house of stone, but when Jesus spoke these words, He introduced His disciples to an entirely new concept of a dwelling place. He did not tell them they would build another building or establish a new place of worship. He told them He Himself would build a house of God which human hands could not construct. Those who read the Greek text of Matthew's gospel understand that Jesus said He would build "the calling out." The Greek word translated church in every English Bible is *ekklesia*, but it does not mean church. It means "a calling out." There is no such thing as "church" in the Greek text of the Bible.

NT:1577
ekklesia (ek-klay-see'-ah); from a compound of NT:1537 and a derivative of NT:2564; **a calling out**, i.e. (concretely) a popular meeting, especially a religious congregation (Jewish synagogue, or Christian community of members on earth or saints in heaven or both):

You should understand that Strong's primary definitions are very accurate, but they often contain appended interpretations, which attempt to further clarify the literal definition of a word. These interpretations are often helpful, but not always. The exact meaning of *ekklesia* is "a calling out," but Strong's "concrete" explanation is derived from his own observation and has no biblical application. *Ekklesia* has nothing to do with meetings or religious assemblies. In the Bible *ekklesia* only refers to the people called out to be the spiritual dwelling place for God. The people are the Church, and we do not need to assemble together in order to worship God or to facilitate His dwelling in us. He dwells in us continually, and we worship Him continually wherever we are and in whatever we may be doing. We assemble for fellowship, not for worship.

Jesus introduced the disciples to a radically different concept of a house, and our word "church" subtly obscures the spiritual reality Jesus intended. There is no such thing as a church per se in the Bible. The disciples were not going to build a building or establish a new meeting place. They understood that they would be part of "the calling out." They understood that the calling out would not build a house, but that they would be the house. They understood that they would be the Church. The calling out is nearly always designated with the definite article to repeatedly emphasize that "the" calling out is one calling out. The Church is literally the one calling out of the Father. As the Father draws each of us to His Son, (John 6:44) He places each member into the fellowship of the one calling out by the Spirit. Many are called (Matt 22:14) to be members of the Church, but the calling out of God is one calling out—one unified spiritual Church.

In the physical sense there may be many local congregations, and these fellowships clearly consist of separate individuals, some of whom may be members of the spiritual Church and some may not. Our eyes cannot determine who is chosen and who is not. God alone determines membership in the spiritual Church, and He uses spiritual vision to determine who is holy, who is righteous, and who is living in His Son and being led by the Spirit. God alone knows who is responding to His call and who is participating in the one, unified, spiritual calling out of God. We have a responsibility to remove overt lifestyle sin from our congregation, but ultimately God will choose the elect for the one calling out—the one Church.

One Virgin

In the culture of ancient Israel, virginity was imperative, if a woman expected to attract a husband, marry, bear children and live a respected life. The "tokens of virginity" were carefully preserved by the parents of the bride to refute any allegations of fornication. Any woman who was defiled sexually before marriage became an outcast of society and was doomed to a life of shame and poverty.

In our society sexual promiscuity has become so commonplace that couples are assumed to have had previous relationships before they finally make the commitment to marry. Virginity has ceased to be an issue in Western culture. Statically, less than ten percent of brides and grooms preserve their virginity for the wedding day. Virginity has become yet another causality of our permissive society along with marital commitment and fidelity.

In the spiritual realm, however, God still highly prizes virginity, so the Church His Son will marry must be a chaste virgin. The spiritual body God is creating for His Son must be undefiled by the world. The one virgin Church may not commit fornication through illicit relationships with human governments the way Israel committed adultery with the nations around her. A church may not become unequally yoked together through covenants with unbelievers. (2 Cor 6: 14-17) Each church must depend entirely on God for its provision, protection and care. Every church must adhere to the laws of God and only obey the directions of the Lord in order to retain the virginity of the spiritual body of Christ.

> For I am jealous over you with godly jealousy: for I have espoused you to one husband, that I may present you as **a chaste virgin** to Christ. (2 Cor 11:2)

Just as there are not many callings-out, neither are there are many virgins. When Paul asserted that he desired to present "you" as a chaste virgin, he used the plural form of the second person pronoun to indicate that the whole church would be part of "a chaste virgin," not each individual member apart from others. Paul's statement is not a figurative reference, as if each physical member might be a spiritual virgin. The plural pronouns indicate that the spiritual body must remain spiritually pure and chaste, so the Spirit can unite every faithful church into the one virgin Church. God is only preparing one undefiled virgin body for His Son. Our eyes may deceive us into thinking there are many virgins, but only one virgin Church will marry Jesus Christ. There will be only one undefiled spiritual Church, which has not lost its virginity by engaging in fornication with the world through covenants with human governments.

One Nation

As the word of God continues to sharpen our spiritual vision, we will see that physical race or nationality does not distinguish the members of the Church, but that all have become one chosen family and one nation to serve as a royal priesthood for our High Priest.

> But ye are a chosen [family], a royal priesthood, **an holy nation**, a [purchased] people, that ye should shew forth the praises of him who hath called you out of darkness into his marvelous light. (1 Pet 2:9)

We must use spiritual vision in order to see that the physical characteristics which can distinguish the individual members of a congregation are of no consequence to the nature of the Church, and members must ignore them when the congregation meets. God has eliminated the physical distinctions which tend to divide a nation, because the citizens of God's spiritual nation are not physical, but spiritual. The concept of a raceless, classless and genderless Church may test the spiritual vision of many believers unless we remember the Church is spiritual. The Church cannot be physical, because there are indeed racial, social and gender differences in every fellowship. Consider the spiritual reality in Galatians 3:27-28.

> For as many of you as have been baptized into Christ have put on Christ. **There is neither Jew nor Greek, there is neither bond nor free, there is neither male nor female:** for ye are all one in Christ Jesus.

Paul clearly explains that there are no racial, social or gender distinctions in Christ's body. All such physical attributes have no relevance for a spiritual church. The color of one's skin, the curvature of one's body and the level of one's status in society must be ignored when the members meet for fellowship. Every physical characteristic has disappeared from the church, because our physical bodies are not part of the church. Only the spirits of the faithful are one body in Christ Jesus, so that we, collectively, reflect His image, not our own. God has rendered all physical distinctions irrelevant, so we may live equally as citizens in one spiritual nation.

The Church has already achieved the objective of many social activists. Each of us has been purchased by the Lord and washed in His blood, and each of us has become part of a new Creation. We have become one nation of one blood, each of us being called out of the darkness of racial, social and sexual bigotry into the light of the spiritual reality that every race, all classes and both sexes may lead and serve equally in a church. Every visible distinction is irrelevant, because God only places our human spirits into the body of Christ, where we are, collectively, one spiritual nation in Him.

One Location

The spiritual reality of one location may severely test your ability to believe the words of God. Paul revealed that the Church does not live on earth, but that God has blessed the whole Church with the opportunity to sit together as one unified Church in heaven in Christ. We are not waiting for a future fulfillment. Our presence in heaven is now. We are in one location now. The reality is now!

> Blessed be the God and Father of our Lord Jesus Christ, who hath blessed us with all spiritual blessings in heavenly places in Christ: ...And [He] hath raised us up together, and made us sit together in heavenly places in Christ Jesus: (Eph 1:3, 2:6)

Many ignore these words, because they just can't grasp the reality. Spiritual reality is beyond the ability of the natural mind to comprehend. We must exercise faith and simply believe the words of God are true. It may be helpful to recall the nature of covenant, wherein covenant partners become one with each other. Recall that, through covenant, we have exchanged places and natures. We live in Christ, and Christ lives in us. We do not live on earth with our old sinful nature, but we live in Christ, and we are holy. Christ's place is in the right side of God in heaven, so we should not be surprised that the Bible says we live in heaven in Him. On the other hand, Christ lives in each of us as a new Man on earth, and He walks and talks through our physical bodies. Peter revealed the parallel reality that Christ is appearing in these last times through us. (1 Peter 1:20) We live in heaven in Him, and He appears on the earth through us. The inspired words of God sharpen our spiritual vision.

God blesses us with every spiritual blessing He has to offer, because we sit together in Christ, Who sits in the right side of God. (Eph 1:20) We are all one in Christ. The true spiritual Church is not divided. Our eyes are just deceiving us, because we cannot see the Spirit uniting us together as one body, and we can't see the spiritual body growing together in heaven. Can you begin to understand how deceptive your eyes are? Can you begin to grasp the reality of the unity of the Church? The Church is the calling out of one unified spiritual body which resides in heaven in Christ. No figurative language—no hocus pocus—just spiritual reality.

One Faith

The reality of one faith may test your spiritual vision as much as one location does, partly because of accepted usage and expression, but perhaps primarily because of imprecise English translations of the Greek text. References to "your faith" are scattered throughout the apostles' writings in English Bibles, so most churchgoers have become accustomed to referring to a believer's walk with God or a Christian's set of beliefs as my faith or your faith or his or her faith, as if my faith might be different from your faith or from any other member's faith. However, in the Greek text of the Bible, there is only one faith—the faith of the Son of God. Any faith other than THE faith is not really faith at all, but only an unfounded trust or a blind belief in whatever one might imagine to be true. Any faith other than THE faith of Jesus Christ is dead faith.

Only one faith was once delivered to the saints, (Jude 3) and any faith outside the one faith cannot fulfill the will of God. We cannot rely on our own faith or our own beliefs to gain God's acceptance. We must trust entirely in the one faith of the Son of God to direct our actions and produce good works in our lives, so the work of the whole body can be pleasing to God. God unites each member with every other member of a church and each church with every other church, as He unites us all in one unified Church. One of the vital unifying factors is the one faith of Jesus Christ.

> There is one body, and one Spirit, even as ye are called in one hope of your calling; one Lord, **one faith**, one baptism, (Eph 4:4-5)

The uselessness of our own faith occasionally becomes apparent in our English translations, particularly when the word faith is not being modified by a genitive pronoun. In a familiar example Paul described how his physical life was no longer under his own control, but that now the faith of the Son of God directed his life. Paul wanted us to know the one faith of Jesus Christ directs all believers.

> I am crucified [to] Christ: nevertheless I live; yet not I, but Christ liveth in me: and **the life which I now live in the flesh I live by the faith of the Son of God**, who loved me, and gave himself for me. (Gal 2:20)

Paul used his own life in Christ as an example of how the one faith directed his life, because he couldn't be absolutely sure anyone else was living by the faith of the Son of God. Likewise, the one faith of Jesus Christ directs the lives of all the faithful in Christ. Each of us lives as a slave in Christ's body, so we all take direction from Him. He directs us by His faith, so we all walk according to the same faith, live by the same standard and avoid schisms in the body. There can be no division in the body, so we cannot be directed by our own faith or by a church leader's faith. Each of us must be directed by the one faith of Jesus Christ.

Each of us has been crucified with Christ and buried in a watery grave, where we are spiritually dead on earth, yet we live in heaven in Him. Our new life in Christ is completely under His direction. We have relinquished control over our bodies on earth, and now the Lord is our Head. Since we are living in heaven in Him, we are no longer in charge of our physical bodies on earth, because He has taken our place as the Head of our physical lives through Covenant with God. He is directing everything we do through the Spirit. Wherever each of us might be on earth, He can be seen walking and talking through each of us, and we are living and growing together into a new spiritual body for Him in heaven. He directs every action of our bodies on earth, and the means by which He directs us is His very own faith. He cannot depend on any of us using our own faith, because our own faith is useless. The body of Christ can only please God and accomplish His purposes when a single faith directs it, and that faith is the faith of the Son of God. The one faith of the Son of God is the means by which God is testing us to see if we are willing to yield to His will in our lives.

Unfortunately, mistranslation has led many of us to believe that God is testing our faith. Such testing would be an exercise in futility, because human faith has been tested since the Garden of Eden and found to be completely useless to God, so God sent His Son and tested Him to see if He would be faithful to carry out the Father's will. Jesus passed the test, so now His faith is the standard by which God tests each of us. Our faith is not being tested. We are.

> Knowing this, that **the trying of your faith** worketh patience. (James 1:3)

Two identical phrases in the epistles of James and Peter were mistranslated the same way and have errantly led Bible students to believe "the trying of your faith" might produce patience or other spiritual fruit. (Jas 1:3, 1 Pet 1:7) Each compound phrase includes a noun of action (gerund), "trying;" a genitive pronoun, "of you;" and a genitive phrase, "of the faith." Literally, this compound phrase reads "the trying of you of the faith." A detailed explanation of the grammar of this phrase could be tedious for those who might be grammatically challenged, but suffice it to say, the genitive pronoun (of you) acts as an accusative and indicates the object of the testing, and the genitive phrase (of the faith) is a normal genitive and indicates the agent of the testing. The object of the testing is "you," and the agent of the testing is "the faith." Regrettably, these relationships have not been accurately conveyed to English readers. Among several possible literal translations, "your testing by the faith" is concise, flows fairly well and accurately reflects the relationships asserted by James and Peter. God wants us to know that He is testing us—that He is testing Christ's body—and that He uses the one faith of Jesus Christ to accomplish that purpose.

The faith of Jesus Christ reflects a single standard through which we are all tested and by which we all live. There are not many faiths in the Church, because there cannot be many standards governing a single living body. Jesus Christ is our Standard, and He is our Law, which applies to each of us equally without respect of persons. The faith of the Son of God unifies the Church under one Law and one Standard of conduct, so each member of the body lives by the same principles of the one faith.

Although the faith of Christ reflects the same principles by which we all should live and the one faith of Christ directs each of us in our daily walk with Him, the faith of Christ applies to each of us uniquely and produces unique actions in each unique member of the body. The faith of Christ remains constant and unchanging, just as laws or principles of conduct remain constant and unchanging, but the one faith speaks to each of us differently, because each of us is a unique member of the body and each of us has a unique role to fulfill in the body. Faith may direct me differently than it may direct you, but the same faith directs each of us. Faith will not direct any of us to sin, but, within the limits of permitted activity, the one faith of the Son of God directs each of us differently.

Since the one faith of Christ directs all of us, personal faith does not exist in the sense that different members of the Church might possess his or her personal faith or live by a different standard of conduct. Personal faith is a function of the one faith, so one member cannot possess his or her own personal faith apart from the other members. The Greek language expresses our relationship to faith differently than the translators have expressed it in English Bibles, so our perception of our relationship to faith has been completely distorted in the English-speaking community. God did not inspire the apostles to describe faith as "my" faith or "your" faith, as if we might each possess a different faith, but He inspired them to express faith as "concerning" each of us. In the Greek text personal faith is a function of the genitive case of the pronoun rather than the possessive case, so I am not directed by "my faith" and you are not directed by "your faith," but rather I am directed by "the faith of me" and you are directed by "the faith of you." Each of us is directed by THE faith, but we are directed by the faith which concerns each of us uniquely, because each of us has a unique responsibility to fulfill in the body. We accomplish a wide variety of purposes, but unity is constantly maintained in the body, because there is only one Law—one Standard—one faith in the unified body of Jesus Christ.

One Bread

Baptism and communion are the only rituals correctly associated with Christianity, but neither is required for salvation. Members participate in them voluntarily. They are essentially a bath and a meal, the former being a sign of initiation into a church and the latter being a continuing sign of membership in the church. Unlike the rituals of many religions, these practices are common to all of mankind, so they cannot be effectively mimicked or stereotyped to bring ridicule or shame upon the Christian community.

Communion is very simple in its practice, yet it has profound meaning for all those who participate in it. The Lord reduced the Passover meal of the old covenant to its essential elements of bread and wine in order to symbolically picture the union of the Church in Christ. Communion is the means by which a member associates him or herself spiritually with a church. The whole congregation becomes united together as one bread in Christ. Communion unites each member who participates in it with every other member of the church who participates in it. The whole congregation becomes united as one bread in the Lord.

> The cup of blessing which we bless, is it not the communion of the blood of Christ? The bread which we break, is it not the communion of the body of Christ? For we being many are **one bread**, and one body: for we are all partakers of that **one bread**.
> (1 Cor 10:16-21)

The inseparable unity of the Church is once again pictured by a substance which has unmistakable integrity. There is no division in a loaf of bread. It is a simple analogy, but many miss the point, because they attempt to imagine how a church could possibly be one bread physically. Consequently, the analogy is either relegated to a figurative interpretation or limited in its scope to only picture each member united with Christ as a separate individual. A church may even attempt to create the appearance of physical unity through congregational participation in certain rituals. The complete spiritual picture that each faithful member of the church becomes united to every other member in Christ is often lost.

The reality of a congregation united together as one bread is a spiritual reality, not a physical reality. A congregation can never become one bread physically, because each member is a separate individual. We will need to depend upon the spiritual vision of the word of God through faith to see all the members united together by the Spirit as one bread in Christ. The one bread of communion pictures the one, unified, spiritual Church living in Christ in heaven.

Since participation in communion is voluntary and scripture does not prescribe it nor the time and manner in which it is observed, God holds each believer responsible to determine whether he or she should participate in communion with any given fellowship. In the first century, the churches led by the apostles could safely depend upon their capable leadership and sound instruction in the word, so that one might safely take communion with any of the first century congregations; however, today you must choose carefully with whom you participate in the symbols of fellowship. It is very unwise to casually "church-hop" and take communion wherever you might find fellowship. When you participate in communion, you must always be careful not to share communion with an individual you know is living in sin. If you share the symbols of communion with an individual who is an adulterer or a liar or a drunkard or a thief or with an individual who is participating in any lifestyle sin, you unite yourself spiritually with that sinner and risk the same destruction the sinner may suffer. (Matt 5:29-30) As a faithful believer, you must walk circumspectly and avoid taking communion with reprobate believers who have become sinners once again. If a church allows any sinner to remain in the congregation, you should arrange to celebrate communion privately and only with faithful members of the body of Christ.

The unity of communion goes beyond simple togetherness and implies a duty and responsibility to the members of the church. As members of the spiritual body, we are responsible to fellowship together as brothers and sisters. (Heb 10:25) We are to love one another, (John 13:34) and provide for one another. (Matt 25:34-40) We are particularly encouraged to know those who lead and serve in the congregation. (1 Thess 5:12) Leaders are specifically responsible to encourage, exhort and admonish us in our walk together with the Lord, (Titus 2:15) but each of us bears a personal responsibility to acknowledge our own sins (Jas 5:16) and forgive the sins of others.

(Matt 6:14-15) We have also been charged to provoke one another to love and good works (Heb 10:24) as well as rebuke those who are sinning in the congregation. (Tim 5:20) Salvation depends upon the diligence of all the members to prevent lifestyle sin from dividing a church into a holy loaf and an unholy loaf. We must remain one holy loaf of bread in God's eyes.

We remain one bread and one body by keeping lifestyle sin out of our congregation, not by acquiring a uniform set of doctrines or traditions. Rather than a physical uniformity in ritualistic worship, commonality of belief and practice or nearby geographical location, the unity of the body is a spiritual state of being. If the body consisted of members who were all uniformly gifted or held an identical practice, the body would be rendered impotent. The members of a body must be a widely diverse group, so we should not be surprised that all the unique members contribute a wide variety of gifts, talents, experiences and perspectives to flavor the one loaf of bread—the one, united, spiritual Church.

One Salvation

Although salvation depends on each of us maintaining a holy, faithful relationship with God, none of us will receive the gift of eternal life alone. Contrary to popular belief, salvation is not a matter between you and God alone. Salvation depends on unity. We must all be part of the one nation—part of the one virgin Church—part of the one spiritual body of Christ. Just as communion pictures the one spiritual loaf of bread, none will receive salvation apart from the faithful members of the body of Christ. Paul admonished the Corinthian church to value every member of the body, not only because every function is necessary, but because there is only one salvation. Salvation for each member depends upon the salvation of the whole congregation.

> Know ye not that they which run in a race run all, but **one receiveth the prize**? So run, that ye may obtain. (1 Cor 9:24)

There is only one salvation, because only one holy nation—one spiritual body—one unified Church will win the prize. Only one, undefiled, virgin Church will be united to Jesus Christ in marriage.

Each faithful church will be united by the Spirit to every other faithful church, so that one united Church will obtain salvation in Jesus Christ when He returns to receive us unto Himself. Salvation for one member is not possible apart from the body or without the other faithful members of a church.

One of the most destructive lies extant in mainstream Christian culture is the assertion that believers will become independent, self-directed spirit beings in the kingdom of God. Such a teaching undermines the concept of a united Church and implicitly absolves members of their biblical responsibility to one another. When a member views his salvation as a matter between himself and God alone, he is far less likely to become personally involved in other members' lives or willing to confront a member about questionable practices. Members invariably defer to church authorities to resolve matters of discipline, and the instructions of the Lord for problem resolution (Matt 18:15-17) are abandoned in favor of the rules set forth by the church organization. We cannot obey laws of God and the rules of men. Only those churches living by the laws of God will win the race. The race we are running is a race between churches, not a race between individual members. It is a race only one spiritual Church will win. Unless your church is a spiritual church united by the Spirit to every other spiritual church, your entire church is in danger of loosing the race.

God is only saving one body now. Jesus Christ only needs one body to be complete. Only one united Church of holy slaves will participate in the marriage supper of the Lamb. Anybody can build a church building, but only those churches which are holy—only those churches enslaved to Jesus Christ—only those churches free from human rulership and authority will win the race and be saved as part of the one, united, spiritual Church.

One Government

Human organizations require human governments, so physical churches organized by men will be governed by men. The common perception of physical churches will blind most churchgoers to the spiritual nature of Church government. Spiritual vision is required to see that God has not arranged His churches in hierarchical order or ordained men to direct them through human reason, but that God lives in us and governs faithful churches through theocracy.

Earlier in this chapter (pp. 180-181) I explained that a physical, temporal body of Christ no longer exists and that no church today can be described as a physical body of Christ. Since the Church is entirely spiritual and there is no physical aspect to the Church, it should be at least intuitively true that a church cannot be governed by human beings. The Church has been set in the heavenly places in Jesus Christ (Eph 2:6) where human beings have no ability to control its members or to organize its members. God has set the members in the body of Christ as it has pleased Him, (1 Cor 12:18) and He governs the Church through theocracy. The Father rules the Church, Jesus Christ is the Head of the Church, and the Holy Spirit empowers the Church to live according to the laws of God and obey the directions of the Lord. The theocracy of God governs the Church apart from human intervention.

In spite of the spiritual nature of the Church, human beings still assume the right to rule churches and stand in authority in churches, and that corruption has been longstanding in the organized Christian community. Very early in church history, the apostle Peter was alleged to have been the first authority in the church, and Jesus' words in Matthew have been misinterpreted to assert that the Church was built upon Peter. We encountered this verse earlier, but we need to focus on a different aspect of Jesus' statement.

> And I [Jesus] say also unto thee, That thou art **Peter**, and upon this **rock** I will build my church; and the gates of hell shall not prevail against it. (Matt 16:18)

Bible students who only read English or only have a superficial understanding that the Greek word for Peter and the Greek word for rock are related words might assume that Jesus said He would build His Church upon Peter or that Peter would be the cornerstone of the Church, but those who read Greek do not get that impression at all. Although related, the Greek words for Peter and rock convey very different meanings. The Greek name for Peter is *Petros*, and the Greek word for rock is *petra*. *Petros* and *petra* should not be confused or assumed to mean the same thing. *Petros* is a piece of rock, and *petra* is a mass of rock. Peter's name describes a piece of rock which has been broken from a larger crag, while Jesus said He would build His Church on a whole, unbroken mass of rock.

In this verse Jesus referred to Himself as the massive, unbroken Rock upon Whom the Church is being built. In other verses Christ is described as a stone (1Pet 2:8) or as the stone the builders rejected, (Luke 20:17) but every reference to the One upon Whom the Church is being built is always in terms of an unbroken rock or whole stone. Peter was a part of the foundation of the Church, and he played a significant role in the history of the Church as an apostle to Israel, the author of two epistles and perhaps vicariously one gospel, but Christ alone is the unbroken Rock upon Whom the Church rests.

The rock, or cornerstone, of a building determines the entire character of the building. When the cornerstone is plumb, level and square, the entire building will be true. Peter was part of the foundation of the Church, but he was not the cornerstone upon which the Church was built. Peter was a human being. Peter made mistakes. (Matt 26:73-75; Gal 2:11-13) Peter's character was not plumb, level and square. The Church could not be built upon Peter. Peter and the other apostles along with the Old Testament prophets played key roles in the foundation of the Church, but scripture fails to reveal that Peter or the other apostles even held any positions of authority over the first century churches. Indeed the prophets were already dead, so the question of delegated authority among the prophets is moot. The apostles fulfilled their roles to support the Church, but the sole Authority in the Church is Jesus Christ Himself. He alone is the Head of the Church and the Cornerstone of faith.

> Now therefore ye are no more strangers and foreigners, but fellowcitizens with the saints...And [ye] are **built upon the foundation of the apostles and prophets, Jesus Christ himself being the chief corner stone;** (Eph 2:19-20)

Jesus Christ is the Rock—the Cornerstone—the unbroken Cliff upon Whom the entire Church is being built. He is the Head, the Chief Leader and the Commander of the Church. His role as the perfectly placed Cornerstone insures the character and integrity of the entire building of God. God is not building a physical building. He is building a spiritual house in which He can dwell. He cannot build anything spiritual on a man. The Church is the living temple of God, and He is building it upon Jesus Christ.

The reality of the Church as one body confirms the supremacy of Christ and the equality of all members in the Church. Among the various descriptions Jesus used in his teaching and the apostles used in their writings, the body is the most fitting description of both the function and government of the Church. This analogy pervades the New Testament and more clearly conveys the nature of the Church and the nature of Church government than any other analogy.

God inspired Paul to write in considerable detail about the body, so His people would know how a church should function. Once again, I encourage you to become familiar with the entire chapter of 1 Corinthians 12. The general subject is the equipping of each member for service in the body. God places each member in the body where He wills, and the Spirit distributes gifts to each of the members, so each member can fulfill God's purpose in the body.

God is creating a spiritual body for His Son, typed by the physical body Jesus had when He walked the earth in the first century. Every living body God has ever created works the same way, so one might expect that this new body God is creating will function the same way as every other body He has ever created. Indeed Paul seems to be describing a spiritual body which functions exactly like my physical body functions.

I will compare the various functions of my physical body to the functions of the spiritual body described by Paul in 1 Cor 12, so you can see the parallel. The many members of my body are one body; likewise, Paul said the members of the Church are one body. (v. 20) Each member of my body is designed to perform a special function; likewise, Paul said each member of the body receives special gifts. (v. 11) The function of my heart is very important, but my skin, my liver and my many glands are no less necessary for good health; likewise, Paul explained at length that no function of the spiritual body is more or less necessary, but that some functions are more important. (vs. 21-31) My body has some parts which are pleasing in appearance, but the others God has hidden within my body; likewise, Paul said some members of the body are more comely than others. (vs. 23-24) Each member of my body is unique; likewise, Paul said each member is a member in particular. (v. 27) There are no racial, sexual or social distinctions among the members of my body; likewise, Paul said there is neither male nor female, bond or free, Jews or Gentiles among the members of the Church. (Gal 3:28)

I am uniquely the head of my physical body; likewise, Paul said the Church has only one Head. (Col 1:18)

This description of the spiritual body God is creating for His Son exactly parallels the nature of your body or my body in the way the members are uniquely equipped, the way each member is needed, the way some perform more critical functions, and the way the whole body is unified. Since the analogy holds true in respect to gifts, necessity, importance and integrity, we should expect that the analogy also holds true in respect to governance. If the analogy of the body is a valid analogy, God must govern the Church in the same manner that a physical body is governed.

> And [Jesus Christ] is the head of the body, the church: (Col 1:18)

The human spirit living in a physical body is its head, and the divine Spirit living in a spiritual body is its Head. Jesus Christ is the divine Spirit living in the Church, so Paul confidently explained that Jesus Christ is the Head of the Church. Jesus Christ has authority over all the members of His spiritual body, just as I have authority over all the members of my physical body. He directly controls the members of His body, just as I directly control the members of my body. Clearly, the analogy holds true for governance.

In Paul's simple statement he addresses both the nature and government of the Church. Paul describes the Church as a body, and he tells us the body has a Head. This description of the Church helps us understand that the spiritual body functions like a physical body and is governed like a physical body. The Church is a spiritual body with one spiritual Head, Jesus Christ.

In my body I am the head and director of each and every member of my body. The members of my body do exactly what I direct them to do, because I live in every member. I do not direct my leg through my arm or my ear through my mouth. I do not direct any member through another member, because each member is unique. There is only one head (that's me) in my body, and there is no hierarchical structure in my body. None of the members of my body has authority over other members of my body. I am the head and sole director of the members of my body.

The spiritual body God is creating for His Son is a living body, just as our physical bodies are living bodies, so we should not be surprised that the Church is governed in exactly the same way your body or my body is governed. Jesus Christ is the Head of His body, which is the Church, and He directs His body the same way I direct my body. Each member of His body is a unique individual, so He gives each member of His body individual and personal direction. He does not direct one member of a church through another member of the church. There is no hierarchical structure or member-run government in the body of Christ. No member has authority over another member of Christ's body. Scripture does not designate members as heads in the body. Jesus Christ is the only Head, and He directs each member of the Church individually, because He lives in each member personally.

> I am crucified with Christ: nevertheless I live; yet not
> I, but **Christ liveth in me**: (Gal 2:20)

Paul used his own life in Covenant with God to explain that his human spirit was dead on earth and that now "Christ liveth in me" as his Head and Director. Likewise, the spirit of every faithful member is dead on earth, and the Lord is now directing the activities of those members. This covenant reality has profound implications for the nature of church government. If the Lord is in charge of each of our physical lives, no member can even be in authority over his or her own life, let alone be in authority over another member.

In the mid twentieth century a best-selling book popularized the expression "Jesus is my copilot," and even yet today T-shirts, bumper stickers and license plate frames continue to perpetuate the misconception that such might be true. Sadly the concept is not true. Jesus is not our copilot. He is our Pilot. He has replaced each of us as heads in our physical bodies, because we have died on earth, and now we live in heaven in Him. The covenant relationship makes it so. While we are living in heaven in Him, He is living on earth in each of us as our Head and Director. We have no need for human direction, because our Head lives in each of us and directs each of us from within. One member cannot exercise authority over another member, because Jesus Christ will not allow any human being to be in authority over Himself.

There is a constant struggle in the Christian community over the correct structure of church government. Churches sometimes divide because they cannot agree. Theologians and Bible historians have searched the scriptures in vain to find the scriptural government of God for churches, and they have failed to find it, not because it is not there, but because they have been looking for a church structure which includes human authorities rather than looking for the theocracy of God. They have failed to find it, because there is no human governmental structure in the Church. The Church is a body, not an organization. A spiritual church must have a spiritual government. The government of God is not physical, and it is not external. The government of God provides spiritual direction from within us. Our Boss lives in each of us.

Although from a physical point of view, individual members still live and operate in the world, God has called the collective Church out of the world, and it does not participate in world affairs or in the lifestyle of the world. The Church cannot be arranged according to the structure of worldly governments or organizations. Each member is placed in the Church as it has pleased God. (1 Cor 12:18) The Church lives in heaven under the government of God, and Paul described the government of God in all its fullness in his letter to the Corinthian church.

> But I would have you know, that the head of every man is Christ; and the head of the woman is the man; and the head of Christ is God. (1 Cor 11:3)

God the Father is sovereign and Head over all. Jesus Christ is the Head of every member of the Church, and every man is the head of his wife. That's all there is to the government of God in the Church. God and Christ are one. Christ and every man are one. A man and his wife are one. All are one in Christ. There is no hierarchical structure or external government for the body of Christ.

The Church does not live in this world, so it is not possible for human governments to rule over the Church. The Church lives in Jesus Christ in heaven, so it is not possible for any man to stand in authority in the Church. Although the individual members of a church live in the world and God requires each of us, as individuals, to subject ourselves to the rulership and authority of human governments, the Church, as a unified spiritual body, may never submit to the rulership of any human government or to the authority of any human being. The government of God must direct every congregation at all times. When men rule or stand in authority in a church, they create division and they destroy the unity of the church, because no one can serve two masters. (Matt 6:24) God must always rule every church, and Jesus Christ must always direct the actions of every church. Every congregation must reject human rulership, and every congregation must reject human authority in order to be part of the one spiritual Church, which alone possesses salvation and always remains united, holy and free.

Responsibilities of a Local Church

Freedom, holiness and salvation are among the many gifts of God. We cannot earn them or maintain them. When we respond to the call of the Father to the Son and acknowledge our lost and sinful state, God extends His grace and places the faith of Jesus Christ in us. The blood of Jesus Christ justifies us before God, and the indwelling of the Holy Spirit makes us holy before God. God sets us in the heavenly places in Jesus Christ, where the perfect Law of liberty frees us from the rulership and authority of men and sets us on the path of freedom toward salvation. We are free to follow the Law of God and depend entirely upon the faith of Jesus Christ to direct every step we take. Every deed we do is a good deed, because His faith is directing every deed we are doing. We may sin various sins from time to time, but the blood of Christ immediately removes every incidental sin we might commit, and we remain holy and blameless before God continually. The indwelling of the Holy Spirit has made each church holy, and the blood of Christ maintains the holiness of the churches at all times. We cannot attain or maintain these blessings by our own works or by the direction of men. Freedom, holiness and salvation are entirely the work of God.

While freedom, holiness and salvation are gifts of God and we can do nothing to achieve or maintain them, God does not guarantee them without contingency. We must work out our own salvation with fear and trembling. (Phil 2:12) Each of us plays a role to retain these blessings. God will not allow anybody to take our freedom, holiness or salvation away from us, but God does not take our free moral agency away from us either. Each of us must continually make decisions as we walk the path of freedom, and we must continually choose to rely on the faith of Jesus Christ to direct every step we take. We must continually choose freedom, holiness and salvation. We must hold on to them, because they can slip out of our hands. We should not neglect them. (Heb 2:1-3) We must diligently listen as the Lord speaks to us through the Spirit and act according to the faith of the Son of God, so we do not fall away from God's blessings. (Heb 6:4-6) We cannot achieve salvation by what we do, but we may indeed loose salvation because of what we may be doing. We cannot attain freedom on our own, but we may loose our freedom, if we are living on our own. We cannot maintain our holiness, but we may loose our holiness, if we are acting in an unholy manner. Our actions will never gain us any gift of God, but our repeated actions in defiance of the Spirit may cause us to forfeit the gifts which God only promises to faithful believers.

A simple belief that God exists is insufficient to attain freedom, maintain holiness or guarantee salvation. We must demonstrate our belief by the way we live our lives. Even demons believe, (Jas 2:19) but their faith results in nothing from God, because their actions demonstrate that they are living in unbelief. Similarly, we cannot say we believe in God and then live our lives as if we do not believe. Faith without works is dead. (Jas 2:17-26) Works do not produce salvation, but, if our works are mixed with lifestyle sin, God can plainly see that we are living in unbelief in spite of what we might say. We may sin from time to time, but the faith of Jesus Christ working in us will always direct us away from lifestyle sin.

The presence of the Holy Spirit in us and the faith of Jesus Christ working through us demands we continually move away from sin in our lives. We will never become sinless, but we must always grow in grace, as we continually align our lives to the standard of the faith of Jesus Christ. We need do nothing more than accept God's gifts and allow Him to maintain them in our lives, but we have a responsibility to avoid sin and to confess any sin we may discover in our lives, either individually or collectively. As we avoid sin and confess sin, we contribute to the holiness of a church by what we are not doing. When we avoid sin, we are acting according to faith, and, when we confess sin, we stop sin immediately. As long as we do not sin repeatedly, we do not threaten our own holiness or the holiness of a church. Christ's blood has removed every sin, but unrecognized or unconfessed sin tends to be repeated, and repeated sin threatens the holiness of an individual member as well as the holiness of the whole congregation. No sin of any sort may continue to exist in a holy church. God has charged each of us to listen to the Spirit and diligently heed the Word, so we can recognize and confess our own sin, admonish others to avoid incidental sins and humbly expose and rebuke the lifestyle sins of other members. (1 Tim 5:20) Christians retain holiness by not participating in lifestyle sins of unbelief. Christians retain holiness by what we are not doing.

The responsibility to avoid sin and stop sin not only applies to each of us introspectively, but each of us has a responsibility as a watchman to insure that sin does not continue in other members of the congregation. Each of us is united with the other members, and the sinful state of one member is offending every member of the body. Just as cancer rapidly spreads in a physical body and threatens the life of the whole body, so also lifestyle sin spreads in a spiritual body and threatens the freedom, holiness and salvation of the entire congregation. Lifestyle sin cannot remain in a holy church.

Jesus Himself outlined the proper way to resolve conflicts and to approach an ignorant or unrepentant member of the congregation to do our part to retain the holiness of our church. His formula initially protects the privacy of the offending member, but it gradually increases peer pressure until the whole congregation becomes involved. If congregational rebuke produces a confession, the integrity of the church can be maintained and the congregation can remain holy, but, if the offending member maintains an unrepentant attitude, particularly in the face of congregational agreement and admonition, further correction is useless, and the brother or sister must be considered to be an unbeliever.

> Moreover if thy brother shall trespass against thee, go and tell him his fault between thee and him alone: if he shall hear thee, thou hast gained thy brother. But if he will not hear thee, then take with thee one or two more, that in the mouth of two or three witnesses every word may be established. And if he shall neglect to hear them, tell it unto the church: but if he neglect to hear the church, let him be unto thee as an heathen man and a publican. (Matt 18:15-17)

When a member becomes a heathen and a publican, he or she has become a sinner once again. The inability to recognize a sin in the face of congregational agreement and rebuke indicates the member may be standing against the Spirit to hinder the resolution of the problem. The initial sin may have been an incidental sin, but an unrepentant attitude is a lifestyle sin. The member's recalcitrance indicates that he or she may have entered a state of unbelief and that the member is offending the congregation.

As individual Christians, we all sin, and the blood of Christ removes every sin, but when a member commits a sin repeatedly or continually, that member is offending the congregation. The church becomes spotted and defiled when a member sins continually. Those members of the church who engage in lifestyle sin must be cut off from the church, so the blood of Christ can cleanse the church and maintain its spiritual garments without spot or wrinkle. Jesus used the analogy of the body to describe how the church should remove offending members from the church, and He warned the members of impending danger to the whole congregation, if they fail to remove lifestyle sin from their fellowship.

> And if thy right eye [is offending] thee, pluck it out, and cast it from thee: for it is profitable for thee that one of thy members should perish, and not that thy whole body should be cast into hell. And if thy right hand [is offending] thee, cut it off, and cast it from thee: for it is profitable for thee that one of thy members should perish, and not that thy whole body should be cast into hell. (Matt 5:29-30)

A correct interpretation of this passage is of vital importance, because every organized church misinterprets Jesus' words. He did not speak figuratively about cutting off a physical hand or removing a physical eye when a person might have sinned with his hand or his eye, but Jesus applied the analogy spiritually to explain that individual members of a church who are sinning and offending the congregation must be literally plucked out and cut off from the church in order for the church to remain holy and spotless. If the member who is the eye of the church is sinning, the church must remove its eye. If the member who is the right hand is sinning, the church must cut off its right hand. These words of Jesus constitute a stern admonition to every congregation that a church should not allow lifestyle sin to continue among its members. Do not miss the obvious implication of this statement. A congregation which allows lifestyle sin to remain in its midst will be cast into hell, and the whole congregation will loose its salvation.

A holy church cannot allow spiritual cancer to remain among the members, and a holy member should not continue to associate with sinning members. When lifestyle sin is recognized in any member, those with the spiritual vision to judge righteous judgment must rebuke the member before the entire congregation. (1 Tim 5:20) When the congregation agrees that the member is sinning and the member fails to respond positively to congregational admonition, the faithful members must spotlight the member's sinning by refusing to fellowship or even eat a meal with that member. Our love for our own spiritual body—for our own congregation—for the Church as a whole—demands we remove ourselves from offensive members and no longer keep company with them.

> But now I have written unto you **not to keep company**, if any man that is called a brother be a fornicator, or covetous, or an idolater, or a railer, or a drunkard, or an extortioner; **with such an one no not to eat**. (1 Cor 5:11)

Notice carefully that Paul advises faithful members to withdraw themselves from a brother, if he BE a fornicator, not necessarily from a brother who has only committed a single act of fornication. We examined the difference between these two types of statements in chapter 6. One who has become a fornicator has changed his nature by committing repeated acts of fornication. One has become a drunkard only after repeated drunkenness. One has become a thief only after many robberies. We must withdraw ourselves from members whose nature has changed because of lifestyle sin. Faithful members of a congregation must disassociate themselves from any member who repeatedly exhibits the same sin. Faithful members may not continue to associate themselves with members who repeatedly engage in adultery, fornication, covetousness, slander, lying, drunkenness, or any other repeated sin. Faithful believers are required to exercise this minimal responsibility to avoid the outward appearance of evil and to separate ourselves from those who have become overtly wicked through the practice of lifestyle sin.

> Therefore put away from among yourselves that wicked person. (1 Cor 5:13)

We should not be surprised that Paul's direction for disciplinary action in a church is similar to God's direction for Israel regarding capital matters. (Deut 17:7) The whole congregation was involved. The whole congregation stoned the offender. We do not literally put members to death as Israel did, but removing a member from fellowship typifies the spiritual death of the member. Such an action should be carefully considered to insure the member is truly guilty of a lifestyle sin. From time to time the sins of high ranking church leaders make headlines, and the nation is shocked to learn that these highly respected men might have committed adultery, embezzled from a church, used illegal drugs or any one of a number of sins a lay member might commit without any public notice. Yet those of high rank in the organized Christian community frequently loose their responsibilities and may even be expelled from their church for nothing more than a single sin. However, in a church led by the Spirit, members may not be removed for a single indiscretion. A church has no right to take disciplinary action against a member for one transgression. Only lifestyle sin must be quickly removed from a congregation, and the whole congregation must be informed and participate in the removal of the offending member. There is no provision in the Bible for unilateral action by either a pastor or other denominational leaders. Matthew 18:17 plainly states that a matter must come before the church—all the members—the whole body, not just the leadership. Church leaders have no biblical authority to disfellowship a member. When an assembly of the entire church recognizes the sin, such congregational agreement is evidence that the member has been judged by Jesus Christ Himself, and faithful members must withdraw themselves from the offending member and refuse to share a meal, particularly communion, with that person. Having fulfilled Paul's direction to stop sin and avoid the outward appearance of evil in the local congregation, God assumes the responsibility to deal with the unrepentant individual spiritually.

Although God ultimately removes an individual from the spiritual body, each member has the responsibility to do his or her part to avoid or stop sin so that the local church can remain a pure and chaste virgin without spot or wrinkle for the Lord. Paul gave this direction in the context of one man's sinning, but we may also apply it more broadly to fellowships and churches. A faithful believer must also remove him or herself spiritually from a congregation which allows overt lifestyle sin to dwell among its members. A faithful believer should not associate with a sinning church.

The standards requiring remedial action toward an individual and remedial action toward a congregation are somewhat different, because individuals live in the world, but the church does not. We should clearly understand the difference between the responsibilities of a church as part of the body of Christ and the responsibilities of each member of a church regarding civil government. There is a difference between a church's relationship to civil government and a member's relationship to civil government. Scriptures abound which make it very clear that every soul—each individual member living in the world—is required to be subject to civil authority, unless that direction contravenes the laws of God.

> Let every soul be subject unto the higher [authorities]. For there is no [authority] but of God: the [authorities] that be are ordained of God. Whosoever therefore resisteth the [authority], resisteth the ordinance of God: and they that resist shall receive to themselves damnation. (Rom 13:1-2)

Paul did not address the church as a whole in this statement, but he specifically addresses each individual church member in this admonition to the Roman church. "Every soul" must be subject to the civil authorities. As long as we are physical human beings, God requires that individual members must all respect the civil rulers and authorities and submit to the laws of the land. Each member living in the world must be subject to civil government. However, we must carefully heed—we must make no mistake—we must clearly understand that God does not permit the collective body of a church to be subject to any human government or civil authority. Churches may never become unequally yoked with unbelievers.

> **Be ye not unequally yoked together with unbelievers:** for what fellowship hath righteousness with unrighteousness? and what communion hath light with darkness? and what concord hath Christ with Belial? or what part hath [the believing] with [the disbelieving]? and what agreement hath the temple of God with idols? for ye are the temple of the living God; as God hath said, I will dwell in them, and walk in them; and I will be their God, and they shall be my people. **Wherefore come out from among them, and be ye separate,** saith the Lord, **and do not [attach yourselves to] the unclean;** and I will receive you, and will be a Father unto you, and ye shall be my sons and daughters, saith the Lord Almighty. (2 Cor 6:14-18)

Christians who individually employ these words as a principle of life might avoid the multitude of difficulties which can arise from entering into marriages and partnerships with the unbelievers of the world, but Paul's words were not directed specifically to individual believers. Notice Paul's use of the plural pronoun, "ye," which refers to the entire congregation as the temple of God. Paul's directive is not for "every soul," as it was regarding civil authority, but He spoke to the collective membership of the church as a body with an imperative verb and an explicit negative. Paul's directive absolutely forbids a church to be unequally yoked with unbelievers. Paul admonished the church to be completely separate from the world.

Unlike the individual members of a church, we have seen with our spiritual vision that the one unified Church comprised of every faithful congregation lives in heaven, not on earth. (Eph 1:3, 2:6) We may individually make agreements, sign contracts and enter into covenants with anyone in the world, but God prohibits such activities for a church. Congregations and fellowships may not make covenants with the rulers and leaders of the world or with its citizens. Just as God did not allow Israel to enter into covenants with the heathen people or with their gods, so also God does not allow a church to make any covenant with unbelievers or with their rulers. A church may have no communion—no covenant—no agreement with the unbelievers of the world.

Consequently, faithful Christians must also withdraw from churches which have become unequally yoked with unbelievers and have entered into covenant agreements with civil governments. We cannot associate ourselves with churches which claim to trust in God but have demonstrated by their actions that they are living in sin and unbelief by making covenants with the rulers of this world. Every congregation should carefully heed Paul's instructions and avoid any relationship with the world.

Complete unity exists now in the one true Church. The faithful of every age have been united together by the Spirit, and we are growing together into one spiritual body for Jesus Christ. He is the Head—the Spirit living in the body—and we are His body—an integral part of His Person. He completes us as our Head, and we complete Him as His body. When God has placed all the members in the body, the Lamb will be complete. The Church presently lives in heaven under the theocracy of God far above any rule, authority or power of men, but, when the body is complete, the Church will reign with Jesus Christ on the earth. (Rev 5:10)

When Jesus walked on the earth as a Man, He lived in a unified physical body and He subjected Himself to the laws of Moses and the laws of the Roman Empire. Today His presence is apparent as He walks the earth in each of the physical members of the Church, and He, through the Spirit, likewise submits Himself to human laws, because He requires each of us to submit ourselves to the laws of civil governments and the direction of civil authorities whenever such submission might be required.

However, our Lord Jesus Christ—our resurrected, complete and perfect High Priest in heaven—is no longer subject to the governments of physical nations. He lives in heaven high above human rulers and authorities, and He has overcome the rulers and authorities of this world. He has divested Himself of all human rule, authority and power existing on earth. (Col 2:15) He is only subject to God the Father. Consequently, those of us who live in Him in heaven as members of His spiritual body are likewise free from the oppression of human rulers and authorities. The spiritual Church is free from the laws of earthly governments and the injunctions of human beings. The united Church is only subject to the laws of God. We only take direction from our Lord Jesus Christ.

Similarly, each congregation must exhibit the same freedom and unity granted to the united spiritual Church of heaven by remaining free from earthly governments. Each congregation must remain free from human rulership and authority. A congregation must never become unequally yoked with unbelievers. Each local congregation must carefully guard its virginity and "make no covenant with them or with their gods." (Ex 23:32)

God has unified the Church by one Spirit through one calling to one salvation for one body at one location under one government. The united body of the one true Church has the responsibility to retain the unity of the Church by continually depending on God to supply all its needs. The one spiritual Church remains free by depending on Jesus Christ to direct every action of the body as we walk the path of freedom in holiness, continually growing in the grace of God and in the knowledge of our Lord Jesus Christ.

> I therefore, the prisoner of the Lord, beseech you that ye walk worthy of the vocation wherewith ye are called, with all lowliness and meekness, with long suffering, forbearing one another in love; endeavouring to keep the unity of the Spirit in the bond of peace. There is one body, and one Spirit, even as ye are called in one hope of your calling; one Lord, one faith, one baptism, one God and Father of all, who is above all, and through all, and in you all.
> (Eph 4:1-6)

Chapter 8

The Nature of Church Leadership

True freedom depends on human leadership in a congregation but rejects all ecclesiastical authority of men. Members who enjoy the freedom of the New Covenant seek advice, receive encouragement and admonition, and submit themselves to able church leaders, but faithful believers refuse to obey any leader's command. God has freed us from all prescriptive direction, and faith in Jesus Christ requires us to obey only Him. Respect for godly leaders demands we consider the merit of their suggestions, but we should never consider their suggestions to be commands we should obey. We are responsible to give reasoned consent to able and wise leaders and allow them to persuade us to believe the simple spiritual realities God describes in the Bible, but we only take direction from the Lord. Leaders practice the faith in the congregation as they also obey the Word, but they allow the Head and Commander to direct the activities of every member. Faithful leaders know the Way, go the Way and show the Way, but knowledgeable, considerate and wise church leaders never rule, never command and never force their will upon the members of faithful congregations.

Theologians have equated biblical leadership with authority, but that assumption has contributed to the apostasy of every organized church. Even secular leaders do not always enjoy the privilege to command those they lead. The leader of my hike in the woods may be very capable and well trained, and he may have an intimate knowledge of the terrain where I will be hiking, but his training and knowledge grant him no authority over me at all. I would be wise to follow him very closely, but I am not under his authority. I am not bound to obey any particular command he might give me, nor am I obligated to do exactly what he does. Likewise, we often recognize members of the community for their examples of leadership, but such recognition does not grant them authority over the citizens of the community. The citizens may applaud the leaders' actions, and the citizens may be encouraged to follow their lead, but no one in the community is placed under a community leader's authority simply because that person exhibited leadership in the community. Leadership cannot always be equated with authority.

Scripture specifically tells us leaders existed among the members of first century congregations, but we may not automatically assume those leaders were authorities. We may not assume church leaders possess the authority to command members of a congregation unless God has specifically granted leaders the privilege of authority in the Bible. The Bible implies all authority has been given to Jesus Christ in heaven and in earth, (Matt 28:18) but the Bible does not specifically say Jesus delegated any of His authority to the apostles. If Jesus delegated any of His authority, we should be able to see who received it in scripture or used it to direct the churches.

In the next sections, I would like to focus your attention on a number of English words which always indicate authority and then examine the inspired words in the Greek text to see if they support the English translation. These word studies will not comprise an exhaustive study of the subject, but they will focus on the concepts which form the foundation of authority in organized churches. When the foundation of authority crumbles from our English translations, it should be evident that the whole system of hierarchical church government is destined to collapse. I will examine five words in this study: 1) authority; 2) command; 3) obey; 4) rule; and 5) ordain.

Authority appears in translation from several Greek words, but in most cases *exousia* is the Greek word behind the authority we see in English Bibles, and it is the only Greek word which has the ability to indicate hierarchical authority in scripture. Consider Strong's definition of *exousia*.

NT:1849
exousia (ex-oo-see'-ah); from NT:1832 (in the sense of ability); **privilege**, i.e. (subjectively) force, capacity, competency, freedom, or (objectively) mastery (concretely, magistrate, superhuman, potentate, token of control), delegated influence:

Exousia means "privilege," not necessarily authority. Although it may indicate authority, it cannot always be correctly translated as authority, because the context always determines the nature of the privilege held by an individual. The exact English meaning of *exousia* in any given passage is entirely contextually discerned. The hierarchical concept of authority, as we use it in twenty-first century

American culture, did not exist in a single word in first century Roman culture, although *exousia* is the central concept which may indicate authority as we understand it, particularly if the privilege is associated with certain prepositions such as *hupo*, under, or *huper*, over. When Jesus healed the centurion's servant, we can clearly see that the centurion was vested with authoritative privilege.

> For I also am a man set under authority, (NT:1849) having under me soldiers, and I say unto one, Go, and he goeth; and to another, Come, and he cometh; and to my servant, Do this, and he doeth it. (Luke 7:8)

The centurion was a man set "under privilege," so the translators have correctly concluded that he was under authority, and he also held a position of authority over other soldiers. He exercised the privilege to direct the soldiers under his command to do whatever he needed them to do in order to obey the orders of his superiors. If a church leader possesses a similar privilege to command members of the church, we should find scriptural support for ecclesiastical authority in passages containing the word *exousia*.

Christ's authority in the Church is unquestioned, but the translators have even camouflaged His authority in mistranslation, arbitrarily granting Him all power, even though Jesus explicitly denied having any power of His own. (John 5:30)

> And Jesus came and spake unto them, saying, All **power** (NT:1849) is given unto me in heaven and in earth. (Matt 28:18)

Translators are blind to the plain words of Jesus, which explain to us that Jesus, as the eternal Word, has no power to do anything of Himself. (John 5:30) Power is a function of the Holy Spirit, not the Word. Christ functions as the supreme Authority in the theocracy of God, not the supreme power. The Father expressly granted the Son all privilege, so we may reasonably conclude Jesus Christ has been given all authority in heaven and in earth. If Jesus conferred any of His privilege to the apostles, we should be able to find it within the context of passages using the Greek word *exousia*.

As Jesus was preparing to return to heaven and sit at the right hand of the Father, Jesus gave the disciples an analogy to encourage them to diligently work and watch while He was away. In the analogy the man taking the journey gave privilege to his slaves.

> For the Son of man is as a man taking a far journey, who left his house, and gave [privilege] (NT:1849) to his [slaves], and to every man his work, and commanded the porter to watch. (Mark 13:34)

This analogy plainly states that Jesus gave privilege to His slaves, i.e., believers, but the nature of the privilege is not specifically stated. One could conclude from this rather ambiguous general statement that all believers hold authority, but such an interpretation would seem meaningless. A more reasonable interpretation might be that Jesus gave each slave a specific responsibility and granted each of them a certain privilege which would allow them to fulfill their responsibility. If we scour the New Testament to find all the *exousia*, i.e., privilege, Jesus granted to leaders or members of the churches, we may glean the following list of privileges:

And when he had called unto him his twelve disciples, he gave them [privilege] against unclean spirits, to cast them out, and to heal all manner of sickness and all manner of disease. (Matt 10:1)(also Luke 9:1, 10:19)

Behold, I give unto you [privilege] to tread on serpents and scorpions, and over all the [power] of the enemy: and nothing shall by any means hurt you. (Luke 10:19)

But as many as received him, to them gave he [privilege] to become the sons of God, even to them that believe on his name: (John 1:12)

Have we not [privilege] to eat and to drink? Have we not [privilege] to lead about a sister, a wife, as well as other apostles, and as the brethren of the Lord, and Cephas? Or I only and Barnabas, have not we [privilege] to forbear working? (1 Cor 9:4-6)

For though I should boast somewhat more of our [privilege], which the Lord hath given us for edification, and not for your destruction, I should not be ashamed: (2 Cor 10:8)

Therefore I write these things being absent, lest being present I should use sharpness, according to the [privilege] which the Lord hath given me to edification, and not to destruction. (2 Cor 13:10)

These things speak, and exhort, and rebuke with all [authoritativeness]. Let no man despise thee. (Titus 2:15)

Then laid they their hands on them, and they received the Holy Ghost. And when Simon saw that through laying on of the apostles' hands the Holy Ghost was given, he offered them money, Saying, Give me also this [privilege], that on whomsoever I lay hands, he may receive the Holy Ghost.* (Acts 8:17-19)

* The designated privilege is of questionable merit, because it is based in Simon Megas' personal observation. Several verses state that God gives His Spirit to whom He wills and when He wills, (2 Cor 5:5, 1 John 3:24) regardless of human intervention. In a similar manner, God bestows the gifts of the Spirit. (Eph 4:8-11)

The principles of sound exegesis prevent me from including the ability to give the Holy Spirit among the privileges Jesus granted to church members, but, if I summarize the remaining privileges, or authorities, given to leaders or members of the churches and collect them together, I can glean the following list: 1) privilege to cast out evil spirits; 2) privilege to heal sickness and disease; 3) privilege to tread on serpents and scorpions; 4) privilege over, i.e., authority over, all the power of the enemy; 5) privilege to become the sons of God; 6) privilege to eat and drink, 7) privilege to marry; 8) privilege to forbear working; 9) privilege to edify the church; 10) privilege to speak, exhort and rebuke with authoritativeness.

Since the foregoing list is an exhaustive list of privileges granted in scripture, we can see that church leaders' privilege over members of a church is conspicuously missing from the Bible. Scripture does not grant church leaders any privilege over the members, and it does not indicate that church members are under privilege, as was the centurion. The Greek word, *exousia,* is not used to define the relationship between leaders and members anywhere in the Bible.

Commands in scripture implicitly expose delegated authority, so we should consult the epistles to determine whether the apostles commanded the churches they served. Any apostolic command given to a church should validate apostolic authority from scripture. Of course anyone who has ever studied an English Bible will certainly recall that Paul commanded some of the first century congregations and that his commands at least constitute empirical evidence that the apostles possessed authority over the people and the churches they served. Many of us have read these misleading translations and have intuitively imputed authority to all church leaders, but the Greek text reads differently in every case.

One of the most remarkable verbs in the Greek language is *paraggello*. The English language offers no single word which even remotely approaches the meaning of this authoritative Greek word. *Paraggello* can be very deceptive, if we do not fully understand its Greek meaning. The essential meaning is "to command," but only in a very narrow and specific way. A careful study of authoritative apostolic directions will reveal that every time the apostles commanded the churches or members of the churches, they always used the word *paraggello*.

The Greek verb *paraggello* occurs 30 times in verses scattered throughout the New Testament, including several of Paul's letters, and we might easily misunderstand its intended meaning when this frequently occurring word underlies the English text. Simplistic translation without any marginal notation gives us the illusion of a subservient relationship between the apostles and the members of the churches in our English translations. In each case *paraggello* is translated command, charge or declare largely at the whim of the KJV translators. The Greek word underlying each of these English words is *paraggello*. Carefully observe the literal definition of this remarkable Greek verb.

NT:3853
paraggello (par-ang-gel'-lo); from NT:3844 and the base of NT:32; **to transmit a message,** i.e. (by implication) to enjoin:

Five Greek words carry injunctive force in the Greek New Testament, and four of these five injunctive words virtually disappear from the New Testament after the book of Acts. These four words describe the injunctions of God, Jesus Christ and human rulers and authorities mostly in the gospels and the book of Acts, and then they disappear from the apostles' writings. By contrast *paraggello* is liberally sprinkled throughout the epistles, and Paul frequently used it when he addressed the members of the churches. When the apostles commanded the people of God, they only used the word *paraggello*. This verb and its noun form, *paraggelia*, are the only injunctive words church leaders used to command the members of the first century churches.

If you only read an English translation, you will get the mistaken impression that Paul assumed personal authority to command the churches, but such is not the case. Paul transmitted an authoritative message, but he did not personally command the congregations by his own authority. Those who *paraggello* do not command by their own authority, but they transmit an authoritative message on behalf of another in whom the authority to command is vested. In one verse even the English translation reveals that Paul was not commanding by his own authority, because Paul expressly stated that the One commanding was the Lord, (see 1 Cor 7:10 below) so even those of us who only read this verse in English can see that Paul was simply transmitting a message from Jesus Christ.

Unfortunately, Paul rarely tells us his commands came from the Lord, and English Bibles usually offer "command" to translate *paraggello*, which completely loses the literal sense of this Greek verb. We have no single English word which remotely conveys the Greek concept of *paraggello*. Although "to command" is the essence of the meaning, the true sense of the Greek, "to transmit a message," is always lost in translation. The meaning of *paraggello* is not simply "to command," but it conveys the sense that what has been enjoined has come from an authority not always readily visible in the context. If you look carefully, you might recognize the word "angel" in the middle of the word. The Greek word *aggelos* means messenger. *Paraggello* literally means "to be a messenger near" or to act as an angel or messenger on behalf of one who has authority to command. Thus, when Paul used this word to command the people of God, he was not speaking by his own authority, but on behalf of the Lord. Paul was the messenger, not the commander.

Paraggello is the only verb used by any of the apostles to command the people of God in the epistles to the churches. For an exhaustive list of the thirty verses using *paraggello*, consult a Greek concordance. I have listed here the twelve verses from the epistles which mistakenly imply Paul spoke by his own authority, but the whole concordance list gives additional insight into situations where various men spoke on behalf of a superior. The bolded word(s) in each verse is translated from the Greek word, *paraggello*.

And unto the married I **command**, yet not I, but the Lord, Let not the wife depart from her husband: (1 Cor 7:10)

Now in this that I **declare** unto you I praise you not, that ye come together not for the better, but for the worse. (1 Cor 11:17)

And that ye study to be quiet, and to do your own business, and to work with your own hands, as we **commanded** you; (1 Thess 4:11)

And we have confidence in the Lord touching you, that ye both do and will do the things which we **command** you. (2 Thess 3:4)

Now we **command** you, brethren, in the name of our Lord Jesus Christ, that you withdraw yourselves from every brother that walketh disorderly, and not after the tradition which he received of us. (2 Thess 3:6)

For even when we were with you, this we **commanded** you, that if any would not work, neither should he eat. (2 Thess 3:10)

Now them that are such we **command** and exhort by our Lord Jesus Christ, that with quietness they work, and eat their own bread. (2 Thess 3:12)

As I besought thee to abide still at Ephesus, when I went into Macedonia, that thou **mightest charge** some that they teach no other doctrine, (1 Tim 1:3)

These things **command** and teach. (1 Tim 4:11)

And these things **give in charge**, that they may be blameless. (1 Tim 5:7)

I **give** thee **charge** in the sight of God, who quickeneth all things, and before Christ Jesus, who before Pontius Pilate witnessed a good confession; (1 Tim 6:13)

Charge them that are rich in this world, that they be not highminded, nor trust in uncertain riches, but in the living God, who giveth us richly all things to enjoy; (1 Tim 6:17)

Now that we have a more complete understanding of the meaning of *paraggello*, we can plainly see that apostolic directives based on their own authority vanish from the Bible when we read these verses with an educated perspective. There are no examples anywhere in the New Testament of any church leader unilaterally commanding the churches, except for Jesus Himself. The Lord is our Commander, and men have no vested authority to command in the body of Christ.

The noun, *paraggelia*, a mandate or command, is derived from the verb above and carries the same connotation as *paraggello*. *Paraggelia* is the command itself—the authoritative mandate of an authority, which was transmitted by a messenger, who may or may not have been vested with authority of his own. Verses using either of these two Greek words cannot validate ecclesiastical authority.

NT:3852 (noun)
paraggelia (par-ang-gel-ee'-ah); from NT:3853; **a mandate:**

This noun is obviously derived from NT:3853, the root verb, so I won't belabor the point. Any such mandate or command recorded in the Bible for a church or any member of a church had been issued by the authority of the Lord, and the messenger who delivered it possessed no authority based on his delivery of the message or the mandate itself. We cannot impute authority to the apostles based on their use of this word. *Paraggelia* is used five times in the New Testament. There are two interesting verses in Acts regarding the mandates of civil leaders and three more in the epistles, two of which involve mandates from the Lord transmitted to the members of the church through Paul, as indicated below. The bolded word in each verse has been translated from *paraggelia*.

For ye know what **commandments** we gave you by the Lord Jesus. (1 Thess 4:2)
This **charge** I commit unto thee, son Timothy, according to the prophecies which went before on thee, that thou by them mightest war a good warfare; (1 Tim 1:18)

Since all apostolic commands and mandates were messages transmitted from the Lord rather than orders based on their own authority, a significant portion of the authoritative language in the epistles vanishes from the text when we understand the full meaning of this unique Greek concept of transmitting authoritative direction. Unfortunately, these are not the only words which mislead English Bible students. There are many more.

Obedience is an important concept in respect to our search for authority in church leadership, so we should see if God requires members to obey church leaders. Obedience in the Greek mind was associated with listening, as it is also in Hebrew. The Greek verb, to obey, is *hupakouo*, and the noun, obedience, is *hupakoe*. They mean to listen as a subordinate or to render obedience to an authority.

NT:5219 (verb)
hupakouo (hoop-ak-oo'-o); from NT:5259 and NT:191; **to hear under** (as a subordinate), i.e. to listen attentively; by implication, to heed or conform to a command or authority:

NT:5218 (noun)
hupakoe (hoop-ak-o-ay'); from NT:5219; **attentive hearkening,** i.e. (by implication) compliance or submission:

Hupakouo and *hupakoe* are translated "obey" and "obedience," respectively, in almost every occurrence, and they are always associated with authority, because each use of these words occurs in context with subordinate relationships of some kind. *Hupakouo*, or "to hear under" in literal English, means to listen, but it means to listen with the understanding that an authority is speaking. The noun form, *hupakoe*, carries the same implications.

I will examine the subordinate relationship in each verse where *hupakouo* and *hupakoe* appear. I have provided a concordance listing of partial verses for the sake of space, not exactly quoted, but containing the essence of the subordinate relationship indicated in each passage. The lists include every use of the word *hupakouo* and *hupakoe* in scripture. You should notice that in each case a subordinate relationship exists between the implied authority and the one who obeys. One contains a mistranslation. Can you find it? If any of these partial verses seems ambiguous, consult the full text in your Bible. We will begin with the verb *hupakouo*.

Matt 8:27	The winds and the sea obey *(hupakouo)* Jesus
Mark 1:27	The unclean spirits obey *(hupakouo)* Jesus
Mark 4:41	The wind and the sea obey *(hupakouo)* Jesus
Luke 8:25	The winds and water obey *(hupakouo)* Jesus

Luke 17:6	If you had faith...a tree should obey *(hupakouo)* you
Acts 6:7	The priests were obedient *(hupakouo)* to the faith
Acts 12:13	A damsel hearkened *(hupakouo)* to the door
Rom 6:12	[Christians] should not obey *(hupakouo)* sin
Rom 6:16	His [slaves] you are to whom you obey *(hupakouo)*
Rom 6:17	[The Romans] obeyed *(hupakouo)* that doctrine
Rom 10:16	Not everyone obeyed *(hupakouo)* the gospel
Eph 6:1	Children, obey *(hupakouo)* your parents
Eph 6:5	[Slaves], be obedient *(hupakouo)* to your masters
Phil 2:12	As you have always obeyed *(hupakouo)* [no object]
Col 3:20	Children, obey *(hupakouo)* your parents
Col 3:22	[Slaves,] be obedient *(hupakouo)* to your masters
2 Thess 1:8	...them who obey *(hupakouo)* not the gospel
2 Thess 3:14	If any man obey *(hupakouo)* not our word
Heb 5:9	Salvation to all them who obey *(hupakouo)* [Christ]
Heb 11:8	By faith Abraham obeyed *(hupakouo)* [God]
1 Pet 3:6	Sarah obeyed *(hupakouo)* Abraham, calling him lord

Similarly, the following list shows each occurrence of the noun form, *hupakoe*, to complete our examination of verses prescribing obedience in the New Testament.

Rom 1:5	We [give] obedience *(hupakoe)* to the faith
Rom 5:19	Many are made righteous by the obedience *(hupakoe)* of Christ
Rom 6:16	To whom you yield yourselves [slaves] to obey, *(hupakoe)* his [slaves] you are...
Rom 6:16	Obedience *(hupakoe)* [will yield] righteousness
Rom 15:18	Christ...has made the Gentiles obedient *(hupakoe)*
Rom 16:19	Your obedience *(hupakoe)* has come to all men
Rom 16:26	The mystery was made known for the obedience *(hupakoe)* of faith
2 Cor 7:15	Titus remembers the obedience *(hupakoe)* of you all
2 Cor 10:5	Bring every thought captive to the obedience *(hupakoe)* of Christ...
2 Cor 10:6	...[so] your obedience *(hupakoe)* is fulfilled
Philemon 21	[Paul] has confidence in [his] obedience *(hupakoe)*
Heb 5:8	Christ learned obedience *(hupakoe)* by suffering
1 Pet 1:2	The elect are sanctified unto obedience *(hupakoe)*

1 Pet 1:14   Gird up your mind as obedient *(hupakoe)* children
1 Pet 1:22   Seeing you are obeying *(hupakoe)* the truth

I hope you found these lists informative. Clearly, subordinate relationships are integrally associated with *hupakouo* and *hupakoe*, and their translation "to obey" or "obedience" is not only consistent, but fully justified. Since we are searching for some indication that church leaders have authority to command the members of the body of Christ, and since these lists contain groups of people and individuals who are subordinate to others, this seems like a logical place to find a scripture which indicates a person should *hupakouo* (obey) or give *hupakoe* (obedience) to a church leader. Although we can see one such example in our English translations, the precision of the Greek text reveals a subtle, grammatical manipulation.

> And if any man obey not **our word** by this epistle, note that man, and have no company with him, that he may be ashamed. (2 Thess 3:14)

Paul, Silas and Timothy collaborated together to write this letter to the Thessalonians, so the plural pronoun "our" implies that the members of the church in Thessalonica ought to *hupakouo* (obey) Paul, Silas and Timothy's word, thus establishing their authority to command the members of the Thessalonian church. At least that's how it reads in our English translation. However, those who read Greek will see that the phrase "our word" is a misleading translation of the Greek phrase, which reads "the word from us." The translators have transformed the case of the pronoun from a genitive, "from us," into a possessive, "our." Such grammatical changes frequently result in misleading translations. The construction of the Greek sentence indicates "the word" is the object of the members' obedience, not "our word." "The word" is a phrase which frequently implies the word of God. The apostles were not exalting their own words. The precision of the Greek language clearly and accurately reveals that the Thessalonians should obey "the word from us," not obey "our word." Paul's instruction to the Thessalonians encouraged them to obey the word of God, concerning which Paul, Silas and Timothy had written to them.

Rulership is implied in the most powerful single verse supporting ecclesiastical authority in the Bible. Hebrews 13:17 is the cornerstone of hierarchical authority in churches. Whenever I have challenged any biblically knowledgeable individual on the subject of church authority, Hebrews 13:17 is always the first scripture quoted to support the hierarchal structure found in all organized churches. Hebrews 13:17 is the scripture big gun organizations use to validate the existence of human authority in their churches. Without this verse hierarchical church government looses any explicit validation, and church authorities are left with only implicit references, such as command and obey, to support the presence of human government in churches. There is no verse in the whole Bible which validates the existence of human authority in churches more than Hebrews 13:17, at least in our English translations. However, yet again the inspired Greek text exposes the corrupt English translations.

We will begin by examining this verse in the New International Version (NIV).

> Obey your leaders and submit **to their authority**. They keep watch over you as men who must give an account. Obey them so that their work will be a joy, not a burden, for that would be of no advantage to you. (Heb 13:17) (NIV)

Of all translations the NIV offers the most corrupt interpretation of this verse. The phrase "to their authority" appears nowhere in the Greek text. Any quality Bible program will easily confirm that the word *exousia* does not appear here and, indeed, that no Greek words appear here to support this English phrase. The phrase "to their authority" has been arbitrarily and errantly inserted by the NIV translators. At the very least the translators should have placed the phrase "*to their authority*" in italics. It has no textual support. The translators presumptuously embellished what the author of Hebrews wrote, and they introduced their own words into the text of scripture rather than faithfully translating what is plainly there. This is not a grammatically difficult verse to translate. The NIV translators simply lacked faith in the literal words of God.

I will continue with the KJV, since the NIV tends to be more a subjective paraphrase than a literal translation.

> **Obey them that have the rule over you,** and submit yourselves: for they watch for your souls, as they that must give account, that they may do it with joy, and not with grief: for that is unprofitable for you.
> (Heb 13:17) (KJV)

First consider the obedience stated here. You may recall that this verse did not appear in the list of verses we examined above where *hupakouo* and *hupakoe* appear. Therefore, you should immediately suspect that the Greek word underlying "obey" in this verse means something other than obey.

The Greek word underlying obey in this verse is *peitho*, Strong's NT:3982. *Peitho* has nothing to do with obedience. Remarkably, *peitho* is the root verb for the Greek noun meaning persuasion. *Peitho* should be translated "persuade" in most contexts, however it occurs here in the passive imperative mood, so it must be translated "be persuaded" in this verse. Under no circumstances does *peitho* mean obey. Consider Strong's definition of *peitho*.

NT:3982
peitho (pi'-tho); a primary verb; **to convince** (by argument, true or false); by analogy, **to pacify or conciliate** (by other fair means); reflexively or passively, **to assent** (to evidence or authority), **to rely** (by inward certainty):

It is highly unusual to find a word with more than one definition, let alone four, so these four definitions should definitely raise a red flag of suspicion regarding Mr. Strong's definitions of *peitho*, but we will consider each one. He undoubtedly intended these four definitions to cover various nuances of meaning suggested in different contexts, but any direct association with obedience is conspicuously missing from all four of his definitions. Among his choices are *convince*, *pacify*, *assent*, and *rely*. Mr. Strong hints at obedience in his description of assent, which means "to give reasoned consent" or "be persuaded," but assent can only be an option when the authority does not give a command. In every case evidence must be the motivating factor to assent, not authority, because the command of an authority always requires obedience. Obedience has no place in any of these definitions of *peitho*.

One fairly reliable way to determine the meaning of a word is to examine its use in other contexts in the Bible. If you consult a Greek concordance and examine each verse in which *peitho* is used, you will see that *peitho* is translated "persuade" in almost half of the fifty-six verses in which it appears. In the remaining verses the KJV offers "trust" or "have confidence" where trust in men is not implied. Remarkably, not one of Strong's four definitions of *peitho* is ever explicitly used in the Bible, however, an obvious relationship exists between persuade and the definitions Strong offers. Convince is becoming an obsolete word, and its only remaining definition is persuade. Assent is simply persuade in the passive sense, and rely also carries a passive sense of persuasion. Three of Strong's definitions imply persuasion, and pacify, if it is not a spurious definition, has no applicable context in the Bible. Even from Strong's four definitions, "persuade" emerges as the primary and essential meaning of *peitho*.

Additionally, several other Greek dictionaries of more recent copyright, including Zodhiates' and Mounce's, have abandoned Strong's archaic and spurious definitions and embraced persuade as the first and primary definition of *peitho*, but they also include trust and assent as valid definitions, because trust and assent represent persuade in the passive sense. Therefore, we may conclude that the primary definition of *peitho* is "persuade," but it may be translated "assent" when the text requires a passive voice verb. It may also be translated "trust" or "rely" when the context does not imply church members should trust or rely upon men. *Peitho* should never be translated "obey."

Vine's *Expository Dictionary of Biblical Words* also contributes considerable scholarly insight to the meaning of this word:

2. peitho NT:3982, "to persuade, to win over," in the passive and middle voices, "to be persuaded, to listen to, to obey," is so used with this meaning, in the middle voice, e. g., in Acts 5:36-37 (in v. 40, passive voice, "they agreed"); Rom 2:8; Gal 5:7; **Heb 13:17**; James 3:3. **The "obedience" suggested is not by submission to authority, but resulting from persuasion.**

Vine's comment to the effect that "the obedience suggested is not by submission to authority, but resulting from persuasion" is a significant statement given the body of evidence we have already accumulated. When we consider that *peitho* is the primary root verb for the Greek noun which Strong's dictionary defines as persuasion, the evidence seems conclusive that persuade is the essential meaning of *peitho*, and obey is excluded, if for no other reason than the lack of scholarly support. In spite of very strong evidence against the use of obey as a legitimate definition of *peitho*, the KJV translators have substituted "obey" for "persuade" in several verses of the apostles' writings. These are all mistranslations. The translators' purpose should be to convey the meaning of the author's stated expression, not their own arbitrary interpretation. Sadly, most translators have forgotten that they are handling the inspired words of God.

Since we can see that *peitho* has been frequently translated persuade, that it is related in word family to persuasion, that its definition in more recent dictionaries is persuade, and that Greek scholars and lexicographers have been unwilling to include "obey" among their primary definitions of *peitho*, one stands on very solid ground to reject "obey" and accept "persuade" as the true meaning of *peitho* in this context. God wanted believers to know that faithful church leaders should persuade us through sound instruction, but He did not shackle us with a blanket obligation to obey any church leader, let alone a false one.

As we continue to examine Hebrews 13:17 in the literal Greek text, consider the rulership explicit in the phrase "have the rule over," which the KJV offers from the single Greek word, *hegeomai*.

NT:2233
hegeomai (hayg-eh'-om-ahee); middle voice of a (presumed) strengthened form of NT:71; **to lead**, i.e. command (with official authority); figuratively, to deem, i.e. consider:

Hegeomai is a verb meaning "to lead." It has nothing to do with rulership. It may imply authoritative leadership, if the person leading has authority, but any vested authority exists outside the meaning of *hegeomai* and we cannot impute authority to church leaders based on the word itself. *Hegeomai* should be translated "lead" in each occurrence of the word, and translators should allow the context to determine whether the leader holds any duly constituted authority.

During the reign of Queen Elizabeth I, the ruling British monarch became the head of the church of England, and, from that time to the present, the kings and queens of England have been the rulers of the church of England. When King James ascended the throne in 1603, he authorized a new English translation of the Bible, and the translators did him a favor by imputing his rulership over the church of England to church leaders in the Bible, so everyone could see that the king and his bishops now ruled both church and state. Since they indeed ruled the church of England, it probably seemed a small matter to morph persuasion into obedience and leadership into rulership. Thus, we can witness here two of several politically driven mistranslations in the KJV Bible. Those who understand that God rules His people and Jesus Christ commands faithful believers will find the translators' allegations in this verse preposterous. The Father alone rules the Church. We only obey the Lord.

A leader may lead from a position of authority, or not, depending on the type of leader he is, because the word "leader" carries no inherent authority. The leader of a division of infantry definitely has the authority to command the troops, but the leader of a hike in the woods has no authority over the hikers at all, although they may be wise to follow him very closely. He is the leader, but he is not the commander. He must persuade the hikers that he knows the way.

As the evidence against authoritarian leadership is mounting, we should examine another word in the context of Hebrews 13:17 which further refutes the notion of authority among church leaders in this verse. Consider submit, *hipeiko* in the Greek text. This word means "to surrender" or "to submit," and every version translates *hipeiko* correctly. Submit means exactly what it says.

NT:5226
hipeiko (hoop-i'-ko); from NT:5259 and eiko (to yield, be "weak");
to surrender:

The Old Testament lacks even the concept of submission in the Hebrew text, even though our English word "submit" appears there five times in the KJV. Unfortunately, it is a mistranslation of either *to bow down*, *to be untrue*, or *to prostrate before* those in authority. God first introduces submission to His people in the New Testament as a working concept for members of churches. The mere presence of the concept of submission in Hebrews 13:17 indicates there is no authority to command implied in this admonition. If the leaders of a church had the authority to command the people, the Greek word for obey, *hupakouo* (NT:5219), would surely have been used, and there would have been no need to request submission.

Obedience and submission cannot apply to the same individual in the same context. Obedience is always a required response to an authority, but free agency is implicit in submission. Submission is only an option when a leader has no authority. We may obey or we may submit depending on the type of leadership, but we need not obey a suggestion, nor can we assume the prerogative to submit, or not, to a command. If an authority gives us a command, we have no choice but to obey, but, if we are led by a spiritual guide, we are free to be persuaded and submit, or not, depending upon how persuasive the leader might be. The hard reality of life is that human leaders make mistakes no matter how well intentioned they might be. God intentionally inspired Hebrews 13:17 to insure that an uneducated, unpersuasive or false leader has no authority to shackle even a babe in Christ to his doctrines or directives.

Since Hebrews 13:17 has been so poorly translated and it is so important to understand exactly what the author wrote here, I will provide a straightforward, literal translation, so you may gain a more accurate understanding of what the author of Hebrews intended to convey in this verse. *Peitho* appears in the Greek text as a passive imperative verb, so it must be translated "be persuaded." *Hegeomai* appears as an active participle, so it must be translated "leading." When a number of other grammatical errors are also corrected, Hebrews 13:17 can be understood more literally as follows:

Be persuaded by those of you leading and submit *yourselves*, for they are watching over your souls, as they will be giving an account in order that they may be doing this with joy and not grieving, for this *is* unprofitable to you.

Paul's admonition in Hebrews 13:17 encourages younger or less experienced members of the church to yield to those who lead with sound logic and a firm grounding in the word. Those with greater education and experience in the scriptures have the responsibility to edify, encourage and exhort those who are newer in the faith, but they hold no vested authority to command even the newest member of a church. The less experienced only have a responsibility to yield to those with more experience, if the leaders are able to persuade them by rightly dividing the word of truth. If leaders fail to persuade the congregation, they may be in error or need more training. God places mutual responsibility upon both leaders and members to submit themselves to one another, (Eph 5:21) but God does not vest any authority to command in spiritual leaders. God has vested all authority in Jesus Christ alone.

Note the qualifications of the bishop (watchman) in Titus 1:7-9: "For a bishop must be blameless, as the steward of God; not selfwilled, not soon angry, not given to wine, no striker, not given to filthy lucre; but a lover of hospitality, a lover of good men, sober, just, holy, temperate; **holding fast the faithful word as he hath been taught, that he may be able by sound doctrine both to exhort and to convince the gainsayers.**" Paul upholds the responsibility to teach, exhort and convince (persuade) rather than command, and this scripture mirrors our revised translation of Hebrews 13:17. An able leader should be able to encourage and persuade dissident believers by offering them rational advice based on sound instruction, but leaders never command members of the church, except by *paraggello*.

Hebrews 13:17 is one of the most egregious examples of spurious translation in the Bible. The translators have assumed that the authority they saw in their hierarchically organized, contemporary churches accurately reflected the way God governed the first century churches, so they superimposed contemporary church governance over the inspired words of God. When diligent Bible students carefully examine the translators' assertions based on the work of scholars, thousands of such translation errors will become painfully apparent. Beginning with the concordance and especially now with Bible programs on the computer, you can equip yourself with powerful research tools, which are able to free you from the interpretations of men and give you access to the originally inspired words of scripture, even if you cannot read a word of Hebrew or Greek. God blesses those who question the translators' interpretations and assume a personal responsibility to look carefully into the inspired texts of scripture.

Ordination is another English concept which comes to us from seventeenth century England and the church ruled by the king and his bishops. Ordination is the ceremony which recognizes the accomplishments of humble leaders and dedicated servants of a church, transforms them from leaders and servants into ecclesiastical authorities, and inducts them into the hierarchy of the church. The concept is derived from another Latin word which has no basis or counterpart in the Greek vocabulary of the Bible. Ordination is entirely a figment of the translators' imaginations.

Translators have used this Latin-based verb as an extraordinarily versatile substitute for fourteen different Greek verbs in the inspired text. Consequently, the intended meaning of all these Greek words has been lost to those of us who only read English. Among the definitions of these fourteen Greek words are "to make," "to cause to be," "to distinguish," "to predetermine," "to arrange," "to prepare," and even "to vote." How, I wonder, can one expect to be able to delve deeply into the mind of God when the translators gloss and obfuscate multiple inspired words in the original Greek text with a single English word? Additionally, the official connotation which ordination has come to represent in ecclesiastical culture compounds the problem. The use of this word in our English Bibles injects an official-sounding rhetoric, which the writers of the New Testament never intended. The concept of ordination exists nowhere in the inspired Greek text.

The following is an exhaustive list of the twenty-one scriptures which use the word ordain in the KJV Bible. I will examine the Greek word underlying each appearance of the concept of ordination in order to properly understand the inspired sense of each verse. Strong's definition of the underlying Greek word accompanies each verse followed by a short commentary.

Mark 3:14
And [Jesus] **ordained** twelve, that they should be with him, and that he might send them forth to preach.
NT:4160
poieo (poy-eh'-o); apparently a prolonged form of an obsolete primary; **to make or do** (in a very wide application, more or less direct):

Jesus "made" the twelve disciples so they would be with him, and afterwards He would send them out to preach the gospel. There is no sense from the Greek word or from the context that Jesus conferred any authority upon them. Jesus simply made them disciples. We might say He chose them, but no ordination is implied. Indeed, the Greek sense implies He created them to be who they were.

John 15:16
Ye have not chosen me, but I have chosen you, and **ordained** you, that ye should go and bring forth fruit, and that your fruit should remain: that whatsoever ye shall ask of the Father in my name, he may give it you.
NT:5087
tithemi (tith'-ay-mee); a prolonged form of a primary theo (theh'-o) (which is used only as alternate in certain tenses); **to place** (in the widest application, literally and figuratively; properly, **in a passive or horizontal posture**, and thus different from NT:2476, which properly denotes an upright and active position, while NT:2749 is properly reflexive and utterly prostrate):

Jesus' stated purpose was to send them forth to bring forth fruit and to allow them to receive what they asked of the Father. Neither the Greek word nor the context carries any connotation of ordination or authority. Notice that the stated placement is "in a passive or horizontal posture," not what one might expect John to say if Jesus raised them to a rank or position of authority through their placement or ordination. If such were the case, John would have used the word *histemi*, NT:2475.

In contrast to *tithemi*, *histemi* means "to stand" in an upright or active position, and scripture uses this word to refer variously to: those who stand in the gospel (1 Cor 15:1); those who stand by faith (2 Cor 1:24); those who stand with the armor of God (Eph 6:14); and those who stand in the grace of God (1 Peter 5:12). The use of *histemi* indicates that it is through the gospel, through faith, through the grace of God and by using the armor of God that all of us stand in the congregation and before God, but none through ordination. We all stand (*histemi*) by faith, but none stands in authority. God has placed (*tithemi*) each member in the body as He has seen fit, and in the same manner He placed the apostles to bring forth fruit to God. None has been placed by the ordination of men.

Acts 1:22
Beginning from the baptism of John, unto that same day that he was taken up from us, must one **be ordained to be** a witness with us of his resurrection.

NT:1096

ginomai (ghin'-om-ahee); a prolongation and middle voice form of a primary verb; **to cause to be** ("gen"- erate), i.e. (reflexively) to become (come into being), used with great latitude (literal, figurative, intensive, etc.):

After Judas' death one of the disciples who were with Jesus from the beginning of His ministry to the time of His resurrection was caused to be a witness of the Lord in Judas' place. Ordination should not be assumed when the Greek text simply says "was caused to be." This disciple was likely caused to be an apostle by God just as Jesus "made" the other apostles. (see Mark 3:14 above)

Acts 10:42
And [Jesus] commanded us to preach unto the people, and to testify that it is he which was **ordained** of God to be the Judge of quick and dead.

NT:3724

horizo (hor-id'-zo); from NT:3725; **to mark out or bound** ("horizon"), i.e. (figuratively) to appoint, decree, specify:

The literal sense here is that Jesus was "marked out" or set apart by God to judge all people. In the figurative sense, we might think of God's action as an appointment, but this word provides no basis to assume God ordained Jesus to a position of authority. Jesus has authority because He is divine, not because God appointed Him.

Acts 13:48
And when the Gentiles heard this, they were glad, and glorified the word of the Lord: and as many as were **ordained** to eternal life believed.

NT:5021

tasso (tas'-so); a prolonged form of a primary verb (which latter appears only in certain tenses); **to arrange in an orderly manner**, i.e. assign or dispose (to a certain position or lot):

God organizes the Church by arranging the members and placing us in the body as it pleases Him. (1 Cor 12:18) He also arranges our eternal life; however, His arrangement does not imply He has granted commanding authority to those assigned to eternal life. If such were the case, we would all be authorities in the Church.

Acts 14:23
And when they had **ordained** them elders in every church, and had prayed with fasting, they commended them to the Lord, on whom they believed.

NT:5500

cheirotoneo (khi-rot-on-eh'-o): from a comparative of NT:5495 and teino (to stretch); **to be a hand-reacher or voter** (by raising the hand), i.e. (generally) to select or appoint:

Many pious churchgoers would be shocked to learn that the apostles voted to select the elders. Such an approach to choosing men of authority would indeed seem flippant, but, if the designated elders were only chosen to fulfill certain responsibilities in their congregations, voting would seem more reasonable. The exact method of voting is not described, but Matt 18:19 indicates full agreement must have been reached regarding each elder before the appointment would have been validated by the Lord.

Acts 16:4
And as they went through the cities, they delivered them the decrees for to keep, that were **ordained** of the apostles and elders which were at Jerusalem.

NT:2919

krino (kree'-no); properly, **to distinguish**, i.e. **decide** (mentally or judicially); by implication, to try, condemn, punish:

These decrees were the result of an agreed decision in Acts 15 based on the scriptures and the apostles' knowledge of Jesus' teachings. One does not ordain decrees, but people are ordained to authority; however, neither is implied here. The apostles simply agreed on a course of action and made a decision.

Acts 17:31
Because [God] hath appointed a day, in the which he will judge the world in righteousness by that man whom he hath **ordained;**

whereof he hath given assurance unto all men, in that he hath raised him from the dead.

NT:3724

horizo (hor-id'-zo); from NT:3725; **to mark out or bound** ("horizon"), i.e. (figuratively) to appoint, decree, specify:

God "marked out" or appointed Jesus Christ to judge the world. As in Acts 10:42 above, Jesus Christ's authority to judge is not established by this Greek word. God's appointment specified Jesus Christ to be the Judge of the world, but He requires no "ordination" to fulfill that role.

Rom 7:10

And the commandment, which was **ordained** to life, I found to be unto death.

NT:9999

inserted word {x}

This word has no support at all in the inspired Greek text. The translators arbitrarily added this word, assuming we needed it for better understanding. Such words should be displayed in italics to indicate they are not supported by the original text. However, it was not displayed in italics, so those who trust the KJV have no way of knowing the ordination implied here is a figment of the translator's imagination. Simply read the verse without "ordained" to gain the literal sense of the verse.

Rom 13:1

Let every soul be subject unto the higher [authorities]. For there is no [authority] but of God: the [authorities] that be are **ordained** of God.

NT:5021

tasso (tas'-so); a prolonged form of a primary verb (which latter appears only in certain tenses); **to arrange in an orderly manner**, i.e. assign or dispose (to a certain position or lot):

The context here is civil authority. God has unquestionably left human authority in human governments for the safety and protection of society. God arranges those authorities in an orderly manner according to His will. God allows men to wield the authority they have assumed to themselves, but His arrangement of them does not convey their authority. Certainly God does not ordain unbelievers.

1 Cor 2:7

But we speak the wisdom of God in a mystery, even the hidden wisdom, which God **ordained** before the world unto our glory:

NT:4309

proorizo (pro-or-id'-zo); from NT:4253 and NT:3724; to limit in advance, i.e. (figuratively) **predetermine:**

God predetermined that Christians would be able to comprehend and discuss the wisdom of God and that unbelievers would not understand. God's predetermination does not imply or establish ordination nor does God ordain an abstract concept like wisdom.

1 Cor 7:17

But as God hath distributed to every man, as the Lord hath called every one, so let him walk. And so **ordain** I in all churches.

NT:1299

diatasso (dee-at-as'-so); from NT:1223 and NT:5021; **to arrange thoroughly,** i.e. (specially) institute, prescribe, etc.:

This word is one of several Greek words which will imply authority if the one making the arrangement has authority. If one has no authority, using this word does not impute it. Paul's arrangement was to make no changes in a member's physical circumstances based on conversion and particularly within the context of marriage. Since Paul prescribed nothing for the members here, any assertion of authority in ordination based on this verse is essentially moot.

1 Cor 9:14

Even so hath the Lord **ordained** that they which preach the gospel should live of the gospel.

NT:1299

diatasso (dee-at-as'-so); from NT:1223 and NT:5021; **to arrange thoroughly,** i.e. (specially) institute, prescribe, etc.:

The Lord has arranged for the well-being of those who preach the gospel by allowing them to receive contributions from members who have benefited spiritually from their preaching. However, such contributions are freely given. Church leaders never demand them. The Lord possesses authority, and His arrangement is law, but His arrangement for the well-being of those who preach the gospel does not establish ordination, nor does it grant any member the authority to demand support.

Gal 3:19
Wherefore then serveth the law? It was added because of transgressions, till the seed should come to whom the promise was made; and it was **ordained** by angels in the hand of a mediator.

NT:1299

diatasso (dee-at-as'-so); from NT:1223 and NT:5021; **to arrange thoroughly**, i.e. (specially) institute, prescribe, etc.:

Angelic messengers arranged the law and delivered it through Moses. They acted by God's authority to arrange the law, but *diatasso* neither states nor implies that the law was ordained.

Eph 2:10
For we are his workmanship, created in Christ Jesus unto good works, which God hath **before ordained** that we should walk in them.

NT:4282

proetoimazo (pro-et-oy-mad'-zo); from NT:4253 and NT:2090; **to fit up in advance** (literally or figuratively):

The primary root word NT:2090 is prepare. God has prepared in advance that Christians should have the capacity to continually serve Him by doing good works. Our ability to accomplish good works is possible, because we live in Christ and He does the work. God does not need to ordain good works.

1 Tim 2:7
Whereunto I am **ordained** a preacher, and an apostle, (I speak the truth in Christ, and lie not;) a teacher of the Gentiles in faith and verity.

NT:5087

tithemi (tith'-ay-mee); a prolonged form of a primary theo (theh'-o) (which is used only as alternate in certain tenses); **to place** (in the widest application, literally and figuratively; properly, **in a passive or horizontal posture,** and thus different from NT:2476, which properly denotes an upright and active position, while NT:2749 is properly reflexive and utterly prostrate):

Again, we find God placed His apostle in the Church in a passive way, which works contrary to the notion that apostles were ordained to positions of authority to command the members of the body. See comment on John 15:16.

Titus 1:5
For this cause left I thee in Crete, that thou shouldest set in order the things that are wanting, and **ordain** elders in every city, as I had appointed thee:
NT:2525
kathistemi (kath-is'-tay-mee); from NT:2596 and NT:2476; **to place down** (permanently), i.e. (figuratively) to designate, constitute, convoy:

This verse provides powerful support for ordination of elders, but that support vanishes when we examine the inspired Greek text. Elders were certainly leaders, but they were not ordained. They were not authorities. They were "placed down" or designated to lead the church, but no authority is implied by the Greek word. *Kathistemi* tells us elders were set in place or designated in every city.

Heb 5:1
For every high priest taken from among men is **ordained** for men in things pertaining to God, that he may offer both gifts and sacrifices for sins:
NT:2525
kathistemi (kath-is'-tay-mee); from NT:2596 and NT:2476; **to place down** (permanently), i.e. (figuratively) to designate, constitute, convoy:

The high priest was "placed down" in his position, indicating the permanence of the responsibility. The high priest was the head of the priesthood, and he certainly held a position of authority over the priests, but *kathistemi* tells us he was placed in his responsibility, not that he was given authority by ordination.

Heb 8:3
For every high priest is **ordained** to offer gifts and sacrifices: wherefore it is of necessity that this man have somewhat also to offer.
NT:2525
kathistemi (kath-is'-tay-mee); from NT:2596 and NT:2476; **to place down** (permanently), i.e. (figuratively) to designate, constitute, convoy:

God placed the high priest according to heredity, and his placement to offer gifts and sacrifices was permanent. (see Heb 5:1)

Heb 9:6
Now when these things were thus **ordained**, the priests went always into the first tabernacle, accomplishing the service of God.

NT:2680

kataskeuazo (kat-ask-yoo-ad'-zo); from NT:2596 and a derivative of NT:4632; **to prepare thoroughly** (properly, by external equipment; whereas NT:2090 refers rather to internal fitness); by implication, to construct, create:

After Moses built the furniture of the tabernacle, set it in place and thoroughly prepared the tabernacle, the priests went in to minister to God. This verb emphasizes the thoroughness of the preparation, not the ordination of the furniture.

Jude 4
For there are certain men crept in unawares, who **were before** of old **ordained** to this condemnation, ungodly men, turning the grace of our God into lasciviousness, and denying the only Lord God, and our Lord Jesus Christ.

NT:4270

prographo (prog-raf'-o); from NT:4253 and NT:1125; **to write previously**; figuratively, to announce, prescribe:

Jude's epistle addresses similar concerns as Peter's epistles, which, written previously, revealed that ungodly men would be destroyed. It is also possible Jude is referring to the Old Testament prophecies. In either case this translation is in error. Jude wanted his readers to know the fate of these men had been previously written.

These twenty-one verses contain every appearance of the concept of ordination in the KJV Bible. The translators have collectively obscured the meaning of more than a dozen informative Greek words, which were inspired to reveal some detail of the truth of God. The context of these verses provides no justification for ordination in churches, and indeed several of the inspired words contradict the assumption that men were ordained to positions of authority in first century churches. Ordination vanishes from the Bible when we are able to examine the underlying Greek words. The practice of ordaining any person to a position of authority in a church flies in the face of the humble service Jesus and the apostles taught. God is not a respecter of persons.

Hierarchical leadership is also generally assumed based on a very well known passage in 1 Corinthians 12. Church leaders frequently quote this passage to validate the hierarchy in organized churches, but notice the context very carefully.

> And God hath set some in the church, **first** apostles, secondarily prophets, thirdly teachers, after that miracles, then **gifts** of healings, helps, [pilotages], diversities of tongues. Are all apostles? are all prophets? are all teachers? are all workers of miracles? Have all the **gifts** of healing? do all speak with tongues? do all interpret? But covet earnestly the best **gifts**: and yet shew I unto you a more excellent way. (1 Cor 12:28-31)

The main point in this context and the parallel passage in Ephesians 4 is the manner in which God places gifts in the body for the benefit of the whole congregation. Examine 1 Corinthians 12 in its entirety and watch carefully as Paul intertwines the thread of spiritual gifts throughout. It should become clear that the gifts God has set in the Church are not positions of authority but are simply gifts of the Spirit listed in an order of importance to the Church, not in an order of rank or authority. The Greek word, *proton*, translated "first" in verse 28, verifies this conclusion.

NT:4412
proton (pro'-ton); neuter of NT:4413 as adverb (with or without NT:3588); **firstly (in time, place, order, or <u>importance</u>)**:

This Greek adjective means "first" in importance, not rank. If Paul had intended rank, he would have used the Greek word *arche*. Carefully compare the definitions of the two Greek words.

NT:746
arche (ar-khay'); from NT:756; (properly abstract) a commencement, or (concretely) **chief (in various applications of order, time, place, or <u>rank</u>)**:

Therefore, I can only conclude that Paul listed these gifts of the Spirit in order of their importance to the Church, not in an order of rank. This list cannot be ranks of hierarchical authority.

We should also consider Paul's use of the anarthrous construction in the Greek text for the various gifts listed above. Anarthrous refers to a word or group of words which appear in the Greek text without a definite article. Paul omitted the Greek definite article, *ho*, before each noun. (Koine Greek has no indefinite article, "a" or "an," as we have in English, although it is sometimes appropriate to supply an indefinite article for English translations.) Anarthrous constructions most often point out the quality of something, and such is the case here. By omitting the definite article, Paul placed emphasis on the quality of the gift or responsibility, not on the individual who receives it. Had the author intended to focus on the gifted individuals, he would have used the definite article before the noun, "the" apostles, "the" prophets, etc., rather than the anarthrous construction. The combined force of the anarthrous construction and the use of *proton* instead of *arche* precludes the possibility that a hierarchical ranking of positions of authority can be based on this passage. Paul simply listed these gifts of the Spirit in the order of their importance to the Church.

We have observed numerous verses and passages containing significant mistranslations, which have led unsuspecting Bible students to believe God has placed a hierarchical order of leadership positions in the Church. We saw that the apostles were granted no explicit authority and delivered no commands to the congregations based on their own authority. We corrected the two egregious mistranslations in Hebrews 13:17, which change the whole tone of the verse and eliminate both rulership in church leadership and the necessity to obey those who lead us. We learned that ordination is an unscriptural ceremony, and we observed verses which teach members to obey God, Jesus Christ, the gospel, the word and the faith, but none which teach us to obey any church leader. There are many other individual verses containing mistranslations of inspired Greek words which may lead us to believe that the Lord vested church leaders with the privilege of authority. I will not belabor the point here, but you may examine an exhaustive list of such verses with their corrected translations in appendix 1.

Hierarchical authority in church leadership cannot be supported by the Greek text of scripture. Every hint of authority in the first century churches vanishes under the scrutiny of the inspired text. God conferred all authority to Jesus Christ, (Matt 28:18) and there is no evidence the Lord delegated any of it to the apostles. Jesus Christ alone is our Head and Commander. He is our Chief Leader, but He is not the chief authority. He is the Chief among many leaders, but He is not the chief over any authorities. Church leaders lead, but they do not command. Leadership in churches is not by authority, but by example and practice. Leaders stand before the congregation and practice the faith of Jesus Christ before the members, but they become transparent as they point each member to the one and only Commander of the Church for personal direction.

In the absence of any indication that church members were required to obey church leaders or that the apostles commanded the members, ruled the churches or ordained authorities in the churches, church leaders have no biblical support for ecclesiastical rulership or authority anywhere in scripture. Additionally, dozens of verses plainly teach that church leaders should not practice authoritarian leadership. Jesus Himself addressed the issue of rulership and authority among those He knew would be the most respected men in the Church. He specifically condemned authoritarian leadership and admonished the apostles not to be authorities.

The twelve disciples and the mother of James and John were alone with Jesus when she asked Jesus to allow her sons to sit on His right hand and His left hand in the kingdom. The other ten disciples became indignant, and God directed Jesus to give all twelve disciples, later apostles, the following instruction:

> But Jesus called them unto him, and said, Ye know that the [rulers] of the Gentiles [lord against] them, and they that are great exercise authority upon them. but **it shall not be so among you**: but whosoever will be great among you, let him be your [servant]; and whosoever will be chief among you, let him be your [slave]: even as the Son of man came not to be [served], but to [serve], and to give his life a ransom for many. (Matt 20:25-28)

If you read carefully, you will see that Jesus described the nature of the apostles' leadership. He specifically addressed who they should be and who they should not be. Church leaders are not to be like the rulers of the Gentiles or like the great ones in the world. The rulers of the world rule over their subjects, and authorities exercise dominion over their subjects. Gentile rulers and authorities are able to do what they do, because they have been granted the privilege to be who they are. They are rulers, and they are authorities.

Jesus specifically instructed the disciples not to be rulers and not to be authorities. If the disciples desired greatness, Jesus told them to become servants and slaves. His words condemn the mere thought of superiority. Jesus' instruction strongly discourages any exaltation of church leaders and implies that a church leader should not strive to attain any position or title in his or her congregation. If Jesus did not allow the apostles to become rulers or authorities, our church leaders today should certainly not assume any position of authority.

Scattered references in various English translations use the word "rule" in reference to church leaders. Every such reference is a mistranslation. Sometimes the Greek text simply says "lead" and other times it refers to a realm of influence, but never to the rulership of leaders over a church. The word "rule" in our English Bibles also hides a Greek word which means "to practice before." An important aspect of church leadership is a leader's practice of the faith in the sight of the congregation, but the inspired text never says church leaders rule. God rules the Church.

Contrary to widespread belief, the original Greek text of the Bible never says any church leader rules a church or that a leader is over the members in authority. Scripture never says that the apostles commanded the people unilaterally or that church leaders direct the activities of the other members of a church. In the inspired text leaders have no office and are not ordained to positions of authority. The two verses which imply Christians should obey church leaders both contain mistranslations. Although all ecclesiastical authority in scripture is imputed by mistranslation, numerous verses clearly indicate that we must remain free from human direction in our walk with God. I have found twenty-four passages indicating a church member's freedom from human authority. They are listed for your consideration in appendix 2.

Two leadership responsibilities existed in the first century churches, and these are indicated in scripture with biblically defined qualifications. Paul addressed the two groups of leaders specifically in his letter to the Philippians, (Phil 1:1) and we find the qualifications for both responsibilities listed in Paul's letters to Timothy and Titus. (1 Tim 3:1-13, Tit 1:7-9) These are vital Christian leadership responsibilities, and the inspired text describes one as a watchman (bishop) and the other as a servant (deacon).

The watchman, variously translated overseer or bishop, fills the responsibility to watch out for the congregation much like the watchman of Ezekiel 33. A watchman is responsible to warn the congregation when enemies intrude from without or errant behavior occurs within. Unfortunately, hierarchical connotations have crept into the translation of the Greek word, *episkopos,* and even scholars have allowed hierarchical and bureaucratic connotations to distort their definitions.

NT:1985
episkopos (ep-is'-kop-os); from NT:1909 and NT:4649 (in the sense of NT:1983); **a superintendent,** i.e. Christian officer in genitive case charge of a (or the) church (literally or figuratively):

Strong's definitions of leadership responsibilities always contain official-sounding authoritative rhetoric, because he assumed the hierarchical structure of the churches of his time was a valid biblical model. We may ignore Strong's personal interpretations following the "i.e.", such as officer, official, and charge. Even his primary definition of *episkopos,* "a superintendent," fails miserably to reflect the literal sense of this simple compound word. It is a particularly egregious definition, because we can never remove the bureaucratic and hierarchical connotations from it. Even translators have avoided this definition, most preferring the more restrained "overseer," but even overseer conveys a sense of privilege absent from the Greek word. The Greek preposition *epi* does not mean over or imply superiority, but it means "upon" in the sense of a location above. The compound word *epi* (upon) and *skopos* (a watch) implies one who watches upon or watches out for someone or something. The watchman was responsible to watch upon the congregation to find and expose enemies. He did not watch upon the congregation in an authoritative sense. Therefore, "watchman" is the most literal translation possible without imputing any authoritative connotations. Although "guardian" and "caretaker" are less literal, they also reflect the essence of the meaning of *episkopos*.

Literally, the watchman, or guardian, is one who watches over or guards the church, but this vital responsibility does not carry any inherent authority. A watchman must have good spiritual vision and the ability to warn the people of danger. Military watchmen fill an important responsibility to guard the camp, but the responsibility does not imply any authority over the troops at all. Frequently the lowest ranking soldiers stand watch over the camp, but, obviously, a private standing watch has no authority over any of the troops. Similarly, a spiritual watchman watches out for spiritual enemies like a scout scanning the perimeter or a sentry at the gate. Watchmen stand as guardians to protect the congregation from danger and warn the members when enemies threaten the salvation of the church. Watchmen do not supervise or oversee the people in the church. They watch out for enemies.

The qualifications for a watchman are listed in 1 Timothy 3:1-7 and generally repeated in Titus. The watchman's responsibility to watch out for enemies is most apparent in Titus 1:7-9.

> For a [watchman] **must be** blameless, as the steward of God; not selfwilled, not soon angry, not given to wine, no striker, not given to filthy lucre; but a lover of hospitality, a lover of good men, sober, just, holy, temperate; holding fast the faithful word as he hath been taught, that he may be able by sound doctrine both to exhort and to convince the gainsayers.

Watchmen are stewards of God, and the English word "steward" quite adequately translates the Greek word, *oikonomos*, which literally means "a house distributor." A steward distributes the provisions of the master to all of the slaves. Stewardship is a responsibility, not a management position or a rank of authority. A steward of God is firmly grounded in the word of God and equipped to be able to distribute the truth God has given him or her to the rest of the members of the church. A steward of God is a slave of the Lord and a fellow servant among the members of a church.

Notice carefully that this list of qualifications describes the watchman's state of being, not his deeds. It describes who he is, not what he does. It describes who he **must be**, not what he must do. A watchman is qualified by his gifts from the Spirit and his dedication to the faith, not by either the quality or quantity of his good deeds. Men cannot judge his service, because these qualifications are not a list of dos and don'ts which can be evaluated by observation to determine whether he is doing a good job. His service is not based on what he does, but it is based on the calling of God, the direction of the Lord and his gifts from the Holy Spirit.

A watchman is most often an elder, although age is not a specifically stated qualification. Paul told Timothy not to allow anyone to despise his youth. (1 Tim 4:12) God specially gifted Timothy, but leadership skills often require years of faithful study and practice to develop. Scripture frequently associates elders and watchmen in the same context, but elder does not describe a separate responsibility in a congregation. *Presbuteros* is an adjective which describes an older person or, as a noun, indicates a senior. Elder is not a biblically designated responsibility in the congregation, but a description of the leader himself. A watchman must exhibit the spiritual maturity most often found in older members, so the responsibility of watchman is usually filled by seniors. Elder describes the person; watchman is his job.

The servant, sometimes transliterated directly into our English Bibles as deacon, fills the responsibility to serve the congregation as necessary and in whatever way the Spirit may move him or her to serve. Like watchmen, servants attend to the needs of a congregation but possess no authority over the congregation.

NT:1249
diakonos (dee-ak'-on-os); probably from an obsolete diako (to run on errands; compare NT:1377); **an attendant,** i.e. (genitive case) a waiter (at table or in other menial duties); specially, a Christian teacher and pastor (technically a deacon or deaconess):

The Greek word *diakonos* occurs thirty times in the New Testament, and it always means servant. Whenever it appears as minister or deacon, it is mistranslated. There is no such word in the

Greek text as minister or deacon apart from servant. There are no offices, no ministers and no deacons in the Greek text. Strong's special and technical notations reflect his observations of organized church practice and have no basis in scripture. *Diakonos* means servant—nothing more, nothing less.

The qualifications of a servant parallel those given for a watchman, and they describe who the servant **must be** rather than what a servant must do. A servant cannot be evaluated by men to determine whether he is worthy of the responsibility, because a servant's calling of God and gifts of the Spirit qualify him for the responsibility to serve, not the type or quality of his deeds.

> Likewise **must** the deacons be grave, not doubletongued, not given to much wine, not greedy of filthy lucre; holding the mystery of the faith in a pure conscience. And let these also first be proved; then let them use the office of a deacon, being found blameless. Even so must their wives be grave, not slanderers, sober, faithful in all things. Let the deacons be the husbands of one wife, ruling their children and their own houses well. For they that have used the office of a deacon well purchase to themselves a good degree, and great boldness in the faith which is in Christ Jesus. (1 Tim 3:8-13)

This passage is full of mistranslations. I have underlined them in the text and listed them in the chart below, indicating the line in the above text where the error occurs, the word or phrase in question, and the literal meaning of the Greek word. Notice that the translators inserted two whole phrases, "use(d) the office of a deacon," in place of a single Greek verb, *diakoneo* NT:1247, which means "to serve."

line	KJV translation	literal Greek
1	deacons	servants
5	use the office of a deacon	serve
8	deacons	servants
8	ruling	stand (practice) before
10	used the office of a deacon	served

Every biblical reference to hierarchical structure for church government vanishes from the text when we carefully examine the underlying Greek words. Every gift of the Holy Spirit Paul listed in 1 Corinthians 12 and Ephesians 4, as well as guardianship and service, carries the responsibility to serve the congregation, not control it. They function to edify the church, not lord over it. The Spirit has given these gifts "for the [furnishing] of the saints, for the work of [service], for the edifying of the body of Christ." (Eph 4:12)

Ordained church authorities often claim they are servants of their churches, but authoritarian service is a contradiction in terms. Many appear to serve the congregation, and they certainly ought to be servants, but their authority stands in the way. When they become authorities, they cease to be servants. One cannot be an authority and be a servant at the same time. The contradiction of authoritarian service pervades the organized churches, and many have accepted the deception of ordained service. Don't believe a lie. The pride of authority and the humility of service stand in opposition to one another and cannot exist together in any human being. Men love to have the preeminence. (3 John 9) They love to sit in the chief seats in meetings and stand in the high places of worship, (Mark 12:39) but Jesus said they will only reap the greater damnation. (v. 40)

The biblical responsibilities of the early church leaders reflected a different tone than we see in churches today. Every church leader attended to the physical needs of the members, while faithful church leaders allowed the Lord to attend to the members' spiritual needs. Leaders served the church in the literal, biblical and menial sense of the word. Not every leader was equipped to teach, but every leader attended to the member's physical needs. Church leaders were not vested with authority, because they were specifically forbidden to rule, exercise authority (Matt 20:25-28) or to be lords over God's heritage. (1 Peter 5:3).

Watchmen and servants are priceless assets to a church. They keep the church focused on Jesus Christ, Who appoints them to lead the members of the church into the full freedom of new covenant faith in Jesus Christ. They are able to discern between the spiritual and the physical, between what is important and what is not, and between what is of God and what is of man. Those who lead well deserve double honor, (1 Tim 5:17) not ordination to authority.

Submission to authority is a contradiction in terms, and Paul's instruction for the Ephesian church to submit themselves to one another provides further evidence that there were no authorities in the first century churches. Submission can only be an option where no authorities exist.

Submission was entirely unnecessary in Israel, because the law and the judges of Israel resolved every dispute which arose among the Israelites. In churches, however, the law and the judges have been replaced by Jesus Christ, and we live by the descriptive laws of the New Covenant. Unfortunately, descriptive laws do not prescribe solutions to the physical problems which may arise among the members of a church, and differences of opinion about physical matters may cause friction between otherwise faithful members. In an effort to provide a way to resolve these disagreements, God has created a new operating system for churches, and this operating system requires no human authorities to direct its function. Mutual cooperation has become the means by which members, who are free from prescriptive laws and human judges, avoid conflicts in the congregation, much the same way yield signs will help to avoid conflicts at otherwise unregulated intersections. Submission has replaced prescriptive laws and serves as the grease which eliminates friction between faithful members. Both leaders and members of a church submit themselves to one another as equals in a cooperative effort to discern and accomplish the will of God, as the Lord directs the church by the Spirit. God requires both leaders and members of the church to cooperate together by "submitting [themselves] one to another in the fear of God." (Eph 5:21)

From time to time disagreements may also arise over the direction a church should take regarding outreach, discipleship, evangelism, fellowship or any other activity the whole church may undertake. Indeed, the distorted perception that these activities are spiritual matters can exacerbate their resolution. However, these issues are simply physical matters involving the preferences of the whole congregation rather than the preferences of an individual member, and such disagreements are resolved in essentially the same way we resolve a disagreement between any two members.

Once again we employ cooperation and submission to resolve the conflict, and the church moves forward when all of the members agree on an appropriate course of action. Since the government of a church is theocracy and not a monarchy or a democracy, the body must depend on its Head, Jesus Christ, to lead each member of the church to agreement. The church does not act by either the will of an authority or the will of the majority, but by the agreement of all of the members. The church cannot move forward until all the members agree. The congregation has discerned the will of God for the church and followed the direction of the Lord and the lead of the Spirit when the all the members reach agreement on the matter.

We should not be surprised that a congregation may not reach full agreement on some issues, and such disagreement may be evidence that the Lord is directing one or more of the members to accomplish a different purpose than the rest. When the entire church cannot agree on a single purpose, the church may pursue two or more purposes, as Jesus Christ directs each group in agreement. Indeed a church will be functioning more like a body when each member is personally led by the Spirit to fulfill a different purpose than any of the other members. Unity in the church is not created through human authority. Unity is not accomplished by doing the same thing. The unity of the body is a spiritual state of being, which is evident when each member listens to the direction of the Lord and follows the lead of the Spirit in everything he or she should do.

The nature of godly church leadership has been camouflaged and corrupted in every organized church. Ordination has elevated the role of church leaders far beyond the inspired biblical model, and the rift created between the clergy and the laity has degraded the role of members to the point that they serve little purpose beyond the funding of the organization. Authorities deny members their gifted roles of service, and even gifted leaders are forbidden to speak in assemblies until they are thoroughly indoctrinated into the teachings of the organization. Flagrant mistranslation is solely responsible for the degenerate state of leadership in organized churches, because translators have imputed contemporary church practice to the words of scripture. English Bibles reflect the translators' experience, which reflects ecclesiastical practice, then ecclesiastical practice shapes a churchgoer's experience to validate what every English Bible says. This circular reasoning cannot be broken until professing believers care enough about the word of God to take the time necessary to carefully examine the inspired Greek text.

Godly church leaders neither assume authority nor do they allow themselves to be ordained to positions of authority. Godly men and women are gifted by the Spirit and placed in leadership roles by God apart from human intervention. Leaders seldom experience a blinding light, which transforms their lives as the apostle Paul did, but rather they are gifted by patience, perseverance, experience and maturity over time, as they practice the faith before the members of their congregations. Leadership is always a function of humility, submission and love as each leader esteems others better than him or herself. Godly leadership is entirely a matter of following the Lord's direction and using the gifts of the Spirit. It has nothing to do with the recognition of authorities for ordained service. God has removed politics from faithful churches, because faithful leaders do not answer to men, but only to the Lord.

Consequently, faithful pastors are free from all organizational responsibility. Pastors are free from the direction of denominational authorities. No one tells a pastor what to do. Pastors are free from bureaucracy and free from paperwork. There is no need to go to the bank or send out offering receipts, because faithful churches do not store up treasure on earth. There is no need to count the offering, because it will be immediately distributed to those in need. There is no need to take attendance, because a spiritual church has no attendance goals to achieve. There is no need for concern about the budget, because holy churches do not have budgets. There are no concerns about being audited by the IRS, because unincorporated groups are free to give as the Spirit leads them, and holy churches have no need to keep records of their members' freewill offerings. A pastor is not at risk to be arrested for excluding a sinner from a meeting, because nonprofit corporate law does not apply to an unincorporated congregation. Church leaders, like members, have absolutely no prescriptive responsibilities. When the Truth makes us free, our leaders are also free indeed.

Chapter 9

The Nature of Organized Churches

True freedom is denied to the members of organized churches. They have established a physical existence through articles of incorporation. They are part of this world. They are not part of the one true Church. The world we see with our eyes is full of illusions, and the visible churches are among those illusions. We can be easily deceived, if we depend on our eyes to determine what is true. Christians must depend entirely on the word of God to reveal what is true and what is false—what is real and what is an illusion. Organized churches are an illusion and a great deception.

The one true Church and the many organized churches embrace opposite realities. One is spiritual and the others are physical. One is true and the others are false. One is a unified spiritual body, and the others are hopelessly divided physical corporations. One depends on God as Ruler, and the others depend on the rulership of men. One depends on Jesus Christ as her Head and sole Authority, and the others depend on human heads and human authority. One knows the Truth, and the others teach and believe lies. One will participate in the wedding feast of the Lamb, and the others God will destroy.

We can see the organized churches, but they are illusions. They are a masterful deception conceived by the great deceiver. Men have created them, but they only exist on paper. This illusionary existence gives them the appearance of serving God, but they are only serving Satan and accomplishing the will of men. Their codified doctrines stand as substitutes for faith, and they embrace the commandments of men instead of the laws of God. They may appear to bear good fruit, but their fruit is corrupt, because their fruit is the product of the tree of the knowledge of good and evil. Their leaders may claim God dwells in them, but the spirit of deception is their god. Pride has lifted up their leaders to stand as antichrists in their churches, and arrogance has allowed them to depreciate and oppress their naïve congregations. Organized churches are products of this world, and their leaders are enemies of God. Their leaders may hypocritically demonstrate an outward appearance of righteousness and piety, but, spiritually speaking, organized churches and their leaders are dead.

The black and white comparison I have drawn here is a contrast between physical and spiritual reality, but the deception of corrupt churches is often difficult to perceive, because a very fine line exists between truth and error. We often consider error to be contrary to truth, but that misperception significantly reinforces the deception. Notice Paul's mistranslated warning to the Roman church.

> Now I beseech you, brethren, mark them which cause divisions and offences **contrary to** the doctrine which ye have learned; and avoid them. (Rom 16:17)

When men speak contrary to truth, their errors are obvious, but Paul's instruction here is much more enlightening. Notice the literal definition of *"para,"* which is translated "contrary to" in this verse.

NT:3844
para (par-ah'); a primary preposition; properly, **near;** i.e. (with genitive case) from beside (literally or figuratively), (with dative case) at (or in) the vicinity of (objectively or subjectively), (with accusative case) to the proximity with (local [especially beyond or opposed to] or causal [on account of]):

Paul was not so concerned about men who might teach doctrine which was opposite to the truth, but he warned the Roman church about men who caused division by teaching things which were very close to the truth. He warned them to reject instruction which was only near to the doctrine they had learned. Jesus Himself warned the disciples about those who would claim He was the Christ but would deceive many. (Matt 24:5) How is that possible? Because they teach doctrine which is very close to the truth. They exalt English Bibles which are only near to the inspired text. Those who speak contrary to scripture are easy to spot, but the inspired text of scripture warns us not to be deceived by pastors whose instruction is only near to the truth or by churches which function very close to the biblical model. Religion can be easily mistaken for godly worship, but we cannot allow ourselves to be deceived by ornately appointed sanctuaries, polished orators and choreographed worship shows.

Satan has been able to wholly deceive organized Christianity for several reasons. Lack of personal Bible study among members is a major factor, and wide dependency on English translations among pastors contributes significantly to the deception, but the primary reason that most people have difficulty recognizing the deception of organized churches is because few grasp the true nature and inherent evil of the world. Before you can understand the nature of organized churches, you need to first consider the nature of the world and understand it in terms of Greek thought.

God's perspective of the world is very different from the world most of us perceive. We may think we know what the world is, but, unless we view the world through the eyes of the apostles, we may not be able to perceive its exact nature or the extent of its corruption. A biblical perspective is required to reveal its true nature. Spiritual vision is required to reveal its corrupt state. When we view the world from a purely human perspective, we are likely to think the world is not all that bad, and we're likely to miss the inherent evil in the organized systems of government we all take for granted.

The English word "world" appears in our Bibles as the equivalent of four Greek words, each of these having its own specific meaning, so our translations will convey a less precise meaning than those four inspired words conveyed to their Greek readers. The four Greek words translated "world" in our English Bibles are *oikoumene*, *ge*, *aion*, and *kosmos*. I offer here a more focused definition of each Greek word in bold type within a brief description. The notation in brackets is my own observation based on an exhaustive Greek concordance study of each Greek word.

NT:3625 *oikoumene*	The world in the sense of the **land** or **territory,** including its inhabitants. [There is such a world to come. (Heb 2:5)]
NT:1093 *ge*	The world in the sense of the **soil** or **ground**, particularly the earth. [There is such a world to come. (2 Pet 3:13)]
NT:165 *aion*	The world in the sense of an **age**, either a long period of time or perpetual time. [There is such a world to come. (Eph 2:7)]
NT:2889 *kosmos*	The world in the sense of its **orderly arrangement**, particularly as the universe is organized. [There is no such world to come.]

Immediately apparent is the wide diversity of underlying Greek concepts which English translations obscure with the single word "world" in our Bibles. The apostles used the first two listed above, *oikoumene* and *ge*, in matter-of-fact references to either the people of the earth or the earth itself, and they invoke neither praise nor condemnation from the various Bible writers. *Aion* is primarily a reference to an "age" of time, most frequently to the period of the present age. The Bible contrasts the present age with the age to come, but it rarely portrays the former in an overtly negative light. However, passages discussing the *kosmos* almost always portray the world in a negative light, and they are often replete with overtly judgmental rhetoric. Of the four worlds of Greek thought, only the *kosmos* has no future counterpart in the age to come.

Based on an accumulation of facts gleaned from a selection of verses which include the Greek word *kosmos*, the following composite picture of the *kosmos* emerges. The *kosmos* is the evil world of which Satan is the prince. This world has not known either God or us. God will reprove this world, and the saints will judge it. The lust of the flesh, the lust of the eyes and the pride of life are promoted and indulged in this world. This world is guilty before God, and God deems this world's wisdom to be foolishness in His eyes. Corruption is in this world as well as the spirit of the antichrist. One who is a friend of this world is an enemy of God. We are in this world, but not of it, and it is from this world we are to remain unspotted. We are chastened of the Lord, so we will not be condemned with this world. We should not love this world or the things in it, since we have already escaped the pollution of this world. We have trouble in this world, but Christ has overcome this world, which lies in wickedness and will pass away forever.

The contrast between the *kosmos* and the other three worlds of the Greek text is profound. Although none of the four worlds is exalted and each will end, almost all the condemnation of the world appears within the context of the *kosmos*. What is it about the *kosmos* that is so inherently evil and invokes the wrath of God?

The literal definition of *kosmos* will shed significant light on the Greek concept of the world, and this definition will begin to expose the underlying cause of much of the evil suffered by human beings living in this world, believer and unbeliever alike. Notice the literal meaning of *kosmos* from Strong's Greek Dictionary.

NT:2889
kosmos (kos'-mos); probably from the base of NT:2865; **orderly arrangement**, i.e. decoration; by implication, the world (in a wide or narrow sense, including its inhabitants, literally or figuratively [morally]):

At first glance you might wonder what "orderly arrangement" has to do with our world. Indeed, *kosmos* has nothing directly to do with the natural state of the earth or the people living on the earth, but it is more directly a description of the nature of the universe, and it aptly describes the precision of the entire physical creation. The Greeks stood in awe of the perfect order they saw in the heavens and the inerrant predictability of the courses of the heavenly bodies. God's arrangement of the universe in an orderly manner inspired the Greek concept of the *kosmos* and God has blessed us with even more spectacular views of the beauty of the universe and the order of the galaxies through the stunning photographs astronomers have been able to capture. *Kosmos* derives its essential meaning from the orderly arrangement of the celestial bodies of the universe.

Even the naked eye can track the orderly arrangement of the bodies of our solar system, and astronomers predict their courses centuries in advance, but the telescope has opened an even more profound reality to our view, and modern imaging techniques allow us to see our home in the universe from a much broader perspective. Spectacular spiral galaxies display an even more complete picture of the orderly arrangement of the universe.

A galaxy is a complete star system, and all the stars in a galaxy revolve around the central core of the galaxy. Within each solar system planets, asteroids, comets and meteors orbit their stars in various patterns. Also within these systems, moons revolve around many planets of the solar systems. A galaxy is a star system with an orderly arrangement, and the arrangement is naturally hierarchical.

A most interesting phenomenon of our Milky Way galaxy, which is also suspected to be true of most galaxies, is the black hole which exists at the center of our galaxy. A black hole is a star so massive that even light cannot escape its powerful gravitational pull. A black hole attracts every body in the galaxy toward itself. The nature of our galaxy is a hierarchically ordered system with a black hole at its center. Billions of such systems comprise the universe.

Although the Greek word *kosmos* was directly inspired by the orderly arrangement of the bodies of the universe, the apostles used it in the narrower sense of the earth or the world, specifically the earth's inhabitants. Within most contexts of the Bible, it can only be understood this way. The apostles clearly had people in mind rather than our planet or the universe when they wrote about the *kosmos*. Therefore, we must consider the possibility that in some way the earth, or more specifically the earth's human population, has been altered to reflect orderly arrangement.

Every single body in the universe is unique, and the earth is no exception. Our planet is not naturally an orderly arrangement, but a single body with a white-hot core, a warm heart and a thin fertile skin upon which we all live. Our planet is unique, and all forms of life on the earth are unique. No two trees are exactly alike. No two birds are identical. Each blade of grass is unique. Unlike the galaxies of the universe, the earth is a single body producing unique living things, which exist apart from any natural hierarchical order.

Likewise, the earth's human inhabitants are each unique. Most of us enjoy uniqueness, and we like people to treat us uniquely. We like people to call us by name. We don't like to take a number. We like to talk directly to the person in charge. We don't like bureaucracies. We like to be special. We don't like to wait in line. We like to do it "my way." We don't like others to tell us what to do. Human beings are not easily ordered in any type of arrangement, because unique things are not easily organized. Orderly arrangement is unnatural to us. We would, on the other hand, be perfectly suited to be members of a body, because each member of a body is unique, and each member of a body performs a unique function.

On this unique planet filled with unique beings and unique things, you may have difficulty recognizing how the earth has become arranged to reflect the orderly system plainly visible in the heavens above. Indeed, orderly arrangement does not occur naturally in our planet, but you can only see it in the unnatural order which men have imposed upon human society. Men have organized the earth's population into an orderly arrangement through the influence of the prince of darkness—the one who is typed by the black hole of our galaxy. Men's sinful desire to dominate other men, especially politically and economically, has driven men to organize the unique human beings of God's creation into governments and corporations with Satan at the center of the arrangement, just as each galaxy is a hierarchically ordered system with a black hole at its center. Although we can appreciate the beauty and precision of the orderly arrangement of the universe, God intended the entire human creation to remain free from the type of orderly arrangement seen in the universe. The orderly arrangement of the human population into governments and corporations is unnatural to the uniquely created and uniquely functioning inhabitants of the earth.

The beauty of the universe and the inherent evil of the world both reflect hierarchical order. God created and ordered the physical universe, but human rulers and authorities under the influence of Satan have organized the world. Every form of organization one might observe in the world, whether governmental, corporate, political, educational or any other type of human organization, is a hierarchically ordered system. Rulers make rules and authorize authorities to enforce the rules within the organization. The larger the organization, the more oppressive and cumbersome the hierarchical system becomes. Layers upon layers of bureaucrats and bureaucracy increasingly shield those at the bottom from those at the top so that communication becomes extremely difficult and oppression and injustice invariably result. Hierarchical order is the essence of the world of Greek thought and is by nature a system of oppression, injustice and bondage. Contrary to God's will, men have established the same hierarchical system of oppression, injustice and bondage in every organized church. One might rightly suspect that organized churches have become what they ought not to be.

God was not surprised by Satan's influence in the world and men's desire to dominate their fellow humans. Since the world's population has been transformed into an orderly arrangement, God has assumed the responsibility to choose and establish the human rulers in the world and use them to accomplish His purposes on earth. Civil authority maintains a certain level of peace and safety in society, so God requires each of us to respect the authorities He has placed in the world. Each of us as a separate creation of God may allow our individual physical lives to be arranged according to the ritualistic rules and regulations of a government or a corporation, but God requires that we as a body—we as the temple of God—we as His Church—remain free from the orderly arrangement of the world and reject hierarchical human organization in churches.

Any hierarchical order stands contrary to God's purpose for a church. God is about the business of creating a body for His Son, and the rulership of human organizations stands opposed to God's purpose to rule all churches personally through His Law. The commands of human authorities also stand opposed to Christ's role to live within a church as its Head and to command all the members of the church individually and personally to do God's will and to accomplish His purposes.

The language barrier shields those of us who only read English from the true spiritual nature of the world to which the apostles alluded. Our English word "world" refers only to the globe upon which we live or to the people living in it. The world of the English language speaks only of a place or its inhabitants. In the mainstream Christian perspective, the world conjures up images of an inherently bad place where its people are sinful and indulge themselves in unspeakable evils. Since sinful people and sinful acts occur in the world, some might see sin as the evil of the world. Since wealth, power and immorality are frequently involved with the worst evils of the world, others might see the world as a place where powerful men and seductive women wallow in the lifestyle of the rich and the famous. In the minds of many churchgoers, the world is simply an evil place where evil people do evil things.

However, the Koine Greek language offered early Christians a completely different image of the world. Rather than an evil place or type of people, the apostles described the world of the first century as a system—a social order—a particular arrangement of its people. When the writers of the books of the New Testament described the world as an orderly arrangement, they asserted that the evil was inherent in the system of government rather than in the planet or the people. In the minds of Greek speaking believers, the inherent evil of the world was its hierarchical system of human government.

God created human beings to function independently, so we could be free from external human governance, and especially so God could rule us and the Lord could direct each of us from within. The inherently evil system of men ruling over men in a hierarchical system stands opposed to God's purposes, and orderly arrangement usurps His prerogative to rule all churches and command His people personally through His Word.

Human orderly arrangement dominates and controls every person living under its oppressive system. The evidence of the world of the *kosmos* is all around us, and every orderly arrangement from governmental bureaucracies to corporate conglomerates reveals its presence. Mega-malls and big box stores, world banks and stock exchanges, highway systems and traffic signals, assembly lines and credit card purchasing are only possible because of the hierarchical system of human rulership and authority. These creations of human minds are not necessarily evil of and by themselves, but they are all symptomatic of the inherently evil system of hierarchical order, which attempts to organize and control our lives in spite of our natural autonomous function. There are increasingly fewer activities of life which the tentacles of this inherently evil system of human governance do not control. God has allowed men to impose all this organization upon society in the present age, but the orderly arrangement of the world's inhabitants will end after Christ returns. His second coming will signal the end of hierarchical order on the earth. The Bible indicates that there will be no *kosmos*—there will be no orderly arrangement—there will be no human rulers or human authorities to organize and regulate life in the government of the kingdoms of the earth in the age to come.

The mainstream Christian view of sinful people occupying their time with sinful activities in a sinful society is a smoke screen which camouflages the real spiritual evil in the world. The earth is not an inherently evil place, but a beautiful, productive garden created for our benefit and pleasure. Sin is not the inherent evil in the world, because sin occurs in both the world and the Church. Wealth is not the inherent evil of the world, because some people are able to manage disproportionate amounts of this world's wealth in a wise and generous way. All these perceptions of the world combine to obscure the real evil of the world from English speaking Christians. However, the inherent evil nature of the organized systems which increasingly dominate and regulate nearly every aspect of our physical lives was impressed upon the minds of Greek-speaking Christians every time they uttered the word *kosmos*.

Paul described the triumph of Jesus Christ over the evil nature of the *kosmos*—the world's hierarchical systems of government—in his letter written to the Colossian church. This passage contains several mistranslations which obscure the literal meaning of the inspired Greek text. Literal translations appear in brackets.

> Beware lest any man spoil you through philosophy and vain deceit, after the tradition of men, after the [principles] of the [orderly arrangement], and not after Christ. For in him dwelleth all the fulness of the Godhead bodily. And ye are complete in him, which is the head of all [rule] and [authority]: ...And having spoiled [rulers] and [authorities], he made a shew of them openly, triumphing over them in it. Let no man therefore judge you... (Col 2:8-10, 15-16)

Could Paul's insight and admonition be plainer? Christ has overcome the organized systems of the world. He has spoiled their rulers and their authorities. Theocracy dwells in Him, and we are complete in Him. He is above the rulers and authorities of the world's systems of government. The Church lives in Him in heaven, and we cannot allow rulers and authorities to govern a church at all. A church has no need of a hierarchical system of government, because our Ruler and our Authority live in us, and we in Him.

In the literal Greek text Paul says Christ "wholly divested himself of" the human rulers and the human authorities of the world. Having departed this world in glory, Jesus Christ now lives above and apart from any human rulership or authority, and those who live in Him are complete in Him. We do not need human rulers and human authorities to govern the churches or to direct the activities of the members, because the theocracy of God lives in us through His Son. We are not to be spoiled or "led away as booty" through philosophy, vain deceit, the traditions of men, or the corrupt principles of orderly arrangement. We must not permit any human ruler or any human authority to judge us in our spiritual walk with Christ, but we allow the Spirit to lead each of us, as God accomplishes His will for the Church through us. God rules us through His Son from within, so humanly imposed external order is not required within churches. Human rulership and authority in a church is anathema.

The Church lives by God's rules, not man's. His laws are a higher standard than any human standard, and the standard of Jesus Christ renders all codified law obsolete. Man's rules prescribe uniformity in society which is not required within churches, and, indeed, human standards of uniformity oppose God's laws and compromise the uniqueness of each believer. Codified laws work contrary to God's purposes and contravene the requirement that each member of the body performs a unique function in the body of Christ. All of man's prescriptive laws and authoritative commands stand opposed to the spiritual freedom granted to every church under the New Covenant. Every church must live by God's laws and remain free from the hierarchical systems of social order.

A church cannot live by the laws of God and the laws of men. The rules and regulations of human governments are contrary to the laws of God. The civil laws of man prohibit a church from any discrimination. The laws of God require the church to discriminate between the righteous and sinners, the holy and the profane, the just and the unjust. Civil law requires churches to accept those of every socially accepted lifestyle, but God requires His people to disassociate themselves from those who live in any sinful lifestyle. (1 Cor 5:4, 5, 13) Civil law makes the whole congregation liable for the mistakes of church leaders. The laws of God hold each of us responsible for our own sins. (Deut 24:16) Civil law requires the doors of a church to be open to anyone who wants to come in and watch and listen. The direction of the Lord commands us not to give what is holy to the dogs. (Matt 7:6) Civil law requires organized churches to comply with IRS rules and regulations. God says He alone is the Lawgiver. (Jas 4:12) No one rules a faithful church, except the sovereign God.

Jesus frequently stood against the rulers and the authorities of Jewish society. The Jewish people generally liked Jesus, because He healed them, removed demons and restored sound minds to those who were lunatic, but the religious rulers and authorities hated Him, because He severely rebuked them when they confronted Him about matters of their law. Jesus stood opposed to their rules and their laws and condemned their hypocrisy. While each of us, individually, should respect civil rulers and authorities, we, collectively, comprise the body of Christ in heaven, and we must, as Jesus does, stand opposed to all human rule, human authority and human power within every church, as we fellowship together in freedom as unique and equal members of His body.

When Jesus returns as the conquering King, the world's governments will be overthrown. The kingdoms of this world will become the kingdoms of our Lord and of His Christ, and He will reign forever and ever. (Rev 11:15) Jesus Christ will put down all rule, all authority and power and remove human government from the nations of the earth. Although this passage describes the future demise of human governments, notice Paul's comments in his letter to the Corinthian church. What does Paul reveal about the nature of rule, authority, power and death? What does each of these four elements have in common?

> Then cometh the end, when he shall have delivered up the kingdom to God, even the Father; when he shall have put down <u>all rule</u> and <u>all authority</u> and <u>power</u>. For he must reign, till he hath put **all enemies** under his feet. The last **enemy** that shall be destroyed is <u>death</u>. (1 Cor 15:24-26)

If you read carefully, I believe you will see that rule, authority, power and death are all enemies of God. Human rule stands opposed to God's rule. Human authority stands opposed to Christ's authority. Human power stands opposed to the power of the Holy Spirit. Human rule, authority and power are naturally enemies of God. Do you believe God would intentionally place His enemies in a church? Would God place rulers and authorities in a church, if rulers and authorities contravene His purposes? God has left civil rulers and civil authorities in the world to maintain relative peace, order and safety in the societies of the world until Christ returns, but He has stripped them from the Church where God alone rules, where Jesus Christ is the Head and sole Authority and where power comes from the Holy Spirit alone to give encouragement, protection and strength to churches living by the faith of Jesus Christ.

The orderly arrangement of the world and the enemies of God are deceptive evils. There are certain worldly advantages to human government and organization, and we often benefit physically from their existence in the world. Organization is a product of the tree of the knowledge of good and evil, so it will invariably provide some benefit and some detriment in our lives. Governments provide civil order, relative safety and many services individuals could not provide for themselves. Corporations are able to produce quality products at reasonable prices, such as the computer which made my biblical research and this book possible. However, when a church allows human rule and human authority to exercise human power over the church, the enemies of God and the essential evil of the world have come to dwell in that church.

Notwithstanding, even casual observation will reveal that human government has been established in every organized church to one extent or another. The world is in a church when any leader is in a position of authority in the church. The world is in a church when any hierarchical order is in the church. Some human governments in churches may be blatantly controlling, while other human governments may be almost invisible to the average member. However, the degree to which such governments exercise their authority does not determine whether or not the world is in a church. The mere presence of human government in a church indicates that the world is in that church. Human government cannot be *in* a church, nor can human government be *in authority over* a church.

The nature and goals of all organizations are diametrically opposed to God's nature, His purposes for the Church and the nature of the Church itself. The nature of all organizations is to rule, to command and to exercise power to enforce its will. Every organization, whether governmental, corporate or ecclesiastical controls the actions of those within the organization by making rules to standardize performance and by empowering authorities to enforce the rules by commanding the people in specific situations. In the United States the federal and state legislatures, as well as local governments, rule our lives by enacting laws, and they empower a hierarchical bureaucracy of federal, state and local authorities to enforce the laws by demanding compliance in various routine or emergency situations. Under the authority and regulation of the government, corporations also make rules to regulate worker performance, and they employ a hierarchical system of management personnel to command their employees in specific situations in an effort to guarantee the uniformity of their products. Sadly, the world's churches are similarly organized and oppressive. Ordained apostles, prophets, pastors and priests control and manipulate their members to serve the purposes of their church organizations. These organizations mandate their doctrines as a substitute for truth, and the rules and regulations of men substitute for the laws of God and faith in Jesus Christ. The goal of every organization, whether governmental, corporate or ecclesiastical, is to rule and control its citizens, employees or members to produce a uniform product which must meet the standards of the organization.

Ultimately, the goal of every organization is to produce exact replicas. The goal of a governmental organization is to produce a society, in which every citizen obeys its prescriptive laws. The goal of a corporate organization is to produce products of exactly the same type and quality. The goal of an educational organization is to produce "A" students, who all know the correct answers to the standardized tests. Similarly, the goal of a church organization is to produce members who conform to the standards set forth in the catechism or doctrine of the organized church. Few seem to consider the obvious nature of organizations and their overtly stated purposes, which inevitably produce exact replicas.

God is not creating a body of penguins. God is creating a fully fitted spiritual body, arranged just like a physical body, in which every member is unique and every member has a unique responsibility to fulfill. A body cannot fully function unless each member is performing its unique task. Likewise, we, as members of the body of Christ, must be free to perform our unique responsibilities as the Lord directs us. To the extent that a member conforms to the doctrine of a church organization and follows the direction of a church leader, the member becomes an exact replica of the organization. One becomes a spiritual penguin. Christianity is not about *doing* certain things or even about doing *any* thing. Christianity is about *being* holy. Christianity is not about what we do. It is entirely about who we are. Paul criticized some of the members of the Corinthian church for wanting to be like other members of the congregation. (1 Cor 12:14-20) Paul encouraged the members to cherish their uniqueness, because he knew those who imitated men would become replicas of the men they imitated.

In an effort to impose orthodox religion upon their members, organized churches frequently prescribe arbitrary rules for their congregations, some of which include priestly celibacy, abstinence from alcohol, the requirement to tithe on income, as well as a host of arbitrary, prescriptive regulations from card-playing, movie-going, dancing and gambling to cosmetic make up and the wearing of hats.

Church organizations invariably claim to derive their rules from the Bible, so pastors often twist or misapply scripture to support the enforcement of all sorts of rules enjoined upon their congregations. Most churches carefully avoid overt rulership, the church-state government of the Vatican being a notable exception, but every organized church rules its members to one extent or the other. Church leaders more frequently use authoritative commands rather than rules, but, as a matter of practice, overt commands are even unnecessary, because members frequently view the mere suggestion of a leader vested with authority as a command to be obeyed.

The otherwise subtle practice of ruling and commanding has become so blatantly oppressive in some church organizations that more moderately governed churches have become outraged by those who blatantly enforce the old covenant laws. The former group has coined an expression to define the nature of what they consider to be wholly unbiblical enforcement of those laws. They call it legalism. Unfortunately, it is a case of the pot calling the kettle black. Legalism exists in every organized church, because authorities exist in every organized church. Legalism is largely a function of human authority in churches. Rare indeed is the case where a layman even tries to govern a fellow member of a church. Legalism is a natural symptom of a systemic problem resulting from hierarchical order in churches, and it is a direct result of human authority in a church. When churches remove the authorities from their congregations, legalism will virtually disappear. Legalism is only a symptom. Authority is the cause.

When a leader assumes authority in a congregation or is ordained to a position of authority in a church, that leader is living in sin. His spiritual state has changed from being a leader to being an authority. Leaders may not be what Jesus told the disciples they should not be. (Matt 20:25-27) A leader may sin, but a leader may not be a sinner. A leader may sin from time to time and legalistically command another member of the congregation, and God will forgive his legalism, but when a leader becomes an authority—when he becomes a commander—when he becomes what Jesus told the disciples they ought not to be, then he is living in sin whether he gives any further commands or not. His actions do not determine his spiritual state, but his pride-filled nature determines it. The leader who has become an authority and stands in the congregation as an authority stands in the place of Jesus Christ. Any leader who has been ordained to a position of authority in a church is living in sin and has made himself a sinner once again. We need not judge such an individual, because he will judge himself. The lifestyle sin of pride will cause him to readily verify that he is an authority in the church. Lifestyle pride has filled all church authorities, and they have all become sinners once again.

When a church leader is living in sin, lifestyle sin will invariably spread like cancer in the congregation and also infect the members. A church member may sin from time to time and allow another member to command him regarding his walk with the Lord, or he may in a time of weakness depend on a man to legalistically order his spiritual life, but, if that member recognizes any man as an authority in his spiritual life and the member is looking to the human authority instead of looking to Jesus Christ, that member is committing idolatry, and he or she is also living in sin. In Old Testament times the people of God went to the groves to commit idolatry. Today they go to organized churches.

Additionally, a church may sin from time to time and receive forgiveness from God, but the church may never allow hierarchical government to be in the church. The church may never allow human rulership or human authority to be in the church. When the world—when the *kosmos*—when the orderly arrangement of hierarchical human authority is existing within a church, that church is no longer part of the spiritual Church. The human authority has become the head of the church, and the existence of a human head in a church separates it from the spiritual Church. The human head is living in sin and the church is living in sin, because the church is allowing the world to live in it. That entire congregation is in danger of hell fire unless the world—the *kosmos*—is removed from it. (Matt 5:29-30)

The love of money is a root cause of all evil, (1 Tim 6:10) and the desire for worldly treasure will further corrupt every organized church. A pastor's desire for money and physical things will lead that church to store up treasures on earth, and his desire to further increase those earthly treasures is the driving force which inevitably lures church fellowships into covenants with the rulers of this world. Unbiblical authoritative leadership is the fundamental cause of illicit covenants and spiritual fornication.

Church leaders know nice buildings and comfortable pews draw people to church, so extravagant amounts of money from church offerings are spent to purchase land and build churches. They know people expect intelligent, qualified pastors trained at the most reputable seminaries, so churches hire the best theologians they can afford. They know people expect an uplifting church meeting with talented musicians and gifted singers, so some churches even hire people to organize the worship service. They know the congregation wants to enjoy the entertainment and hear the message, so they provide the best sound systems with the latest mixing and graphic capability. Church leaders know food draws people to fellowship, so they provide snacks before and after church, if not a full breakfast and lunch. Church leaders know all these things draw people to church, so they want to provide all these things for their members. However, all these physical things cost money, and the expenditure of money first requires the receipt of money.

Unfortunately, any flow of money between citizens of a civil government will very quickly draw the attention of the federal and state revenue agencies. Human governments depend on commerce for their revenue, and all commerce, even gifts, is taxable. Unless a church transforms itself into a nonprofit corporation, all money received by any individual or group in the church is taxable to those who receive it. The pastor, or whoever receives the money, would be required to pay tax on all the church contributions. Additionally, no contribution given to a private individual, like the pastor, or an unincorporated group, like the offering committee, is tax deductible for the contributor. Members of unincorporated churches receive no tax benefit for their freewill offerings to their church. Thus, the church would be required to pay tax on every contribution, and the members would receive no tax deduction for their contributions. The government cannot recognize an unincorporated church, because it has no visible head. A spiritual church has no human head to sign a covenant with the government or bow to the rules and regulations of nonprofit corporate law in order to gain the tax benefit. Unless a church designates a human head to create articles of incorporation and by-laws for the church, it cannot incorporate, and the unincorporated church remains invisible to physical eyes. No tax exemption is possible, because a spiritual body remains invisible to human rulers, human authorities and human governments.

Now, if human rulers had spiritual vision, they could easily see that the Spirit unites the members of every unincorporated church into one spiritual body. (1 Cor 12:20) They could plainly see that the tithes and offerings the members contributed were not really being passed from one body to another, but rather that the money was simply being collected and stored within a single spiritual body. With spiritual vision, the government would plainly see that the members of the church were simply giving to themselves, and, consequently, contributions made by members of the church within the spiritual body of the church would not be taxable. But alas, the government has no such spiritual vision.

However, God indeed has excellent spiritual vision. God clearly recognizes that those who give money to their organized church are really just giving to themselves, so He gives no particular credit in heaven for those who give to their church. He knows they will receive the vast majority of their offerings back again in the form of steepled churches, trained pastors, religious literature and physical sustenance, just to mention some of the lesser, albeit very expensive, benefits of church membership. God does not give us a heavenly reward when we reap an earthly reward.

God only gives us a heavenly reward when we give to the Lord. Jesus specifically gave us the parable of the sheep and the goats, so we would know how to give to the Lord most effectively and, thereby, give to God and store up treasure in heaven.

> When the Son of man shall come in his glory, and all the holy angels with him, then shall he sit upon the throne of his glory: And before him shall be gathered all nations: and he shall separate them one from another, as a shepherd divideth his sheep from the goats: And he shall set the sheep on his right hand, but the goats on the left. Then shall the King say unto them on his right hand, Come, ye blessed of my Father, inherit the kingdom prepared for you from the foundation of the world: **For I was an hungred, and ye gave me meat: I was thirsty, and ye gave me drink: I was a stranger, and ye took me in: Naked, and ye clothed me: I was sick, and ye visited me: I was in prison, and ye came unto me.** Then shall the

> righteous answer him, saying, Lord, when saw we thee an hungred, and fed thee? or thirsty, and gave thee drink? When saw we thee a stranger, and took thee in? or naked, and clothed thee? Or when saw we thee sick, or in prison, and came unto thee? And the King shall answer and say unto them, **Verily I say unto you, Inasmuch as ye have done it unto one of the least of these my [brothers], ye have done it unto me.** (Matt 25:31-40)

Jesus explained that we give to Him by giving to one of His brothers. We might easily misconstrue Jesus' meaning, if we were to assume Jesus meant we should give to one of His brothers, the Jews. Although the context of the passage clearly tells us that God will gather the sheep and goats from all nations, Jesus left no doubt about whom He meant when He referred to His brothers.

> While [Jesus] yet talked to the people, behold, his mother and his brethren stood without, desiring to speak with him. Then one said unto him, Behold, thy mother and thy brethren stand without, desiring to speak with thee. But he answered and said unto him that told him, **Who is my mother? and who are my [brothers]? And he stretched forth his hand toward his disciples, and said, Behold my mother and my [brothers]! For whosoever shall do the will of my Father which is in heaven, the same is my brother, and sister, and mother.**
> (Matt 12:46-50)

Christians give to God when we give to someone in whom the Lord is walking on earth. We give to God by giving to one of Jesus' sheep—one of His disciples—one of His children who is doing the Father's will. We give to God by personally attending to the physical needs of a believer who is sick or hungry. We give to God when we give to a believer who is less fortunate than the rest of us. We receive no tax benefit, but we store up treasure in heaven.

Many church leaders teach that members give to God when they give to their church, but that concept is a subtle lie intended to pick your pocket. Don't believe a lie. The Bible doesn't say that. The truth is: no one can give to a church, because a church is a spiritual entity. A church can't be seen. A church is invisible to human eyes until it ordains a human head and becomes a nonprofit organization. Then every time well-meaning people attempt to give to the Church, the authorities divert the funds to the organization, and the Church—the holy ones—the body of Christ—never receives a cent. No one can give to a church. One can only give to the organization. The only way to give to God is to give to an individual in whom God dwells.

Some may recognize the implications of Jesus' words and try to circumvent the difficulty by earmarking their church offerings to benefit a specific individual whom they may feel is in need of assistance. Unfortunately, the Internal Revenue Service (IRS) restricts the ability of a church member to earmark contributions for a particular individual. IRS Publication 1828 states: "…net earnings [i.e. church contributions] may not inure to the benefit of any private individual." Thus, IRS regulation prohibits a church member from giving to an individual through a church organization. Federal law makes it illegal to give to God through a church! Once you give to a church organization, the money is out of your control, and you can claim no reward from God for what an organization does with the money. There is no heavenly reward for giving to any organization.

There is a simple way to determine whether you have given to God or given to an organization, because the government grants no tax deduction for giving to an individual. If you have given to a church and your contribution is tax deductible, you have given to an organization. If you have given to a believer who is hungry, thirsty, homeless, naked, sick or in jail, you will receive no tax benefit, but God will consider your gift as a gift to Himself, and your heavenly account will receive full credit. You can only give to God on an individual basis, and you should not expect to receive anything in return for your gift. If you receive a tax deduction for your freewill offerings, you have received your reward, and you should not expect to receive any additional reward from God.

God expects each member to be personally involved in providing for the physical needs of other believers, but God alone provides all the needs of a church. A church is a spiritual body, and a church has no physical needs. Human beings have no power or ability to provide for the needs of a church. A church has no need of a house.

A church has no need of clothing or food or water. A church has no need of anything physical. A church certainly has no need of money. Each spiritual church lives in heaven as part of the united body, where God alone provides every need for every church.

Just as a physical body has physical needs, a spiritual body has spiritual needs. God alone has the power to provide spiritual needs, and God provides all the needs of a church. He has provided the Word as our spiritual food, and He has provided Christ's blood as our spiritual drink. (John 6:48-58) God has clothed us with humility (1 Pet 5:5) and righteousness. (Rev 19:8) so that the church is not spiritually naked. The church has no need of collective shelter, because the church lives in heaven in Christ. Even physically, we each have a body, so our individual bodies are temporary shelters for the members of the church. The church is living in booths, so to speak. The Lord is preparing a permanent place for us to live within Himself, and He will gather us all together and shelter us in that spiritual abode upon His return. (John 14:1-3)

Since God provides all the needs of a church, Jesus knew the church would have no need for money or for any other physical things, so He prohibited any church from storing up any treasure on earth, where that treasure can deteriorate, be stolen or devalued by inflation. A church may collect money and goods and immediately dispense them to those in need, but a church may not lay up any treasures on earth.

> Lay not up for yourselves treasures upon earth, where moth and rust doth corrupt, and where thieves break through and steal: But lay up for yourselves treasures in heaven, where neither moth nor rust doth corrupt, and where thieves do not break through nor steal: For where your treasure is there will your heart be also. (Matt 6:19-21)

Few really grasp the grammar of this verse. Most overlook the plural pronouns and the explicit negative it contains. Jesus' words entirely prohibit laying up any treasures on earth for those addressed in this context. Although we easily understand that all lying is sin when scripture says we should <u>not</u> lie, and we never consider that some stealing might be permitted when scripture says we should <u>not</u>

steal, somehow the little word "not" alludes many interpreters. Most seem to intuitively know Jesus could not possibly forbid all savings of money or goods and demand they give every penny they earn to Him and live in continual poverty, but few are able to discern the context to determine exactly what Jesus is saying.

Unfamiliarity with second person pronouns has frequently led pastors to read over the context of this verse and misapply Jesus' words. The plural forms of the second person pronouns in this verse set the context for Jesus' instruction. Many have ignored the context and misinterpreted this instruction, because they have failed to understand that plural pronouns address churches, not individuals. Since we know a spiritual body has no need for physical things, we may more easily understand why Jesus directed this instruction to the collective body of each church as a whole. We plainly see the plural form here in the reflexive pronoun "yourselves" rather than the singular "thyself," and in the possessive plural pronoun "your" rather than the singular "thy." Jesus' instruction absolutely prohibits any accumulation of wealth or physical possessions for a church. Churches may not lay up any treasures on earth.

Contrary to popular teaching, this instruction does not address individual church members. There is no biblical prohibition for an individual to store up treasures on earth. As wise stewards of God's provision, each of us should prudently prepare for a rainy day, for retirement or for other future needs. The Lord discouraged building larger barns simply for the sake of amassing great wealth, but God does not discourage reasonable savings for vacations, special occasions or major purchases. Even benevolent giving is best done out of what has been laid up rather than taxing the current budget. Not only are we, as individuals, not prohibited from laying up treasures on earth, we are specifically directed by God to lay up responsibly for future generations. God does not expect us to spend every nickel we earn and die in poverty. God requires that we, as individuals and parents, should store up for our children's future.

> ...for the children ought not to lay up for the parents,
> but the parents for the children. (2 Cor 12:14)

The Greek verb, *thesaurizo*, is translated "lay up" in both this verse and the one above. God does not prohibit individual Christians from laying up treasure on earth, but He has indeed prohibited every church from making any accumulation of money or goods for the obvious reason that a church is a spiritual entity and has no need for physical possessions. When churches buy land and build buildings, they are storing up treasure on earth. When churches have savings accounts and certificates of deposit, they are storing up treasure on earth. When churches make any purchases of goods, they are storing up treasure on earth. When churches take up any collection which they do not immediately dispense to those in need, they are in direct violation of Jesus' words. Churches have no need for anything physical. All the needs of a church are spiritual, because the church is spiritual, and God continually provides all those spiritual needs. A congregation's trust in God for all its needs is the essence of faith.

On the other hand, an organization absolutely needs money. Money is the lifeblood of an organization. Any physical or spiritual body can live without money, but an organization without money is dead. A church organization is no different, so a church organization without money will also die. The people—the calling out—the members don't die, but the organization dies. Don't waste your money on church organizations, but rather give personally to those in need. Church organizations divert money intended to preach the gospel to build monuments to themselves, and we stand in awe of the magnificent cathedrals and sacred buildings where no one is allowed to live. Corrupt church organizations try to protect their own, so they squander hundreds of millions of dollars of their members' offerings on abuse settlements and other lawsuits. Some churches spend thousands of dollars to advertise for more members, so the offering baskets can be filled even fuller. Organized churches are desperate for money to preserve their organizations, because they are all corrupt, and they all operate contrary to the laws of God. They depend on money, not on God.

Spiritually blind church leaders seem unaware that God does not dwell in a house or that a church has no need of a physical dwelling. Contrary to the direct prohibition of the Lord, they have ignorantly set their hearts on building houses for God and meeting places for the church, when such investments of money and effort serve no purpose for God or the church. These leaders are frequently able to convince unsuspecting members that God will be served, if they support the endeavor financially. The greater the membership, the more feasible the undertaking will be, but small congregations are often heavily burdened by the realities of a mortgage and the cost of building maintenance. Building fund collections can become an overriding priority, and, combined with normal congregational giving, members' personal budgets may become strained. Dozens of church organizations collapse each year under the weight of the fiscal responsibilities of property ownership and management. When the money dries up, church organizations die.

When an unincorporated church lays up money to buy land and build church buildings, the church has sinned. Congregational sins, as with all individual sins, are removed by the blood of Christ, and God will forgive every sin a congregation may commit. However, as is frequently the case, one sin leads to another sin, and the worldly effort to lay up treasures on earth is often further combined with worldly wisdom, and many church leaders recognize the opportunity to maximize their church's treasures on earth by reorganizing their congregation to conform to the civil government's requirements for a nonprofit corporation. Civil law doesn't require a church to become a corporation. These opportunist church leaders are simply acting out of greed. It's all about money, folks!

Church leaders have discovered that they can measurably increase the forbidden accumulation of treasure, if they transform their invisible church into a visible "body" by changing their legally unorganized congregation into an organized church, a nonprofit corporation. When a church leader becomes the head of his church, the church can be transformed from being part of the invisible body of Christ to being a visible organized church with a visible head. The new head of the church, now vested with authority to speak for the church and represent the church, may now act on behalf of the church to create Articles of Incorporation, which qualify a humanly organized church to be a nonprofit corporation. Regarding nonprofit church organizations, the *About Business* website states, "Articles of Incorporation together create the primary incorporation document that is the basis for a corporation coming into existence." Suddenly the church becomes visible. Suddenly the church has a physical existence! "The Articles" are the document which allows the church to have a corporate existence and be seen in the eyes of government officials, thus paving the way for the church to increase its treasure on earth by making a covenant with the government.

As long as Jesus Christ remains the Head of a church and there are no human heads to represent the church, the body and its Head remain invisible to human governments, but when a church ordains a human head to sign articles of incorporation, that church suddenly becomes visible to the government. When a man is ordained with the authority to speak for a church and act on behalf of the church to sign contracts with unbelievers and enter into covenants with human governments, the door opens for the church to engage in spiritual intercourse with the world. The authority of a human head in a church makes it possible to reorganize the church into a corporation, and incorporation makes it possible for a church, previously betrothed to the Lord, to violate its covenant with the Lord, enter into a covenant with the government and commit fornication with the rulers of the nation. When men stand in the place of the Lord, the door is open to make covenants "with them and with their gods." (Ex 23:32) Human authority facilitates spiritual fornication.

Covenants establish a relationship between two parties. One is the greater partner and the other the lesser, and each receives benefits from the other. When God enters into covenant, He assumes the greater role. God rules the church, and the church bows in obedience to worship God and receives blessings and protection from God. Similarly, in the case of a covenant between the government and a church, the government assumes the role of the greater partner and usurps God's prerogative to rule the church. When the church prostrates itself before the government officials in obedience to all federal and state rules and regulations pertaining to charitable corporations, the organized church receives the benefit of tax-exempt status for all the contributions it receives, and the members of the organized church receive the benefit of tax deductions for all their tithes and offerings. The government rules the organized church, and the church bows in obedience to worship its new human rulers and obey all their corporate laws.

Of course none of these benefits extends to unincorporated churches or their members but only to nonprofit corporations, which have established a covenant with the government. The government still does not recognize an unincorporated congregation, because it has no human head or corporate by-laws. It remains part of the invisible, spiritual Church. The civil government only benefits those churches it can rule by covenant agreement.

Every organized church lives under the rulership of the civil government and must obey the laws of the land. The existence of government rules and IRS regulations in churches is frequently a closely guarded secret, and members may need to inquire diligently before the church will make the documents of incorporation and tax exemption available. Since the federal government rules every organized church, these church organizations are explicitly required to impose rules upon their members, so the churches are able to comply with the legal requirements, particularly IRS regulations, imposed upon all nonprofit corporations. IRS regulation mostly affects ordained members of a church, so lay members may be unaware of the relationship between the government and the church and unfamiliar with the rules and regulations imposed upon their church. Curious members should ask to see the church's Articles of Incorporation, tax exemption documents and a copy of their church administration manual, paying particular attention to the rules governing the receipt, accounting and distribution of church contributions. Organized churches are hamstrung by IRS regulations and the rules of the civil government.

When a church creates articles of incorporation, enters a covenant relationship with an earthly nation and submits itself to that human government, the organized church has committed fornication with the world. The church humbles itself before the rulers of the government and lays prostrate before its regulators and regulations. The church subjects itself to government scrutiny, particularly IRS scrutiny, and stands naked before the federal bureaucrats, IRS agents and state regulators to whom the church must submit in obedience to all nonprofit corporate law.

After ancient Israel entered into the old covenant with God, she was repeatedly warned against making covenants with the nations around her. Any covenant Israel made with the neighboring nations constituted spiritual adultery. Besides the adultery, God prohibited covenants with the nations, because He knew those covenants with heathen rulers would inevitably lead to idolatry. God knew the heathen rulers would require Israel to obey their covenant laws and turn Israel away from His laws. God knew Israel would be required to bow to the human rulers and comply with their human laws rather than faithfully obey the covenant laws of God.

Sadly, the Bible records the graphic details of Israel's failure to heed God's words, and the prophets chronicled many of the covenants Israel cut with neighboring nations at various times and for various reasons. As God had prophesied, her adulterous relationships with the nations around her led her to bow down to the rulers with whom Israel cut her covenants and submit to the laws those covenants imposed upon Israel. Israel's repeated adultery and idolatry became the intense focus of God's stern admonition, rebuke and wrath. Adultery and idolatry clearly stand apart throughout the Old Testament as Israel's greatest sins.

Times have changed, but those who call themselves the people of God have not. The death of Jesus ended the covenant relationship God had with Israel, and simultaneously God established a New Covenant with His Church. Once again He expects His holy nation to remain spiritually chaste, unblemished by covenant relationships with the nations around her. The Church must allow God alone to rule her, and she must remain obedient to the Lord and dedicate herself to His direction. The Lord expects His Church to trust completely in Him for her protection, provision and care. He expects the Church to remain unrestrained by illicit covenants with the governments of the nations wherein her members dwell. Her time must be spent worshiping the Lord, to Whom she has been espoused, while she awaits the time when she will consummate her marriage at the wedding feast of the Lamb. (Rev 19:7)

Although the marriage which existed between God and Israel is a type of the marriage which now exists between Christ and the Church, there is a significant difference in the state of the marriage relationship. Israel entered into a covenant with God at Mount Sinai, at which time Moses received the instructions for building the tabernacle. Approximately nine months later Moses finished the tabernacle and installed the furniture. Shortly thereafter, the glory of the Lord descended to fill the tabernacle, and His divine Presence consummated the marriage covenant with Israel. God came to dwell with His wife, Israel.

Unlike the consummated relationship Israel had with God, the New Covenant has been cut, but the Church has yet to experience the wedding feast of the Lamb. Christ and the Church are espoused through the New Covenant, and the marriage is presently in the engagement period of separation and testing. God and Israel consummated their marriage, but the Church has only been espoused to Jesus Christ, and we are presently awaiting the wedding feast. God is testing the churches to see if they will remain chaste in order to be part of the one, holy, virgin Church.

> For I am jealous over you with godly jealousy: for I have espoused you to one husband, that I may present you as a chaste virgin to Christ. (2 Cor 11:2)

God has cut the Covenant, and the Church is espoused to Jesus Christ, but the wedding feast is yet some time away. Christ and the Church are legally married according to the Jewish custom, but the Bridegroom has gone to prepare a place for us to live. The Church must remain a chaste virgin while Christ is away. The Church must avoid all covenant relationships and remain spiritually pure in the sight of God. Any covenant agreement a church might make with a government of the world constitutes spiritual fornication.

Unlike Israel's adultery, which God would have forgiven if she had been willing to abandon her covenants with the nations and turn to God again, a church may not engage in even one single act of fornication with the nations of the world. Any fornication with the world will disqualify a church from being part of the one virgin Church. Any single covenant agreement between a church and a human government will disqualify that church from participating in the wedding feast. Forgiveness is not the issue. Spiritual purity is. Any church which has entered into a covenant with a world government has committed spiritual fornication. It has become spiritually defiled and is no longer fit to be married to the Lamb.

Hardhearted and desperate attempts to find a scriptural basis for divorce have served to blur the distinction between fornication and adultery. Although fornication and adultery involve the same immoral act, the result of fornication is very different from the result of adultery. The act of fornication defiles a body, and God's forgiveness cannot reverse it. Fornication, either physically or spiritually, destroys the virginity of a body, and that body is defiled forever. For that reason fornication cannot be forgiven in the sense that a person or a church may become virgin once again. On the other hand, the act of adultery defiles a marriage relationship. A married person has no virginity to guard, so virginity is not an issue with adultery. Adultery defiles the relationship of trust between the married partners, which can be forgiven. God forgives adultery as long as it does not become a willful lifestyle sin, but God cannot restore virginity to any defiled body. Adultery, either physically or spiritually, is forgivable and the relationship can be restored, but fornication defiles a physical body or a church body forever, because that body has forever lost its virginity.

Marriages in the Jewish culture of the first century were arranged differently than they are today, and you should be careful not to misinterpret the rules God has revealed in scripture which govern the marriage relationship. You should carefully consider the ramifications the Jewish wedding custom holds for churches which commit fornication with human governments. From the time the marriage covenant is established to the time the bridegroom returns, if evidence comes to light that the bride is not a virgin, the marriage covenant could be annulled and the woman put away (divorced). (Deut 22:13-21) Jesus taught the same standard for divorce to His disciples in the Sermon on the Mount. (Matt 5:32)

> But I say unto you, That whosoever shall put away his wife, **saving for the cause of fornication,** causeth her to commit adultery: and whosoever shall marry her that is divorced committeth adultery.

Adultery was not grounds for divorce in a consummated marriage, but fornication during the engagement period of the Jewish marriage covenant was. This unique exception for divorce applied to those who had entered into a marriage covenant but had not yet come together in conjugal union. Even today, God highly respects those who avoid fornication by carefully guarding their virginity before the wedding day, and He guarantees all those who flee fornication the right to choose a mate who has likewise remained sexually pure.

Although this divine law certainly applies to physical marriages, it specifically applies to the covenant relationship between Jesus Christ and His espoused, virgin Church. Christ and the Church must both remain pure and chaste, and God has specifically recorded this law to honor and respect His spiritually chaste Son. God has guaranteed His right to marry the one and only spiritually chaste virgin Church and reject every defiled church. Every defiled spiritual body—every immoral bride—every corporate church which has entered into a covenant with a human government and has thereby committed fornication with the world will be rejected from participation in the wedding feast of the Lamb.

God preserved an example of the proper application of divorce on the grounds of fornication, so those of us who live in the twenty-first century can understand how Jesus' instruction applies to marriages today, both physically and spiritually. However, by far, the most important understanding you must gain is how this law applies in a church's spiritual marriage to Jesus Christ. Your salvation may depend on it. Matthew recorded this typical example of alleged fornication in connection with the immaculate conception of Jesus.

> Now the birth of Jesus Christ was on this wise: When as his mother Mary was espoused to Joseph, before they came together, she was found with child of the Holy Spirit. Then Joseph her husband, being a just man, and not willing to make her a public example, was minded to put her away privily. (Matt 1:18-19)

Joseph established the marriage covenant when he paid a certain price to Mary's father for her care and training, but Joseph and Mary had not come together sexually, and she remained at home with her father until Joseph had prepared a place for them both to live. During that engagement period of separation and testing, Mary became pregnant with Jesus. Joseph initially assumed Mary had committed fornication and prepared to divorce her according to the divine statute, but a messenger of God intervened to assure Joseph that Mary had not acted immorally and that her pregnancy was an act of the Holy Spirit. (v. 20)

In our spiritual marriage, the marriage Covenant has been signed, the Bridegroom has paid the marriage price with His life, and the Bridegroom has gone away to prepare a place for Himself and the Church to live. While He is away, all churches are anticipating His return and expecting to be part of the one virgin Church, but only those churches which do not commit fornication with the world by entering into covenants with the world will be invited to marry the Bridegroom. God will reject every church which enters into any covenant agreement with any civil government, and they will not participate in the wedding feast. God will only invite the members of virgin churches to marry Christ, because those churches will remain holy and chaste and continually look to the rulership of the Father and the headship of Jesus Christ. When He returns, He will select the one virgin Church which has remained spiritually chaste and has not made covenants with the world. He will choose the one virgin Church which has neither submitted to the rulership of human governments nor allowed human authorities to direct her.

The competition for Christ's favor will be intense. We can see many organized churches in the world competing for the privilege to wed the returning Savior, but God is preparing one virgin Church without spot or wrinkle for his Son, and only that one virgin Church composed of all the chaste virgin churches, which are invisible to human rulers, will participate in the wedding feast. Every church which incorporates and becomes a visible church—a separate church with a human head and a human government—a spiritually defiled body—will be rejected. There are many corporate churches seeking the Lord's favor, and all of them are expecting to participate in the wedding feast, but the Lord will reject the corporate churches, because they are rejecting the rulership of God and the authority of Jesus Christ. He will reject them, because they are bowing to human rulership and authority. He will reject them, because they have committed fornication and become defiled by their covenants with the world's governments.

The apostle Paul compared the competition for the Bridegroom's favor to a race. The one virgin Church (comprised of all the faithful unincorporated churches) and all the separate corporate churches are running together in that race, but only one spiritual Church will win Christ's favor. Only one virgin Church will receive the prize.

> Know ye not that they which run in a race run all, but **one receiveth the prize**? So run, that ye may obtain.
> (1 Cor 9:24)

As individuals, we must each work out our own salvation with fear and trembling, but salvation is more than just an individual matter. Salvation is a group matter. Salvation is a church matter. We are not only responsible to remain faithful individually, but churches must remain faithful to the Lord collectively. Each local church must remain free from civil rule and regulation. Each church must remain faithful to the rulership of God and the direction of the Lord. Every congregation which prostrates itself before human authorities and the governments of this world will be rejected by Jesus Christ, removed from the wedding feast and lose the race. Only one virgin Church will receive the prize.

The apostle Paul warned the Corinthian church to avoid becoming unequally yoked with unbelievers by making covenants with the world, but theologians and church leaders are oblivious to Paul's simple instruction, which God inspired and preserved in order to protect every congregation from becoming unequally yoked with this world's governments.

> Be ye not unequally yoked together with unbelievers: for what fellowship hath righteousness with unrighteousness? and what communion hath light with darkness? and what concord hath Christ with Belial? or what part hath [the believing] with [the unbelieving]? and what agreement hath the temple of God with idols? for ye are the temple of the living God; as God hath said, I will dwell in them, and walk in them; and I will be their God, and they shall be my people. Wherefore come out from among them, and be ye separate, saith the Lord, and do not [attach yourselves to] the unclean; and I will receive you…
> (2 Cor 6:14-17)

Church leaders are ignorant of the impact plural pronouns have on the context and the interpretation of scripture. Ignorant church leaders have taught their members that Paul's instruction applies to individual members, but this instruction does not apply to individual members. Paul's instruction specifically applies to churches. If Paul's words applied to individual members, none of us could sign any contract with an unbeliever. None of us could have a credit card. None of us could book an airline reservation. None of us could buy a house. None of us could even operate a computer, because user agreements are required by the software companies. If Paul's words applied to individuals, none of us could function in this world.

Paul's words do not apply to individual members. Paul's words apply to churches. Faithful churches must remain separate from the world. Faithful churches cannot become unequally yoked, especially for the benefit of tax exemptions and tax deductions. Any church which becomes unequally yoked with unbelievers—which engages in contracts with the world—which becomes attached to civil governments through contractual agreements—will be disqualified from the wedding feast. Such spiritual fornication will render that church spiritually impure and defiled, unfit to marry the Lamb. Jesus Christ will reject any church which has entered into a covenant relationship with any nation—with any government—with any individual or organization of the world. Every church which commits fornication with the world will be removed from the body of Christ and disqualified from participation in the wedding feast.

Since the desire for accumulated wealth has led every organized church into covenants with civil governments for the benefit of tax exemptions and tax deductions, it should be obvious that every organized church has committed spiritual fornication and become defiled before God. Organized churches have all lost their spiritual virginity, and they are no longer qualified to be part of the chaste virgin Church of heaven. All organized churches have been disqualified from participation in the wedding feast of the Lamb.

Largely because churches have failed to depend entirely on God to provide their spiritual needs, and because church leaders have failed to properly interpret the words Jesus addressed to churches, misguided church leaders have blindly and ignorantly led countless congregations into forbidden covenant relationships with the world. Just as Israel's kings failed to trust God to provide for His people and sought the protection and favor of the nations around them, so church authorities today have failed to see that God provides all the needs of their churches, and they have blindly sought the protection and favor of the governments of this world. Church authorities, intent on increasing their forbidden treasures on earth, have greedily sought tax exemptions and tax deductions through their covenants with civil governments. Woe unto those churches which commit fornication with this world. There will indeed be weeping and gnashing of teeth when apostate believers realize they missed out on salvation, because they trusted pride-filled church authorities and greedy church organizations.

As surely as the Church will prevail against the gates of hell, the facade of organized Christianity will likewise crumble before the faithful in Jesus Christ. In that day God will break the authoritarian control human organizations have held over believers since at least the third century and usher in the new age of the kingdom of God. From that time forward, every believer will be free from the orderly arrangement of hierarchical government and enjoy the full freedom of the New Covenant promised to those believing in the name of Jesus Christ. As our returning Lord announces victory over the civil rulers and authorities of the world, His united faithful body of believers will likewise announce victory over every ruler and every authority defiling every organized church. Organized Christianity is doomed to the rubbish heap of human endeavor.

Chapter 10

A New Perspective

True freedom is a present reality for those who trust the word of God to sharpen their spiritual vision. Spiritual vision gives us a new perspective of the nature of God, the nature of Jesus Christ and the nature of the Church. When we trust the inspired words of the apostles, we gain a new perspective on the nature of law and the nature of sin and judgment. We become enlightened to the true nature of the world and the defiled nature of all organized churches. Spiritual vision changes our whole outlook on the nature of our walk with God.

Our walk with God is a process of continual spiritual growth over the entire period of our spiritual lives. Whether a person is born into a family of believers or a family of atheists, God calls each of us individually and personally, and He places each of us into the body of Christ and saves us by His amazing grace from the time we first believed; yet faith demands we continue to grow. We cannot rest on our laurels. Just as any living thing will die if it stops growing, so we will also die spiritually if we stop growing. The doctrine of guaranteed security is a myth. We must continually work out our own salvation with fear and trembling. (Phil 2:12) Every believer must grow in grace and in the knowledge of the Lord Jesus Christ. (2 Pet 3:18) Too many believers assume they have salvation in the bag, and they go about living their lives without actively pursuing the salvation God freely provides for them. Far too many believers think they've arrived, when the journey has hardly begun.

In spite of all its faults, God blessed me to be associated with an organization which prescribed daily Bible study for all its members. I have since learned that Bible study is not required for salvation, but I have also come to see that salvation in this age is very unlikely without diligent careful study of the apostles inspired writings. When the apostles led the churches of the first century, the written words of God were largely unavailable to individual believers, but the early churches could safely depend on the personal instruction and gifted leadership of those the Lord had personally taught. Two thousand years later we may appear to possess personal copies of the prophets' and apostles' writings, but the inspired words of God are still not readily available to us, because few read ancient Hebrew or Koine Greek. Additionally, Jesus has personally taught none of those who lead churches today. Churchgoers are tangibly worse off today than the early believers were, because they assume they have personal copies of the inspired words of God, and they don't, and they assume pastors and teachers are intimately familiar with the inspired words of God, and they aren't.

The underlying cause of this significant deception is human authority operating in hierarchical organization. When we depend on a single individual or a private group to translate the inspired words of God, we are starting with a human interpretation of the words of God, and then we are allowing church leaders to further interpret what has already been interpreted in translation. Interpretation upon interpretation creates a recipe for deception and false doctrine. Since translation is, by definition, an interpretation and nearly half of those charged with making translations do not even believe God inspired the words they are translating, the translations they produce will invariably be corrupted. Then, when church authorities study and interpret these corrupted translations and rely on them to determine church doctrine, errors will be compounded by their further interpretation of what has already been interpreted by translation, and heresy will invariably be introduced into church doctrines and taught to unsuspecting members. Church authorities are completely dependent on the authority of the translators to validate their church doctrines, and heresy is perpetuated, because few even think to question the word of an authority. Members rely on the authority of their pastors, who defer to the authority of regional and denominational authorities, who defer to the unquestioned authority of translators to determine doctrine. Men bowing to the authority of men in a closed hierarchical system creates an environment where doctrine is proven in the same way circular reasoning proves a point. Hierarchical authority perpetuates doctrinal heresy.

The same understanding which gives us insight into the nature of organized churches also gives us insight into the nature of seminary education and the role it plays in perpetuating heresy. Although the more obvious victims of hierarchical authority are naïve members, seminary students also suffer from a similar oppression in the study of their religious curricula. Seminaries intentionally perpetuate denominational heresies, because institutions of higher learning for theologians and pastors use the same system of government which perpetuates heresy in churches, so these seminaries will pass the same errors along to their students who graduate to lead churches. When young zealous members attend their denominational seminary to become theologians and pastors, they learn the same heretical doctrines taught in their churches, because hierarchical authority dictates the nature of the curricula. The students learn to bow to the authority of the translators and theologians who preceded them, and, consequently, they become spiritually blind to the errors of translation and accepted doctrinal flaws. They are unable to overcome the power of the words of authorities to be able to listen to the Spirit and learn the truths of God. Students naturally confirm the doctrines, because seminaries teach the same interpretative practices which produced the doctrines originally. Baptist seminaries produce Baptist theologians. Methodist seminaries produce Methodist theologians. Catholic seminaries produce Catholic theologians. Seminaries perpetuate denominational heresies and produce theological penguins, because hierarchical authority has the same effect in seminaries as it does in churches.

Additionally, seminaries teach the same translating practices which have produced earlier translations, because hierarchical authority also dictates the nature of the curricula for those who study Hebrew and Greek. Students confirm earlier translations, because seminaries teach their students the same interpretative translating practices which have produced every English translation. The basic principles of living life in this world may be understood in spite of frequent mistranslations, but corrupt interpretative practices taught in seminaries have obscured a wide variety of spiritual perspectives in every translation, particularly the nature of the Church, the nature of Church government and the reality of lifestyle sin. Spiritual reality is impossible to comprehend by the natural mind, and highly educated translators have allowed their natural minds to influence their translations. They have substituted physical reality for spiritual reality, and they have imputed visible church practice into the text of their translations, ignoring the inspired words of scripture and perpetuating the viscous cycle of circular reasoning required to perpetuate heretical doctrine. Translators have imputed hierarchical human government into every translation, because hierarchical authority in seminaries produces translators who are as blind to spiritual reality and the nature of church government as those who produced earlier translations, particularly the KJV.

The wisdom of the world influences churches and seminaries today, just as it influenced the first century community of believers. Paul taught spiritual realities the natural mind cannot comprehend, and worldly-minded converts began to twist Paul's words very early in the history of the Church. Peter had to deal with that issue in his letter to the scattered believers of Asia Minor.

> ...even as our beloved brother Paul also according to the wisdom given unto him hath written unto you; as also in all his epistles, speaking in them of these things; in which are some things hard to be understood, which they that are unlearned and unstable [twist], as they do also the other scriptures, unto their own destruction. (2 Peter 3:15-16)

The wisdom of God is simple and plain to a spiritually-minded person, but it is foolishness to a worldly-minded person. The wise and educated of the world are unlearned and unstable spiritually, and they cannot comprehend the spiritual realities described by the apostles in their letters. When the wisdom of the world—the wisdom of orderly arrangement—the wisdom of hierarchical authority controls seminary education and highly educated theologians trust the authority of exalted translators and revered translations above the authority of the inspired text, they become spiritually unlearned and unstable, and they allow their minds to twist the inspired words of God and mistranslate them exactly as their predecessors did. The unlearned and unstable teachers of the first century could do little damage beyond the reach of their voices, but today unlearned and unstable authorities have the power of the media to amplify their voices across the country and the power of the printing press to multiply error-infested translations around the world. Peter properly assessed the fate of these self-appointed, unlearned and unstable authorities, and destruction certainly awaits theologians and translators who not only misinterpret and mistranslate the letters of apostles but the Old Testament scriptures as well. Hierarchical authority is primarily responsible for leading unsuspecting believers into idolatry and spiritually blind church leaders into sacrilege.

Although hierarchical authority is the primary perpetuator of mistranslation and heresy, another factor which contributes significantly to these problems at the highest levels is rampant unbelief among theologians. Nearly fifty percent of those who enter seminaries abandon their faith in God by the time they graduate as theologians. They may graduate with an academic understanding of theology and a technical ability to translate a manuscript, but most theologians simply do not tremble before the plain, inspired words of God, and they allow themselves to question the inspired text. When a translator allows himself to question the text he is translating and doubt the inspiration of that text, he has disqualified himself from any involvement in the translating or interpreting process. When a translator allows himself to distort the literal meaning of words or manipulate the accepted grammar of sentences, he has corrupted his translation, and it is unfit for use in the Christian community. Since unbelief has corrupted every translator and human reason has become a substitute for faith in the inspired text, we should not be surprised to find wholesale mistranslations when the work of these faithless translators is examined by sound scholarship. Their work preserves the evidence of their faithlessness for everyone to see, and their own words will convict them when they stand before the judgment seat of Christ.

Since we have encountered a number of inspired truths which unbelieving translators have rejected and hidden in their translations, we have already discovered enough evidence of their faithlessness to indict them for perjury. Translators have not believed Christians are holy, so they have told us Christians are sanctified, and they have transformed the holiness of God's people into a holiness of God's purpose. They could not believe they could possibly be slaves of Jesus Christ, so they have elevated their position, and ours, to that of servants of the Lord, and they have completely distorted our true relationship to Jesus Christ. They have not believed Jesus Christ literally lives in us and walks the earth in us as His spiritual body, so they lied to us about what Peter wrote and told us the contextually irrelevant truth that Jesus walked the earth for our sake. Translators can never write lies without being exposed. God already knows, and sooner or later faithful Christians will discover them. Each of us must hold a childlike faith in God to know that He has been able to preserve the inspired text of scripture. Each of us must hold a childlike faith and trust in Jesus Christ to teach us personally by the Spirit through the scripture God has so carefully preserved. When a translator lacks that childlike faith and trust in the inspired text of scripture, then God deems that translator unlearned in His sight. God will give him over to a reprobate and unstable mind, and the wisdom of the world will allow him to twist the words God inspired.

The only way believers can overcome the perversion of our English translations is to seek direct access to the mind of God by studying the inspired texts of the Bible, particularly the Greek New Testament. The only way we can eliminate the problems inherent in translation is to reject hierarchical authority and allow God to teach us personally and directly through His inspired words. The only way to know God is to know His Word, and He has only preserved His words in Hebrew and Greek. How deep is your desire to know God? How willing are you to know Him better? Is it worth your time to study another language to know Him better? Are you willing to seek and knock and ask so God can open your mind to His thoughts and speak to you directly through His inspired words, or would you rather sit back and allow men to spoon-feed you their personal version of truth? Are you willing to diligently study to show yourself approved unto God—or would your rather watch TV?

God speaks to us individually and personally through His Word. Jesus Christ lives in us, and God speaks directly to us through Him. God does not speak to us through any man. No man stands in authority between God and His people. When men translate the Bible, call it a holy book and pass it off as an authoritative text, they not only place themselves as mediators between believers and God, they also place themselves in authority over the words of scripture. Some dare to claim the Holy Spirit inspired their translations, just as He inspired the original language texts, but such an allegation places the Spirit in authority over the Word. The blatant heresy of their claim ought to be obvious. Just as the spirits of the prophets are subject to the prophets, (1 Cor 14:32) so the Holy Spirit is indeed subject to Christ. God will never allow the Spirit to be in authority over His Word, let alone allow fallible human beings to be in authority over the Word. The translators' claims are preposterous. Faithful members of the spiritual Church must reject the authority of men and rely entirely on God to speak to us personally through the inspired text of scripture.

When we align our beliefs to the plumb line of the inspired text of scripture, we will gain a new perspective of our relationship to God, our relationship to Jesus Christ and our relationship to one another. When we allow the inspired text to teach us, we will gain a deeper understanding of the nature of sin in our lives. Our walk with God will become bold and filled with confidence and courage. The Greek text will also open our minds to the carnality and vanity of the orderly arrangement around us and to the spirituality and eternity of the Church in Christ, and we will be better able to see the world and the Church from an enlightened spiritual perspective. Unfiltered biblical insight frequently opens the door to new perspectives. I am confident that there are other truths to find.

God will reward us with many amazing discoveries, if we are willing to make the sacrifice of our time and effort to investigate the inspired text of scripture and gain a new perspective of the words of God. The most profound discovery I have made is the absence of any human rule, authority or power for the Church in the apostles' inspired writings. Human authority in the Church is a figment of men's imaginations and a function of the wisdom of the world. Human authority defiles a church and separates it from the spiritual Church. God cannot govern a church when men stand in authority over that church. When men direct churches, they will accomplish the purposes of men rather than the purpose of God. Human beings have no role in the government of faithful churches. There is no external government for the faithful of God. Our Ruler lives in us. Our Head directs us from within.

As we began to peer into the inspired text, our perspective regarding Church rulership changed, and we discovered that God is sovereign. We discovered God rules the Church, just as God ruled Israel. God has always made the rules to govern His people, and no man has the right to usurp His sovereign right to rule His Church. God invalidates every rule of man in the Church, but church leaders have allowed themselves to be filled with pride, and they have dared to rule God's people. They are standing in the place of God, and they are living in sin. God will remove them all from the Church.

Organized churches completely ignore the rulership of God, because their covenants with federal and state governments require church organizations to bow to civil rulership. Consequently, most churchgoers have absolutely no knowledge about who rules their church, and incorporated churches blindly accept the civil rules and regulations the government imposes upon them. Although many federal laws significantly influence the operation of churches, by far the most scrutiny comes from the IRS, which imposes volumes of rules and regulations to track and control the receipt, accounting and disbursement of charitable contributions. Since money is the lifeblood of every organized church, these churches are willing to bow to IRS rules and regulations in order to gain the fiscal benefit of tax exemptions and tax deductions. Every organized church is in bed with the government, and anyone who actually believes in the separation of church and state is spiritually blind and has his or her head buried very deeply in the proverbial sand.

Our perspective regarding Church authority and headship has also changed, and the inspired text has revealed that Jesus Christ is the Word of God, and He is our living Law. God plainly prohibited Israel from adding to or diminishing from the law, but God has no need to make such a rule in the New Covenant, because it is impossible to add to or diminish from Jesus Christ. He is the unalterable Law of God. He is the unalterable Standard of faith. We obey the Law, because we obey only Him, but our Law is not a list of dos and don'ts or a ritualistic code. Our Law is a living Law. Our Law directs every action of the Church from within. Our Law is our Commander, and He lives in us and directs our lives every moment of every day. Our slavery to Jesus Christ precludes serving any other master. We have no need for human laws or human authorities in a church. God has placed His Law to be the Head of the Church, and there is only one Commander in the Church, just as there is only one head in any living body. Church leaders have allowed themselves to be filled with pride, and they have dared to assume authority over the people of God. They are standing in the place of Jesus Christ and living in sin. God will remove them all from the Church.

Although organized churches proclaim the authority of Jesus Christ and claim to place Him at the head of their churches, they all reject His direction and allow the civil government to rule them. They all ordain authorities to stand in the Lord's place and oppress God's people with prescriptive rules and the commandments of men. Spiritually naïve members bow before the rules of men and ignorantly commit idolatry by recognizing these ordained authorities, who stand in Christ's place and pridefully teach the mixture of truth and error translators offer as a substitute for the inspired words of scripture. Our new perspective reveals the abject corruption of every organized church because of spiritual fornication through covenant agreements with civil governments. The message of this book is a warning for every believer to come out of organized churches, because scripture strongly suggests that the whole system of organized religion as well as all those participating in it will suffer the fury of the wrath of God. Are you willing to stake your salvation on the integrity of fallible human authorities?

Our new perspective of rulership and authority has provided a new perspective of Paul's words in 1 Corinthians 15, which I had read dozens of times, but I was blinded to its plain meaning until I began to see the corruption in organizations, which rule with authority and use their power to influence the members to do all this church stuff. As long as I was part of the organization—as long as I was part of the problem—I could not see the deception, but not long after I resigned from the organization, the profound meaning of this passage nearly jumped off the page.

> Then cometh the end, when he shall have delivered up the kingdom to God, even the Father; when he shall have put down <u>all rule</u> and <u>all authority</u> and <u>power</u>. For he must reign, till he hath put ALL ENEMIES under his feet. The last ENEMY that shall be destroyed is <u>death</u>. (1 Cor 15:24-26)

We examined this verse earlier, but it is imperative to fully grasp its meaning. Read it again, if you are in doubt. I would not say that these are the only enemies of God, but we may rest assured that rule, authority, power and death are four enemies of God. All rule is an enemy, not just some rule. All authority is an enemy, not just some authority. The political power which enforces the injunctions of human rulers and authorities also falls in the category of an enemy of God. Without question, death is an enemy. Should we assume God has personally authorized any of these enemies in the Church? We may only conclude that God has removed all rule, authority, power and death from the Church. God Himself rules the Church. Jesus Christ is the sole Authority in the Church. The Holy Spirit is the only Power Who leads, protects and empowers the Church.

Death has lost its hold upon the Church, which lives in heaven and possesses eternal life in Christ Jesus. (John 6:54, 1 John 5:13) God has removed all four of these enemies from faithful churches.

The Church is not a physical entity. It is not a building. It is not an organization. It is not a group of men who have been ordained to manipulate and control their members to accomplish the purposes of an organization. The Church is spiritual. It's a spiritual body. The Church is invisible. You can't see the Church. Men can't rule a spiritual entity. Men can't direct something they can't see. Only God can rule the Church. Only Jesus Christ commands us from within. Only the Holy Spirit gives us the power to do what is pleasing in God's sight. The more I contemplate Paul's words, the more preposterous it becomes to think men could possibly rule, command or force their will upon us. Church leaders only have as much control over us as we individually give them. God has given no authority to church leaders, so believers must reject their authority.

Paul's statement to the Corinthians specifically addresses the future time when God will completely remove human rulership, authority and power from the earth, but without a doubt rule, authority and power still exist in the world. Just see what happens when you refuse to do what a police officer tells you to do. Bamm! Right in the slammer. You may have to go to court, maybe pay a fine, or perhaps the county will extend its hospitality until you serve enough time to pay your debt to society for not following their rules and not obeying their authorities. Authority and the power to enforce the law clearly still exist in civil governments.

However, what do you think will happen when I refuse to do what the pastor tells me to do? Nothing! I can walk away from him and do something completely different, and he can't do a thing about it. He can't do a thing to me when I don't follow his orders. He can't make me preach the gospel. He can't make me pray. He can't make me study the Bible. He can't make me serve the church. He can't even make me worship God. I used to bow and scrape to those guys, as if their wish was my command—as if they held the power of eternal life in their hands. What a scam. Ecclesiastical authority is a joke. Even intuitively it should be obvious it is a lie. Ecclesiastical authority is just like *The Emperor's New Clothes*. In reality, church authorities are spiritually naked. The children of God simply have the ability to recognize what is obvious.

We also gained a new perspective of our own nature as members of the Church, and we saw that the inspired text reveals many truths hidden in translation including the holiness of every member. We are holy because the Holy Spirit lives in us, not because we are sinless. Mistranslation has also camouflaged our slavery to Jesus Christ and our role as servants of one another. We are equals as slaves of Jesus Christ, and we are equals as servants of one another. Our slavery to the Lord demands we only take orders from Him, but we serve one another as equals according to His direction. We also learned that the covenant relationship allows us to exchange places with our covenant Partner, so the words of scripture sharpened our spiritual vision and allowed us to see ourselves as a single unified body in the heavenly places in Jesus Christ. Since we are in heaven in Him, it became obvious that God alone places the members in the body of Christ as He sees fit.

The true nature of the Church contradicts almost everything organized churches teach about it. False teachers tell us we are sinners in the church, but the inspired text of the Bible tells us we are the temple of God and we are holy. (1 Cor 3:17) False teachers tell us a church must lay up money to do the work of God, but the inspired text says churches must not lay up any treasure on earth. (Matt 6:19) False teachers tell us each member may have his or her own faith, but the inspired text says there is only one faith. (Eph 4:5) False teachers tell us the church is our spiritual mother, but the Bible plainly says the Church is a chaste virgin. (2 Cor 11:2) False teachers tell us the church voluntarily serves Christ, but the inspired text repeatedly says that the members of the Church are purchased slaves. False teachers tell us they must make rules to guide the church on the path to God, but the inspired text says God is the Lawgiver and He alone rules faithful churches. (James 4:12) False teachers tell us they are authorities in the church, but the inspired text denies authority to church leaders and overturns every hint of the hierarchical system implied by our English translations. False teachers tell us men are ordained by God to their positions in the church, but the inspired text lacks any word to convey the concept of ordination and renders the practice heretical. Scripture contradicts everything false teachers teach about the Church. The Bible reveals the true nature of the Church from God's perspective, a spiritual reality we can only comprehend by faith.

The inspired text of the Bible further changes our perspective of the nature of the world. When read in Greek, our vague and benign English concept of the world as our earthly state of human existence vanishes to reveal the tentacles of an inherently evil system of government. The world of Greek thought reveals a hierarchical system of pride and oppression, and our innocuous concept of a sinful society gives way to God's overt contempt for those who have ordered society into hierarchical governments. The apostles were not inspired to condemn the earth or the evil population living on it, but they were inspired to condemn an evil social arrangement—a satanic system—an inherently corrupt form of government which every society has assumed to be absolutely necessary for its survival. This system of hierarchical human government is thoroughly condemned in scripture, and the people of God are commanded to come out of this world's system of government and allow God to place us under His government, where there is no hierarchical order and there are no human rulers and no human authorities. The revelation of the inspired text stands opposed to human reason and logic, yet that is what faith is all about. We must believe God. We must depend on His wisdom and reject the wisdom of orderly arrangement.

In the inspired text, the wisdom of the world is not the wisdom of the globe or the wisdom of the evil people living on earth. The wisdom of the world is the wisdom of orderly arrangement. The wisdom of the world is the wisdom of hierarchical order. Carnal reason dictates that wise men rule over simple men, and human logic demands that trained authorities teach and direct the general population, but the wisdom of world is foolishness to God. The wisdom of God is Christ in us. The wisdom of God is government from within. God rules us from within, because His Word lives in us and His Spirit empowers us. The body of Christ has no need of external human government. Those who feign faith and continue to live in an unruly manner will indeed become subject to the orderly arrangement of civil authority, but those who live godly lives in Christ Jesus are completely free from the orderly arrangement of human rulership and authority.

As our perspective of the world becomes clearer and we begin to grasp the reality that there is no hierarchical order in the Church, it should become obvious that the playing field is level in the Church. We are all equals before God. None is under the authority of another, and none respects one above another. All the Lord's holy slaves enjoy equal standing in a church, and none of us has the right to judge another Man's slave. (Rom 14:4) Each member is worthy of individual respect as a member of the body, so partiality based on one's perceived position or title is strictly forbidden in the Church. Churches must come out of the world, and we must leave partiality based on intelligence, stature, influence or affluence in the world. Politics is dead in the one true Church.

Hierarchical authority naturally leads to official titles, so Jesus offered churches a new perspective regarding godly leadership and explicitly condemned titles of authority. Jesus condemned the practice of exalting church leaders and the practice of seeking the praise of men, and titles serve to promote both evils. Jesus repeatedly emphasized humility and service over titles and authority. He condemned the hypocrisy of the Pharisees and Sadducees and explicitly prohibited the use of titles to distinguish members in their service to the congregation.

> But all their works they do for to be seen of men: they make broad their phylacteries, and enlarge the borders of their garments, and love the uppermost rooms at feasts, and the chief seats in the synagogues, and greetings in the markets, and to be called of men, Rabbi, Rabbi. **But be not ye called Rabbi**: for one is your Master, even Christ; and all ye are brethren. **And call no man your father** upon the earth: for one is your Father, which is in heaven. **Neither be ye called masters**: for one is your Master, even Christ. But he that is greatest among you shall be your servant. And whosoever shall exalt himself shall be abased; and he that shall humble himself shall be exalted. (Matt 23:5-12)

Jesus emphasized humble service rather than exalted position, and He encouraged the disciples to demonstrate their greatness through physical service to their brothers and sisters in Christ. On one occasion Jesus suggested that the greatest of all should become the slave of the others. (Matt 20:27) His statement condemns the mere thought of superiority and implies those seeking a title should eliminate pride and arrogance by assuming the lowest social position. Jesus condemned titles, because none is superior in Him and He has given none authority in Him. Since we are all slaves of the Lord, Jesus' words make sense. Slaves do not hold titles. Since we are all brothers and sisters in the Church, Jesus' direction is even more logical. Brothers and sisters never use titles among themselves. Titles among believers are the fruit of pride and hypocrisy.

In His instruction to the disciples, the Lord specifically prohibited three titles, including those of rabbi, father and master. Rabbi is Hebrew for teacher, and master is a mistranslation of the Greek word for guide. Titles and authority go hand in hand, and each of these titles reflected a position of authority held by various men in first century religious culture. Two of these, teacher and guide, were popular titles in Jewish religious culture, and father was a popular Roman title. Since there are no authorities in the Church and we are all equals before God, titles are superfluous. Indeed, it is a lifestyle sin to assume or accept any title of respect not shared by the members generally.

Jesus plainly taught that a faithful church leader should not assume any title in respect to his service to the church, yet church organizations confer all sorts of titles by ordination, including Father, Pastor, Reverend, Bishop, Elder, Teacher and many others. All titles, assumed or ordained, violate Jesus' words. Any title used before a leader's proper name usurps Jesus' headship in that role and is a reflection of the pride and arrogance invariably found in the leaders of the world. Where no hierarchical order exists, there can be no titles. Jesus condemned titles, because God has not arranged churches hierarchically and He never intended church leaders to possess authority. As our perspective changes, biblical instruction becomes increasingly clearer.

As we continue to study the inspired text of scripture, we will gain a new perspective regarding the role of women in the Church. An area of constant contention in churches involves the role women fulfill in church leadership and in meetings of the congregation. Even though we can plainly read that women prophesied and prayed in the first century churches, (1 Cor 11:4-5) many denominations prohibit women from participating in these and other activities during their assemblies. Organized churches routinely forbid women to hold leadership positions or address the church during official meetings. Even beyond these prohibitions, gifted female members are subordinated to male authorities in virtually all church activities, resulting in unbiblical discrimination against women throughout the organized Christian community.

Gender discrimination is immediately attributable to hierarchical authority in churches and finds biblical support through an errant interpretation of several passages of scripture. When we carefully consider the context of these passages and understand what Paul intended to convey to his audience, even the strongest arguments for a subordinate female membership evaporate from the Bible. In addition to these misinterpreted scriptures, the lack of a basic understanding of the spiritual nature of the Church also contributes to this discrimination. When we combine the reality of the spiritual nature of the Church with an educated perspective of these passages, we should clearly see that female members are fully equal to male members of a congregation.

At this point I want to be very careful not to confuse the equal relationship between men and women in a congregation with the biblical relationship between men and women in marriage. Although a female member of a church is fully equal to a male member of the church in the spiritual relationship to Christ, the Bible plainly states that a wife should subordinate herself to her husband in the marriage relationship. Indeed, many conclude that a subordinate relationship exists between men and women in a church, because they misinterpret passages of scripture which refer to the roles of wives and assume these passages are discussing the roles of women in a church. Unfortunately, Koine Greek makes no clear distinction between a woman and a wife, so we are entirely dependent on context to discern the difference in any given passage. In reality, however, there are few, if any, general biblical references to women in the early churches, and I have concluded that nearly every general reference to women in the New Testament is a reference to married women and their role in some aspect of married life. Such must be the case in 1 Corinthians 11 & 14 and 1 Timothy 2.

Several passages appear to stand opposed to the equality of women in congregational assembly, so we will examine the two which present the strongest case against the equality of women in a church. When we properly understand these passages and apply our new perspective to the rest, every scripturally based objection to female leadership will evaporate from the Bible. Both verses in question prescribe silence for women, and both discuss the manner in which women should learn. One raises the issue of speaking, and the other raises the issue of teaching.

> 1) For God is not the author of confusion, but of peace, as in all churches of the saints. Let your women keep silence in the churches: for it is not permitted unto them to speak; but they are commanded to be under obedience, as also saith the law. And if they will learn any thing, let them ask their husbands at home: for it is a shame for women to speak in the church. (1 Cor 14:33-35)

> 2) Let the woman learn in silence with all subjection. But I suffer not a woman to teach, nor to usurp authority over the man, but to be in silence. For Adam was first formed, then Eve. And Adam was not deceived, but the woman being deceived was in the transgression. (1 Tim 2:11-14)

We may first consider who the women are in these two passages. The first informs us that these women were to be under obedience according to the law. The law placed women under the authority of their fathers or husbands, but the law did not place the female population under the authority of men generally. A young woman lived under the authority of her father until she married, and then she lived under the authority of her husband. Paul continues to suggest that these women learn from their husbands at home, so it seems obvious that Paul addressed married women in this context. It would seem unreasonable to ask unmarried women to wait until they were married before they could learn about spiritual matters discussed in meetings of the church, especially if some never married. The women in this context can only be wives.

Paul informs us in the second passage that he does not permit a woman to teach or usurp authority over the man. The definite article "the" associated with the singular "man" confirms that Paul was talking about the woman's husband and precludes the possibility that Paul was teaching that women are subservient to men generally.

Under the law, men were not only placed in authority over their wives, but the responsibility to teach the family was placed squarely upon their shoulders, so Paul confidently instructs the woman not to teach or usurp authority over her husband. Once again, the woman in this discussion is a wife, and Paul's reference to Adam and Eve further confirms this interpretation. If there were any single women in the church, Paul did not address them in either of these passages.

Having established that the women addressed here were wives, we should consider the context of these passages. The context of the first passage involves avoiding confusion and maintaining order. All of us understand how difficult it is to concentrate on the message of a sermon when cell phones ring, when children cry or even when people whisper to one another. Imagine how much confusion members would create, if they arbitrarily interrupted the speaker to ask questions or to offer comments. Paul was dealing with such a situation in the Corinthian church. Apparently, some of the women were eager to learn, and they were interrupting the speaker to ask questions. Paul told the women not to speak, or "talk randomly" (literal Greek), in the context of maintaining proper decorum and having respect for both the speaker and the other members of the congregation. Paul admonished the women to ask their husbands at home, if they wanted to learn anything, so it is clear that these women were motivated to talk in church in order to learn about what was being discussed. They were not trying to teach or present their own instructional material. Paul did not expressly deny women the opportunity to address the congregation at the proper time, but he was dealing with the same issues pastors today must occasionally address when congregational activity disrupts the meeting and causes confusion.

The context of the second passage contains instruction regarding the general behavior of wives. The context has nothing directly to do with congregational assembly, and the prohibition for a wife to teach her husband reiterates and emphasizes the authority and responsibility of a husband to teach his wife and family at home. Paul admonished the woman to respect the instruction of her husband and honor his position as head of the family. The context of this passage addresses marital relations, not conduct in churches, so this verse cannot limit anyone's right to speak in church assembly. Most errant interpretations result from ignoring the context of a passage.

An important part of the context of both of these passages is the cultural context of the first century, where men dominated society and women were largely relegated to the status of slaves in respect to their husbands. In Jewish religious culture, women had a separate court at the temple, and the synagogue was primarily attended by men, because they were responsible to teach their families at home. The Christian requirement that men and women assemble together was unprecedented at the time, and few women had previous experience regarding the manner in which men met together and exchanged ideas. Thus, it should be no surprise that Paul needed to give women instructions about how they should conduct themselves in assembly. We should be able to appreciate how delicately Paul needed to walk that very fine line which, on the one hand, required women to be respectful of those speaking and learn from their husbands at home, yet, on the other hand, never infringed upon the right of every member to speak as the Spirit might move him or her in an assembly of believers. (1 Cor 14:29-31)

Paul summarily settled the question when he declared that "every woman who prays or prophesies with her head uncovered dishonors her head." (1 Cor 11:5) Regardless of the wearing of hats issue, Paul clearly allowed women to pray and prophesy. Three chapters later within the context of instructions for conducting church meetings, Paul defined prophesying when he said that one who prophesies speaks to men for edification, exhortation and comfort, (1 Cor 14:3) so we learn that prophesying involves speaking to men in church. Since 1 Cor 11:5 plainly allows women to prophesy, and the Bible defines prophesying as speaking to men and gives the definition in the context of church assembly, we may only conclude that women may prophesy in church, women may speak in church, and women may speak to men in church. Any blanket prohibition regarding women speaking in assembly has no biblical basis.

We may further consider this question from the point of view of the nature of the Church. By far the most powerful argument for the equality of women in congregational assembly lies in the spiritual nature of the Church. A spiritual church contains none of the physical distinctions one might find in an organization. In a church each believer is called a member regardless of gender. In the church we lack the physical distinctions which allow the members to be categorized or organized according to physical appearance.

> For ye are all the children of God by faith in Christ Jesus. For as many of you as have been baptized into Christ have put on Christ. There is neither Jew nor Greek, there is neither bond nor free, **there is neither male nor female**: for ye are all one in Christ Jesus. (Gal 3:26-28)

Spiritual vision should change your whole perspective of church meetings. Each believer who has been baptized into the body of Christ has put on Christ and become a unique member in the body of Christ without physical distinctions. God has placed each of us into a church where there are no racial distinctions, no social distinctions and no gender distinctions. Do you grasp the reality of these words? Can you grasp the impact this truth should have on status of women in churches? Gender distinctions do not exist in churches. There are no men in a church, and there are no women in a church. If gender cannot be distinguished in a church, no one can be denied the right to speak in an assembly of the church, nor is there any basis to deny anyone the right to exercise leadership in the church. If members cannot be distinguished by gender, no woman can be denied any role in a church which scripture may appear to designate for a man.

Let us turn our attention from organizationally assumed speaking and teaching prohibitions, which naturally preclude women from holding church leadership responsibilities, and focus directly on the issue of women in leadership. In an effort to avoid appearing to be stuck in the dark ages, social pressure has forced an increasing number of church organizations to reexamine the contexts of those passages above and at least allow women to teach, speak and pray in their assemblies, however most still stop short of ordaining women to positions of authority. Among these churches the main obstacle to the ordination of women is the issue of authority in the organized church. The ordination of women may present a logistical conflict in the church, not only when an ordained woman is married, but particularly when an ordained woman is married to an unbeliever. The organized church must face the possibility that her husband, who might be a novice, unqualified, or even an unbeliever, and who indeed possesses scriptural authority over his wife, may be holding de facto authority over the church. The very circumstance of the married state, which theologians have ignored or twisted to deny women leadership responsibilities in churches, invariably poses a different dilemma when organized churches allow women to be ordained to positions of authority. Organized churches will inevitably face this difficulty whenever they ordain a woman to any position of authority in their hierarchy.

Since, however, we have seen in previous discussions that there are no human authorities, whether male or female, in any Spirit-led church, the issue of authority in leadership becomes moot and disappears for congregations which are part of the spiritual Church. When a female leader requires no ordination at all, the logistical obstacles to female leadership disappear, and a woman is completely free to serve the congregation according to her gifts of leadership provided by the Spirit. When hierarchical organization and human authority are removed from churches, women are free to speak in congregations and lead congregations based on the same qualifications required of men. When members depend entirely on the authority of Jesus Christ to direct their church, each member is free to be placed by God in the church where He wills, and each member is free to serve the congregation in whatever way the Lord may direct regardless of gender.

As our spiritual vision improves and our perspective changes, we will become increasingly aware that every physical attribute which distinguishes us physically from other members of a congregation has been removed from the spiritual Church. A church is not only genderless, but it is also raceless and classless. There are no blacks. There are no whites. There are no poor. There are no rich. Just as we may not judge members by the curvature of their bodies, so we may not judge members by the color of their skin or their social standing. Paul used these three distinguishing aspects of our physical lives to explain to the Galatians that physical differences and distinctions are entirely irrelevant in the church. When Christians assemble, there is no back-of-the-bus for anybody in the body of Christ. Neither is there any head-of-the-class for members of the body. The playing field is level in the church, and everybody is equal before God. Those of us with spiritual vision see all the members the same way God sees them. Nobody is exalted and nobody is debased. Discrimination and partiality are lifestyle sins, and they cannot exist in a spiritual church.

> My brethren, have not the faith of our Lord Jesus Christ, the Lord of glory, with respect of persons. For if there come unto your assembly a man with a gold ring, in goodly apparel, and there come in also a poor man in vile raiment; And ye have respect to him that weareth the gay clothing, and say unto him, Sit thou here in a good place; and say to the poor, Stand thou there, or sit here under my footstool: Are ye not then partial in yourselves, and are become judges of evil thoughts? (James 2:1-4)

Somehow most Bible students are able to see the discrimination James described in his epistle, but few are able to see the partiality in themselves or in their own congregations. Just as most fail to see the discrimination women suffer and endure in churches, they also fail to see the respect of persons given to pastors and other church authorities. When a pastor has a designated parking place for his personal convenience or a special entrance to the sanctuary, that church is practicing partiality. When a pastor sits or stands in a special place in the congregation, that congregation is practicing partiality. When a pastor receives a gift because of his position in the church, the giver is practicing partiality. When a member cancels a long-standing appointment to accept a last-minute invitation by the pastor, that member is practicing partiality.

Since most churchgoers assume a pastor has been ordained by God to his position of authority in the church, members seldom question the favoritism shown to the pastor or consider their actions to be a violation of the prohibition against partiality. Members often ignore the contradiction created between ordained authority, which demands partiality, and the plain words of God, which prohibit partiality. This contradiction can only be resolved when human authority is removed from churches.

Partiality is inherent in hierarchical organization, and organized churches invariably practice favoritism and discrimination. When a member is ordained to a position of authority, it becomes impossible for the congregation to treat the ordained member the same way they treated him before his ordination. When an organization has recognized the superiority of a leader, it naturally expects the congregation to conform to his direction and depend on his judgment. Partiality naturally follows. Authority demands partiality. An ordained pastor expects special treatment, and congregations don't think twice about giving their pastors special treatment, but, when one member is exalted and treated differently from other members, God calls that respect of persons. We may call it partiality, favoritism or discrimination, but the sin is the same. Whenever a church honors and respects any member above the members generally, and particularly when they honor him because of his title or position, it should be clear that partiality has divided the church and sin is resident in that congregation.

Human authority and lifestyle sin are inextricably bound. Most, if not all, of the difficult issues facing churches today would disappear, if hierarchical authority disappeared from churches. Much of the lifestyle sin, which has cut off organized Christianity from God, would disappear, if congregations would remove human authorities. We must live by faith and not by sight, but, when men stand in authority in a congregation, their visible headship creates a separate body apart from the body of Christ. When men create a church with a physical head and a humanly organized body, they have replaced faith in the Lord with obedience to the ordained human head. Faithful believers should not continue to associate with an apostate church which men have arranged and built.

Proponents of hierarchical organization in churches have claimed authority is necessary to maintain order and avoid anarchy in church meetings, but simple logic should suffice to overturn that assumption and reveal the absurdity of the claim that anarchy will result where no spiritual policemen are present. Anarchy, by definition, is an absence of government or a state of lawlessness, but we know every true Christian lives under the government of God, and our living Law directs every true believer. The new covenant Standard of conduct is higher than any civil code, and Christians are never without government or law. Christians are able to rely on the Authority within to maintain order in meetings. Believers should all know the rules God has provided to insure we conduct meetings in an orderly and godly manner, (1 Cor 14) but even most unbelievers and seekers have the common sense to enter a sanctuary with respect and sit quietly while the meeting is in order. Anarchy is never an issue. Church authorities don't maintain order. Common decency does. Faith does.

On rare occasions a member may intentionally disregard the rules of proper decorum and disrupt a meeting to express a public objection to the speaker's point of view. When verbal rebuke and an invitation to leave the meeting are unsuccessful, the final step to regain order is a call to the police, not the pastor. A pastor is no more likely to be able to quiet a dissident member than anyone else, indeed less likely, because he is often the focus of the individual's anger. Such an individual has long since ceased to reflect a godly attitude, and, having refused polite admonition, there remains no alternative but to call the civil authorities. Ecclesiastical authority is useless to quell a disruption. Disorder in a meeting is a civil matter, not a spiritual matter. Ultimately, civil authority maintains order in church meetings, not spiritual authority. Anarchy is impossible as long as civil authority remains in place.

The rules of organized churches sometimes frustrate sincere, respectful individuals with divergent points of view, because such rules invariably nullify the right of members to speak in meetings as the Spirit may move them. God's rules of order grant every member the opportunity to address the congregation, (1 Cor 14:31) but the rules of most organized churches override God's rules and limit speaking opportunities to those well schooled in the organization's doctrine. The organization expects potential leaders to bow before its authorities and learn the prescribed doctrine of the church before they are allowed to speak in church meetings, so those with different perspectives have no opportunity to present them. Thus, ecclesiastical authority perpetuates the church's doctrine and prevents the expression of divergent perspectives, but it has nothing to do with preventing anarchy. Ecclesiastical authority protects the organization and its purposes, but it has no power to protect a meeting from disruption or its members from harm.

In His wisdom God knew the best way to deter frustration and avoid disruption in meetings, and He inspired the solution to be included in scripture. God has decided in advance to grant every member the privilege to speak in meetings of a church, so each member may express his or her thoughts and the congregation may hear every perspective. No one may refuse any member in good standing. God has placed only one restriction on our freedom to speak in assembly. Members may only speak one at a time.

> But he that prophesieth speaketh unto men to edification, and exhortation, and comfort...Let the prophets speak two or three, and let the other judge. If any thing be revealed to another that sitteth by, let the first hold his peace. **For ye may all prophesy one by one, that all may learn, and all may be comforted.** (1 Cor 14:3, 29-31)

Prophets, or teachers, are not limited to those whom the organization authorizes to speak but include any member who feels the Spirit has given him or her a word of edification, exhortation or comfort for the congregation. Indeed, we saw Paul granted women the right to prophesy, (1 Cor 11:5) even though few organizations recognize a woman's ability to edify, exhort or comfort their church members through inspired speaking. Whenever anyone speaks under the inspiration of the Spirit, scripture says he or she is prophesying, therefore, any member may speak in a meeting to edify, exhort or comfort the congregation. No one may be refused. Members speak one at a time, so everyone can hear and understand what the Spirit has led each member to say. After two or three have spoken, another member, perhaps a leader, is required to give his or her judgment of the inspiration of the previous messages. The process continues until all the members have had an opportunity to share their inspired thoughts. Paul's directions require no spiritual authority to carry them out, because anyone may moderate the meeting and select the speakers one at a time. These directions only require godly patience and respect for the perspectives of the other members of the church, while each member awaits his or her turn to speak.

Organized churches cannot operate by God's rules, because the free flow of information and insights by the inspiration of the Spirit would overturn the doctrines and practices of every organized church. Heresies would be discovered, lies would be exposed, and the true nature of organized churches would be revealed for everyone to see. If churches allowed faithful men and women the freedom to share the inspired text of the apostles' writings with the entire congregation, all the lies and half-truths perpetuated by hierarchical authority would be exposed and overturned. If churches allowed all their members the freedom to scrutinize accepted ecclesiastical practice and speak as the Spirit moved them, the whole system of ecclesiastical government would collapse. Although such a supposition lies beyond a reasonable expectation of fulfillment, God has granted each of us the privilege to scrutinize the messages of those who assume the authority to speak for God. Jesus gives us permission to individually evaluate what authorities say, even if the authorities do not allow us the freedom to express such evaluations openly in the congregation. Jesus described the nature of false prophets and false teachers, and He revealed that we can know who false prophets and false teachers are, because we can evaluate their teachings by comparing their words to the words of the apostles and prophets written under the inspiration of the Spirit.

> Beware of false prophets, which come to you in sheep's clothing, but inwardly they are ravening wolves. Ye shall know them by their fruits.
> (Matt 7:15-16)

False prophets and false teachers distort the inspired meaning of the words of God, and the prophet Isaiah warned us that there is absolutely no light in the messages of false prophets and false teachers. (Isa 8:20) When men teach lies along with truth, they pollute the entire message, much like adding sewage to fine wine. Even the smallest amount of sewage pollutes the whole bottle of perfectly blended grape and oak flavors and renders it repulsive and useless. Truth is like fine wine. When it is polluted with even a small amount of error, it becomes similarly repulsive and useless. When church leaders lie to us and tell us they are authorities in the church, tell us we give to God when we give to the church, and tell us the members of the church are sinners among any number of other lies which have no basis in scripture, then we can know them by their fruits, because the inspired text of scripture exposes their lies and proves them to be false teachers. They do not fool us by their pious countenance, their long prayers or their eloquent sermons, because we know from their lies that, inwardly, they are ravening wolves. Authorities masquerade as sheep, but a spiritual perspective reveals them to be wolves in sheep's clothing.

The Greek text also introduces us to a new perspective of sin and judgment, and it reveals the distinction between incidental sin and lifestyle sin. We learned that the blood of Christ removes every incidental sin we may commit and that we remain holy continually in spite of our occasional sins, but we also learned that the mistranslation of Greek verb tenses completely obscures God's revelation of lifestyle sin. The difference between incidental sin and lifestyle sin is the same as the difference between what we do and who we are. God does not judge us for what we do, because the blood of Christ removes every sin, but He may condemn us for who we are, if sinning has changed our nature. We may sin, but, if any becomes a sinner once again, his or her salvation is in jeopardy.

Our new perspective reveals that a believer may commit adultery from time to time, but, if he is committing adultery repeatedly, he has become an adulterer, and he is living in sin. A believer may use illicit drugs from time to time, but, if he uses drugs repeatedly, he has become an addict, and he is living in sin. A believer may commit a homosexual act from time to time, but, if he engages repeatedly in such acts, he has become a homosexual, and he is living in sin. Similarly, he may commit any sin and remain holy, but he may not commit any sin repeatedly and thereby become unholy.

Organized churches ignore lifestyle sin and focus on eliminating incidental sins, seemingly unaware that the blood of Christ immediately purges our occasional sins. Many pastors are operating under the false assumption that God's purpose is to create a perfect church, and they focus their sermons on eliminating incidental sins and completely ignore lifestyle sin. Sinners are allowed to remain in the congregation, and no one removes them, because congregations are oblivious to lifestyle sin. Church doors remain open to all who care to come in, sit quietly and respect the rules of the organization, so sinners are often welcomed in organized churches. Adulterers are welcomed in organized churches. Drug addicts are welcomed in organized churches. Homosexuals are welcomed in organized churches. Virtually all lifestyle sin is welcomed in organized churches, and church authorities are powerless to do anything about it, because they do not even have the spiritual insight to recognize when repeated sinning turns a believer into a sinner.

Although most visible sins must be repeated before they rise to the level of salvation-threatening lifestyle sins, many sins of the mind are inherently lifestyle sins. Sins of the mind are often difficult to recognize and cannot be directly addressed by prescriptive laws. Lifestyle sins of the mind include hate, anger, disrespect, hypocrisy, pride, arrogance and any other sinful attitude which a person may allow to persist in his mind or control his actions. Sins of the mind can occur in any person, but the lifestyle sins of pride and arrogance particularly affect human beings in positions of authority. Pride is inextricably bound to authority, because ordination vests a person with a feeling of superiority. Arrogance is inextricably bound to authority, because the ordained authority invariably looks down on those who have been placed under his authority. Every habitual sin is a lifestyle sin, but many other mental sins are inherently lifestyle sins, because they reflect a continuing sinful attitude of the mind.

The lifestyle sin of divorce stands apart as one of the most prevalent lifestyle sins, and it is listed among the relatively few sins God specifically says He hates, (Mal 2:16) yet divorce is rampant in the organized Christian community, because civil codes regarding marriage are accepted as the standard for church attendance rather than the laws of God. Organized churches are powerless to control divorce, because they bow to the standards and regulations of civil governments, which allow divorce for any reason—indeed for no reason at all. Organized churches acknowledge civil laws in place of God's laws, so we should not be surprised that the lifestyle sin of divorce is rampant in organized churches.

God has revealed that a man and a woman are one in marriage. (Gen 2:24, Eph 5:31) God's revelation is a spiritual reality, so only those with spiritual vision can perceive the unity of two separate individuals. Faith in the words of God allows us to comprehend the reality. The world cannot see it, because the orderly arrangement has no faith. Those who trust in the authority of men have no faith. They walk by sight and have no respect for the spiritual realities revealed by God in His word.

A single body cannot be divided in half or else both halves will die. Similarly, a head cannot be separated from a body or both it and the body will die. When two believers, united by God spiritually as one flesh, separate and divorce, at least one, maybe both, will die spiritually. The spiritual reality of the unity of marriage is scripturally plain, and the consequence of divorce ought to be obvious to anyone who possesses spiritual vision.

Even without spiritual vision, Jesus made the lifestyle sin of divorce plain for every believer to see, because divorce involves two separate, yet related, lifestyle sins: unforgiveness and judgment. The foundational teachings of Jesus in the Sermon on the Mount make it plain that these two sins are both inherently lifestyle sins.

> For if ye forgive men their trespasses, your heavenly Father will also forgive you: But if ye forgive not men their trespasses, neither will your Father forgive your trespasses. (Matt 6:14-15)

> Judge not, that ye be not judged. (Matt 7:1)

Unforgiveness is a lifestyle sin, because unforgiveness continues until a change of heart allows the member to be willing to forgive. Judgment is a lifestyle sin, because the condemnation and rejection continue until the member lifts his judgment and the relationship is restored. Unforgiveness and judgment are both sins of the mind and are, therefore, inherently lifestyle sins, because these sins continue until the person experiences a change of mind toward the rejected individual. From a spiritual perspective, unforgiveness and judgment are opposite sides of the same deadly coin. Unforgiveness reveals one is judging, and judgment reveals one is not forgiving. God absolutely requires our forgiveness of others, because He has forgiven each of us for a lifetime of sin. God absolutely forbids condemnation of others, because He has lifted his judgment from each of us, even though we deserved condemnation. Jesus' words apply broadly to our relationships with every individual, believer or unbeliever, but they should especially apply to those we have promised in Covenant with God to love as long as we live.

When a husband, for example, divorces his wife, the husband has condemned her and rejected her. He has judged her to be useless and reprobate. The husband has not judged her actions, but he has judged her person. As long as the couple is divorced, the husband's judgment continues. He is living in sin, because he has judged unrighteous judgment. He has considered her useless, condemned her and removed her from his presence. The husband can no longer receive forgiveness from God until he repents of his unforgiveness, withdraws his judgment and reconciles with his wife. His words of repentance must always be followed by action, so the husband must at least extend an offer of reconciliation to provide evidence that he is truly thinking differently.

However, none of us can ever force our will upon another, so the husband's repentance places the proverbial ball of forgiveness into the wife's court. If the wife is willing to forgive, the couple may reconcile, and God's forgiveness and blessing will be extended to them again. Unfortunately, divorce situations frequently become more complicated, so reconciliation is rarely that simple.

Divorce situations become more complicated whenever one of the divorced members remarries. Remarriage adds a third lifestyle sin to the situation. When a divorced member remarries, he or she is living in lifestyle adultery, and the new mate is also living in sin. If a married member commits an act of adultery and returns to his or her own mate, the member can receive forgiveness from God for the incidental sin, but, when a divorced member moves in with a lover to make a life together with or without the benefit of civil sanction, both are living in sin, and their lifestyle adultery cannot be forgiven until they recognize their lifestyle sin and repent.

When an individual adds the lifestyle sin of adultery to the lifestyle sins of unforgiveness and judgment, one may tend to think the situation has become so complicated that it can never be sorted out or that God can never forgive individuals who have messed up their lives so much, but, indeed, that is not true. God is always ready to forgive when we repent, and He has provided a remarkably simple solution for believers who have been deceived by their own lust or allowed to sin by ignorant church leaders. Even those whose lives have been ravaged by youthful lust and the high water mark of social tolerance for sin can receive forgiveness from God, if they are willing to acknowledge the biblical principles of marriage, turn from unforgiveness and judgment and resolve never to divorce again.

God inspired a little known and rarely applied principle in the law of Moses, which He has given us to provide the solution to the most complicated divorce and remarriage situations anyone might imagine. When human relations become so complicated with multiple marriages and multiple divorces, God, in His infinite wisdom, has made a simple provision to wipe a fallen believer's slate clean. Those who are willing to renounce divorce forever and resolve to live faithfully with one mate for the rest of their lives may simply repent—think differently—about divorce and remarriage. Moses provides us with a glimpse into the mind of God to help us deal with situations which have become complicated by the influence of the world and the failure of church leaders to provide godly instruction regarding marriage and divorce.

> When a man hath taken a wife, and married her, and it come to pass that she find no favour in his eyes, because he hath found some uncleanness in her: then let him write her a bill of divorcement, and give it in her hand, and send her out of his house. And when she is departed out of his house, she may go and be another man's wife. And if the latter husband hate her, and write her a bill of divorcement, and giveth it in her hand, and sendeth her out of his house; or if the latter husband die, which took her to be his wife; **Her former husband, which sent her away, may not take her again to be his wife**, (Deut 24:1-4)

When a man and a woman married in Israel and then they divorced, and the woman married another man and they divorced, God did not allow the woman to remarry her first husband, even if the second husband was dead. When a person married a second or a third or a forth time, etc., that individual could no longer remarry any previous spouse. Each time the person remarried, God burned the bridge back to any previous relationship. This provision reveals the mind of God for dealing with marital ignorance and forms the basis for the solution to marriage situations which have become deeply mired in the ignorance of lifestyle sin.

God has effectively decided to treat backsliding believers' deep involvement in lifestyle sin the same way He treats repentant sinners when they come to faith for the very first time. In fact, the situations are identical, because backsliding believers have ignorantly made themselves sinners once again through indulgence in lifestyle sin, just as sinners are ignorant of God and His ways before coming to faith. When backsliding believers acknowledge the laws of God, recognize their sinful state, resolve to turn from lifestyle sin and live faithfully in marriage, God simply wipes the slate clean and allows them to begin living faithfully once again. God never requires an illegitimately married couple to divorce and remarry their original spouses. The present couple must simply think differently about divorce and resolve never to divorce again.

However, notice carefully that repentance from ignorantly living in any particular sin is a one-time blessing. Once a person gains the knowledge of a lifestyle sin and repents, he or she can never engage in the same lifestyle sin without giving up salvation. The primary consideration which allows God to cleanse fallen believers from the twisted complications of lifestyle sin is ignorance. As long as a believer has entered lifestyle sin ignorantly, God is always willing to forgive, but a believer may never knowingly live in sin. Knowledge cancels the opportunity to repent due to ignorance. If a believer enters any lifestyle sin with knowledge, the Bible says he or she is sinning willfully, and there remains no more sacrifice for those who are sinning willfully. (Heb 10:26) Those who fall away in this manner cannot be renewed again to repentance, (Heb 6:4-6) because knowledge precludes ignorance.

However, knowledge is also a prerequisite to repentance when fallen believers are ignorantly living in sin, because they cannot even recognize the need to repent unless they know they are sinning. Lifestyle sin is a very precarious situation for backsliding believers, because they cannot repent unless they know, and they cannot know unless they somehow gain an understanding of the truth. God's simple solution for lifestyle sin remains highly unlikely unless church leaders take the time to carefully study the Bible and teach the truth about godly marriage and the dangers of lifestyle sin.

Unfortunately, most church leaders are filled with pride and living ignorantly in sin themselves. Authorities are ignorant of the principles of godly marriage and have no capacity to teach their members the truth about marriage. Polls show fully fifty percent of Christian marriages have ended in divorce, and many of those have remarried again. This statistic serves an indictment on the leadership of the organized Christian community and exposes their utter failure to teach the basic principles of godly marriage or to promote and uphold marital commitment and fidelity. Christians are living in sin due to lack of knowledge, not because they don't believe God exists. Once again, the prophet Hosea puts his finger on the problem, "My people are destroyed for lack of knowledge." (Hosea 4:6)

Our new perspective of sin, judgment and unforgiveness reveals the spiritual poverty of every organized church. Organized churches are rich and increased with goods, but, spiritually speaking, they are wretched and miserable and poor and blind and naked. Their spiritual nakedness is obvious to anyone blessed with spiritual vision. Their leaders are living in sin and their members are living in sin, because every organized church has been defiled by covenants with the world. Organized churches have become the world, but God is calling His people out of the world. He is calling us out of lifestyle sin. We cannot allow our churches to make covenants with the government. We cannot allow anything to destroy our marriages. We cannot allow unforgiveness to destroy a relationship. We cannot allow judgment to cause division in a holy church. We cannot allow pride to puff up our faithful church leaders and turn them into authorities. We cannot even allow a drunkard to spot a holy church. We cannot allow any of these lifestyle sins to threaten our salvation. We cannot be like organized churches. Every lifestyle sin must be removed from a faithful congregation. Every church must remain holy continually in the presence of God.

The wisdom of the world raises those who show leadership ability to positions of authority over other people, but God knows authority corrupts every human being, and He will remove every human authority from His Church. As God applies spiritual heat to His precious people, those who are puffed up with pride will rise to the top, just as scum rises to the top as heat purifies precious metals. God will skim off and destroy all those whose pride allows them to be exalted and ordained to positions of authority in churches, just as a refiner will skim the scum off the pure gold before it is sculpted into a work of art.

When human authority is removed from our churches, then our churches today can function like the cooperative, communal congregations of the first century. When hierarchical government is removed from churches, each of us will be free to listen as the Lord speaks through the Spirit, and we will be free to follow His direction. There will be no codified church doctrine, because there will be no authorities to codify doctrine. The Spirit will lead each of us to conform to biblical instruction as the Lord directs. There will be no church buildings, because the Lord said we should not store up treasure on earth. Congregational collections of money or goods will be rare, because each of us will give directly to the poor and oppressed to fill their needs. There will be no headquarters organization to support, and there will be no pastor's salary to pay. There will be no great commission to accomplish or church mission statement to fulfill, because only the Lord has vision for the Church, and He will direct each of us individually and personally by the Spirit to act faithfully and pleasingly in God's sight.

The government of God is so simple that very few believe it. The wisdom of the world assumes human authorities must direct the churches, but the wisdom of God designates the Lord as the only Authority in His Church. God cannot govern the Church according to the systems and structures of world governments, and He does not organize it through human direction. He places each member in the Church as it has pleased Him. (1 Cor 12:18) The Church lives under the government of God, and the government of God for the Church is theocracy described in all its fullness by the apostle Paul in his letter to the Corinthian church.

> But I would have you know, that the head of every man is Christ; and the head of the woman is the man; and the head of Christ is God. (1 Cor 11:3)

God is sovereign and Head over all. Jesus Christ is the Head of every member of the Church, and every husband is the head of his wife. That's all there is to the government of God in the Church. God and Christ are one. Christ and each believer are one. A man and his wife are one. All are one in Christ. There is no hierarchical structure in theocracy. There are no human rulers or authorities in the Church.

God is calling individuals who live in the world and continue to function in the world. He is calling individuals who submit to the direction of rulers, authorities, bureaucrats, and bosses. He calls individuals who comply with federal, state and local laws and willingly yield to corporate policies and procedures. He calls individuals who eat physical food, drink physical water, wear physical clothing and live in physical shelters. He calls individuals who occasionally depend on police for protection or doctors for health. God calls individuals who make covenants of all sorts with governments, businesses and individuals in order to earn wages, purchase products and pay for the services we need to maintain our physical lives. Physically, each of us lives in the world, and each of us earns, spends and saves money in order to function in the world according to the world's system of orderly arrangement.

However, while we live in the world physically, He has removed us from the world spiritually and placed us into one united Church. He has joined us together by the Spirit into one spiritual body living in heaven. God is calling to Himself one spiritual nation—one holy temple—one unified Church which will only submit itself to the rulership of God and the authority of Jesus Christ. As a church, we do not live in the world, we do not participate in the affairs of the world, and we do not submit to any rulership or authority in the world. As a church, we do not depend on the police for protection or on doctors for health. As a church, we do not eat physical food, drink physical water, wear physical clothes or live in physical shelters. As a church, we do not need money, and there is no point to accumulate wealth or goods. As a church, we are in Covenant with God, so we do not make covenants with any human ruler, because a church may not worship any man. A church may not bow down to any governmental or corporate laws to increase its treasure on earth, because, as a church, God provides all our needs.

Many sincere churchgoers have been caught up in organized Christianity and have been looking to fallible human beings as authorities on God or as authorities on His Word. If you are beginning to recognize the difference between organized churches and the one true Church, God may be calling you out of the corrupt system of organized religion. When you are ready to step out into the full freedom of new covenant faith in Jesus Christ and trust Him alone to direct your spiritual life apart from any human supervision or direction, simply repent of your trust in human authorities and determine to allow God to rule you and Jesus Christ to be your one and only Commander. You may no longer allow the rules of men to govern your spiritual life or the commands of church authorities to determine your service to God. You must allow the faith of Jesus Christ to direct you as He speaks to you personally through the Spirit every moment of every day. God has called you to experience the freedom of His grace through faith, so He has freed you from every prescriptive direction of every church authority.

Your repentance may involve a significant change in the way you conduct your spiritual life, but very little may need to change in the way you conduct your life in the world. The truth you are embracing is spiritual reality based on the inspired words of God. You are thinking differently. While you must change your focus to the Lord for direction, you may not necessarily need to change your habits. You may still visit with your friends at your church, and you may still serve the people in the same way you have always served them, but you may no longer obey the directions of church authorities to fulfill your service to the Lord, and you may not direct the actions of your fellow Christians. The Lord must direct every activity of every member. You are completely free to allow God to rule your life through His Word and allow the Lord to direct your actions through the Spirit. Church leaders may teach you the principles of love, faith and godliness, and they may describe the nature of the Christian life, but you should never allow church leaders to oversee your activities or pressure you to serve the church in any way. Christianity is not about what you do. It is about who you are. You must be holy, and you can only remain holy, if you are free from human direction and depend entirely upon the Lord to direct your spiritual life.

While you may serve people in the same way the Lord has always directed you and participate in the same activities, you should carefully consider the admonition of the apostle Paul regarding your fellowship with members who are living in sin. It is very important to live by every word of God.

> But now I have written unto you not to keep company, if any man that is called a brother be a fornicator, or covetous, or an idolater, or a railer, or a drunkard, or an extortioner; with such an one no not to eat. (1 Cor 5:11)

You may no longer fellowship with anyone in the congregation who claims to be a Christian and, at the same time, that individual is living in sin. You may eat with unbelieving friends and relatives, but you may not associate or share a meal with anyone who is called a brother or sister in the faith, if that person denies the faith by the way he or she is living. Anyone holding an ordained position of authority in your church, such as a pastor, an elder or a deacon, is living in sin; therefore, you should not share communion with any pastors, elders or deacons. You should set an example of obedience and faithful Christian conduct by not eating or keeping company with ordained men or women from any church.

Your change in perspective will allow you to become more focused on who you are rather than just on what you do. You must see yourself as a citizen of the kingdom of God. You must be a member of the united Church of heaven. Spiritual awareness of who you are should cause you to realize you cannot be a Catholic or a Protestant. You cannot be a Baptist or a Methodist or a Mormon or a Seventh Day Adventist. You may not associate yourself with any organized church. You may not participate in communion with any organized church.

You need not be concerned that your name might appear on the membership roster of an organized church, because nominal membership in an organization is irrelevant to your salvation, but you should not associate yourself with any organized church. You associate yourself with an organized church when you take communion with that church. You must see yourself as a member of the spiritual Church, which God has placed in heaven in Jesus Christ. When your membership in the Church of heaven becomes a reality, you should realize you cannot participate in the symbols of unity with any organized church. Organized churches are separate bodies with separate heads. You may not share communion with any church which is living in sin, because communion unites you spiritually with that apostate church. You may only share communion with faithful members and with leaders who hold no office and claim no authority over you. Since participation in communion is not required for salvation, you may choose to abstain from communion altogether, or you may arrange to take the symbols of the bread and wine with a small private group by personal arrangement. You do not need a pastor to bless and serve the communion. Any member may ask the Lord to bless the bread and wine. Our heavenly Pastor is always present with us in our very midst, even when we meet in small groups. "Where two or three are gathered together, there I am in the midst of them." (Matt 18:20)

Your example will be a powerful witness to the members of an organized church. They may ask why you are doing what you are doing, and you may have the opportunity to tell them that your life in Covenant with God is now entirely under His rulership and under the authority of the Lord. You may tell them that you no longer rely on human authority for direction on the path of salvation. You may also want to encourage your friends to look into the biblical basis for their trust in church authorities, and you may express your concern for those who have allowed the facade of organized Christianity to deceive them. These, of course, are only suggestions, because you should follow the lead of the Spirit in everything you say or explain to your friends.

However, your confidence in the Lord is bound to bring you persecution. Faithless or convicted individuals may criticize your behavior, judge your character or ridicule your beliefs, but do not despair, because "all those who will live godly in Christ Jesus will suffer persecution." (2 Tim 3:12) You may be questioned by church authorities or even removed from the organization, but remember, men have no power to remove anybody from the spiritual body of Christ. Only God can remove a member from the Church of heaven.

At some point you may even feel your efforts are being wasted, and you may feel you also need to remove yourself physically from a faithless congregation, but remember that you should continue to seek Christian fellowship and assemble together (Heb 10:25) with believers who claim no authority over you. You should seek fellowship with those who also live godly lives in Jesus Christ and are not puffed up by the pride of authority. You are free to seek fellowship wherever faithful believers assemble. You are free to go wherever the Spirit leads you to go, and you are free to do whatever the Spirit leads you to do. Faith in the Lord Jesus Christ leaves you free to pursue any godly course.

The faith of Jesus Christ has opened the strait gate before you, and the Spirit of God is leading you through the narrow Way which few have been able to find. You have come "unto mount Sion, and unto the city of the living God, the heavenly Jerusalem, and to an innumerable company of angels, to the general assembly and church of the firstborn, which are written in heaven, and to God the Judge of all, and to the spirits of [righteous] men made [complete], and to Jesus the mediator of the new covenant." (Heb 12:22-24) God has placed you in the heavenly places in Jesus Christ, where there is no organization to join, no offering basket to fill, and no codified rules and regulations to follow. The spiritual vision of the Word of God has allowed you to see yourself assembled among the righteous as an equal with all true believers. Welcome to fellowship among the called and faithful who are experiencing true freedom in Christ.

Appendix

1	Mistranslation Exposed	333
2	Scripture Denies Ecclesiastical Authority	357
3	Nailed to the Cross	363
4	Comparison of the Covenants	369

Appendix 1

Mistranslation Exposed

The following pages contain an exhaustive list of scriptures, each of which will tend to validate the assumption that God intended men to rule churches and ordain authorities to direct the churches. Each contains one or more mistranslated words. These errors will imply that the Bible supports hierarchical organization in churches. The passages in question are listed in biblical order so you can more quickly find a particular verse should that become necessary. I use the King James Version (KJV) as my English text. Less significant mistranslations, corrections or clarifications of the KJV text are indicated in brackets. All definitions of Greek words are quoted directly and unedited from Strong's *Greek Dictionary of the New Testament*. The word(s) in **bold type** is the focus of the discussion. Where necessary, I offer a corrected translation of the verse. The corrected translation is underlined.

Matt 24:45
Who then is a faithful and wise [slave], whom his lord **hath made ruler** over his household, to give them meat in due season?
 NT:2525
kathistemi (kath-is'-tay-mee); from NT:2596 and NT:2476; **to place down (permanently)**, i.e. (figuratively) to designate, constitute, convoy:

Two errors obscure the meaning of this verse. Our English Bibles imply that Jesus Christ will appoint church leaders to rule over other members in the Lord's household. The translators' assumption of rulership presumptuously embellishes the Greek text, which merely states that He has placed some members permanently in their responsibilities. A simple literal translation would be "designated." Additionally, the English translation errantly leads the reader to believe that a faithful and wise slave will be placed over the lord's household. In the Greek text the phrase "over his household" is associated with the lord rather than the slave. This verse should be translated: Who then is a faithful and wise slave, whom the lord over his household **has designated** to give them meat in due season.

333

Mark 3:14
And [Jesus] **ordained** twelve, that they should be with him, and that he might send them forth to preach
NT:4160
poieo (poy-eh'-o); apparently a prolonged form of an obsolete primary; **to make or do** (in a very wide application, more or less direct):

This verse tells us that Jesus "made" the twelve disciples, so they would be with him and afterwards they would be sent out to spread the gospel. There is no sense from the Greek word or from the context that any authority was transferred or that an ordination ceremony took place. The simple English sense is that Jesus chose them. (see John 15:16) The Greek vocabulary of the New Testament contains no concept of ordination to a position of authority.

Mark 13:34
For the Son of man is as a man taking a far journey, who left his house, and gave **authority** to his [slaves], and to every man his work, and commanded the porter to watch.
NT:1849
exousia (ex-oo-see'-ah); from NT:1832 (in the sense of ability); **privilege**, i.e. (subjectively) force, capacity, competency, freedom, or (objectively) mastery (concretely, magistrate, superhuman, potentate, token of control), delegated influence:

Rather than authority, the Lord has blessed each of His slaves with various privileges which facilitate the Lord's work on earth. Although Mark alludes to specific privileges, he does not list them in this verse. If we conduct a thorough search of the New Testament, we may accumulate the following list of privileges granted to members of the Church: 1) privilege to cast out spirits and to heal sickness and disease (Matt 10:1, Luke 9:1); 2) privilege to tread on serpents and scorpions (Luke 10:19); 3) privilege over the power of Satan (Luke 10:19); 4) privilege to become the sons of God (John 1:12); 5) privilege to eat, to drink, to marry, to forbear working, etc. (1 Cor 9:4-6); and 6) privilege to edify (2 Cor 10:8, 13:10). Indeed Jesus gave privileges to His slaves as this list indicates, but He grants no privilege over other members and no privilege to command the members. There are no other privileges granted to church leaders or members anywhere in the Bible.

Luke 12:42

And the Lord said, Who then is that faithful and wise steward, whom his lord **shall make ruler** over his household, to give them their portion of meat in due season?

The KJV translation of this verse contains identical errors as those found in Matthew 24:45. See explanation above.

Luke 12:44

Of a truth I say unto you, that he will **make** him **ruler** over all that he hath.

NT:2525

kathistemi (kath-is'-tay-mee); from NT:2596 and NT:2476; **to place down (permanently)**, i.e. (figuratively) to designate, constitute, convoy:

Once again the translators have erroneously imputed rulership to those whom He has placed permanently in their responsibilities.

John 15:16

Ye have not chosen me, but I have chosen you, and **ordained** you, that ye should go and bring forth fruit, and that your fruit should remain: that whatsoever ye shall ask of the Father in my name, he may give it you.

NT:5087

tithemi (tith'-ay-mee); a prolonged form of a primary theo (theh'-o) (which is used only as alternate in certain tenses); **to place** (in the widest application, literally and figuratively; properly, **in a passive or horizontal posture**, and thus different from NT:2476, which properly denotes an upright and active position, while NT:2749 is properly reflexive and utterly prostrate):

Jesus' placed the disciples so they would bring forth fruit and so they would receive what they asked of the Father. Neither the Greek word nor the context carries any connotation of authority. Notice that *tithemi* means to place "in a passive or horizontal posture," not what one might expect John to say, if the disciples were raised up to a position of authority through their placement or ordination. If such were the case, John would have used the word *histemi*. (NT:2476) See the definition of this word in your concordance. The Greek vocabulary of the New Testament contains no concept of ordination to a position of authority.

Acts 1:20
For it is written in the book of Psalms, Let his habitation be desolate, and let no man dwell therein: and his **bishoprick** let another take.
    NT:1984
episkope (ep-is-kop-ay'); from NT:1980; **inspection (for relief)**; by implication, superintendence; specially, the Christian "episcopate":
    The inspection asserted here is "for relief" only. The Greek word carries no implications of superintendence. *Episkope* is derived from NT:1980. The definition of this root verb is "to visit." *Episkope* means "visitation." ...and his **visitation** let another take.

Acts 1:22
Beginning from the baptism of John, unto that same day that he was taken up from us, must one **be ordained to be** a witness with us of his resurrection.
    NT:1096
ginomai (ghin'-om-ahee); a prolongation and middle voice form of a primary verb; **to cause to be** ("gen"- erate), i.e. (reflexively) to become (come into being), used with great latitude (literal, figurative, intensive, etc.):
    After Judas' death, one of the disciples who were with Jesus from the time of His baptism to the time of His resurrection needed to be appointed to take Judas' place among the apostles. That individual was caused to be a witness with the eleven. If the other apostles can be shown to have the authority to command members, so will this person. No authority is stated or implied here. The Greek vocabulary of the New Testament contains no concept of ordination to a position of authority. ...one must **be caused to be** a witness with us of his resurrection.

Acts 6:3
Wherefore, brethren, look ye out among you seven men of honest report, full of the Holy Ghost and wisdom, whom we may appoint **over** this business.
    It is interesting that some use this correctly translated verse to impute authority to these seven men and, therefore, to deacons in a church, even though Luke plainly tells us they were appointed over the business, not over the people.

Acts 10:48
And [Peter] **commanded** them to be baptized in the name of the Lord.
NT:4367
prostasso (pros-tas'-so); from NT:4314 and NT:5021; **to arrange towards**, i.e. (figuratively) enjoin:
Command or enjoin can only be used in the figurative sense, but Luke's statement is a history of literal events. Peter literally arranged for their baptism. And [Peter] **arranged** for them to be baptized in the name of Christ.

Acts 14:23
And when they had **ordained** them elders in every church, and had prayed with fasting, they commended them to the Lord, on whom they believed.
NT:5500
cheirotoneo (khi-rot-on-eh'-o); from a comparative of NT:5495 and teino (to stretch); **to be a hand-reacher or voter** (by raising the hand), i.e. (generally) to select or appoint:
Some may be surprised to learn that Paul and the other leaders of the churches designated elders by voting. Their appointments were not confirmed by majority vote, but by full agreement. (Matt 18:19)

Acts 17:15
And they that conducted Paul brought him unto Athens: and receiving a **commandment** unto Silas and Timotheus for to come to him with all speed, they departed.
This remarkable account that Silas and Timothy received a command to come to assist Paul may have the appearance of an authoritative injunction from Paul, but it is not definitive. The historical record Luke preserves for us is unclear whether the command was issued by Paul or from one of those who conducted him to Athens. Even if Paul issued the command, we may only have a record of an apostle's sin and not necessarily clear evidence Paul exercised the privilege of vested ecclesiastical authority. Since this incident is a matter of the historical record of what actually took place and apostolic authority is not otherwise supported by clear biblical teaching, the historical record of this incident is not suitable to establish or refute authority. We must see supporting evidence

from the words of the Lord or church teaching in the epistles before we may assent to ecclesiastical authority for churches.

Acts 20:28

Take heed therefore unto yourselves, and to all the flock, **over** the which the Holy Ghost hath made you **overseers**, to feed the church of God, which he hath purchased with his own blood.

One error of translation and one error of interpretation combine to skew the intended meaning of this verse. First, the Greek preposition is "in," not "over." If Luke had intended to say "over," he would have used the Greek preposition *huper*, NT:5228.

NT:1722
en (en); a primary preposition denoting (fixed) position (in place, time or state), and (by implication) instrumentality (medially or constructively), i.e. a relation of rest (intermediate between NT:1519 and NT:1537); **"in,"** at, (up-) on, by, etc.:

The preposition describes a fixed position in, not over, and offers no figurative sense. Overseers have been literally placed IN the flock, not figuratively over it. Of 122 uses in the New Testament, *en* is never translated "over," except in this verse. Had the author intended to convey authority over the flock, he would have used the Greek word *huper*.

NT:5228
huper (hoop-er'); a primary preposition; **"over"**, i.e. (with the genitive case) of place, above, beyond, across, or causal, for the sake of, instead, regarding; with the accusative case superior to, more than:

Additionally, the word overseer is a very clever manipulation of both component parts of this compound Greek word and carries a bureaucratic connotation in our culture which did not exist at all in the first century Greek or Jewish culture.

NT:1985
episkopos (ep-is'-kop-os); from NT:1909 and NT:4649 (in the sense of NT:1983); a superintendent, i.e. Christian officer in genitive case charge of a (or the) church (literally or figuratively):

Notice that *episkopos* is a compound word comprised of NT:1909 "upon," and NT:4649, "a watch." The preposition "over" (NT:5228 above) is not part of this word. Strong defines NT:4649 as a "watch" rather than a "seer," so it becomes clear that theologians have transformed the role of a church leader from being "a watch upon" a church into being an overseer of a church. Strong's definition of *episkopos*, "a superintendent," further corrupts it by abandoning any literal basis in the original Greek word in order to cement the concept of ecclesiastical authority in churches, as indicated by his appended notes. The Greek word indicates the *episkopos* is one who diligently watches upon the flock, not one who has authority over the flock. He was given the responsibility to watch out for enemies of God, not to rule over the people of God. He serves the church, but he does not control it. "Watchman" and "guardian" more literally reflect the responsibility indicated by the Greek word.

Rom 11:13
For I speak to you Gentiles, inasmuch as I am the apostle of the Gentiles, I magnify mine **office:**
NT:1248
diakonia (dee-ak-on-ee'-ah); from NT:1249; **attendance** (as a servant, etc.); figuratively (eleemosynary) aid, (official) service (especially of the Christian teacher, or techn. of the diaconate):

Strong's reference to official service is an assumption based on his observation of the practices of organized churches. All references to offices in the Bible are mistranslations. Paul esteemed his service to the Gentiles. For I speak to you Gentiles, inasmuch as I am the apostle of the Gentiles, I magnify my **service.**

Rom 12:4
For as we have many members in one body, and all members have not the same **office:**
NT:4234
praxis (prax'-is); from NT:4238; **practice**, i.e. (concretely) an act; by extension, a function:

There are no offices in the Church. There is no Greek word for "office" in the New Testament. For as we have many members in one body, and all members have not the same **practice.**

Rom 12:8
Or he that exhorteth, on exhortation: he that giveth, let him do it with simplicity; he that **ruleth,** with diligence; he that sheweth mercy, with cheerfulness.

NT:4291
proistemi (pro-is'-tay-mee); from NT:4253 and NT:2476; **to stand before**, i.e. (in rank) to preside, or (by implication) to practise:

No one rules the Church but God. This church leader practices his faith as he stands before the congregation, and Paul encouraged him to be diligent and eager to serve in this capacity. No rulership or authority is stated or even implied by the Greek text.

Rom 13:1-2
Let every soul be subject unto the higher [authorities]. (NT:1849) For there is no [authority] but of God: the [authorities] that be are **ordained** (NT:5021) of God. Whosoever therefore resisteth the [authority] resisteth the ordinance of God: and they that resist shall receive to themselves damnation.

NT:5021
tasso (tas'-so); a prolonged form of a primary verb (which latter appears only in certain tenses); **to arrange in an orderly manner**, i.e. assign or dispose (to a certain position or lot):

The context of this verse demands that "every soul" should be subject to civil authorities, which God has "arranged in an orderly manner" (NT:5021) in human governments. It is absurd to assume that God might ordain authorities in civil governments. Each church member should submit to all civil authority, but this passage does not imply a hierarchical structure for churches. The context here is limited to civil authority, so no valid conclusions can be drawn from this passage regarding church authority.

1 Cor 7:10
And unto the married I **command**, yet not I, but the Lord, Let not the wife depart from her husband:

NT:3853
paraggello (par-ang-gel'-lo); from NT:3844 and the base of NT:32; **to transmit a message,** i.e. (by implication) to enjoin:

The commands Paul gave were based on the authority of the Lord, not on his own authority to command. Paul acted as a messenger from God, not an authority.

1 Cor 7:17
But as God hath distributed to every man, as the Lord hath called every one, so let him walk. And so **ordain** I in all churches.

NT:1299

diatasso (dee-at-as'-so); from NT:1223 and NT:5021; **to arrange thoroughly**, i.e. (specially) institute, prescribe, etc.:

This word is one of several Greek words which will convey authority, if the one who is making the arrangement has authority. If one has no authority, using this word does not impute it. Paul's arrangement was to prescribe no changes in a member's physical circumstances based on conversion and particularly in respect to marriage. The Greek vocabulary of the New Testament contains no concept of ordination to a position of authority.

1 Cor 9:12
If others be partakers of this [privilege] over you, are not we rather? Nevertheless we have not used this [privilege]; but suffer all things, lest we should hinder the gospel of Christ.

Paul concedes that "others" have privilege (NT:1849) over the members, but Paul never specifically stated that the apostles exercised the same authority to demand financial support from the members of the church. The "others" to whom Paul refers is unclear. Perhaps it refers to publicans or other government officials who indeed had authority to collect taxes from the people. Paul had the privilege to forbear working and to receive freewill offerings from the church, a privilege listed among those granted to church leaders (1 Cor 9:6), but Paul had no authority to demand money from the members. Those who preached the gospel had the privilege to receive whatever voluntary support the congregation might offer for their necessity, but they neither held authority over the members nor the authority to demand contributions from them.

1 Cor 11:17
Now in this that I **declare** unto you I praise you not, that ye come together not for the better, but for the worse.

NT:3853

paraggello (par-ang-gel'-lo); from NT:3844 and the base of NT:32; **to transmit a message,** i.e. (by implication) to enjoin:

The commands Paul gave were based on the authority of the Lord, not on his own authority to command. Paul acted as a messenger from God, not an authority.

1 Cor 12:28-31
And God hath set some in the church, **first** apostles, secondarily prophets, thirdly teachers, after that miracles, then **gifts** of healings, helps, governments, diversities of tongues. Are all apostles? are all prophets? are all teachers? are all workers of miracles? Have all the **gifts** of healing? do all speak with tongues? do all interpret? But covet earnestly the best **gifts**: and yet shew I unto you a more excellent way.

The main point in this context, as well as the context of Ephesians 4, is the gifting of each member by the Spirit for the benefit of the whole body. I encourage you to study 1 Corinthians 12 in its entirety and watch carefully as Paul intertwines the thread of gifting throughout. It will become clear that the gifts God has set in the Church are not positions of authority, but are simply gifts of the Spirit listed in the order of their importance to the body. They are not given in an order of rank of authority. Such is verified by the Greek word *proton*, translated "first" in verse 27.

NT:4412
proton (pro'-ton); neuter of NT:4413 as adverb (with or without NT:3588); **firstly (in time, place, order, or importance)**:

This Greek word for "first" refers to importance, not rank. If rank were intended, Paul would have used the Greek word *arche*. Carefully compare the definitions of the two Greek words.

NT:746
arche (ar-khay'); from NT:756; (properly abstract) a commencement, or (concretely) **chief (in various applications of order, time, place, or rank)**:

Therefore, we may only conclude that the gifts given to the members of the body are listed in order of importance, not in order of rank. This list cannot be a list of hierarchal positions in the body.

One might also consider that the gifts are listed here without a definite article. Had Luke intended to emphasize the role of those who received the gift rather than the quality of the gift, he would have used the definite article before each noun, e.g., "the" apostles.

1 Cor 16:1
Now concerning the collection for the saints, as **I have given order** to the churches of Galatia, even so do ye.

NT:1299

diatasso (dee-at-as'-so); from NT:1223 and NT:5021; **to arrange thoroughly**, i.e. (specially) institute, prescribe, etc.:

Once again Paul has thoroughly arranged for a certain activity. This word does not imply or impute authority to Paul.

2 Cor 10:13
But we will not boast of things without our measure, but according to the measure of the **rule** which God hath distributed to us, a measure to reach even unto you.

NT:2583

kanon (kan-ohn'); from kane (a straight reed, i.e. rod); **a rule** ("canon"), i.e. (figuratively) **a standard** (of faith and practice); by implication, a boundary, i.e. (figuratively) **a sphere** (of activity):

The problem with this verse is as much a matter of semantics as mistranslation. Paul used *kanon* in a figurative sense, referring to the geographical area where Paul had personally preached the gospel and established churches. He admonished the Corinthians to heed his instruction and avoid other "super" apostles, who berated Paul for his slight build and clumsy manner of speech. Paul was asserting his right to be their apostle. This transliterated word has come into English to define the "canon" of scripture, i.e., those writings which meet the "standard" of the Word of God and have been accepted into the "sphere" of the inspired writings of scripture.

2 Cor 10:15
Not boasting of things without our measure, that is, of other men's labours; but having hope, when your faith is increased, that we shall be enlarged by you according to our **rule** abundantly...

NT:2583

kanon (kan-ohn'); from kane (a straight reed, i.e. rod); **a rule** ("canon"), i.e. (figuratively) **a standard** (of faith and practice); by implication, a boundary, i.e. (figuratively) **a sphere** (of activity):

Again Paul speaks of his sphere of influence in respect to the Corinthian church. (See comments on 2 Cor 10:13 above for a more complete explanation.)

2 Cor 11:5
For I suppose I was not a whit behind the **very chiefest** apostles.
   NT:5244 a
huperlian. (hoop-er-lee'-an); See NT:5228 and NT:3029: **beyond measure, exceedingly**.

   At first glance one might assume "super" apostles existed in the Corinthian church, but Paul was actually speaking sarcastically regarding those who had exalted themselves in the congregation. Read the immediate context to gain a clearer understanding of Paul's statement. However, context aside, the translators' "chiefest" is horrible English, and it is also a poor translation for Paul's inspired word meaning "exceedingly," perhaps implying most accomplished; but keep in mind that this was a tongue-in-cheek embellishment of those apostles' value to the church.

2 Cor 12:11
I am become a fool in glorying; ye have compelled me: for I ought to have been commended of you: for in nothing am I behind the **very chiefest** apostles, though I be nothing.
   NT:5244 a
huperlian. (hoop-er-lee'-an); See NT:5228 and NT:3029: **beyond measure, exceedingly**.

   The same error occurs here which appears in the verse above. See comments on 2 Cor 11:5.

Eph 4:7-8, 11-12
But unto every one of us is given grace according to the measure of the **gift** of Christ. Wherefore he saith, When he ascended up on high, he led captivity captive, and gave **gifts** unto men... And he gave some, apostles; and some, prophets; and some, evangelists; and some, pastors and teachers; for the perfecting of the saints, for the work of the ministry, for the edifying of the body of Christ:

   This section in Ephesians parallels 1 Corinthians 12. These gifts of the Spirit were special blessings bestowed upon certain individuals for the edification and growth of the body. They were listed in the order of their importance to the body. They are neither a ranking of offices for churches nor a list of positions of authority in the body. (See comments on 1 Cor 12:28-31 above.)

Phil 1:1
Paul and Timotheus, the servants of Jesus Christ, to all the saints in Christ Jesus which are at Philippi, with the **bishops** and **deacons**:

Many assume bishops and deacons hold offices of authority in churches, but such is not supported by biblical evidence. For an explanation of the meaning of the word bishop (overseer) see under 1 Timothy 3:2, and similarly for deacon see under 1 Timothy 3:8.

1 Thess 4:2
For ye know what **commandments** we gave you by the Lord Jesus.
 NT:3852
paraggelia (par-ang-gel-ee'-ah); from NT:3853; **a mandate:**

One should carefully observe that this Greek noun is derived from the verb NT:3853, "to transmit a message." Paul transmitted several commands to the Thessalonians, which he received from the Lord. He did not command by his own authority, but acted as a messenger of the Lord.

1 Thess 4:11
And that ye study to be quiet, and to do your own business, and to work with your own hands, as **we commanded** you;
 NT:3853
paraggello (par-ang-gel'-lo); from NT:3844 and the base of NT:32; **to transmit a message,** i.e. (by implication) to enjoin:

The commands Paul gave were based on the authority of the Lord, not on his own authority to command. Paul acted as a messenger from God, not an authority.

1 Thess 5:12
And we beseech you, brethren, to know them which labour among you, and are **over** you in the Lord, and admonish you;
 NT:4291
proistemi (pro-is'-tay-mee); from NT:4253 and NT:2476; **to stand before**, i.e. (in rank) to preside, or (by implication) to practise:

The translators' presumption of ecclesiastical authority resulted in this gross mistranslation. Those who labor among the brethren "stand before" or "practice" their faith among the members, but they are not over them in authority. The sense of "practice" is probably preferred. No authority is implied by this word. If one could show that leaders held a rank of authority in a church, this Greek word could be translated "preside," but it can never be translated "over." Leaders lead by standing (practicing) before the members.

2 Thess 3:4, 6, 10, 12
And we have confidence in the Lord touching you, that ye both do and will do the things which **we command** you...Now **we command** you, brethren, in the name of our Lord Jesus Christ, that ye withdraw yourselves from every brother that walketh disorderly, and not after the tradition which he received of us...For even when we were with you, this **we commanded** you, that if any would not work, neither should he eat...Now them that are such **we command** and exhort by our Lord Jesus Christ, that with quietness they work, and eat their own bread.

NT:3853

paraggello (par-ang-gel'-lo); from NT:3844 and the base of NT:32; **to transmit a message,** i.e. (by implication) to enjoin:

The commands Paul gave were based on the authority of the Lord, not on his own authority to command. Paul acted as a messenger from God, not an authority.

2 Thess 3:14
And if any man obey not **our word** by this epistle, note that man, and have no company with him, that he may be ashamed.

The fundamental error in this verse is not a mistranslation of the word "obey," but the translators' carelessness to properly reflect the exact grammar of the Greek sentence structure. This translation implies that the members of the church in Thessalonica ought to *hupakouo* (obey) Paul, Silas and Timothy who wrote this epistle to them. However, the Greek text reveals that the phrase "our word" is a mistranslation of the Greek phrase which plainly states "the word from us." The object of the obedience is "the word," not "our word." There is a vast difference between obeying "the word from us" and obeying "our word." Paul's intent here is to admonish the Thessalonians to obey Jesus Christ, the Word of God, of Whom Paul, Silas and Timothy were messengers, a concept examined at length in chapter 8. <u>And if any man obey not **the word from us** by this epistle, note that man and have no company with him, that he may be ashamed.</u>

1 Tim 1:3
As I besought thee to abide still at Ephesus, when I went into Macedonia, that **thou mightest charge** some that they teach no other doctrine,
NT:3853
paraggello (par-ang-gel'-lo); from NT:3844 and the base of NT:32; **to transmit a message,** i.e. (by implication) to enjoin:

The commands Paul gave were based on the authority of the Lord, not on his own authority to command. Paul acted as a messenger from God, not an authority.

1 Tim 1:18
This **charge** I commit unto thee, son Timothy, according to the prophecies which went before on thee, that thou by them mightest war a good warfare;
NT:3852
paraggelia (par-ang-gel-ee'-ah); from NT:3853; **a mandate:**

One should carefully observe that this Greek noun is derived from the verb NT:3853, "to transmit a message." Paul transmitted several commands to Timothy which he had received from Jesus Christ. He did not command by his own authority, but acted as a messenger of the Lord.

1 Tim 2:7
Whereunto I am **ordained** a preacher, and an apostle, (I speak the truth in Christ, and lie not;) a teacher of the Gentiles in faith and verity.
NT:5087
tithemi (tith'-ay-mee); a prolonged form of a primary theo (theh'-o) (which is used only as alternate in certain tenses); **to place** (in the widest application, literally and figuratively; properly, **in a passive or horizontal posture**, and thus different from NT:2476, which properly denotes an upright and active position, while NT:2749 is properly reflexive and utterly prostrate):

Again, we find God placed His apostle in the church in a passive way, which works contrary to the notion that apostles had authority to command the members of the body. See John 15:16 above. The Greek vocabulary of the New Testament contains no concept of ordination to a position of authority.

1 Tim 3:1
This is a true saying, If a man desire **the office of a bishop**, he desireth a good work.
NT:1984
episkope (ep-is-kop-ay'); from NT:1980; **inspection (for relief)**; by implication, superintendence; specially, the Christian "episcopate":

One should carefully observe that the inspection described here is for the purpose of relief or assistance only. The definition of the Greek root verb *episkeptomai* (NT:1980) is "visit" as in James 1:27. *Pure religion and undefiled before God and the Father is this, To visit (episkeptomai NT:1980) the fatherless and widows in their affliction, and to keep himself unspotted from the world. Episkope* is the noun form and means "visitation." It has nothing to do with the official inspection invariably implied in our cultural understanding of inspection. It carries the concept watchful protection and care rather than official inspection. It is never translated inspection in the Bible. In this context *episkope* describes visitation in the sense of providing aid or relief. This is a true saying, If a man desires **visitation** [for relief], he desires a good work.

1 Tim 3:2
A **bishop** then must be blameless, the husband of one wife, vigilant, sober, of good behaviour, given to hospitality, apt to teach;
NT:1985
episkopos (ep-is'-kop-os); from NT:1909 and NT:4649 (in the sense of NT:1983); a superintendent, i.e. Christian officer in genitive case charge of a (or the) church (literally or figuratively):

The English word, bishop (or superintendent), carries a bureaucratic connotation in our cultural understanding of the word which did not exist at all in the first century Greek or Jewish culture. Strong's definition further obscures the literal meaning of this word, which you can clearly see is a compound of NT:1909, "upon," and NT:4649, "to watch." The verb form (NT:1983, *episkopeo*) is translated "looking diligently" in Hebrews 12:15. The Greek sense indicates a bishop is one who carefully watches out for the flock, not one who has authority over the flock. Watchmen were given the responsibility to guard the congregation, not to rule over it. They serve the church, but they do not command or control it. Mr. Strong's comments about the "Christian officer" are spurious. A bishop fulfills the same responsibility in a church that a watchman fulfilled in Israel. (Ezek 33) <u>A **watchman** (or guardian) must be blameless, the husband of one wife, vigilant, sober, of good behaviour, given to hospitality, apt to teach.</u>

1 Tim 3:8
Likewise must the **deacons** be grave, not doubletongued, not given to much wine...
   NT:1249
diakonos (dee-ak'-on-os); probably from an obsolete diako (to run on errands; compare NT:1377); **an attendant**, i.e. (genitive case) a waiter (at table or in other menial duties); specially, a Christian teacher and pastor (technically, a deacon or deaconess):

   Diakonos is the Greek counterpart for our English word "servant," which is its simple, literal and intended meaning in this context. Do not be confused by Strong's notation that the literal definition of *diakonos* might have anything specifically to do with a Christian pastor, teacher, deacon or deaconess. Mr. Strong simply acknowledges that organized Christianity has created these offices based on the word *diakonos*. Our English word "deacon" has obviously been transliterated from the Greek word, but for no good reason. In three instances out of thirty occurrences of *diakonos* in the Bible, the translators have chosen not to translate the word, giving the English reader the mistaken impression that those mentioned in this context have been conferred biblical authority in their function as church servants. <u>Likewise must **servants** be grave, not doubletongued, not given to much wine...</u>

1 Tim 3:10
And let these also first be proved; then let them **use the office of a deacon**, being found blameless.
   NT:1247
diakoneo (dee-ak-on-eh'-o); from NT:1249; **to be an attendant**, i.e. wait upon (menially or as a host, friend, or [figuratively] teacher); techn. to act as a Christian deacon:

   The technical notation in Strong's definition is spurious. See comment on 1 Tim 3:8. <u>And let these also first be proved, then let them **be servants**, being found blameless.</u>

349

1 Tim 3:12
Let the **deacons** be the husbands of one wife, [standing before] their children and their own houses well.
NT:1249
diakonos (dee-ak'-on-os); probably from an obsolete diako (to run on errands; compare NT:1377); **an attendant**, i.e. (genitive case) a waiter (at table or in other menial duties); specially, a Christian teacher and pastor (technically, a deacon or deaconess):
See notation on 1 Tim 3:8. The special and technical notations are spurious. <u>Let the **servants** be the husbands of one wife, standing before their children and their own houses well.</u>

1 Tim 3:13
For they that **have used the office of a deacon** well purchase to themselves a good degree, and great boldness in the faith which is in Christ Jesus.
NT:1247
diakoneo (dee-ak-on-eh'-o); from NT:1249; **to be an attendant**, i.e. wait upon (menially or as a host, friend, or [figuratively] teacher); techn. to act as a Christian deacon:
The technical notation in Strong's definition is spurious. See comment on 1 Tim 3:8. <u>For they that **are being** good **servants** purchase to themselves a good degree, and great boldness in the faith which is in Christ Jesus.</u>

1 Tim 4:11
These things **command** and teach.
NT:3853
paraggello (par-ang-gel'-lo); from NT:3844 and the base of NT:32; **to transmit a message,** i.e. (by implication) to enjoin:
The commands Paul gave were based on the authority of the Lord, not on his own authority to command. Paul acted as a messenger from God, not an authority.

1 Tim 5:7
And these things **give in charge**, that they may be blameless.
NT:3853
paraggello (par-ang-gel'-lo); from NT:3844 and the base of NT:32; **to transmit a message,** i.e. (by implication) to enjoin:

The commands Paul gave were based on the authority of the Lord, not on his own authority to command. Paul acted as a messenger from God, not an authority.

1 Tim 5:17
Let the elders that **rule** well be counted worthy of double honour, especially they who labour in the word and doctrine.
    NT:4291
proistemi (pro-is'-tay-mee); from NT:4253 and NT:2476; **to stand before**, i.e. (in rank) to preside, or (by implication) to practice
    The translators assumed church leaders rule churches. Those who labor among the brethren "stand before" or "practice" their faith among the members, but they never rule. "Practice" is probably preferred. If one could show that leaders held a rank of authority in a church, this Greek word could be translated "preside," but it can never be translated "rule." Let the elders that **stand before** the congregation well be counted worthy of double honor…

1 Tim 6:13
I give thee **charge** in the sight of God, who quickeneth all things, and before Christ Jesus, who before Pontius Pilate witnessed a good confession;
    NT:3853
paraggello (par-ang-gel'-lo); from NT:3844 and the base of NT:32; **to transmit a message,** i.e. (by implication) to enjoin:
    The commands Paul gave were based on the authority of the Lord, not on his own authority to command. Paul acted as a messenger from God, not an authority.

1 Tim 6:17
Charge them that are rich in this world, that they be not highminded, nor trust in uncertain riches, but in the living God, who giveth us richly all things to enjoy;
    NT:3853
paraggello (par-ang-gel'-lo); from NT:3844 and the base of NT:32; **to transmit a message,** i.e. (by implication) to enjoin:
    The commands Paul gave were based on the authority of the Lord, not on his own authority to command. Paul acted as a messenger from God, not an authority.

Titus 1:5
For this cause left I thee in Crete, that thou shouldest set in order the things that are wanting, and **ordain** elders in every city, as I had **appointed** thee:

NT:2525 (ordain)
kathistemi (kath-is'-tay-mee); from NT:2596 and NT:2476; **to place down (permanently)**, i.e. (figuratively) to designate, constitute, convoy:

NT:1299 (appointed)
diatasso (dee-at-as'-so); from NT:1223 and NT:5021; **to arrange thoroughly**, i.e. (specially) institute, prescribe, etc.:

Once again church leaders are said to have been "placed down" with an implication of permanence rather than raised up to positions of authority. Paul had made a "thorough arrangement" to fill these responsibilities, but we cannot assume from this verse that either Paul or Titus exercised authority to accomplish the task. The Greek vocabulary of the New Testament contains no concept of ordination to a position of authority.

Titus 1:7
For a **bishop** must be blameless, as the steward of God; not selfwilled, not soon angry, not given to wine, no striker, not given to filthy lucre;

NT:1985
episkopos (ep-is'-kop-os); from NT:1909 and NT:4649 (in the sense of NT:1983); a superintendent, i.e. Christian officer in genitive case charge of a (or the) church (literally or figuratively):

See note on 1 Timothy 3:2. For a **watchman** (or guardian) must be blameless, as the steward of God, not selfwilled, not soon angry, not given to wine, no striker, not given to filthy lucre;

Titus 2:15
These things speak, and exhort, and rebuke with all **authority**.

NT:2003
epitage (ep-ee-tag-ay'); from NT:2004; an injunction or decree; by implication, **authoritativeness**:

Paul described the manner in which Titus was to speak. Titus was to speak, exhort and rebuke with command or authoritativeness. This verse does not say that Titus had authority over anybody.

Philemon 8-9
Wherefore, though I might be much bold in Christ to **enjoin** thee that which is convenient, yet for love's sake I rather beseech thee, being such an one as Paul the aged, and now also a prisoner of Jesus Christ.

NT:2004 (verb)
epitasso (ep-ee-tas'-so); from NT:1909 and NT:5021; **to arrange upon,** i.e. order:

This verse provides a most remarkable window into the relationship God has inspired between leaders and members in the body of Christ. This Greek word, properly translated "enjoin," is not used after the book of Acts, except for this one notable passage in Philemon 8.

In his letter to Philemon regarding the runaway slave, Onesimus, Paul first expresses his human inclination to command Philemon to reinstate Onesimus, but then relents "for love's sake." Paul really wanted to step into this situation and solve Onesimus' problem with a command, but the Spirit moved him not to step over the line of proper Christian conduct. Instead, he employed what he knew to be the Christian approach. Had Paul felt the necessity to command Philemon, he would have undoubtedly used the word, *paraggello*. **This is the only record of the use of an injunctive word by a church leader in relation to a member of the church in any of the epistles to the churches.**

Heb 13:7
Remember them which **have the rule over** you, who have spoken unto you the word of God: whose faith follow, considering the end of their conversation.

NT:2233
hegeomai (hayg-eh'-om-ahee); middle voice of a (presumed) strengthened form of NT:71; **to lead,** i.e. command (with official authority); figuratively, to deem, i.e. consider:

The KJV translators imputed rulership to church leaders based on the de facto rulership of King James over the Anglican church. This blatant error is obvious to anyone who realizes God alone rules the Church. Remember them that lead you, who have spoken unto you the word of God:

Heb 13:17
Obey them that **have the rule over** you, and submit yourselves: for they watch for your souls, as they that must give account, that they may do it with joy, and not with grief: for that is unprofitable for you.

NT:3982 (obey)
peitho (pi'-tho); a primary verb; **to convince** (by argument, true or false); by analogy, **to pacify or conciliate** (by other fair means); reflexively or passively, **to assent** (to evidence or authority), **to rely** (by inward certainty):

NT:2233 (have the rule over)
hegeomai (hayg-eh'-om-ahee); middle voice of a (presumed) strengthened form of NT:71; **to lead**, i.e. command (with official authority); figuratively, to deem, i.e. consider:

This grossly mistranslated verse is the foundation of hierarchal human authority in churches. The imputed rulership and implied authority of church leaders vanishes from the Bible when this verse and many others like it are correctly translated. It is beyond the scope of these short notes to deal with all the issues which could be raised here, but one can plainly see that *pietho* has nothing to do with obedience and *hegeomai* has no other meaning than "to lead." No one rules except God, and obedience to church leaders is never enjoined upon Christians in the Greek text of the Bible. See a more complete explanation in chapter 8, page 231-236. **Be persuaded** by them that **lead** you, and submit *yourselves*: for they watch for your souls, as they that must give account, that they may do it with joy, and not with grief: for that *is* unprofitable for you.

Heb 13:24
Salute all them that **have the rule over** you, and all the saints.
NT:2233
hegeomai (hayg-eh'-om-ahee); middle voice of a (presumed) strengthened form of NT:71; **to lead**, i.e. command (with official authority); figuratively, to deem, i.e. consider:

At least the translators are consistent in their error. The Hebrew brethren are encouraged to greet their leaders on behalf of the author of Hebrews. Salute all them that **lead** you, and all the saints.

2 Pet 3:2
That ye may be mindful of the words which were spoken before by the holy prophets, and of the commandment **of us** the apostles of the Lord and Saviour:

NT:5216

humon (hoo-mone'); genitive case of NT:5210; **of** (from or concerning) **you**

We should immediately recognize that the genitive phrase "of us" is a mistranslation of the Greek word which forms a genitive phrase "of you" (pl). In the Greek text the phrase in question modifies "the apostles," not "the commandment," therefore, you may notice that inserting "of you" back into the sentence makes no sense. Obviously, the brethren do not make commandments, nor are all the brethren apostles. A complete explanation of the translators' manipulation of this verse is beyond the scope of this book, but I offer here a corrected translation of the apostle's inspired thought. That ye may be mindful of the words, which were spoken before by the holy prophets, and the commandment of the Lord and Savior from the apostles of you (NT:5216), i.e., from your apostles.

Conclusion

God frequently walks a very fine line in His word to define the strong, persuasive nature of skilled leaders who speak, exhort and rebuke authoritatively, all the while God carefully avoids any explicit expression that might imply authority has been bestowed upon church leaders. Although strong leadership is imperative in every congregation, hierarchical authority in that leadership is not, and it cannot be supported by the Greek text of the Bible. In the literal Greek text Jesus Christ is described in four verses in the New Testament as the Chief Leader (Acts 3:15, 5:31, Heb 2:10, 12:2). He is never described as the chief authority. Jesus Christ is the Head of many leaders in the Church, but He is not the chief over any authorities for the simple reason that there are no human authorities in the body of Christ. There is only one authority in any body. There is only one Authority in the body of Christ.

Having spent several years scouring the New Testament for passages of scripture which even remotely imply hierarchical authority for churches, the verses in this appendix represent the result of that search. This appendix contains every scripture in the

Bible which could possibly be construed to imply hierarchical authority in the Church, and the errors in these several dozen scriptures have been exposed by the work of Greek scholars. Perhaps you have now experienced the same enlightenment I experienced as, one by one, hierarchical authority crumbled from the Bible. Whereas the authority of civil leaders can be easily verified in scripture, there is not even one verse in the Greek text which implies authority for congregational leaders.

I'm convinced that such an omission is not an accident. Do we think God forgot to include the structure of church government in the Bible? Do we think one of the most important subjects a Christian needs to understand was inadvertently omitted from scripture? I think not. The government of God is not obscured in the Bible—indeed it is obvious. The government of God is theocracy.

Although most churches claim their government is a theocracy, none are. They are all structured hierarchically. The broad diversity of church structures attests to the theological struggle to find an explicit biblical model for church government. Theologians and church leaders have searched the scriptures in vain to find any explicit government of God for their churches, and they have failed to find it, not because it is not there, but because they have been looking for a church structure which includes human authorities rather than looking for the government of God. They have failed to find it because there is no human governmental structure in the Church. The Church is a body, not an organization.

The Church is one body, and Jesus Christ is the Head of His body. He governs His body from within it. Jesus Christ lives in each faithful member of the Church, and He governs each of us individually and personally. There is no need for hierarchical structure in the Church. If Jesus Christ lives in each member of the Church, do you think He would allow a man be in authority over Himself? Such a circumstance seems ludicrous.

The fundamental problem, I'm convinced, is that many professing Christians simply don't believe Jesus Christ lives in them. They don't believe they have put on Christ or that they are clothed in Him. Most simply don't understand the covenant relationship. God is in us. Christ is in us. The Spirit is in us. Our government lives within us. Men cannot exercise authority over those in whom God dwells, because God will not allow a man to be in authority over Himself.

Appendix 2

Scripture Denies Ecclesiastical Authority

A number of scriptures struck me as having a more profound significance as I gained a new perspective of the nature of the Church and the nature of Church government. Perhaps you will also find these verses more meaningful than you have realized in the past, particularly as you consider them in the light of this study.

1 Cor 11:3
But I would have you know, that the head of every man is Christ; and the head of the woman is the man; and the head of Christ is God.

This verse describes the entire structure of government in the Church. God is the Head of Christ, Christ is the Head of everyone, and a husband is the head of his wife. It is impossible to fit the hierarchal structure of churches into Paul's description of governance for the Church. The Church is a spiritual entity, so government in the Church is a spiritual matter and must be observed from a spiritual perspective. Can a believer have more than one spiritual head?

Matt 6:24 (also Luke 16:13)
No man can serve two masters:

No one can serve two spiritual authorities. Either a man is in authority over you or Jesus Christ is in authority over you. Which do you choose?

Matt 28:19-20
Go ye therefore, and teach all nations, baptizing them in the name of the Father, and of the Son, and of the Holy Ghost: **Teaching** them to observe all things whatsoever I have **commanded** you: and, lo, I am with you alway, even unto the end of the world. Amen.

Why do you think Jesus told the disciples to teach what He had commanded them? Why not tell the disciples to command the members to do what Jesus had commanded the apostles to do? Could it be Jesus did not grant them any authority to command?

1 Tim 2:5
For there is one God, and one mediator between God and men, the man Christ Jesus;

Every denomination and most churches ignore this plain revelation of scripture by placing men in positions of authority to stand between the members and God by assuming the right to judge and direct their members. Leaders of faithful churches must lead by setting a godly example, by teaching, by encouraging, by exhorting and by admonishing, but not by commanding. Those who command usurp the authority of Jesus Christ. No man stands in authority between God and a believer, except the Man, Jesus Christ.

Gal 2:20
I am crucified with Christ: nevertheless I live; yet not I, but Christ liveth in me:

Do you really believe Jesus Christ lives in you? If Jesus Christ lives in you, do you think He would allow a man to have authority over Himself? The Lord's presence in each member of His body precludes the possibility that men have authority over any member.

Rom 6:16
Know ye not, that to whom ye yield yourselves [slaves] to obey, his [slaves] ye are to whom ye obey; whether of sin unto death, or of obedience unto righteousness?

This verse plainly says that anyone who obeys a man as an authority is a slave to that man. Since no one can be enslaved to two masters, we must choose between obeying the Lord and obeying a church authority. Whom do you choose?

1 Cor 15:24-26
Then cometh the end, when he shall have delivered up the kingdom to God, even the Father; when he shall have put down **all rule and all authority and power**. For he must reign, till he hath put all **enemies** under his feet. The last **enemy** that shall be destroyed is death.

This verse reveals that rule, authority, power and death are enemies of God. Do you think God would intentionally place any of these enemies in a church?

Matt 20:25-28 (also Mark 10:42-45)
But Jesus called them unto him, and said, Ye know that the princes of the Gentiles exercise dominion over them, and they that are great exercise authority upon them. **But it shall not be so among you: but whosoever will be great among you, let him be your [servant]; And whosoever will be chief among you, let him be your [slave]: Even as the Son of man came not to be [served], but to [serve], and to give his life a ransom for many.**

Jesus described the nature of church leadership in this verse. He said leadership should not be the way it is in the world. He strongly implied that leaders should not be rulers or authorities.

1 Cor 7:23
Ye are bought with a price; **be not ye the [slaves] of men.**

A slave is one who obeys the orders of a master. Paul admonishes the Corinthian brethren not to take orders from church leaders. We can only have one spiritual Authority in our lives.

Gal 1:10
For do I now persuade men, or God? or do I seek to please men? for **if I yet pleased men, I should not be the [slave] of Christ.**

Since even the desire to please men is condemned, how much more should we condemn the practice of obeying the commands and wishes of self-proclaimed church authorities?

Luke 18:8
Nevertheless when the Son of man cometh, **shall he find faith on the earth?**

Faith is trusting in Jesus Christ to be your Lord and Master, your Leader and your Guide. Faith trusts Him for everything. Those who trust in human authority lack faith in Christ. No wonder Jesus was apprehensive about finding faith on the earth at His return. Indeed, the Greek interrogative implies a negative answer to the question.

Acts 10:34
God is no respecter of persons:

God does not consider one member above another. Would it be possible for God to grant the privilege of authority to any church member without being a respecter of persons?

Gal 5:18
But if ye be led of the Spirit, **ye are not under the law**.

Consider the difference between the old covenant and the New Covenant. In the old covenant there were over 613 laws prescribing the ritualistic observances of holy times, holy places and holy things. The enforcement of codified law requires human authority. Under the New Covenant God has freed us from the standard of prescriptive law, and now we live by the spiritual standard of the faith of Jesus Christ. Since codified laws do not define our conduct, there is no need for human authorities. If we have been freed from prescriptive laws, one may logically conclude we have been freed from human authority. Why do we need human authorities in the Church when there are no humanly enforceable laws to uphold? Is not the authority God has left in the civil sector sufficient to control the belligerent and unruly?

Rom 14:4
Who art thou that **judgest another man's [slave]?** to his own master he standeth or falleth. Yea, he shall be holden up: for God is able to make him stand.

I am Jesus' slave, therefore no man can judge me but the Lord. Since I am Jesus' slave, no man can command me or give me orders. Jesus Christ alone directs each of His slaves.

1 Cor 1:24
Not for that we have dominion (NT:2961, to be lord of) over your faith, but are helpers (NT:4904, co-laborer) of your joy: for by faith ye stand.

This statement could be no plainer. Paul said he did not function as a lord or an authority over the Corinthians. The apostle claimed he was a co-worker with the members. We stand by faith, not by the commands of church leaders—not by the authority of men.

Mark 9:35
And he sat down, and called the twelve, and saith unto them, If any man desire to be **first,** (NT:4413 foremost or superior) the same shall be last of all, and [slave] of all.

The mere desire to be first, foremost or superior is condemned. We are all the lord's slaves, and we are all equals in Him.

Matt 23:8-12
But be not ye called **Rabbi**: for one is your Master, even Christ; and all ye are brethren. And call no man your **father** upon the earth: for one is your Father, which is in heaven. Neither be ye called **masters:** for one is your Master, even Christ. But he that is greatest among you shall be your servant. **And whosoever shall exalt himself shall be abased; and he that shall humble himself shall be exalted.**

Rabbi, Master and Father were the most commonly used and highly acclaimed Hebrew and Roman titles in religious culture. Jesus strongly implies that those who assume any kind of religious title exalt themselves beyond Christian propriety. This verse serves as a stern warning to those who call themselves Pastor, Reverend, Father, Teacher, Elder or any other title in a church. Titles are a function of human pride and vanity, and they have no place in the Church. "Wherefore let him that thinketh he standeth take heed lest he fall." (1 Cor 10:12)

1 Cor 2:15
But he that is spiritual judgeth all things, **yet he himself is judged of no man.**

A spiritually minded member has the capacity to judge every deed, but he cannot be personally judged by anyone. When we judge deeds, we judge sin, and the congregation may act to cut off sinners and remove themselves from those who are sinning, but none stands in authority to judge another unilaterally.

1 Peter 2:9
But ye are a chosen generation, **a royal priesthood**, an holy nation, a peculiar people...

The Bible upholds the universal priesthood of all believers, and the Church is typed by the priesthood of Israel. Although the government of Israel contained a hierarchical judgeship and, after Israel asked for a king, a hierarchical military, the Mosaic form of the priesthood described no hierarchy. The high priest typed Jesus Christ, but the remainder of the priesthood served at the tabernacle or taught in the community as equals. As the antitypical new covenant priesthood, each of us similarly serves our great High Priest as equals before God.

Matt 28:18 & Col 2:9-10
And Jesus came and spake unto them, saying, All [authority] is given unto me in heaven and in earth...For in [Christ] dwelleth all the fulness of the Godhead bodily. And ye are complete in him, which is the head of all [rule] and [authority]:

Jesus Christ possesses all authority, and He is supreme in authority over all human rulers and authorities. Any authority vested hierarchically in church leaders should be revealed in scripture, but it is conspicuously missing. Although the Bible plainly upholds civil rulers and authorities and explicitly tells each of us to submit ourselves to them, any mention of church authorities is absent from scripture. Was that an unfortunate oversight on God's part, or is it a strong indication there are no human authorities in the Church?

1 Peter 5:2-3
Feed the flock of God which is among you, [watching over *them*], not by constraint, but willingly; not for filthy lucre, but of a ready mind; **Neither as being lords over God's heritage**, but being [dies] to the flock.

Speaking to the elders of the church, Peter specifically denied them the right to be lords over God's people. A first century lord was the master of slaves, and a lord's essential function was to command his slaves to do whatever the lord wanted them to do. Only a lord possessed vested authority to command his slaves. In this passage Peter specifically denied elders the right to command God's people or to exercise authority over them. Since this statement is given within the context of directions for the leadership in the scattered Hebrew churches, Peter's directive is one of the most explicit statements in the Bible denying church leaders the right to exercise authority over the churches.

Appendix 3

Nailed to the Cross

Jesus was begotten of God, born of the virgin Mary and lived a perfect life in the flesh. In spite of His sinlessness, Jesus was condemned by the Jews, crucified by the Romans and forsaken by God in order to pay for the sins of the whole world. Salvation is only possible because of the selfless sacrifice Jesus made on the cross. As far as our salvation is concerned, Jesus was nailed to the cross, and only Him. This much is plain.

However in Colossians 2:13-14 Paul's letter to the church at Colossae implied that something besides Jesus had been nailed to the cross.

> And you, being dead in your sins and the uncircumcision of your flesh, hath he quickened together with him, having forgiven you all trespasses; blotting out the handwriting of ordinances that was against us, which was contrary to us, and took it out of the way, nailing it to his cross;

Beyond Jesus' literal crucifixion, Paul's statement indicates that "the handwriting of ordinances that was against us" was blotted out, taken out of the way and nailed to the cross. This, of course, is figurative language, because, except for a sign Pilate wrote which declared, "Jesus of Nazareth, the King of the Jews," nothing was nailed to the cross except Jesus.

Paul's statement has become one of the more perplexing and controversial scriptures in the Bible. Some claim this verse says the law was nailed to the cross, which would imply that the law is no longer in effect. Others assert the law was not nailed to the cross, even though they admit the law is not the standard of Christian conduct. Yet others deny the law was nailed to the cross in order to defend their faith in the law.

Most will at least agree that the language of this verse is difficult and that its meaning is obscure at best, yet within every church or fellowship there will be some who read it one way and some who see it the other. Intense arguments sometimes ensue.

In an effort to resolve the disagreement surrounding this verse and bring peace to those who are willing to let the Bible interpret itself, we will examine scriptures which verify the law is still in force and show that a contradiction arises when we assume it is not. We will also expose the hidden meaning of Colossians 2:14 through a careful examination of the Greek words which underlie our English translations and explain how the first century custom of dealing with indebtedness provides a clear and simple solution to the perplexing nature of this verse.

The Law is Holy, Just and Good

We may effectively approach the exegesis of this verse by assuming a particular interpretation, and then we can see if any contradictions arise as a result. We will begin by assuming "the handwriting of ordinances" means the law. If that were the case, Paul would clearly be saying the law was nailed to the cross. Of course one might wonder why he didn't just say so rather than using such obscure language.

If "the handwriting of ordinances" means the law, then this verse also says the law is against us and contrary to us. Yet plain scriptures tell us the law is good for us.

> For that which I do I allow not: for what I would, that do I not; but what I hate, that do I. If then I do that which I would not, I consent unto the law that it is good. (Rom 7:15-16)

The law is the means through which we become aware of sin at an observable level. The law measures deeds to see if they fall short of the old covenant standard of conduct. The law is not against us or contrary to us. The law is good. It is good, because it shows us something about our sinful actions. It shows us that we sin. Sin is exposed by the law. Our awareness of sin does not make the law inherently bad. The law is not against us. The law is not sin.

> What shall we say then? Is the law sin? God forbid. Nay, I had not known sin, but by the law: for I had not known lust, except the law had said, Thou shalt not covet. (Rom 7:7)

The law is not sin. The law defines sin. Without the law, we would lack an observable standard for sin, and we would not be able to recognize or condemn sinful actions. Even more than that, the law is holy and spiritual.

> Wherefore the law is holy, and the commandment holy, and just, and good... For we know that the law is spiritual: (Rom 7:12, 14)

Since God tells us through Paul that the law is spiritual, we learn that the law is eternal. God will never abolish it. It is illogical to even assume God would abolish a good law.

Apparently, some believers at Rome thought that faith abolished the law, but Paul made it clear to them that the law was not abolished. Paul asked essentially the same question in his epistle to the Romans which we are now considering in Colossians 2:14.

> Do we then make void the law through faith? God forbid: yea, **we establish the law.** (Rom 3:31)

Faithful believers not only establish the law, but we fulfill the law. We fulfill the law, just as Christ fulfilled the law. Jesus did not come to destroy the law; He came to fulfill it. (Matt 5:17) Even so believers also fulfill the law in Christ. Our Lord wants to fulfill the law as He lives in each of us who walk after the Spirit, just as He did when He walked the earth in His own flesh.

> For what the law could not do, in that it was weak through the flesh, God sending his own Son in the likeness of sinful flesh, and for sin, condemned sin in the flesh: **that the righteousness of the law might be fulfilled in us,** who walk not after the flesh, but after the Spirit. (Rom 8:3-4)

What could be plainer? The law is good. The law is holy. The law is spiritual. Jesus Christ establishes the law and fulfills the law in those who live by faith. Of course, that is not difficult for those of us who walk after the Spirit in love for God and in love for our neighbors, because love fulfills the law.

> Love worketh no ill to his neighbour: therefore love
> is the fulfilling of the law. (Rom 13:10)

Since we come to a contradiction with a number of plain scriptures when we assume the law was nailed to the cross, we must search for another explanation for this difficult verbiage. Let's consider the meaning of two key words in this context.

Dogma

The Greek word, *dogma*, which underlies "ordinances," is only used five times in the New Testament. It means "a law" in a general sense, but is not related to or derived from *nomos*, which is used 198 times in the New Testament and specifically refers to legislated law, mostly to the law of Moses. Had Paul wanted to refer to the law of Moses, he would likely have used the Greek word *nomos*.

We should also notice that references to the law of Moses never appear in plural form in the New Testament. They always appear in singular form. Thus, Paul's use of *dogma* in the plural form should immediately raise suspicions that it does not refer to the Mosaic law.

Cheirographon

Also of interest is the Greek word for "handwriting." According to Strong's dictionary, *cheirographon* literally means "something hand written, i.e., a manuscript (specifically a legal document or bond)." Our English Bibles accurately reflect the Greek meaning, so those who would abolish the law—the ten commandments in particular—point out that the decalogue was written by God and specifically that He wrote it with His finger. However, they fail to recognize that His method of writing produced an engraved document on stone. One can do nothing else on stone. One may write on parchment or paper, but not on stone. This circumstance precludes the possibility that the law might simply be blotted out, as Paul asserted. God wrote the ten commandments on stones, not only to symbolize its inflexibility, but its permanence. An engraved document cannot simply be blotted out. Thus, Paul's reference to *dogma* rather than *nomos* indicates a document other than the law of Moses, and his reference to the blotting out of the *cheirographon* cannot be a reference to the decalogue.

Thayer's Greek lexicon sheds considerable light on the meaning of *cheirographon* and its application in first century culture.

NT:5498 cheirographon
1) a handwriting, what one has written by his own hand
2) a note of hand or writing in which one acknowledges that money has either been deposited with him or lent to him by another, to be returned at the appointed time

Thayer describes *cheirographon* as a certificate of debt personally handwritten by the debtor, so this definition excludes any reference to a document written by God. The certificate became a legally binding document, or *dogma,* and the individual to whom the debt was owed held the note written by the debtor. Luke recorded an example of such a legally enforceable handwritten note of debt in the parable of the unfaithful steward.

> And he said also unto his disciples, There was a certain rich man, which had a steward; and the same was accused unto him that he had wasted his goods. And he called him, and said unto him, How is it that I hear this of thee? give an account of thy stewardship; for thou mayest be no longer steward. Then the steward said within himself, What shall I do? for my lord taketh away from me the stewardship: I cannot dig; to beg I am ashamed. I am resolved what to do, that, when I am put out of the stewardship, they may receive me into their houses. So he called every one of his lord's debtors unto him, and said unto the first, How much owest thou unto my lord? And he said, An hundred measures of oil. And he said unto him, **Take thy bill,** and sit down quickly, and write fifty. (Luke 16:1-6)

Although the main point of the parable seems to be an attempt by the steward to ingratiate himself to the debtors, we may also learn how men handled debts in first century culture. The "bill" which the steward renegotiated with the debtor is particularly relevant to this study. Although "bill" is a reasonable translation, our English translation obscures the precise nature of the document.

In our twenty-first century culture we think of a bill as a document produced by the lender of money or the seller of goods, not by the borrower or buyer. However, in the cultural setting of the New Testament, the borrower wrote his own bill. In collaborative support of Thayer's definition of *cheirographon*, the Greek text of verse six reads, "Take your WRITING..." The debtor had written his note of debt with his own hand, which became a legal document, and the lord to whom the debt was owed held the note. Since the steward handled the lord's financial affairs, the handwritten note of debt was in the steward's possession, so he could execute it on behalf of the lord according to the terms of the note. In an attempt to gain favor with the debtor, the steward prematurely returned the legal note of debt to the debtor and suggested he make a new writing on the spot which reflected a fifty percent discount, apparently anticipating a personal favor from the debtor after the steward's dismissal from his stewardship. This example of a legal handwritten note of debt forms the basis for the figurative use of it in Col. 2:14.

Having resolved the cultural differences we encounter here as we attempt to interpret the words of God, it becomes a simple matter to analyze what Paul is trying to convey. The handwriting which was against us was the sin debt each of us owed God for breaking the law. Each of us has figuratively written certificates of indebtedness by hand, i.e., our sinful deeds executed by our own hands, which attest to our indebtedness to God. These figurative certificates were legally enforceable against us, because the law, rather than being abolished, still stands to condemn sinful actions. As God's Steward, Jesus held the certificates of debt which acknowledged we owed God our lives. His blood blotted out our handwritten notes of debt for sin, which were indeed against us, and took those sin debts out of the way when He was nailed to the cross.

Appendix 4

Comparison of the Covenants

Aspect of Covenant	Abrahamic Covenant	Old Covenant	New Covenant
† covenant established	covenant cut (Matt 26:28)	covenant cut (Ex 24:1-11)	covenant cut (Matt 26:28)
§ participants with God	Abraham and the patriarchs (Ex 2:24)	Israel (Ex 34:27, Deut 29:1)	all believers (John 1:12)
‡ redemption from	Slavery to sin in Ur (Gen 11:31, 12:1)	slavery to sin in Egypt (Ex 13:3)	slavery to sin in the world (Rom 6:17-18)
‡ mediator	Melchizedek (Gen 14:18)	Moses (John 1:17)	Jesus Christ (Heb 12:24)
† blood (sacrifice) of the covenant	Jesus Christ (Matt 26:28)	animals (Ex 24:5-8)	Jesus Christ (Matt 26:28)
§ promises offered	a seed, a nation, blessings and a land (Gen 15:4-7, 18)	freedom, prosperity, security and a land (Ex 6:4-8)	salvation & inheritance through Jesus Christ (Gal 3:29)
‡ sign of initiation	undetermined	baptism (1 Cor 10:2)	baptism (Acts 2:38)
† sign of the covenant	circumcision (Gen 17:10-11)	the Sabbath (Ex 31:13)	circumcision (Luke 2:21)
‡ commemoration sign of the covenant	bread & wine (a meal) (Gen 14:13)	Passover meal (Ex 12)	bread & wine (a meal) (1 Cor 11:23-26)
‡ calling	personal (Gen 12:1)	national (Deut 29:1)	personal (1 Cor 7:17)
‡ achievement goal	completion (Gen 17:1)	keep the law (Deut 6:4-9)	completion (Matt 5:48)
‡ standard of righteousness	faith (Gen 15:6)	obedience (Ex 19:5-6)	faith (Rom 3:21-22)
‡ duration	forever (Gen 17:7)	Exodus to Jesus' death Gal 3:19)	forever (Heb 13:20)

‡ priesthood	Melchizedek (Gen 14:18)	Aaronic (Ex 29:9)	Melchizedek (Heb 5:5-6)
§ holy place	each individual (Gen 17:4)	tabernacle (Ex 40:34)	each individual (Rom 8:9-11)
§ obligations	hear My Word (Gen 26:5)	hear My Word (Ex 19:3)	hear My Word (Matt 17:5)
‡ standard of conduct	Word of God (Gen 26:5)	the law (Ex 20 / Deut 5)	Jesus Christ (Gal 6:2)
‡ relationship to God	friend (Jas 2:23)	servant (Lev 25:55)	friend (John 15:15)

† These aspects of covenant establish the unity of the Abrahamic and the New Covenants.

‡ These aspects of covenant support the unity of the Abrahamic and the New Covenants.

§ These aspects of covenant will necessarily be different in some way even though the Covenant is the same.

www.ingramcontent.com/pod-product-compliance
Lightning Source LLC
Chambersburg PA
CBHW022059150426
43195CB00008B/194